About the Author

Kevin D. Randle retired from the military in 2009 as a lieutenant colonel. He flew combat missions in Vietnam as a helicopter pilot and recently received the Bronze Star Medal for his service in Iraq. In 1974 he got his first credit as a freelance writer with an article about UFO landing traces. He has investigated such cases all over the United States, including the famous Roswell crash of 1947. Randle has written more than two dozen books on the topic, is a frequent guest on radio and television, and is one of the participants in Discovery Canada's newest UFO program. He continues to research the topic but at a most leisurely pace than before. He lives with his wife in Iowa.

ALSO FROM VISIBLE INK PRESS

Alien Mysteries, Conspiracies, and Cover-ups
by Kevin D. Randle
ISBN: 978-1-57859-418-4

Conspiracies and Secret Societies: The Complete Dossier, 2nd edition
by Brad Steiger and Sherry Hansen Steiger
ISBN: 978-1-57859-368-2

Hidden Realms, Lost Civilizations, and Beings from Other Worlds
by Jerome Clark
ISBN: 978-1-57859-175-6

The Horror Show Guide: The Ultimate Frightfest of Movies
by Mike Mayo
ISBN: 978-1-57859-420-7

Real Aliens, Space Beings, and Creatures from Other Worlds
by Brad Steiger and Sherry Hansen Steiger
ISBN: 978-1-57859-333-0

Real Encounters, Different Dimensions, and Otherworldly Beings
by Brad Steiger and Sherry Hansen Steiger
ISBN: 978-1-57859-455-9

Real Ghosts, Restless Spirits, and Haunted Places, 2nd edition
by Brad Steiger
ISBN: 978-1-57859-401-6

Real Miracles, Divine Intervention, and Feats of Incredible Survival
by Brad Steiger and Sherry Hansen Steiger
ISBN: 978-1-57859-214-2

Real Monsters, Gruesome Critters, and Beasts from the Darkside
by Brad Steiger
ISBN: 978-1-57859-220-3

Real Nightmares, eBooks 1–8
by Brad Steiger

Real Vampires, Night Stalkers, and Creatures from the Darkside
by Brad Steiger
ISBN: 978-1-57859-255-5

Real Zombies, the Living Dead, and Creatures of the Apocalypse
by Brad Steiger
ISBN: 978-1-57859-296-8

Unexplained! Strange Sightings, Incredible Occurrences, and Puzzling Physical Phenomena, 3rd edition
by Jerome Clark
ISBN: 978-1-57859-344-6

The Vampire Book: The Encyclopedia of the Undead, 3rd edition
by J. Gordon Melton, Ph.D.
ISBN: 978-1-57859-281-4

The Werewolf Book: The Encyclopedia of Shape-Shifting Beings, 2nd edition
by Brad Steiger
ISBN: 978-1-57859-367-5

Please visit the Visible Ink Press website at www.visibleinkpress.com.

THE GOVERNMENT
UFO FILES
THE CONSPIRACY
OF COVER-UP

THE GOVERNMENT UFO FILES
THE CONSPIRACY OF COVER-UP

Visible Ink Press®
43311 Joy Rd., #414
Canton, MI 48187-2075

Visible Ink Press is a registered trademark of Visible Ink Press LLC.

Most Visible Ink Press books are available at special quantity discounts when purchased in bulk by corporations, organizations, or groups. Customized printings, special imprints, messages, and excerpts can be produced to meet your needs. For more information, contact Special Markets Director, Visible Ink Press, www.visibleinkpress.com, or 734-667-3211.

Managing Editor: Kevin S. Hile
Art Director: Mary Claire Krzewinski
Typesetting: Marco Di Vita
Proofreaders: Aarti Stephens and Dorothy Scott
Indexer: Larry Baker
Cover images: Shutterstock.

Cataloging-in-Publication Data

Randle, Kevin D., 1949-
  The government UFO files : the conspiracy of cover-up / by Kevin D. Randle.
    pages cm
  Includes bibliographical references and index.
  ISBN 978-1-57859-477-1 (pbk. : alk. paper)
    1. Unidentified flying objects—Sightings and encounters—United States. 2. Government information—United States. 3. Conspiracies—United States. I. Title.
  TL789.4.R359 2014
  001.9420973—dc23   2013048353

Printed in the United States of America

10 9 8 7 6 5 4 3 2 1

THE GOVERNMENT UFO FILES

THE CONSPIRACY OF COVER-UP

Kevin D. Randle

VISIBLE
INK
PRESS

Detroit

CONTENTS

ACKNOWLEDGMENTS

The problem with acknowledgments is that someone important is almost invariably overlooked. A book is a project in which one or two people sit in rooms in front of a computer screen and attempt to put together something that is interesting and entertaining. But to pull this off it requires assistance from many others. Sometimes it is a simple email answer to a question and other times it is reviewing portions of the manuscript for accuracy. This work is no exception. Without the help of many people, great chunks of this book might not have been included. If there is an order to here, other than by chapter, it is unintentional.

Keith Chester and his work on the Foo Fighters was a wonderful resource. Clas Svahn reviewed the Ghost Rockets chapter, providing insight into that case and making sure that the Swedish names were spelled correctly. Wendy Connors and Rod Dyke told me about the early days of the unofficial investigation at Wright Field. Steven Bassett and his Paradigm Research Group provided the opportunity to meet with several of those interviewed for this book. Robert Hastings was helpful in understanding the intrusions at various military installations, and Robert Salas provided a first-hand account of his experiences at Maelstrom Air Force Base. Salas also provided an introduction to others who had witnessed similar activities at other Air Force installations. John Callahan, formerly of the FAA, gave me his personal account of his investigation into the JAL 1628 incident. Others who contributed by answering questions include Tom Carey, Jerry Clark, Michael Swords, Barry Greenwood, John Steiger, Don Ecker, Frank Warren, Mark Rodeghier, Nick Redfern, and probably a dozen others whom I have left out inadvertently.

PHOTO CREDITS

INTRODUCTION

More than 12,000 reports on unidentified flying objects (UFOs) exist in the government files known as Project Blue Book. Included among them are tens of thousands of pages of related material, reports, surveys, letters, and investigations that need to be reviewed and studied to gain a complete understanding of the Air Force program of UFO research.

There are thousands of pages of documents that relate to Project Moon Dust, an intelligence function that began in the late 1950s and continued until 1985, when the code name was compromised. At that point, rather than end the project, the code name was changed and classified, and those assigned to the various UFO projects went back to work.

The files of the U.S. Department of State, the Central Intelligence Agency (CIA), the Federal Bureau of Investigation (FBI), the Federal Aviation Administration (FAA), the Army, Navy and Air Force all have documents relating to UFOs, UFO investigations, and UFO activities that inhibited or affected their operations at various times. All of these documents tell a story of deceit, deception, and duplicity, leading the public away from the truth by wrapping it in ridicule, misinformation, and secrecy.

Buried deep in the National Archives in Washington, D.C., are additional documents in various files that are labeled in odd ways or located in strange places. The question is how to figure out where these documents are kept and finding a way to access them.

To end the discussions about UFOs by the public, in the late 1960s the Air Force dedicated more than half a million dollars to a civilian university to study UFOs. The government files reveal that rather than desiring a scientific investigation, the University of Colorado study, known as the Condon Committee, was actually a way to end Air Force investigation of UFOs and to stymie civilian interest in the topic. The mission was clearly stated in documents found in both Project Blue Book government files and those held by private institutions.

One of these documents, known as the Hippler Letter, was written by Air Force officer Lieutenant Colonel Robert Hippler to James Low of the Condon Committee.

In it, Hippler spells out exactly what the Air Force expected for its money, including the requirement that the leader of the study, Dr. Edward U. Condon, say something positive about the Air Force investigation. Low acknowledged Hippler's request and responded that the committee would fulfill the mission. Hippler wrote in the letter that if UFO investigation didn't end now (the late 1960s), the Air Force would be stuck with the issue for another twenty years.

The problem is that there is so much information hidden in those files that it is nearly impossible to figure out what has happened and what the government might know about UFOs. In addition, the government has wrapped the enigma of UFOs in a blanket of ridicule that makes witnesses afraid to mention a sighting. Military personnel have been ordered not to talk about the sightings they have made and civilian employees have been forced to sign nondisclosure agreements that threaten huge penalties for violation, all for something that doesn't officially exist.

Allegations about a government cover-up about UFOs have been swirling for years. It is evident in official statements, including the one issued by the Condon Committee, which claims that they found no evidence of government secrecy. The committee made this claim even though they reviewed files that were labeled "Secret." In fact, some of the scientists on the committee were not even allowed to review all the available material because they didn't have the proper security clearances.

Examples of this cover-up can be found elsewhere in the government files. In the mid 1990s, when U.S. Senator Jeff Bingaman asked the Air Force about Project Moon Dust, he was told, officially, by an Air Force officer that no such project existed. Presented with documents from the Department of State that were clearly marked "Moon Dust," revealing a UFO component as part of the Moon Dust mission, a higher ranking Air Force officer conceded the existence of the mission but declared that it had never been deployed. Other documents revealed this to be untrue also.

As the Condon Committee researched UFO sightings during the late 1960s, they asked for information about a UFO over the Minuteman missile silos in North Dakota. That entire investigation seemed to consist of a letter from Dr. J. Allen Hynek, the Air Force consultant on UFOs, to the headquarters at the Minot Air Force Base. A first lieutenant was charged with finding the answers to Hynek's questions and responded in detail. The problem was that the Project Blue Book file contained an important observation made about radio communications by an officer on the base at the time. The information was not communicated to the Condon Committee, but Hynek must have known about it. According to this report, while the UFO was nearby, radio communications between the Air Force security team and the officers in the launch capsule were interrupted. This was a matter that could affect national security, that demonstrated the UFO interacting with the environment, and that provided an avenue for further investigation. However, all this was ignored, and the Condon Committee concluded that the UFO sightings were an overreaction by lonely, sleepy, or hysterical airmen.

There is also evidence of cases in which the CIA participated in UFO investigations but reported that the event never happened. The CIA told witnesses that they, the CIA, were not present even as they collected documentation and moved it elsewhere. The solution offered by the skeptics was quickly found to be inaccurate by

UFO researchers, and the official solution offered by various government representatives ignored the testimony of witnesses.

In the government files, I also found evidence that official notice of UFOs, although the phenomenon was called many other things, did not begin in 1947 as nearly everyone suggested, but in 1940, with the Foo Fighters. Reports about UFO sightings, although not referred to as such before 1944, began just prior to the entry of the United States in World War II and continued until the war ended, when the reporting structure and mechanism for recording the sightings collapsed.

As I searched the government files, I found discrepancies between the studies in those files and public announcements about UFO sightings. The Green Fireballs were reported as merely meteors, though the top expert in the field, Dr. Lincoln La Paz, was convinced that they were not. The Ghost Rockets were nothing more than Soviet attempts to intimidate the Swedish government, except that searches of the Russian files after the dissolution of the Soviet Union show that the Soviets had nothing to do with Ghost Rockets.

Skeptical answers, offered by various self-labeled experts, are easily disproved. In one case, it was suggested that a helicopter was responsible for a national security violation, except the helicopter identified as the culprit wasn't there until two weeks after the sighting, and even then it was seen more than 120 miles from the site. Even more interesting, the Air Force, charged with protecting the weapons storage facility, didn't bother to chase down that helicopter and didn't bother to have anyone arrested for the violation. The Air Force was not able to find this helicopter, but a skeptical researcher was.

In May 2013, Steven Bassett of the Paradigm Research Organization put together the Citizen Hearing on Disclosure, bringing together former members of both the House of Representatives and the Senate, as well as witnesses and researchers. Over five days, the committee heard testimony about UFOs from those who had experiences with them and those who had researched them for decades. Among the best testimony was that of former missile officers who reported, based on personal experience, that UFOs had affected the national security of the United States and the government. They stated that the Air Force Office of Special Investigation had worked to bury this information. It would be easy to ignore a single voice, discussing a single incident, but the testimony came from several former officers from several missile sites scattered across the northern tier of states.

Pilots told of UFO intercepts in which the craft were fired on, but the bullets and missiles had no effect on the alien craft. Government documents from one South American country covering this issue were in evidence for the committee. Commandant Oscar Santa Maria Huertas, a retired Peruvian Air Force pilot, said that on April 11, 1980, an object like a balloon was hanging suspended over the end of the runaway. He was ordered to take off and bring down the object.

Huertas took off in an SU-22 fighter, reached an altitude of some 8,000 feet, and got into position. He fired a burst of 64 30 mm cannon shells. He said that some of the rounds "deviated" from the target and fell away, but others hit it with no effect. He said that it seemed as if the rounds had been absorbed by the "balloon," which then began to rise rapidly and turned away from the base.

The "dogfight" didn't end there. According to Huertas, he gave chase, but the UFO always stayed in front of him. He was in full pursuit when the object stopped suddenly and he had to turn to avoid a collision. From that point on, he was unable to get another shot at the UFO. Each time he was prepared to fire, the UFO would "escape by ascending vertically" seconds before he would open fire.

At the National Press Club in Washington, D.C., I saw the official Department of Defense documents about this case. They said that he had fired on the UFO "without results." I asked Huertas if he had hit the UFO, and he confirmed that he had.

Interviewed at the end of the Citizen Hearing on Disclosure held in Washington, D.C., in May 2013, former Utah Representative Merrill Cook said, "I do not believe there has been any strong, credible evidence of [alien visits] at this point, but I do think there has been some credible evidence of things that are unidentified that had been flying about."

Cook would not say that the offered testimony and documentation provided enough proof that we have been visited by alien creatures, but he said there was enough credible evidence that something unidentified is flying around. That might be splitting a hair, but I understand what he was thinking when he said that. Besides, he agreed that something unidentified was flying around and that is more than enough.

What all this points to is a long and ongoing attempt by the government and the Air Force to suppress the information about UFOs. The government files are filled with excellent cases with multiple witnesses and multiple chains of evidence suggesting that something strange is happening. The government files contain documented evidence that UFOs are a threat to national security when they penetrate nuclear weapons storage facilities and when they are able to shut down missile guidance systems and force the missiles "off-line." The government files contain evidence that a legitimate scientific study of the cases could provide information of value.

How do I know?

The conclusion to one of the cases studied by the Condon Committee stated, "This unusual sighting should therefore be assigned to the category of some almost certainly natural phenomenon, which is so rare that it apparently has never been reported before or since."

The report came from an airline crew over Labrador on June 30, 1954. The Condon Committee seemed to believe that the cause was some sort of optical illusion, while the Air Force wrote it off as the planet Mars seen under unusual circumstances.

But the real point is that neither of those solutions is satisfactory. And if, in fact, the flying objects can be explained as a new natural phenomenon, whatever it might be, that in itself is enough cause for exploration and would advance scientific knowledge. Rather than acknowledging this, Condon, in keeping with the tradition evidenced in the government files, said that nothing useful would be found by a continued study of UFOs.

This study of the government files changes the history of the UFO field and proves that the government has been less than candid about UFO sightings. Once all the files are examined, it will be clear that something is going on. It is something real, and it is something that requires additional research. Even if it doesn't lead to the extraterrestrial, it will advance our knowledge, and isn't that the point of science?

The Foo Fighters

Nearly every book about Unidentified Flying Objects (UFOs) suggests that the "Modern Era" began on June 24, 1947, when Kenneth Arnold saw nine crescent-shaped objects near Mount Rainier, Washington. But the truth of the matter is that flying saucers, also referred to by many other names, were reported regularly from the beginning of the 1940s. These early manifestations were eventually labeled the "Foo Fighters," and they were described in ways that made it clear they were much more than just blobs of light seen in the distance.

Though much of the literature about Foo Fighters suggests that they first appeared in the late stages of World War II, and it is true that the name Foo Fighters wasn't used until 1944, it is also true that the sightings began much earlier than that. On February 26, 1942, just weeks after the American entry into the war, a Dutch sailor in the Timor Sea, near Australia and New Guinea, reported seeing a large, illuminated disk approaching at what he thought was an incredible speed.

According to what the witness told Australian UFO researcher Peter Norris many years later, "It flew in big circles and at the same height ... the craft suddenly veered off in a tremendous burst of speed ... and disappeared."

In the European Theater, on March 25, 1942, the tail gunner in a Royal Air Force bomber flying over the Zuider Zee, Holland, returning from a raid on Essen, Germany, saw a glowing, orange disc or sphere following them. He told the pilot, who also saw the object closing in on them. When the object was about 100 or 200 yards from the plane, the gunner fired and hit the object, with no effect. The object finally disappeared.

Paul C. Cerny and Robert Neville, two UFO investigators with the Mutual UFO Network, reported in the July 1983 issue of the *MUFON UFO Journal* that a sailor with the fleet off Guadalcanal in August 1942 reported sighting a disk-shaped object that circled overhead. According to them, "... a chief at the time aboard the U.S.S. *Helm* ... had an excellent observation of an incredible encounter with an unknown, unidentified intruder. At 10:00 A.M. the fleet received a radar report from one of the cruisers and a little later a visual sighting of the object was made from their destroyer."

This was one of the first Foo Fighter reports and it began, not with a visual sighting, but with radar contact. The object was then seen by the sailors of the

The modern era of UFO sightings starts with aviator and businessman Kenneth Arnold, who, in 1947, reported seeing nine crescent-shaped objects near Mount Rainier, Washington.

fleet as it approached. According to the witness, because it was not coming from the correct direction known then as the radio beam, the object was assumed to be hostile. When it was still over a mile away, the fleet opened fire.

According to Cerny and Neville, "The unknown then made a sharp right turn and headed south from an approach heading of 320 degrees. The UFO increased its speed and then circled the entire fleet."

The witness, who refused to let his name be used, said that he had a pair of 7 × 50 binoculars so that he had a chance to see the object quite well. According to him, it was fairly flat, silver in color, with a slight dome in the center of the top.

Having circled the fleet, the object departed to the south. It had been fired upon, but the speed at which it was traveling made it difficult for the fleet to hit the object. The antiaircraft fire seemed to have no adverse effect on the object.

Just days later, with Marines on the islands, a sergeant with the 1st Marine Division, Stephen J. Brickner, reported another encounter with a silver object. He said:

> The sighting occurred on August 12, 1942 about 10 in the morning while I was in bivouac with my squad on the island of Tulagi in the southern Solomons [Tulagi being near Guadalcanal].... I was cleaning my rifle on the edge of my foxhole, when suddenly the air raid warning was sounded.... I immediately slid into my foxhole.... I heard the formation before I saw it.... It didn't sound at all like the high-pitched "sewing machine" drone of the Jap formations. A few seconds later I saw the formation of silvery objects directly overhead.

> At the time I was in a highly emotional state; it was my fifth day in combat with the Marines. It was quite easy to mistake anything in the air for Jap planes, which is what I thought these objects were. They were flying very high above the clouds, too high for a bombing run on our little island. Someone shouted in a nearby foxhole that they were Jap planes searching for our fleet. I accepted this explanation, but with a few reservations. First, the formation was huge; I would say over 150 objects were in it. Instead of the usual "V" of 25 planes, this formation was in straight lines of 10 or 12 objects, one behind the other. The speed was a little faster than Jap planes, and they were soon out of sight. A few other things puzzled me: I couldn't seem to make out wings or tails. They seemed to wobble slightly, and every time they wobbled they would shimmer brightly from the sun. Their color was like highly polished silver. No bombs were dropped, of

course. All in all, it was the most awe-inspiring and yet frightening spectacle I have seen in my life.

About the same time, on the evening of August 11 and the morning of August 12, bomber crews of the Royal Air Force (RAF), flying near Aachen, half a world away, saw "a phenomenon described as a bright white light" climbing up from the ground. When it reached about 8,000 feet it leveled off for about two minutes.

While all these sightings are interesting, and they show that some sort of unidentified flying objects were seen over major areas of conflict early in the war, they didn't spark any real official or high-level interest. Some of the sightings were not reported at the time simply because the flight crews didn't know what to make of them and they didn't want others to think they were suffering from war nerves or combat fatigue. Others were noted but not passed on in the chain of command because there was nothing of intelligence value in them.

Author and researcher Jerome Clark has written down the accounts of UFO sightings in the 1940s in his *UFO Encyclopedia.*

These sightings, some reported at the time and others not mentioned until long after the Kenneth Arnold sighting of June 24, 1947, continued in all theaters of the war. According to Jerome Clark in his *UFO Encyclopedia,* second edition, "Among the relatively rare reports from 1943 is an account from a bombardier who remembered that 'round, speedy balls of fire' sometimes followed Allied bombers back from night raids on Tokyo (*Wisconsin State Journal* [Madison], July 8, 1947)."

Clark also reported on an event on October 14, 1942 as B-17s of the 384th Bomb Group were returning from a mission over Germany. Clark wrote:

> [B-17's] … spotted a cluster of "discs" in front of them. The objects were moving in their direction, and one pilot attempted to evade what he was certain was an imminent collision. As he later told debriefers, his "right wing went directly through a cluster with absolutely no effect on engines or plane surface." He and his crew heard one of the objects strike the tail section of the bomber, but no explosion or other effect followed. He also said that 20 feet or so from the disc there was a "mass of black debris of varying sizes in clusters of three by four feet." The fliers had two subsequent encounters with the discs and accompanying "debris." [Caidin, Martin. *Black Thursday.* New York: Dell Publishing Company, 1960.]

This sighting and others of a similar nature are important because they were reported in the debriefings and were recorded in government files. But they are also important because they show that some of the Foo Fighters were not solid ob-

The phenomenon of St. Elmo's Fire has been observed for many years, as can be seen in this 1866 illustration of a ship at sea. It is a natural phenomenon resulting from a coronal discharge eminating from sharp or pointed objects, such as a ship's masts, when there is a strong electrical charge in the atmosphere, usually during a thunderstorm.

jects, but glowing balls of what has been called St. Elmo's fire, though the exact nature of these objects was never determined.

There was official interest in these sightings and British government documents reflect this. On October 12, 1942, Bomber Command, in a memorandum called "Enemy Defenses—Phenomenon," alerted the headquarters of the eight bomb groups about the sightings. They wrote, "The Operational Research Station at this Headquarters has carried out an investigation into enemy pyrotechnic activity [meaning the glowing balls of light] which has recently been experienced over Germany. The AOC [Air Officer in Charge] has issued instructions that the information contained in this report be brought to the notice of all crews. We would remind you that Consolidated FLO [Flak Liaison Officer] Reports issued by MI14(E) refer to Phenomenon when reported and given possible explanations."

Essentially, they were telling the flight crews that something was going on, and though they weren't sure what it was, they wanted information about the sightings reported. They were also searching for explanations for what was being seen.

British government files reveal that on December 2, 1942, Headquarters of RAF Station Syerston sent a classified memorandum to Major Mullock, who was the Flight Liaison Officer at the headquarters of the No. 5 Group. The memo referenced an object seen by Captain Lever and his crew, members of the 61 Squadron during an attack on Turin on the night of November 28/29, 1942. The government file said, in part:

> The object referred to above was seen by the entire crew of the above aircraft. They believe it to have been 200–300 feet in length and its width is estimated to at 1/5 or 1/6 of its length. The speed was estimated at 500 m.p.h., and it had four pairs of red lights spaced at equal distances along its body. The lights did not appear in any way like exhaust flames; no trace was seen. The object kept a level course.
>
> The crew saw the object twice during the raid, and brief details are given below:
>
> (i) After bombing, time 2240 hours, a/c [aircraft] height 11,000 feet. The aircraft was some 10/15 miles South West of Turin traveling in

northwesterly direction. The object was traveling South-East at the same height or slightly below the aircraft.

(ii) After bombing, time 2245 hours, a/c height 14,000 feet. The aircraft was approaching the Alps when the object was seen again traveling West-South-West up a valley in the Alps below the level of the peaks. The lights appeared to go out and the object disappeared from view.

The Captain of the aircraft also reports that he has seen a similar object about three months ago North of Amsterdam. In this instance, it appeared to be on the ground, and later traveling at high speed at a lower level than the heights given along the coast for about two seconds; the lights went out for the same period of time and came back on again, and the object was still seen to be traveling in the same direction.

This sighting is important, not because of what the report contains, but because of who eventually saw the report. It was sent through the normal military channels, but six copies were sent to the U.S. Army Air Forces and six to the U.S. Naval Intelligence.

Leonard Stringfield, a well-respected UFO researcher who eventually had his own sighting of the Foo Fighters, reported that up until December 1942 the majority of the sightings had been over Germany and Holland. According to Stringfield, a sighting that didn't make it into government files showed that these things were seen all over Europe. This sighting came from a submarine patrol craft along the coast of England, where the crew reported spotting a strange craft with no wings.

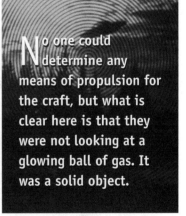

No one could determine any means of propulsion for the craft, but what is clear here is that they were not looking at a glowing ball of gas. It was a solid object.

What is important about this sighting is one of the side effects observed. According to the witness, the aircraft intercom began to malfunction as the object neared. The intercom became a "jumbled mess of incoherent squawks," while the object was close by. No one could determine any means of propulsion for the craft, but what is clear here is that they were not looking at a glowing ball of gas. It was a solid object.

Three years later, just days after the Japanese surrender, Stringfield, at the time an Army intelligence NCO, was on an aircraft heading for Tokyo. Three tear-shaped objects, in a tight formation and traveling on a course that was parallel to that of the aircraft on which Stringfield was a passenger, appeared. The sighting would have been just one more in the list of sightings reported from the Pacific Theater, except that in this particular instance, the left engine of the transport began to act up.

A few moments later, the co-pilot left the cockpit and told the passengers that they were in trouble. Both engines were sputtering and the pilot was preparing for an emergency landing.

Stringfield, based on his intelligence training, was familiar with the aircraft in the inventories of the world's air forces at the time. He knew that the three objects in the sky were not jets, and were certainly nothing built by either the Germans or the Japanese. As he watched, the three objects disappeared into a cloud bank. As they vanished, the aircraft's engines began to function normally. They began to climb again.

In both these cases, neither of which was reported through official channels, witnesses reported some sort of effect on their aircraft. This sort of interference would later be called "electromagnetic effects" and would be reported more frequently after Arnold's sighting.

The Silver Discs

Sightings of the balls of fire, of disk-shaped craft, of strange things in the sky in Europe and Asia continued. Some of the sightings were clearly not of any sort of piloted craft or of extraterrestrial origin. They were too small to carry a crew and it seemed that they were an experimental type of anti-aircraft launched by the Germans.

According to the government files, on September 6, 1943, a huge bombing raid was made on Stuttgart, Germany. Captain Raymond P. Ketelson was the 384th

Blobs of light like the ones shown here were seen many times by pilots during World War II. They were definitely unusual, but whatever they were was never fully established. (This photograph, while illustrating what the Foo Fighters looked like, is of suspicious origin).

Bomb Group leader on that day. They were near the target flying above 22,000 feet when two of the crews reported "objects resembling silver discs about the size of half-dollars" floating down.

The information was published in a classified document called, "384 BG memorandum, ATTN: A-2 Duty Desk Section 'A'," which was updated with "Additional Information On The Observations of Silvery Colored Discs On Mission to Stuttgart. 6 Sept. 1943":

> This observation was made by two crews of the 384th Group and was the only place it was noted. At this time from 2 to 4 FW-190's or ME-109's and 1 JU 88 [German fighter aircraft] were flying 2 or 3000 feet above and a little ahead of our formation. These E/A [enemy aircraft] were not seen to drop the material out. It came from above our A/C [aircraft]. As to its shape, it was a mass of material, kept a good pattern, did not dissipate as it streamed down and fell comparatively slow. In one instance, the cluster appeared to be about 8 ft. in length and about 4 feet wide as it streaked down. Another observation stated it was about 75 feet long and 20 feet wide. These dimensions in length being the size from top to bottom as it fell. The cluster was composed of small round objects, silvery in color. In all instances, the objects fell in the path of our A/C. Some was observed to fall on the wing of a B-17 belonging to our group. The wing immediately started to burn. The a/c did not return. No further information available.

It is clear from this report that these "Foo Fighters" did not fit the classic definition but may have been some new form of anti-aircraft. It seems, based on this report, that this new form of anti-aircraft weaponry appeared to be successful, though it could be argued that it might not have been worth the effort to deploy it.

That didn't stop the intelligence analysis. There had been a report sent on to General "Hap" Arnold about the silver discs. On September 16, according to the government files, Major Bauman, the chemical warfare officer, wrote that the discs were "white phosphorous and a sticky substance which would cause it to cling to the plane ... Thermite with some sort of igniting compound inherent in a sticky substance ... or ... Flat round glass containers loaded with either of the above incendiary compounds."

There were additional sightings of these tiny silver discs on later missions, and of other, similar weapons that included flying doughnuts and pie plates. A large number of reports were generated as the flight crews reported seeing these things during debriefing after their missions. Analysis suggested that these were enemy anti-aircraft weapons dropped from above the bomber formations with the hope of hitting and destroying Allied aircraft, causing them to catch fire.

Investigators doing research into UFOs, and those who were attempting to identify these things during the war, seem to have lumped these events in with all the other Foo Fighter accounts. The Foo Fighters, however, were described as large balls of light, balls of fire, or as large, solid objects that paced aircraft and bomber formations. These silver disks were obviously something else.

There were also sightings that were not of tiny silver saucers, and did not happen during German fighter attacks on Allied bombers. In May 1943, for example, there were a number of such reports. According to the government files, on May 12/13 a flight crew saw a meteor that they called an "object ... reddish-orange in color ... that emitted a burst giving off a green star." Ten days later, on May 23/24 a large number of rockets were seen by the flight crews. On May 27/28 near Essen, Germany, a flight crew saw a cylindrical object with several portholes evenly spaced along the side. It hung motionless until it flew off at several thousand miles an hour.

Balls of Fire

The Pacific Theater sightings weren't of the little silver disks but of glowing balls of fire. Keith Chester, in his book *Strange Company*, details these reports of balls of fire. He found, in government files, a document from XXI Bomber Command dated March 29, 1945, which said, "Japs Have A Bagful Full of Tricks, *But They Don't Work!* In the European Theater of Operations, the Germans have experimented with a great variety of 'secret weapons' and special antiaircraft devices. None of these has proved effective against our bombers. It seems that the Japs—with their usual flare for imitation—have likewise tried a number of weird weapons against B-29's of the XXI Bomber Command."

The intelligence officers, in debriefing the flight crews, heard about the balls of fire. The flight crew mentioned that they had seen two orange-red bursts with tails, or three green balls that appeared to float down, and balls of fire traveling at very high speeds. They also described two large red balls of fire that were apparently attached and that were floating down.

> The Foo Fighters ... were described as large balls of light, balls of fire, or as large, solid objects that paced aircraft and bomber formations. These silver disks were obviously something else.

Like their counterparts in Europe, these crews called the lights "flares" in some instances. According to Chester, in his examination of government files, one flight crew reported they had seen "three flares" approaching them as if they were radar controlled. The flares turned with and followed the aircraft through a series of maneuvers.

During a raid on the Mitsubishi Aircraft Engine Works on the night of March 30/morning of April 1, 1945, there were multiple encounters with the balls of fire. They seemed to approach the B-29s and then explode. They did no damage, just raised the stress level of the flight crews on the raids as they watched the fire come up at them.

In the government files found by Chester was a report from a B-29 crew that had seen a dark object flying at them. They said that object "disintegrated" before it reached them, falling to the ground and then exploding. This same crew reported that something had followed their B-29 as they approached land's end. As the object caught up to them, the pilot increased his speed and made a series of

The 29th Bombardment Group is shown here in Guam in 1945. Government file reports reveal the military thought the Japanese were using some kind of silver disks to, ineffectively, attack these bombers.

turns, which the object followed. There were two long streaks of fire that, at another time, might have been thought of as missiles and then this object exploded.

A different crew, according to the government files, saw something coming up off the ground. It was a long, red streak of flame, observed by everyone on the aircraft. The object climbed steeply, turned right, and came around the front of the aircraft, but well ahead of it. Circling around the plane, the UFO now approached from the rear, and then it exploded without doing damage to the B-29.

Two days later, on April 3, according to the XXI Bomber Command's Tactical Report, flight crews mentioned "Balls of Fire" as the only enemy opposition. According to Chester, the best of these reports came from a crew of the 73rd Bombardment Wing. Chester wrote:

> According to Lt. Althoff, they had just completed bombing the secondary target and were approaching land's end. Their altitude was 9,000 feet at the time when he first saw the "ball of fire" coming in on his B-29 at about the five o'clock [position]. It was about 300 yards behind his B-29 and the "ball of fire was about the size of a basketball." Immediately, evasive action was taken, but the ball of fire cut to the inside of the plane and continued to follow. Lt. Althoff said that it appeared that the ball of fire could not keep up with the B-29's evasive maneuvers, weaving turns, but

when the bomber was flying straight, the ball of fire caught up to them. One of the other crewmen said he saw a "streamer of light behind the ball of fire, which was faint and not steady." The light faded as it turned with the B-29, but increased in intensity on the straightaway.

Playing cat and mouse, the B-29 and its pursuer were over the Pacific Ocean. Diving to 6,000 feet, the B-29 was able to obtain additional air speed, and the ball of fire fell behind, eventually turned around, and gave up its pursuit, heading back to the coast. Watching the object retreat, Lt. Althoff noticed a "streamer of light," but then the light "faded abruptly." The blister gunner thought he had seen a "wing in connection with ball of fire; and it had a navigation light burning on left wing tip." But now the chase was over. It had followed them for approximately six minutes.

Lt. Schmidt was in another B-29. His plane had departed the target area, which they bombed from 6,100 feet. Gaining another 900 feet, he noticed a ball of fire, emitting a "steady phosphorescent glow," following him. Immediately the B-29 took evasive action, "gaining and losing 500 ft. and also changing course as much as 35 degrees and varying airspeed from 205 to 250." Flying into the clouds, they thought the maneuver had worked, but as they emerged, the ball of fire was right on the B-29's tail. Twice more the pilot steered his bomber into the clouds and twice more when he came out, the ball of fire was right there behind his plane. Then, over Tokyo Bay, the ball of fire "disappeared" not too far behind the fleeing B-29.

These sorts of reports would continue throughout the Pacific Theater and throughout the rest of the war. As had been noticed in Europe, the aircraft were not damaged by the encounters. The aircrews reported them, as they would anything else that might affect future missions. As in Europe, intelligence officers and the command staffs were worried about the deployment of a new type of anti-aircraft weapon. They investigated carefully, but they could find nothing to explain these balls of fire or what they might be.

The Foo Fighters

It wasn't until late in 1944 that the term "Foo Fighter" was used for the first time. The reports of these objects, in late 1944, were made by members of the 415th Night Fighter Squadron. On November 23, one of the squadron's aircraft, commanded by Lieutenant (some sources identify him as a captain) Edward Schluter (sometimes spelled Schlueter), took off from Dijon, France, for a night patrol. Near Strasbourg, the intelligence officer, Lieutenant F. Ringwald, glanced out of the aircraft and spotted eight to ten balls of red fire moving at what he thought of as a "great velocity."

Both ground radar and airborne radar showed nothing. In the aircraft, Lieutenant Donald J. Meiers (identified in other sources as Myers) told Schluter that he had no enemy fighters on his radar.

The light blobs of the Foo Fighters can been seen here, vaguely, above the plane on the right. The Foo Fighters had the ability to appear and disappear suddenly. Like many of the pictures of Foo Fighters, the provenance of this photo is clouded.

The pilot maneuvered the aircraft toward the lights and they seemed to vanish. A minute or two later, the lights reappeared, but they were much farther away. They seemed to be reacting to the night fighter and after five or six minutes, they began to glide, leveled out and finally disappeared—this time for good.

During their debriefing, according to one version in the government files, Meiers called the objects "Foo Fighters" for the lack of a better term. Due to the unusal nature of their report, Schluter and Meiers began to take all kinds of ribbing from their fellow flight crews, at least until others made similar sightings.

On December 15, 1944, according to an operations report in the government files, another flight crew reported that they, "Saw a brilliant red light [that appeared to be 4 or 5 times larger than a star] at 2000 feet going at 200 MPH in the vicinity of Ernstein. Due to AI (Air Intercept radar) failure could not pick up contact but followed it by sight until it went out. Could not get close enough to identify object before it went out."

Another Foo Fighter report was found in the Operations Report for a December 23, 1944 mission. It said, "In vicinity of Hagenau saw 2 lights coming toward A/C from ground. After reaching the altitude of the A/C they leveled off and flew on tail of Beau [their aircraft] for 2 minutes and then peeled up and turned away. 8th mission—sighted 2 orange lights. One light sighted at 10,000 feet the other climbed until it disappeared."

There were other sightings in which it seemed that the lights or objects paced the aircraft, following them through turns, climbs, and dives; in fact, they seemed to be observing the bombers. Government files from the Pacific Theater on May 2, 1945 reveal the following:

> The crew of plane #616 over FALA ISLAND, TRUK ATOLL, at 021802Z [May 2 at 6:02 P.M. Greenwich Mean Time] observed 2 airborne objects at their 11,000 foot altitude, changing from a cherry red to an orange, and to a white light which would die out and become a cherry red again. These objects were out on either wing and not within range of caliber .50 machine guns. Both followed the B-24 thru [sic] all types of evasive action. A B-24 took a course for Guam and one of the pursuers dropped off at 021900Z [May 2 at 7:00 P.M.] after accompanying the B-24 for an hour. The other continued to follow never approaching closer than 1000 yards and speeding up when the B-24 went through the clouds to emerge on the other side ahead of the B-24. In daylight it was seen to be bright silver in color.

Because the Foo Fighters only seemed to show up over enemy territory in Europe and over the Pacific Ocean in areas that were controlled by neither the Japanese nor the Allies, it suggested to intelligence officers that the Foo Fighters represented some sort of enemy technology. In some of the cases it seemed that the Foo Fighters were new enemy anti-aircraft weapons rather than some sort of advanced fighter, but in most of the cases intelligence officers had no real answers. They assumed that the flight crews, even under the stress of combat missions that lasted for hours, after repeated attacks by enemy fighters, flak over targets, weather that created problems, horrible flying conditions, and equipment failures, would be providing accurate information. They certainly wanted to learn more about these strange lights and weird objects.

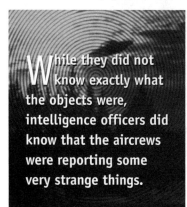

While they did not know exactly what the objects were, intelligence officers did know that the aircrews were reporting some very strange things.

While they did not know exactly what the objects were, intelligence officers did know that the aircrews were reporting some very strange things. Since it was more than one crew, and since it happened with greater regularity as the war continued, it became imperative for them to discover if there was a sudden increase in the enemy technologies.

In 1944 the Allies formed the Combined Intelligence Objectives Committee (CIOS), which met for the first time on September 6. Some of those in attendance who would later figure in the study of UFOs were Howard Robertson and the Chief, Air Technical Section, Colonel Howard McCoy, whose name would surface in many other UFO-related activities. According to the government files, their mission was to coordinate intelligence field teams and their handling of reports, including those of the Foo Fighters. They referred, at the time, to these objects as "pirate bodies." The CIOS had other activities, but it is interesting that one of the main functions was to discover the nature of the Foo Fighters, and that some of those involved would appear in later, other UFO investigations.

Various commands at various levels created numerous documents and reports about the Foo Fighters and the balls of fire that have been examined in today's world. Government files suggest, and in fact, a later investigation into UFOs supports this assumption, that thinking about the Foo Fighters went beyond just the enemy and new technologies. In January 1953, the CIA sponsored a review of the material that had been reported to the Air Force Projects Sign, Grudge and Blue Book, which studied UFOs and UFO sightings. Known as the Robertson Panel after the leader, Dr. H. P. Robertson, it noted, "If the term 'flying saucers' had been popular in 1943–1945, these objects would have been so labeled."

Jerome Clark, in his massive *UFO Encyclopedia* (second edition), reported that Dr. F. C. Durant, a member of the Robertson Panel, in his *Report on the Meetings of Scientific Advisory Panel on Unidentified Flying Objects Convened by Office of Scientific Intelligence, CIA,* wrote that:

General Hap Arnold, shown here, commanded U.S. Army Air Forces during World War II, and he was the one who ordered David T. Griggs to investigate the Foo Fighters.

> Instances of "Foo Fighters" were cited. These were unexplained phenomena sighted by aircraft pilots during World War II in both European and Far East theaters of operation wherein "balls of light" would fly near or with the aircraft and maneuver rapidly. They were believed to be electrostatic (similar to St. Elmo's fire) or electromagnetic phenomena or possibly light reflections from ice crystals in the air, but their exact cause or nature was never defined. Both Robertson and [Luis Alvarez] … had been concerned in the investigation of these phenomena, but David T. Griggs is believed to have been the most knowledgeable person on this subject.…

The David T. Griggs mentioned above was a scientist who had been "drafted" from MIT to work on radar during World War II. Griggs was sent into the European Theater in 1942 where he worked under Generals Hap Arnold, Jimmy Doolittle, and Carl Spaatz, meaning he was at the highest levels of the Army Air Forces' command structure. He flew both training missions and combat missions and was in a position to hear the stories of the "anomalous" phenomenon, or Foo Fighters. Although Griggs was a scientist, the air crews trusted him because he was there with them and he flew missions with them. He was the guy to unravel the mystery of the Foo Fighters, and given their apparent interest in the Allied bombing campaigns in all theaters of the war, it was something that needed to be done quickly.

David T. Griggs

While the government files do not document an official project, groups of committees dedicated to learning the identity of the Foo Fighters were formed and there were various individuals who were tasked with finding more about the Foo Fighters. Griggs was part of one of these groups. As he worked to improve the radar systems in the European Theater, and as he traveled around to Europe, he had an opportunity to investigate the Foo Fighters at the request of Hap Arnold. He later told Dr. James McDonald, a scientist with a deep interest in UFOs that he, Griggs, had written reports about the Foo Fighters, but he had no copies of those reports and he didn't know where they might be located in the government files.

According to what Dr. Michael Swords wrote in *UFOs and Government: A Historical Inquiry*, Griggs told McDonald in the 1960s....

> [about] his musings about jet exhausts being misinterpreted, about dark nights with no background leading to tricks of perception, about war nerves, and all that. He then related how he and a crew had been temporarily fooled by the Moon rising under just the wrong (or right) conditions. [This referred to a mission on the night of June 19/20, 1945. Griggs was in the navigator's position on a B-29. One of the waist gunners yelled, "Fireball coming in." The problem was that the crew had been so anxious to show Griggs a fireball that they had misidentified the moon.] But Griggs did not really believe that such things explained all the foo fighter reports.

Which, when you think about it, is exactly what nearly everyone says about UFO reports. There are widespread and long lists of solutions for UFO sightings that range from astronomical phenomena, to misinterpretations of manmade objects, to hysteria, and psychological problems. Nearly every sighting of a UFO is explained by careful research, but there is a residue which has no conventional explanation, no matter how thorough the investigation might be. Griggs had confirmed, for McDonald, that he had found the same sort of thing for the Foo Fighters some years before anyone was talking about UFOs and flying saucers.

Griggs said that he didn't think that every sighting was explained or explainable. He thought there was something to the real, as opposed to imaginary, sightings, but he just didn't know what that might be.

Griggs said that he didn't think that every sighting was explained or explainable. He thought there was something to the real, as opposed to imaginary, sightings, but he just didn't know what that might be. According to Swords, Griggs said, "The air observers' reports were all over enemy territory—never over our ground. Anxiety that the enemy might have something we needed to know about kept the checking under way. [And], there were reports of engine disturbances over [what could have been the "Reich," meaning Germany]."

When the war in Europe ended in May 1945, Griggs was sent to the Pacific Theater with a similar assignment. European sightings of the Foo Fighters described a variety of different types and shapes, but in the Pacific, the majority of descriptions seemed to describe mainly "balls of fire." Griggs was part of the Compton Scientific Intelligence Committee, and he wanted to specifically to track down Japanese military technology with an eye to finding more about their electromagnetic beam experiments. There had been some discussion that these beam weapons could interrupt the smooth function of engines, as had been reported in some of the European Foo Fighter cases and, of course, was what Len Stringfield would report about his sighting at the very end of the war in the Pacific.

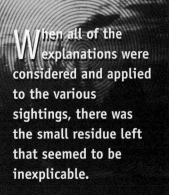

When all of the explanations were considered and applied to the various sightings, there was the small residue left that seemed to be inexplicable.

Griggs did find, according to the government files, some information about this electromagnetic "ray" technology. The ray was something primitive, but "[They could] stop the engines at short range … and one massive device could kill a rabbit.…" The document is somewhat difficult to decipher, but it seemed to suggest that the ray killed a rabbit at a distance of about three feet. Apparently the device was discovered and captured, complete with its thirty-four foot dish. According to Swords, the dish and its equipment were shipped to the U.S., but there is no record of it arriving in the country and there seems to be no follow up about what happened to it.

The Final Solution

Throughout the war, the Allies in all theaters were interested in these objects, lights, Foo Fighters, and balls of fire because they might represent an advance in the enemy ability to control the air. They were seen as a threat to air operations, though the Foo Fighters didn't seem to engage in aerial combat and the balls of fire did no damage to Allied aircraft.

There are reports where enemy fighters dropped some tiny silver disks, which were some kind of anti-aircraft device. These cases are clearly describing some sort of weapons system, and these reports do not belong in the category of Foo Fighters.

In other cases, the Foo Fighters were small "balls of fire," sometimes referred to as St. Elmo's fire. The thought being that they were some sort of ionization of the air around the aircraft but that simply doesn't work. Why were sightings of these balls of fire only reported over enemy territory, and why are they not reported today around airports? While there are certainly times when the air is electrified in some fashion in the world today, the area does not glow, and the phenomenon are extremely rare.

The exception to this seems to be the Japanese experiments into electromagnetic radiation and weapons. They seem to have been able to develop a beam weapon that could stall an engine, but the range was only two or three feet so there was no practical military application for it. Had they been able to extend the range to several thousand feet, it might have become a significant weapon. Interestingly, all information about this has disappeared.

When all of the explanations were considered and applied to the various sightings, there was the small residue left that seemed to be inexplicable. There were sightings, such as one on 19/20 June by a B-29 crew in which the crew shot at the object. According to the government files, the gunners fired on it, but either missed or they hit it with no apparent results.

Griggs, in his investigation of the balls of fire, learned of one other such incident. Wanting to see one of the balls of fire himself, Griggs accompanied an aircrew on an operational mission. They told him that they had fired at one once but they didn't tell him, or he didn't report, the results of that incident in any official document. Griggs did note the report in a telephone interview with Dr. James McDonald, as described to UFO researcher Jan Aldrich.

In Europe, a B-17 crew flying over the North Sea toward Berlin on the morning of April 7, 1945, saw something very strange. The navigator, Captain Louis Sewell, thought they were being attacked by a German fighter. According to the government files, Sewell said that the fighter dived at them, leveled and then rolled under the B-17. It did not attack and they realized it wasn't a fighter but something that looked more like a V-2. It was maneuvering intelligently, but it didn't seem to have any wings.

In 1945, Captain Louis Sewell, piloting a B-17 much like this one over the North Sea, saw something that looked like a V-2 but it was maneuvering intelligently.

Importantly, the object, which held its position relative to the B-17 for a short time and then accelerated to "two thousand miles an hour," was seen by others in the formation. The radio operator in Sewell's aircraft took several pictures of the object. Once on the ground, the film was taken away and the crew heard nothing more about it, which, according to Sewell, wasn't all that unusual.

Here was something that was seen in the daylight, was seen by others in other aircraft, and which was photographed. Like the Japanese "beam" weapons, those photographs disappeared into the great maw of the military machinery.

There is one point that needs to be made. In all the reports, documents, and government files available about Foo Fighters and the balls of fire, no one was thinking of the extraterrestrial. Everyone involved thought that these things were something that the enemy was developing, and that thought worried all concerned. If the Germans, or the Japanese, had developed aircraft or anti-aircraft weapons with the capabilities observed, then that could tilt the war in their favor and prolong the fighting.

There was almost no discussion of the Foo Fighters as spacecraft in the government files. In the end, no conclusions were drawn about the Foo Fighters or the balls of fire. It was just one of the strange things that happened during the war.

The Scandinavian Ghost Rockets

Following reports of the Foo Fighters, and before sightings of flying disks, there were sightings of objects called the Ghost Rockets. Beginning with reports of sightings over Scandinavia early in 1946, the sightings later expanded to the European continent. In the end, there were a number of official investigations, a number of cases with recovered physical evidence, and an indirect request for assistance from the United States.

The report that seems to be the origin of the Ghost Rockets was made on February 26, 1946, when a radio station in Helsinki noted "numerous meteors" that had fallen in northern Finland. The objects, which glowed, blazed, and fell, acted like meteors and were considered to be meteors by many who saw or investigated them, but there was something unusual about them.

It is odd that these objects would be considered anything other than meteors, but Jerome Clark, in his *UFO Encyclopedia* (second edition), provides what could be the inspiration for either the reports in Finland or the explanation of them. He wrote:

> At 11 P.M. on January 18, 1946, as an American C-54 transport plane was passing over rural France at 7000 feet, the pilot observed what he took to be a brilliant meteor at 35 degrees above the eastern horizon. The object fell and was lost to view—but only momentarily. To the witness' astonishment the "meteor" ascended, then "described a tiny hyperbola of perhaps one degree altitude and fell again from sight."

> Whatever the phenomenon was, it clearly had not been a meteor. Soon Europeans and others would call such phenomena "ghost rockets" and ascribe them to secret Soviet experiments with captured V-2 missiles. Many of the "rockets" *would* be meteors, but none, so history attests, were missiles from Russia, which at the time, possessed only a primitive missile technology …

The next reported sighting in 1946 came on May 24, when two night watchmen saw a "wingless, cigar-shaped body of dimensions of a small airplane." At regular intervals, sparks or fire spurted from the rear. It was at a very low altitude and moving at the speed of an airplane to the southwest, according to what they said.

Analysis of the sighting appeared two days later in *Dagens Nyheter*:

Even if reports of a wingless aircraft spurting fire over Landskrona are to be treated with a certain reserve, it is very possible that what people saw were V-1 bombs fired by the Russians from some experimental station on the Baltic Coast. This statement was made by an air expert, to whom *"Dagens Nyheter"* submitted reports in yesterday's telegram. The experts state that the whole of Germany has been fine-combed by the occupying powers for robot bomb material and experiments are being carried out zealously. Just as with the Germans, a number of projectiles went on courses not intended ... bombs from the Continent can naturally now land in or make short-cuts over Sweden. The observations made by the inhabitants of Landskrona, namely that sparks from the tail come at intervals, agrees with the V-1 bomb's manner of operation. It is true that the witnesses have given the length of the projectiles now seen as considerably less than the V-1 bomb's 6–7 metres but it is easy to err on such points. Of all parties interested in robot bombs, the Americans appear to have come the farthest.... Finally, it remains to report that a chauffeur in Huddinge saw a shining projectile at 12 o'clock at night on Friday/Saturday and he considered that it could not have been either an aircraft or a meteor. When he spoke of the matter, he had not heard of what happened in Landskrona so he could not have been influenced by it.

On May 28, 1946, there were other reports of what were being described in some newspapers as fireballs. These came from Karlshkrona and Halsingborg, as well as many people in the Stockholm area, who said they had seen the same thing in Huddinge and Hagalund. According to the newspaper *Morgon-Tidningen*, many aviation experts were suggesting experiments with secret, long-range weapons.

The same thing was seen in Katrineholm on May 31. This time the object was said to be a glistening, silver rocket shaped like a giant cigar. There were no hints of wings, but there might have been a stabilizer on the rear. It moved quickly and interestingly, the newspaper reported that "many observers" said that it was faster than a fast airplane. It was at about 1,000 feet.

On the same day, the *Adronbladet* reported "Mysterious objects, considered to be some kind of peculiar 'meteors' or some new V-bomb, have flown over Helsingfors [Helsinki]. The mysterious wingless projectiles, which fly on a north-east–southwest course, appear to have their 'bases' somewhere north of Lake Ladoga."

It was on June 1 that the British Air Attaché in Stockholm sent a communiqué to the Assistant Chief of Staff (Intelligence) at the Air Ministry, that said, "Flying missiles observed over Sweden.... Both myself and members of my staff have discussed the ... reports with representatives

On January 18, 1946, an American C-54 transport plane was flying over France when it encountered what looked like a bright meteor, but then witnesses saw it change course.

The UFO spotted over Katrineholm, Sweden, in 1946 was described as looking like a giant cigar.

of the Swedish Air Force, who, although interested, are as yet unable to confirm the observations officially, but they have agreed to pass on to us any information that may be of interest." It was signed by Group Captain Simpson, Air Attaché.

The Ghost Rockets moved from Sweden to Denmark according to the *Aftonbladet* on June 4, 1946. Swedish government files seem to confirm that a farmer in the Ringsted area reported seeing a shining object early in the morning. He alerted his wife and both of them watched it for what they said was a long time. They said it moved too slowly to be a comet, but apparently meant that it was too slow to be a meteor. They saw a trail of sparks from it as well.

Helsinki was the scene of a number of sightings on June 9. Witnesses saw a huge light with a long, fiery tail fall toward the ground. Not long after, they heard an explosion. At 10:17 P.M. a "rocket-shaped" light flew over Helsinki at about a thousand feet. It was followed by a smoky trail and a rumbling noise. The afterglow brightened the sky for about ten minutes.

For the next few days there were continuing reports of lights in the sky. The *Morgon-Tidningen* reported that an engineer

who flies daily … [said,] 'I had just put out the light and stood by my window when in the half-darkness I was able to see something come out of a cloud.… The bomb, if it really was such, passed west of the city in a northward direction. It seems as if it was on a descending course … and in such a case ought to have fallen down somewhere in the area.… It could not have been any of our new jet planes, which have a continuous exhaust and thereby look like true rockets. The later V-weapons did the same, but the first had intermittent exhaust.'

The Swedish Defense Staff entered the investigation officially on June 12. According to the Swedish government files, in a document dated December 23, 1946, the Commander in Chief of the Swedish Defense Staff set up a special committee to study the sightings. In that document it was reported, "Headquarters sent out an order on 12 June 1946, to all military units to report all observations which were made. Similar orders were sent to the military attachés in Norway and Denmark."

The consensus seemed to be that there was something going on, the sightings were of something real, not just lights in the distance, and the best solution seemed to be that these were V-weapons created by the Nazis. As the war ended and Allied forces overran Peenemünde from the east and the west, German scientists who had been working on building the rockets were captured by the Allied forces. The sightings over Scandinavia led many to believe that the Soviets were testing their own version of the V-weapons created by the scientists captured in Germany.

On June 24, 1946, the question of who had captured what from the Germans became important. According to government files, Major James P. Hamill of U.S. Army Ordnance, received a confidential message from the Pentagon for Dr. Werner von Braun. They wanted an evaluation of the rocket technicians captured by the Soviets or those who were left behind in the Soviet zone of occupied Germany. They wanted to know how long it might take these scientists to develop intercontinental missiles. Hamill produced an eleven page report about it.

Von Braun seemed to think that the Soviets had captured a number of very capable men. But von Braun also believed that the United States had the advantage because of the research facilities available to them. History would prove that the U.S. had the lead in the development of missiles, even after the Soviets launched the first satellite in 1957. It didn't seem likely they would be testing their missiles over Scandinavia where, if one crashed, the technology would fall into the hands of scientists in Sweden and then, eventually, the United States.

Dr. Wernher von Braun was a German expatriate who led the U.S. program in rocket development. If the Americans were taking advantage of former Nazi scientists, was it possible that other countries were, too, as well as German technology?

In other words, the Ghost Rockets were not evidence of Soviet development of intercontinental missiles, and they were not being produced by someone in Germany testing the V-weapons. Although those who reported seeing an object often reported something that looked like the V-1 buzz bombs of World War II, there was no one who would have been launching them in 1946. It is also clear that there was not an explosive warhead. The solution would not be found in that direction.

On June 26, 1947, there was another report from Finland. It was given a fairly high evaluation and it suggested that a "V-bomb" had been seen over Helsinki. It was believed that the bomb was launched from the Porkkala area, about twenty miles southwest of Helsinki on the Baltic seacoast. Adding to the confusion about the origin of the Ghost Rockets, the area was claimed by the Soviets though it seemed to be part of the Finnish mainland.

The sightings over Scandinavia led many to believe that the Soviets were testing their own version of the V-weapons, created by the scientists captured in Germany.

Photographs and Physical Evidence

It was in July that things changed in the Ghost Rocket investigations. On July 9, Eric Reuterswärd photographed one of the rockets about fifty miles west of Vasteras. Reuterswärd suspected that he had photographed a meteor, but the Swedish military wasn't convinced.

Clas Svahn, a Swedish UFO researcher, told the story in depth in the fall 2002 issue of *International UFO Reporter*. In an interview conducted by Svahn in 1986, Reuterswärd explained that on a hot, Tuesday afternoon, he and his wife, Åsa had just finished a swim and climbed an old forest watchtower so they could look over the landscape. Reuterswärd said:

> I remember the event very well.... We climbed the tower in order to photograph the view.... At the exact same moment as I pushed the shutter button, then right there it was something mysterious in the sky which both observed. I'm not able to remember exactly how it looked, but I know that it was a light which passed us.... We were both startled, and for a long time discussed what it could have been.

Having heard about the Ghost Rockets, and knowing the Ministry of Defense's interest in them, Reuterswärd sent in a report. The government files, as reviewed by Svahn, said:

> We observed a sharp, greenish-white (neon-colored) gleam of light in [a] northwestern direction and in a 45-degree angle, which emerged suddenly and swiftly moved downwards perhaps five moon diameters; after which it disappeared. The disappearance occurred—in my opinion—with an explosion like a burst of flames, and I also thought I heard a hissing sound. We got the impression that it was a meteorite, though we've never seen one in daylight. The whole incident was over in a moment.

> We then went home, the vacation ended, and we sent the roll of film to be developed, and it then became clear that there was something on it. We had no idea that it had been caught on film until we got to see the copy.

UFO researcher Clas Svahn has published interviews with UFO witnesses for such publications as *International UFO Reporter.*

Analysis of the photograph by others, including the Bertil Lindblad at the Stockholm Observatory, suggested, just as Reuterswärd thought, the photograph showed a meteor. He wrote, sometime later, "There is no doubt whatsoever that Mr. Reuterswärd's picture shows a daylight fireball. What is remarkable, however, is that the trajectory is vertical and not horizontal as most fireballs show."

There were two reported crashes as well. At 2:35 P.M., near Ockelbo, Sweden, a "silvery cigar-shaped" craft flying at a very low altitude "tumbled against the ground and was gone in a few moments," according to the *Morgon-Tidningen* on July 11.

On the same day, at Lake Barken, an object with alternating blue and green lights came from the northeast and fell into the lake about 350 feet from the witness.

Also on July 9, at Mockfjärd, a shiny "star" making a whistling sound fell. A 23-year-old man thought that the object crashed near the town. Just before impact, there was a blinding flash and the witness lost sight of the object. He heard what he thought was the impact, and for the next fifteen minutes he smelled a strong, burning odor.

The next day, at Björkön, Sweden, an object trailing glowing smoke crashed into a beach. The *Svenska Dagbladet* of July 11 reported:

> The area is secluded, about 3 km from Björkövägen. One of the summer cabins ... belongs to airline pilot Torvald Linden, who, when the 'meteor' came, had some visiting neighbors around a coffee table outside the cabin.... The projectile gave off a blinding light. It was indeed so bright that the sun's rays happened to dim. The projectile was quite low, its highest speed at 50 meters per second. It descended at a 40-degree dive angle and fell into the sand, yet without any immediate report. At a distance of only 20 meters lay some young girls and bathers, and they saw how the sand spurted up. After some time we found the crater, which however was rather modest in size (couple of decimeters deep and a meter in diameter.) Spread all around was discovered thus a mass left by the mysterious sky-projectile. It mostly looked like porous slag of various colors—from burned yellow to black. Some small bits were in powdered form, and when they were taken in the hands, they began to smart as if from lye....

Jerry Clark later wrote that the "military authorities produced ambiguous results, and in due course the witnesses were accused of imagining things." However, it was also noted by Swedish newspapers that the material was "[s]ent to Defense Staff's Air Defense Division. Sundsvall air base press officer Capt R Westlin said, 'The projectile clearly produced a high temperature and the remains of the same were very hot when found. The slag produced by the projectile was burned black'."

The *Svenska Dagbladet* continued on July 11, 1947:

Tests on the remnants of the projectile were referred on Wednesday to Dr. Birger Bäcklund.… At first he gathered a bit of gray-white loose material under the microscope from a piece of paper or film fragment, which appeared to be divided up into squares something like a checkers or chessboard. The paper or film coating was only a quarter-millimeter in surface. That the material in question was not of any celestial origin we can establish at once, said Dr. Bäcklund. It looked most nearly like carbon carbide which was exposed to weathering. It was somewhat more gray in color than other pieces of the find. When Dr. Bäcklund picked at the object a little piece of paper of about a quarter-millimeter in size came off and under a magnifying glass it appeared that the paper was checkered almost like a checkerboard with white squares with black bottoms. The squares were microscopic but very regular and it was all like a kind of screen which is used in electrotyping. Here it must be a question of an object which was not exposed to any exceptionally high temperature.

Reports of these sorts of events continued. On July 18, two missiles that were described as eight feet long with wings set back three feet from the nose, fell into the water at Lake Mjøsa, Norway, creating some turbulence. The witnesses

Lake Mjøsa in Norway, where in July 1947 two winged missiles were seen plunging into the water.

said that the wings seemed to flutter, as if they were made of cloth and that the objects themselves gave off a whistling sound.

The next day, July 19, at noon, witnesses reported a gray, rocket-shaped object with wings crash into Lake Kölmjärv. Although the Swedish military searched for three weeks, the deep mud on the lake's bottom hid anything that might have fallen into it. Lieutenant Karl-Gösta Bartoll led the search team at the lake. They scanned for radioactivity but apparently found nothing. The bottom of the lake was disturbed, but there was no other sign of an object. Bartoll said that "there are many indications that the Kolmjarv [Kömjärv] object disintegrated itself...."

On July 28, 1946, the Ghost Rockets returned to Norway. According to the *London Daily Telegraph*, two violent explosions were heard in Oslo, accompanied by an "intense white light." A report noted that it was assumed that the noises were caused by the Ghost Rockets, but they had burst into such small pieces that they had, for all practical purposes, disappeared.

A five foot long, cigar-shaped craft, trailing smoke was seen over Southern Sweden on August 12. It flew out over the water until it seemed to land or crash on a small, uninhabited island. Although there were a few who went to search, the tangled undergrowth and thick bushes prevented them from finding anything.

Four days later, on August 16, a Ghost Rocket flying over Malmö, Sweden, exploded. The blast shattered windows and scattered some debris over the area.

This V-1 German bomb bears a strong resemblance to the Ghost Rockets, according to some investigators who examined the debris fround in Sweden.

The last of the reported crashes came in mid-October, when two people on the shore of a lake heard what sounded like a flock of birds taking flight. They looked up in time to see an object fly over the trees. It looked like a dart with small wings and had a ball-shaped tip. It exploded as it crashed into the water.

Small bits and pieces of the debris were recovered and analyzed. There was nothing extraordinary about it, and some of the descriptions of the craft did seem to mirror descriptions of the V-1 buzz bombs used by the Nazis during World War II. Various government agencies in Sweden, Europe, and in the United States were becoming interested in the Ghost Rockets, and classified reports, messages, and information began circulating at the highest levels.

More from the Government Files

It was around June 26, 1946, that communications among various governments, and communications inside those governments, began to heat up. In a secret document entitled, "Memorandum for Commanding General, Army Air Forces, Subject: Reports of 'Rocket Sightings Over the Scandinavian Countries," there was the suggestion that the Ghost Rockets were terrestrially based. Simply put, those who had reviewed the available information and who wrote the report believed that the rockets were of German design, launched by the Soviets.

On July 10, the RAF Air Attaché in Stockholm, sent to ACAS(I), Air Ministry, a memo on the "Subject: Flying Missiles Observed over Sweden":

> This may or may not be more "chaff for the wheat" but the following was obtained from a Finnish news correspondent working for *Associated Press*. This man has been very helpful in the past and spent much of the war in London. For the past few months he has been in Finland where he was following up the "Flying Missiles" reports from a news angle. He states that he considers the probable experimental base to be near Riga, in Latvia. He has sources recently arrived from Estonia and they all confirm that the general direction is from this part of the world. For what it is worth, I believe the above to be his genuine opinion after many enquiries. He will let me know if he obtains anything further.

He signed it, "Simpson Group Captain, Air Attaché."

The next day, Christian M. Ravndal of the State Department, in a secret telegram from Stockholm wrote:

> For some weeks there have been numerous reports of strange rocket like missiles being seen in Swedish and Finnish skies. During past few days reports of such subjects being seen have greatly increased. Member of Legation saw one Tuesday afternoon. One landed on beach near Stockholm same afternoon without causing any damage and according to press fragments are now being studied by military authorities. Local scientist on first inspection stated it contained organic substance resembling carbide. Defense staff last night issued a communique listing various places where

missiles had been observed and urging public to report all mysterious sound and light phenomena. Press this afternoon announces one such missile fell in Stockholm suburb 2:30 this afternoon. Missile observed by member Legation made no sound and seemed to be falling rapidly to earth when observed. No sound of explosion followed however. Military Attaché is investigating through Swedish channels and has been promised results of Swedish observations. Swedes profess ignorance as to origin, character or purpose of missiles but state definitely they are not launched by Swedes. Eyewitness reports state missiles come in from southerly direction proceeding to northwest.... If missiles are of Soviet origin as generally believed (some reports say they are launched from Estonia), purpose might be political to intimidate Swedes in connection with Soviet pressure on Sweden being built up in connection with current loan negotiations or to offset supposed increase in our military prestige in Sweden resulting from the naval visit and recent Bikini tests or both. Soviet political pressure on Sweden in connection with Baltic refugees here has, as recently reported to Dept, been considerably stepped up.

Proving that the U.S. was quite interested in these reports of the Ghost Rockets, on July 16, the USMA (the military—that is to say the army attaché) in Stockholm sent a top secret message to the War Department in Washington, D.C., meaning the Pentagon. The Department of Defense, which combined the Departments of the Army and Navy, wouldn't come into existence for another year. The message said:

Swedish Army Staff studying 300 to 400 rocket incidents Ref your WAR 94001 of 12 July. They advise: 50 points of impact observed. No evidence of radio control and Army Staff believes phenomena not radio controlled. Defense Research Institute studying fragments but key personnel on leave and report being delayed therefore. No large fragments yet found and small fragments appear to be nonferrous. *Aftonbladet* states Russians have established base with Staff of German scientists on Dago Island off Estonia. (Staff checking basis of this report) Staff has rather tenuous hypothesis to support this as follows:

Two circular rocket courses both with radius of approximately 300 kilometers and centres respectively in the 56-57 N latitude, and 19-20 E longitude quadrangle and the 61-62 N latitude, 21-22 E longitude quadrangle with rockets launched from Dago clockwise on both courses. This theory accounts for only portion of the incidents. Staff has not yet processed all reports. Some highly placed officials believe the phenomena are Russian rocket experiments either purely for research or for War of Nerves. Staff very nervous about release of info to United States and United Kingdom for fear Russians will cry "West Bloc." This office urges greatest protection this information.

The army attaché indicated that a detailed report would be included in the next diplomatic pouch, with a follow-up on ultimate findings of the investigation. This was sent to General Stephen J. Chamberlin for action, meaning he was to deal with it in the context of intelligence analysis. Information, meaning the text, was passed to General Carl Spaatz and to General Norstad.

The analysis circulating at the highest levels was that the Ghost Rockets were Soviet experiments, and they were launched from Estonia or Latvia. The information also suggested there were no signs that the rockets were under radio control. Fragments recovered were of non-ferrous.

The Swedish Defense Research Institute claimed that the Soviets might be engaged in a "war of nerves." Given the history of the region and Soviet attempts at expansion after the end of World War II, the Swedes were reluctant to provide specific information to either Great Britain or the United States. They were concerned that the Soviets might see it as proof that Sweden had aligned with the Western Bloc, making them an enemy of the Soviets. In other words, in July 1946, the politics of the world influenced the research into these bizarre aerial phenomena.

In a top secret memo from Stockholm to the British Foreign office on July 22, 1946, it was reported:

Among the high-ranking officers receiving the findings of the investigation was U.S. Air Force Chief of Staff General Carl Spaatz.

> Following is position on missiles over Sweden as seen by Heath and Malone after discussion at Swedish Air Ministry to-day. 1. Too many missiles have been observed and described to allow of explanation as meteorites. Full list of observations being sent separately. 2. Sole remains so far recovered in Sweden are pieces no longer than an egg of porous yellow combustible material, porous black carboniferous material, porous grey ash or slag material and black slate like material. Representative samples of each are being sent separately. 3. Meager remains so far recovered permit no definite conclusions by Swedes or ourselves. 4. All investigations now coordinated by Kjellson of Swedish Air Ministry. Both he and we believe that present evidence suggests athodyd propulsion with yellow and black materials being used as main fuel or to maintain combustion. Kjellson does not exclude electronic propulsion as outlined by Austrian deserter Peters during the war or even atomic propulsion. We see no reason for these latter suggestions. 5. Geiger counter was requested to ask the Swedes to test for radioactivity at point of incident. They will have portable Geiger counter weighing 12 kilogrammes so will only require one from us if ours is lighter and more easily handled....

By the end of July, the situation, at least to the thinking of the Swedish military, had reached nearly crisis level. According to the *New York Times* of July 28,

Director of Central Intelligence General Hoyt S. Vandenberg surmised that the Ghost Rockets might have been launched by the Soviets as an intimidation tactic.

1946, "A limited censorship has been imposed on information concerning unidentified flying missiles—believed to be flying bombs or rockets—that have been sighted over Swedish territory in recent weeks. The authorities have banned the publication of names of localities where the missiles have been sighted and newspapers have been required to use the dateline 'Somewhere in Sweden' when writing about the subject."

Two days later, Norway followed suit, ordering that the locations of sightings not be published, in what would become a wave of censorship. Two weeks later, on August 16, Denmark joined the ban, and two weeks after that, on August 31, Norway banned publication of any Ghost Rocket information, which they hoped would end the sightings.

Proving that interest in the Ghost Rockets was international, and proving that the American military was involved in gathering information, even if they did not provide any technical or military support, on August 1, 1946, a top secret "memorandum for the President," was written. Colonel E. K. Wright, executive to Lieutenant General Hoyt S. Vandenberg, director of central intelligence [the Central Intelligence Group, forerunner of the CIA] at that time, wrote:

1. Since 15 May there have been occasional press reports of "ghost rockets" seen passing over points in Sweden. On 19 July two such "rockets" were reported to have fallen in Norway. The Swedish and Norwegian Governments have now imposed a news blackout with respect to the subject.

2. Official sources, principally the Military Attaché at Stockholm, have confirmed these reports and obtained additional, but inconclusive, information. Although ten such missiles have fallen within Sweden, the Swedish General Staff has as yet been unable to reach firm conclusions on the basis of the fragments recovered.

3. From the information presently available, the Director of Intelligence, WDG8, has concluded that:

    a. The missiles are of the jet-propelled V-1 type (rather than rockets).

    b. They contain only small demolition charges (for self-destruction) rather than a warhead.

    c. They outrange the V-1. This result could be achieved by construction from light, non-ferrous materials, and by the substitution of additional fuel for the heavy warhead. It could also be achieved by the use of a turbo-jet engine such as the Germans were developing at the close of the war. German scientists in Soviet employ are capable of completing this development, and the characteristic noiselessness reported supports the supposition of its use.

d. Their course is apparently controlled, either by radio or pre-set controls. (Turns and circular courses have been indicated).

e. Their launching from some Soviet-controlled point in the vicinity of the Gulf of Finland is probable.

4. Since the interior of the U.S.S.R. affords areas suitable for extensive and undetected experimentation, the launching of these missiles over Scandinavia must be a deliberate demonstration for political effect. In this the Soviet objective might be:

a. Intimidation of Sweden and Norway, by a demonstration of their vulnerability to attack with such missiles.

b. Intimidation of Great Britain, by demonstration of vulnerability of the United Kingdom to such attack from continental areas which the Soviets now control or are capable of seizing.

c. Intimidation of the United States by a demonstration of Soviet capabilities for the scientific development of new weapons.

This memo demonstrates the mindset at the upper levels of the U.S. intelligence community at that time. No one was arguing that the Ghost Rockets were unreal or some sort of mass hallucination. The thinking was that they were real, based on German designs of the V-weapons, and they were being controlled by the Soviet Union. There was no real discussion about the possibility of an extraterrestrial component to the Ghost Rockets. The intelligence community, among all the various countries taking an interest in the Ghost Rockets, was almost unanimous in the opinion that this was some sort of Soviet operation.

Then, on August 16, 1946, in a top secret message from the U.S. Naval Attaché in Stockholm entitled "Reference: MA Stockholm's Top Secret Report R334-46 of 13 August 1946 Subject: SWEDEN Guided Missiles Rocket Sightings Over Sweden, it was reported:

> The intelligence community, among all the various countries taking an interest in the Ghost Rockets, was almost unanimous in the opinion that this was some sort of Soviet operation.

No tangible evidence to date as to nature or origin of rockets reported over Sweden, although Swedish Defense Staff insists that they are rockets. Swedish press and public aroused, but Swedish Air Force officers still on summer leave, aircraft warning not mobilized, and no attempts made to intercept missiles with jet fighters; improbable that rockets, if any, are Russian or British, but possible that they are Swedish. Swedish defense staff evasive and their communiques contradictory and confusing. Sweden may be experimenting with rockets, but is concealing the fact and encouraging belief that rockets of foreign origin are being launched over

Sweden, with civilian observers reporting jet fighters, contrails and meteors as rockets.

1. This report is an attempt to correlate various reports on the recently reported sightings of light phenomena or rockets over Sweden and, in the absence of any tangible evidence, to formulate a hypothesis as to their nature and origin.

2. To date no U.S. military or naval personnel in Sweden have seen any fragments, photographs, radar tracks, points of impact, or other evidence of any kind to prove that guided missiles have actually been seen over Swedish territory.

3. On 12 August the reporting officer asked three Swedish Air Force officers what they thought of the reported sightings. They answered that they believed definitely that these were rockets. On 13 August the reporting officer and the Assistant U.S. Military Attaché were permitted to talk to three Swedish Air Force officers from the Defense Staff, who stated in answer to direct questions that while they had no definite evidence to back their belief, they believed that the reported phenomena were rockets. This may therefore be accepted as the official Swedish military expression as to the nature of the reported phenomena.

4. Although sightings of brilliant light phenomena over Stockholm on 11 August created a great furor in the Swedish press and considerable concern among the Swedish public, the Swedish Air Force has not called back its officers from their summer leave, and the Swedish aircraft warning net has not been mobilized to spot reported missiles. Considering the fact that hundreds of reports from all over the country have described cigar-shaped missiles with fiery tails at altitudes low enough for interception by Swedish jet-propelled aircraft, this apparently unconcern and lack of sustained energy on the part of the military organization is peculiar.

Case 1. Rockets of Russian Origin

5. The Russians might be launching rockets over Sweden in order to pressurize [sic] the Swedes in connection with the proposed Russian-Swedish trade agreement, or to frighten them away from any consideration of joining a Western Bloc. Another motive would be the demonstration of a new weapon to answer our atomic bomb demonstrations. A lesser consideration would be the testing of rockets over a neutral country, as Germany did with the V-2 rockets. Arguments against this theory are that the reported ranges (1000 km) are far in excess of those for any known rocket to date for the flat trajectories described (two or three hundred meters for a cigar-shaped rocket thirty feet long over central Sweden.) This would indicate a new propellant and a far more efficient control system than the best German rockets; it is therefore doubtful that Russia would risk giving away such a secret by launching it over Sweden at altitudes low

enough for it to be shot down by Swedish jet fighters. The Swedish communist press ridiculed this idea, pointing out that no evidence of any kind had been found, and that Russia had all of Siberia to test her rockets. THE RUSSIAN MILITARY ATTACHÉ IN STOCKHOLM ALSO ASKED THE BRITISH ASSISTANT RAF ATTACHÉ FOR INFORMATION ON THE SUBJECT [emphasis added]. (Paragraph 5, Enclosure (A)). The main reason against the theory of Russian origin is the lack of any tangible evidence. However, the Swedes may be concealing any such evidence which they may have, even though they stated emphatically that they have no such evidence. The motive of such conduct would be to avoid trouble with Russia.

Case 2. Rockets of British Origin.

The British Assistant RAF Attaché stated that he believed the reported objects were rockets, and has made a financial wager that tangible evidence will be found. HE ALSO STATED THAT HE WOULD LIKE TO "PLANT" A FALSE CLUE TO WORRY THE RUSSIANS, GIVING A PURPORTED COURSE INDICATING THAT ROCKETS HAD BEEN LAUNCHED FROM DENMARK OR BRITISH-OCCUPIED TERRITORY. [emphasis added] The U.S. Military Attaché in Stockholm reported that the British are extremely worried about the European situation, and that after a recent visit to his former bomber base in England he found it fully operational, even to the fire-trucks. It is known that the British are worried about our demobilization and would like to keep us armed for the blowup which they expect to occur with the Russians. This would be one way to alert us. It would be possible for the British to launch airborne rockets over the Kattegat, set to cross over Sweden and fall into the Baltic. However, it is doubtful if the British would embark on such an undertaking because of the risk of disclosure either to us or to the Russians. Furthermore, a strong protest could be expected from Sweden. Again there is the fact that the Swedish Defense Staff is peculiarly inactive and unconcerned, while the British are reported by MA Stockholm to be extremely worried about the matter, and to have offered, or are offering, two of their best search radar sets to help the Swedes track down the rockets.

At this point, public discussion of the Ghost Rockets faded away given the various governments' embargo on releasing the information and the attempts to halt press reports of the sightings. It didn't mean that the sightings ended, or

Karl-Gösta Bartoll investigates Lake Kölmjärv after a report of a rocket-UFO crash there, 19 July 1946.

that a solution had been found, only that the stories were no longer being published in Scandinavia.

But that didn't stop the international interest in them. A British Air Ministry Intelligence Report in September 1946 said:

> A large number of visual observations have been obtained from Scandinavia. Some of the best came from Norway. An analysis suggests the most notable characteristics of the projectiles to be: a) great speed; b) intense light frequently associated with a missile; c) lack of sound; d) approximate horizontal flight.... Thus, if the phenomena now observed are of natural origin, they are unusual; sufficiently unusual to make possible the alternative explanation that at least some are missiles. If this is so, they must be of Russian origin.

More Ghost Rocket Sightings

Although the Scandinavian newspaper had stopped reporting on Ghost Rockets, the international press continued. The number of sightings was not decreasing significantly, and the descriptions, while often slightly different, seemed to indicate that the Ghost Rockets were basically rocket shapers. It was also clear that these things were still flying over Sweden and the rest of Scandinavia.

On August 8, 1946, the Associated Press reported:

> The Swedish Defense Staff is now firmly convinced that Sweden is being used as a shooting range for foreign rocket-driven projectiles something like the type of the German V1 and V2, said the *Aftonbladet* today.

> Earlier reports were more or less reliable and last night an officer from the defence staff's air defense division himself saw something 'which could not be described as a meteor.' The officer was located in central Sweden and saw a fireball with a luminous tail which tore along at a height of 500–1,000 meters.

> The chief of the air defense division said that many projectile courses have been plotted on a map and their path over Sweden shows a great arc which ends out over the Gulf of Bothnia or the Eastern Sea.

On August 13, another Associated Press (AP) story reported, "Many persons said today that at least one V-bomb exploded over Stockholm last night." There was also a discussion of some sort of a "luminous phenomenon" seen about an hour earlier.

The next day, on August 14, 1946, there was a sighting of such interest that it was detailed in an FBI memo on the "Flying Discs," dated August 19, 1947:

> On 14 August [1946] at 10 A.M. [a Swedish Air Force pilot] was flying at 650 feet over central Sweden when he saw a dark, cigar-shaped object about 50 feet above and approximately 6500 feet away from him traveling at an estimated 400 m.p.h. The missile had no visible wings, rudder

or other projecting part, and there was no indication of any fuel exhaust as had been reported in the majority of other sightings.

The missile was maintaining a constant altitude over the ground and consequently, was following the large features of the terrain. This statement casts doubt on the reliability of the entire report because a missile, without wings, is unable to maintain a constant altitude over hilly terrain.

Four days later, on August 17, 1946, the AP was again reporting about the Ghost Rockets. The story said, "Again last night many places in western and southern Sweden observed luminous projectiles which moved with great speed from south to north. It is regarded now as certain that a new V-weapon is involved. It is also thought that it is radio-directed. Danish scouts who were on a visit in Goteborg discovered a rocket bomb on Monday which suddenly [digressed a good] 30 degrees from its course, then shortly after it resumed it again. The Swedish authorities are considering sending in a fighter plane against the rocket bombs, states the *Aftonbladet*."

"Many persons said today that at least one V-bomb exploded over Stockholm last night."

On August 24, a Norwegian student in Sweden reported in an article published on August 24 that he had seen one of the Ghost Rockets:

On a walking tour through Sweden in the first half of August I met with some acquaintances who took me with them on an evening in a motorboat up one of Sweden's [beautiful] rivers. Suddenly [shooting] out of the evening stillness I saw a bright light which neared us from the southeast with colossal speed. As it came nearer it took the shape of a full moon, perhaps a little more elliptical, but in size like when seen on the horizon. The light was very bright and reminded me of the results when a magnesium bomb explodes. On the edges the light was more blue-green and the tail shimmered. As it came closer there could be seen a thick, almost glowing smoke tail.

As the phenomenon was right over us it lighted everything up strongly, so that you could see as on the brightest day. The fireball or "fiery mass" as the Swedes call it, had till then described a slight arc downward toward us. Now four stars broke off, which with a luminous stripe behind them sank down toward the ground, to be extinguished. The fireball was extinguished momentarily as these stars broke away, and then perhaps for a second, I having accustomed my eyes to the dark, I saw a black elongated projectile go forward through the air in a apparently horizontal course [about] 300 meters up. It was pointed in front, but astern it looked [broken off]. The length was something I only judge at around 3 meters. On the back third the whole tail glowed, and this faint glow was the last we saw of the projectile which disappeared in a direction toward a small village nearby. It did not look like it had either wings or guide fins. The course was directly northwest the whole time.

The owner of the motorboat, a Swedish engineer, looked at his watch when he first saw the phenomenon. It appeared at 20.45 and its whole [duration], he thinks, was only 6–8 seconds. Since he is experienced in tracking [?], moreover, he thinks he could estimate the projectile's speed at between 1500 and 200 [sic] kilometers an hour.

Not a sound was heard from the ghost bomb, neither the object itself not the stars were separated.

The next morning the Swedish press broke a report from the defense staff that a "space ship" was observed over Middle Sweden, and then we each sent in our statements about what we had seen. Those who had sent up the ghost bomb, however, would not be able to read of the bomb's descent through reports from the Swedish defense staff. But next evening when we stayed up in the Central Swedish villages local newspapers broke this report that a "space ship" had passed over the roof the previous day.

The sightings continued into October and the *New York Times* reported, "On October 11 Swedish military authorities announced that they had been unable to discover the origin or nature of the 'ghost rockets' after investigating for four months. Of the 1,000 reports handled, 80 per cent could have been 'celestial phenomena,' they said. The radar study, however, had detected some objects 'which cannot be the phenomena of nature or products of imagination, nor be referred to as Swedish airplanes.'" They were not, the report added, V-type German bombs either.

This photo was taken on July 9, 1946, by Erik Reuterswärd in Guldsmedshyttan, Sweden. The image of the Ghost Rocket was later released by the Swedish military.

A top secret U.S. Air Force report published on November 29, 1946, entitled "Significant Developments of Scientific Warfare in Russia, (Air Intelligence Division Report #100-136-24)" concluded that the Ghost Rockets were of the "V-5," that is, a Swedish military development. Although they didn't have access to the secret Swedish evaluations at the time, it is clear from the documentation in Swedish government files, and from aviation history, that the Ghost Rockets were not a Swedish research and development project.

And still, the sightings continued. For example, the *Lethbridge Herald* reported, "The Moscow radio reported today that a meteor which resembled 'a white-hot flying cannon ball' was sighted Nov. 12 by the Leningrad Arctic Institute's polar station at Providence Bay, at the northeast tip of Siberia across Bering Strait from Alaska. The radio description, particularly as to velocity, coincided to some degree with that of meteor-like objects sighted above Scandinavian countries in recent months."

This points to another problem. While the majority of the publicity about Ghost Rockets focused on Scandinavia, there were reports from other European countries. In Greece, according to newspaper reports, "Acting Foreign Minister Stefanos Stefanopoulos supported a statement in London by Premier Constantine Tsaldaris that flying rockets had been seen over Greece.... The rockets, estimated to be flying at a height of 5,000 to 10,000 yards, had been seen specifically at Drama, 130 miles northeast of Salonika and just below the Bulgarian border."

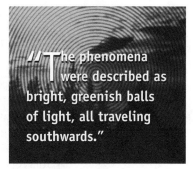

"The phenomena were described as bright, greenish balls of light, all traveling southwards."

The September 6, 1946 issue of the *London Daily Telegraph* reported, "The rocket passing over Salonika ... fell into the sea ... A total of four were seen ... all on the night of September 1st. These were officially reported by military units and confirmed by many reports from civilians. One passed over Mt. Paikon, both in Macedonia.... Another passed over the town of Katharini...."

On September 7, "What is described as a ball of fire was seen traveling in a southwesterly direction.... It was first seen last night and was seen for a second time a few hours later ...," according to the *London Sunday Express* on September 8.

According to the *London Daily Telegraph* on September 19, "Officials at Lisbon [Portugal] observatory were unable yesterday to explain reports that strange lights had been seen moving across the sky.... The phenomena were described as bright, greenish balls of light, all traveling southwards."

The investigations by the Swedish military continued, though with a lower profile. On December 23, 1946, they issued a classified report that remained hidden for nearly thirty years. Eventually, it was declassified.

Swedish Government Files, December 23, 1946

From a December 23, 1946 letter to the Commander in Chief of the Swedish Defense Staff:

I. *Development of the Investigation.* At the end of May 1946, there was brought to the attention of the Defense staff, certain peculiar luminous phenomena over Sweden, partly through press reports, and partly by civilian observers, who reported their observations directly to the Military Authorities. Until the 8th of July, approximately 30 reports had been received, among these, one from the Military Attaché in Finland.

Headquarters sent out an order on 12 June 1946, to all military units to report all observations which were made. Similar orders were sent to the military attachés in Norway and Denmark.

A large number of observations were made the 9th of July (approximately 250). Thereafter the reports continued to come in during the period July–September with a "climax" on the 11th of August … During the period October–November the number of reports was considerably reduced. The total number of reports, up to 6 December 1946, was 987.

On the initiative of the Defense Staff and Aviation Administration, a committee was established 10 July consisting of members of the Defense Staff, Aviation staff, Naval Administration, the Defense Research Institution and the Defense Radio Institution to handle this matter. Col. Bengt Jacobsson was chairman, with Eng. Malmberg as his secretary. While Col. Jacobsson was in America, Maj. Cervell of the Defense Staff served as chairman. The committee met approximately 15 times up to 1 December

Through this committee, the investigation was intensified. Within the Defense Staff, all reports regarding this matter were summarized and forwarded to the Air Administration and Air Defense Sections. Personnel were sent out both from the Defense Staff and the Air Administration section to evaluate important reports. Liaison with the civilian authorities—including Customs authorities—and the lottakåren [women participating as volunteers performing military duties], as well as the Stockholm Observatory, was established. In connection with a communique of 10 July the population was requested to send reports of their observations to the Defense Staff."

II. *Source Material.* Information has been received chiefly from four sources: (a) visual observations (reports, newspaper clippings, reports from military attaches; (b) radar trackings; (c) radio observations (direction finder and intercepts); (d) reports from special sources.

The largest number of reports were visual observations. Incidents were reported throughout the entire country with a concentration in the middle of Sweden.

On 9 July and 11 August, luminous phenomena were observed at the same time over almost all of Sweden. It is possible that these phenomena were of a celestial nature, and if they are excluded, approximately 450 reports remain. Of these, approximately 50% concern luminous phenomena and the rest concern observations of 'real' objects. These objects are mainly of two different types: (a) 'spool-shaped' without any wings or stabilizing surfaces (42%), (b) 'spool-shaped and provided with wings (8%).

The reports have been sent in by various categories of observers, among these several trained observers, military persons, technicians, etc.

Approximately 100 impacts have been reported, together with fragments from 30 of these. All have been investigated by the Defense Research Institution. It has been impossible to make certain that any of the objects originated as parts of projectiles or rockets; they have generally been attributed to other sources. At Kölmjärv, located close to Överkalix, a positive impact was reported in July by two different observers. An intensive investigation gave no result.

There wasn't much additional detail in the Swedish report. It outlined the seriousness of the sightings, which were treated with concern, but in the end, many of the reports were thought to be nothing more than misidentifications of natural phenomena or of human-created craft. Still, there remained the physical evidence recovered, which suggested that something real was going on, and that the answer did not lie with Swedish aviation experimentation. The sightings were of something else, and the most likely answer for the Swedes, and for others, was the Soviet Union.

This was a rather unsatisfying report because it provided no real answers to any of the important questions. Without a complete summary of the incidents, which might have provided some clues, without the details of the sightings, the observations and conclusions of the report have little real weight.

The report seems to suggest terrestrial explanations for the Ghost Rockets, but most

Ludvig Lindbäck, brother to principle witness Knut, at Lake Kölmjärv, site of the 19 July 1946 rocket-UFO crash in Sweden.

sightings were regarded as nothing more than misidentifications, and a few, very few, might have been of Soviet design, or so the thinking went in 1946.

The American Investigation

In 1947, American intelligence continued their investigation into the Ghost Rockets. Looking at the phenomenon from a terrestrial point of view, that the Ghost Rockets were real, that they were tangible, and that a source of them could be found, made sense. The Swedish military had suggested there were one hundred reports of impacts and in thirty of those cases, debris of some kind had been recovered. With something to analyze, even with small samples, there should have been some kind of conclusion. If the Ghost Rockets were some sort of Soviet experiment or an improvement on the German V-weapons, then it was in the interest of American national security to learn more about them.

According to the government documents, Colonel William E. Clingerman, in a letter for Colonel Howard McCoy, asked Lieutenant Colonel George Garrett for all the files on the Ghost Rockets, referred to as the "Swedish incidents." These files would have been accumulated throughout 1946 and 1947 and should have been part of what was the first of the American UFO investigations known as Project Sign, which eventually evolved into Project Blue Book.

What is interesting here is that Clingerman, McCoy, and Garrett were all heavily involved in the UFO investigations in those early years. It might be sug-

Some of the Poject Blue Book staff. Standing, from left to right: Lieutenant William F. Marley, Jr; SSGT Harold T. Jones; Mrs. Hilma Lewis (a temporary typist); Mrs. Marilyn Stancombe (secretary). Seated: Major Hector Quintanilla, chief of Project Blue Book.

gested that much of what they did for the Army and the Air Force was learned as they attempted to determine the source of the Ghost Rockets.

In fact, Dr. Donald H. Menzel, the director of the Harvard Observatory, thought that this long-time involvement was something of a problem. In 1968, he began a correspondence with Lieutenant Colonel Hector Quintanilla, the chief of Project Blue Book, Dr. Edward U. Condon, leader of the University of Colorado study of UFOs, Dr. Robert Low, who was attached to the Colorado project, and a Ph.D. candidate named Herbert Strentz. Menzel's theory was that the Swedish Ghost Rockets had "conditioned" the Air Force into a mindset of acceptance of these strange things in the sky. Menzel wrote, "I think there must have been some briefing of top generals, by CIA or other cognizant authority...."

To Menzel, the theory was validated when Strentz found articles on Ghost Rockets that had been published in American newspapers. All this lead to the Air Force generals being "too accepting of flying saucers." What Menzel didn't know, of course, was that those who were conducting the investigations had been looking at these sorts of reports since the Second World War. But those officers, McCoy and Clingerman, had been gathering Ghost Rocket reports for many months.

The Project Blue Book files list a number of sightings from Scandinavia in early 1948. They came from a variety of sources and all were eventually "identified" as "Astro-meteor." Typical of these is Incident #99, as reported in a government document, the Grudge Report, which came from the Military Attaché in Helsinki who happened to be in Vasa, Finland.

According to the government files, "Helsinki press 10th January reported observation of light phenomena vicinity of Vasa on 3rd January ... brightly shining object with long tail moved west to east visible for 30 seconds."

In a letter to the Director of Intelligence, GSUSA in Washington, D.C., dated January 13, 1948, the sightings are detailed again. It added another sighting from Pietarsaari, on January 5

Dr. Donald H. Menzel, the director of the Harvard Observatory, was an astronomer and astrophysicist who published several books debunking UFO theories.

that was "observed from north to south. Eyewitnesses state flames were objected [sic, ejected] and grey streaks left in the sky."

In a "comment" on the letter, it said, "Finnish press now using term flying saucers reference light phenomena. Last report was 20th December in Utsjoki, Northern Finland near Norwegian border.... Evaluation press reports impossible however press claims many witnesses. May be revival another series of alleged flying phenomena...."

In the government files, the summary listed for these, and other sightings said, "Information given here is too limited for any conclusions to be drawn. The stated heights, the occurrence at [the] same time each night, and their specific direction makes explanation of the objects as meteors unlikely. The green tails are also not characteristic of typical meteors, but would fit into a description of rockets or flares."

What is interesting is that all of these sightings contained on the Blue Book master list are identified as meteors, yet the analysis from the field seems to suggest that meteors are not a viable solution in many of the cases. It seems that the cases listed in Blue Book were all solved in the same fashion. They were all considered meteors, even though the length of the sighting and other aspects suggested that a meteor was not the culprit.

There was additional information contained in the government files. The Grudge Report took note of the Ghost Rockets:

> During the summer of 1946, there were reported to have been seen in Sweden a number of mysterious aerial objects. There were as many different de-

scriptions for the "ghost rockets," as the newspapers tagged them, as there were observers. It soon became quite common for newspapers in Sweden and in the U.S. to refer authoritatively to these objects as guided missiles with the inference that they were test flights from Russia or Russia-dominated areas. The "ghost rockets" were usually seen in hours of darkness, almost always traveling at extremely high speed; shaped like a ball or projectile; bright or incandescent blue, white, red, green or yellow; sometimes associated with noise; and were always seen at too great a distance to observe details.… The Swedish Defense Staff conducted a comprehensive study of the early incidents. Several thousand reports were thoroughly investigated and plotted, with resultant conclusions that all evidence obtained of sightings were explicable in terms of astronomical phenomena.

This report does supply an explanation, then, for writing off all the Swedish sightings as "astro." The Swedish Defense Staff seemed to have suggested that solution themselves. Without further investigation, Project Blue Book and then Project Grudge officers accepted that explanation and applied it to all the sightings.

> The "ghost rockets" were usually seen in hours of darkness, almost always traveling at extremely high speed; shaped like a ball or projectile...."

There is one other aspect to this that requires examination. According to the Grudge Report, "although the Swedes themselves show little concern, they attempt to play up their incidents to the United States, obviously to emphasize their request for radar."

The Air Attaché, Colonel Donald Hardy, in a document dated December 30, 1948, and found in the government files, wrote, "The cooperation of the Defense Staff in securing this information was … given in an effort to emphasize their need for additional U.S. radar equipment.… The members of the Defense Staff, to whom I talked, were eager to point out the good use to which such equipment could be put for both ourselves and the Swedes as … by our mutual interest in unidentified flying objects.…"

The idea that the Swedes were more interested in gaining new radar equipment than in solving the riddle of the Ghost Rockets satisfied those investigating UFOs in the United States. Having found what they believed to be a rationale for suggesting that some of the Ghost Rockets were something other than astronomical phenomena, the American officers could move on.

What Happened to the Ghost Rockets?

While it seems that the majority of the reports took place in 1946, and that they were investigated by the Swedish military, that's not exactly accurate. There were literally hundreds of reports throughout Scandinavia. Once the security curtain came down, once the press stopped reporting the sightings, it seemed that the Ghost Rockets stopped flying. This seems to suggest that many of the sightings were generated by the press. That is, people who would never have thought about mentioning the "light" in the sky prior to the publicity, did so once the press began covering these sightings. When the publicity ended, the sightings stopped.

At least that is the impression given in many places, including the government files. But other sources of information, including secret Swedish government files that were declassified in 1984, show that sightings continued. They were just not mentioned in the newspapers. There were more than 1,500 sightings recorded from early 1946 on. These sightings took place over much of Europe and even into North Africa.

And there is an interesting statement made by the military attaché in 1948 when he wrote, "Finnish press now using term flying saucers reference light phenomena." The sightings of the Ghost Rockets didn't stop flying; they were just called something else. Instead of Ghost Rockets they became flying saucers.

What is interesting is that almost no one, at the time, looked at the extraterrestrial.

There were many theories about these objects, including the idea that they were meteors, Soviet missiles attempting to intimidate their European neighbors, a secret Swedish project (which is untrue based on government records available today), and hoaxes. Some of these theories were floated by the Swedish military as an excuse to build up their forces. What is interesting is that almost no one, at the time, looked at the extraterrestrial. Everyone, regardless of country and regardless of position in their various government organizations, was thinking in terms of the terrestrial.

The Extraterrestrial Component

Jerome Clark, in the second edition of his *UFO Encyclopedia*, brings up the extraterrestrial. He reports that on April 17, 1971, there was a letter published in the *Sjaellands Tidende* from Hans Sorensen, who wrote:

> In the summer of 1946, I was cycling on the way from Jyderup toward Kalundborg. A couple of kilometers outside of Viskinge toward Kalundborg, I suddenly noticed something odd … so I stopped in a clear spot so as to see better. Then I saw three thingamajigs fitting the descriptions of UFOs. They flew vertically overhead.… They were like polished mirrors on top, and in profile almost like a flat and deep saucer. The underside was uneven and dull gray. That was in July, in calm weather. It was about 2 P.M., and the sun was behind me. As I stood there, several people came up, and we concurred that there were no sounds, such as a normal aircraft would make.

The same year, 1971, another report surfaced, first in a Swedish magazine *Allers*, and later recounted in *Flying Saucer Review*. The man who told the story was Eugen Semitjov, who said that he was relating a story told to him by a prominent industrialist, Gösta Carlsson. The year was 1946 and his tale makes the extraterrestrial crystal clear. Semitjov claimed Carlsson told him:

I saw that in the farthest end of the open ground there was a disc-shaped object with a cupola. The cupola seemed to be a cabin with oval windows. Above it there was a mast, almost like a periscope of a submarine. Beneath the disc there was a big oblong fin which stretched from the center to the edge of the underside. There were two metal landing legs. A small ladder reached to the ground from a door beside the fin.

The object was approximately 53 feet in diameter and 13 feet from top to bottom at the middle. I know this because I measured the marks on the following day.... On the ground ... a man in white, closely-fitting overalls was standing. He seemed to be some sort of guard ... Everything was silent. The only thing I heard was the sound from the guard when he walked on the grass. There were three men working at the window, and two more were standing alongside. There were three women as well, and one more came out of the object later.... In all I saw 11 persons.

They all wore short black boots and gloves, a black belt around the waist, and a transparent helmet. The women had ashen-colored hair, but I could not see the hair of the men as they wore black caps. There were all brown-colored, as if sunburned.

I went a few steps closer, but then the guard raised his hand again. After that I stood still. The guard had a black box on his chest which was suspended by a chain around his neck. It looked like an old black camera. He turned it toward me, and I thought he was going to take a picture of me, but nothing happened, except that I thought I heard a click from my forehead lamp. The lamp did not work after that, but that may have been purely coincidental. When I returned home I found that the battery had run out, although it was a new one.

It seemed as if the "cheese-dish cover" of light stood like a wall between us. I think it was created to isolate them from our world and atmosphere. One of the women came out of the cabin with an object in her hand. She went to the edge of the wall of light and threw it beyond the area of light. At the same time I heard her laugh.

I thought the disclike object could be some sort of military device. The whole scene seemed so strange.... I was aware of a smell like that from ozone following an electrical discharge.

Carlsson said that he picked up the thrown object, but when UFO researchers examined it in 1971, they found that it was nothing extraordinary. Carlsson had changed the shape so that it looked like a staff, which seems odd, given that he had an alleged alien artifact in his possession. It was made, partially of silicone.

There also seem to be some contradictions in Carlsson's story. He talked as if he knew it was alien and that they had created a cone of light to separate themselves from the earth's atmosphere, yet he thought it might be a military device.

These tales, and a few others that surfaced long after the initial wave all dated to 1946. If they are accepted at face value, they lead to the extraterrestrial.

But they are single witness cases and the physical evidence that has been offered provides little in the way of corroboration. They add little to our knowledge.

Clas Svahn, who spent eight years investigating the Gösta Carlsson observation, said much later that in 1946, there was no real talk of the extraterrestrial. The thought was that the Ghost Rockets were something manufactured on Earth. He is also very skeptical about the Gösta Carlsson story.

Conclusions

Like the Foo Fighters, the Ghost Rockets preceded the flying saucers. The sightings, when broken down, match many of those that came later. The Ghost Rockets were described by the witnesses as best they could. When compared to the later sightings that began with Kenneth Arnold in the United States, they weren't that different. Many of the sightings were of bright objects trailing sparks and could be thought of as meteors.

Clas Svahn, who had the opportunity in the 1980s to review most of the Swedish Defense Ministry's Ghost Rocket files, wrote:

> The military archives show that the main part of the reports filed were of meteors spotted at night or evenings. But that also leaves us with reports of cigar-shaped and missile-like objects, presumably made of metal, which cruised through the skies in the summer of 1946. Even if the ghost rockets were never identified, the Ministry of Defense never doubted that there really had been intrusions over the Swedish border. Later in 1946, a special ghost rocket committee drew the following conclusion: "There is no doubt that foreign experiments with jet-propelled or rocket weapons have been going on over Sweden."

Svahn finished his report by writing, "It was suspected that these weapons belonged to a new generation of military systems: 'The projectiles are steerable, either by autopilot, and then with a preset trajectory, or steered by radio impulses from a ground station, perhaps with television or by a pilot in the projectile,' wrote the committee."

In 1984, Svahn, found a number of the civilian witnesses and also interviewed Karl-Gösta Bartoll, a retired Swedish Air Force officer who lead the search and who said that there were indications that the object had disintegrated, crashing into a lake.

Bartoll told Svahn, "First of all, Knut Lindbäck saw a second cascade of water after the first impact and, secondly, an old lady living in a cottage near the crash site reported she had heard a muffled thunderclap. The object was probably manufactured in a light-weight material, possibly a kind of magnesium alloy that could disintegrate easily, and not give any indications on our instruments."

Carlsson said that he picked up the thrown object, but when UFO researchers examined it in 1971, they found that it was nothing extraordinary.

In September 2012, Svahn organized an expedition to the lake to see if they could recover some of the material. He told the *Huffington Post*, "It was difficult for divers to photograph underwater as it was quite muddy. What was interesting was when they reached the spot where we think the craft sank, they found that the bottom was nearly bottomless. We don't know how far the mud goes down. At this point, we have no means of continuing our expedition—we cannot go any deeper down in the mud."

He also said that he planned to return when he had more funds and better equipment. What is interesting, and was apparently unknown in the late 1940s, was that a number of the sightings were of green-colored lights. Reuterswärd's photograph, for example, was of a green object. The importance of this observation would not be understood for decades.

Project Saucer

By 1947, there were two things that were obvious, according to the government files. First, that those in intelligence work at Wright Field and the Pentagon were aware that something disk shaped was flying around American skies, and second that there was already an unofficial investigation underway to try and find answers.

Colonel Howard McCoy had been involved with the Foo Fighter investigation during the Second World War. According to Keith Chester in his book *Strange Company,* on September 6, 1944, a group known as the Combined Intelligence Objectives Subcommittee met in London. Chester writes that the committee was set up to coordinate intelligence reports but they also investigated the reports of unconventional aircraft operating over the European Theater.

In 1946, while the Ghost Rockets were flying over Scandinavia, Colonel William E. Clingerman sent a note to Colonel Howard McCoy, asking for all the files on the Ghost Rockets. The files would have accumulated throughout late 1946 and early 1947 and were part of the first of several American UFO investigations. However, for some reason, most of these government files never made it into Project Sign.

McCoy had been involved in investigating the Foo Fighter sightings during the war and later, after the war ended, the Ghost Rocket sightings. At the time, the thinking was that both these were terrestrially based weapons systems, the former launched by the Nazis and the later by the Soviets. Had the Nazis or the Soviets created rockets, missiles, or some other craft capable of the performance described by the witnesses, the American military would have been at a disadvantage. The Americans needed to learn as much as possible about these weapons in order to develop a countermeasure, and thus, investigations into these sightings were regarded as an important intelligence matter.

But no real solutions were found. The Foo Fighters were never identified as some sort of Nazi or Japanese weapon, and when the Soviet Union collapsed in the 1990s, the Ghost Rockets could not be confirmed as Soviet technology. In the mid-1940s, however, American intelligence and Howard McCoy had no way of knowing that.

In early December, 1946, as noted earlier, the Swedish Defense Ministry issued a report on the Ghost Rockets. But there had been other sightings that would

The Smith Signting: July 4, 1947

According to the government files and newspaper accounts, about dusk on July 4, 1947, Captain E. J. Smith was flying a United Airlines DC-4 near Emmit, Idaho, when his first officer, Ralph Stevens, reached down to flash the landing lights. Smith asked him what he was doing, and Stevens said that another plane was coming at them and he wanted to ensure that they were seen. Smith wrote:

> My copilot ... was in control shortly after we got into the air. Suddenly he switched on the landing lights.
>
> He said he thought he saw an aircraft approaching head-on.
>
> I noticed the objects then for the first time.
>
> We saw four or five "somethings." One was larger than the rest and for the most part ... right of the other three or four similar but smaller objects.
>
> Since we were flying northwest— roughly into the sunset we saw whatever they were in at least partial light.

> We saw them clearly. We followed them in a northwesterly direction for about 45 minutes....
>
> Finally the objects disappeared in a burst of speed.

According to the government files, Smith said that they were never able to see any real shape. He thought the craft was flat on the bottom and seemed to be irregular on the top. The object appeared to be flying at their altitude and followed them for ten to fifteen minutes.

The AMC (Air Materiel Command) opinion of the sighting was that it had occurred at sunset, which meant the lighting conditions would be changing rapidly, making conditions ideal for illusionary effects. The objects could have been ordinary aircraft, balloons, birds, or pure illusion. AMC remarked that they had insufficient data to draw any sort of conclusion. In the final Project Blue Book listing, this sighting is marked as "Unidentified."

have interested those at Wright-Field in intelligence. One of the first reports came from the pilot of an Army Air Forces C-54 transport over France.

On August 1, 1946, Captain Jack Puckett was flying a C-47 transport about 40 miles north of Tampa, Florida, when he sighted a cigar-shaped craft. Puckett would later say:

> At approximately 6:00 P.M. while flying a C-47 at 4000 feet northwest of Tampa I observed what I thought to be a shooting star to the southeast over the Atlantic Ocean. My copilot, Lt. Henry F. Glass and my engineer both observed this object at the same time.
>
> This object continued toward us on a collision course at our exact altitude. At about 1000 yards it veered to cross our path. We observed it to be a

long, cylindrical shape approximately twice the size of a B-29, with luminous portholes.

Puckett thought the object was rocket propelled. It trailed fire about half of its length. It remained in sight for two and a half to three minutes, eliminating the idea that it was a meteor.

These sightings, because they involved military pilots, were probably reported through the chain of command and would have arrived at Wright Field. Staff at Wright Field receiving the information would have been part of T-2, the intelligence function, including Howard McCoy and Colonel Albert Deyarmond.

By this time, T-2 had been receiving intelligence reports about these sightings for years. Although initially viewed as a foreign problem (the objects were being sighted over Europe or over the Pacific during the war), sightings were now being made over American territory. McCoy seemed to think that some sort of an investigation was needed, but he did not have authorization or funding to conduct one as he deemed necessary.

That first American investigation began, unofficially, in December, 1946, when, according to records reviewed by Wendy Connors and research conducted by Connors and Michael Hall, McCoy received a telephone call during the 1946 staff Christmas party. McCoy's secretary took the call and McCoy and Deyarmond both returned to T-2, the intelligence section at Wright Field.

Wright Field in southwest Ohio was originally an air field during World War I and became a flight testing facility for the U.S. Army Air Corps and Air Forces.

Edward Ruppelt, shown here in a newspaper photo publicizing his book, was chief of Project Blue Book.

Connors said that she wasn't sure about the exact sequence or authorization, but she believed that General Nathan Twining received the initial order and passed it along to T-2. There may have only been a verbal order to begin the investigation because no documentation for this project has been found in the government files.

McCoy and his staff commandeered a room in the T-2 facility to set up the project, only allowing their team access to the room. McCoy then ordered Alfred Loedding, later the first director of JPL, to begin designing the basic project and to find a way to begin gathering information. All this was done in the months before the Arnold sighting, but not before other sightings were made.

Among the first that would have been sent to them and which would have ended up in their private investigation, is a report mentioned only in Ed Ruppelt's private papers released after 1960. On January 16 and 17, 1947, two fighters based in England attempted to intercept a "violently maneuvering" UFO. Although Ruppelt, who would become chief of Project Blue Book, was aware of these incidents, they do not appear in the government files.

On April 1, 1947, a series of sightings were reported near Richmond, Virginia, involving the U.S. Weather Bureau. This would later become Incident No. 79 in the government files, in this case, the Project Grudge final report. It should be noted that the case disappeared from Project Blue Book files as they were released to the public. According to the information in the Grudge Report:

> A weather bureau observer at the Richmond Station observed on three different occasions, during a six month period prior to April, 1947, a disc-like metal chrome object. All sightings were made through a theodolite while making pibal [balloon] observations.

> On the last reported sighting, the balloon was at 15,000 feet altitude, the disc followed for 15 seconds. It was shaped like an ellipse with a flat level bottom and a dome-like top. The altitude and the speed were not estimated, but the object, allegedly through the instrument, appeared larger than the balloon.

> Another observer at the same station saw a similar object under corresponding circumstances, with the exception that her balloon was at an altitude of 27,000 feet and possessed a dull-metallic luster. There was good

visibility on days of observation. Report of this sighting was not submitted until 22 July 1947.

AMC Opinion: There is no readily apparent explanation. If there were only one such object, it seems amazingly coincidental that it would be seen four times near the pibal of this station only. On the other hand, there would have to be a great number of these objects to rule out coincidence, and as they number of objects increases so do the chances of sightings by other witnesses.

Project Astronomer's Opinion: There is no astronomical explanation for this incident, which, however, deserves considerable attention because of the experience of the observers and the fact that the observations was made through a theodolite and that comparison could be made with a pibal balloon. The observers had, therefore, a good estimate of altitude, of relative size, and of speed—much more reliable than those given in most reports.

This investigation would like to recommend that these and other pibal observers be quizzed as to other possible, unreported sightings.

This series of reports made by Walter Minczewski, are not mentioned in the Project Blue Book index, which lists only a couple of reports made prior to the Kenneth Arnold sighting. All were reported after the press coverage of the Arnold sighting, so there is no way to document the actual date of the sighting, except for Minczewski's reports.

Dr. James McDonald did interview Minczewski, but twenty years after the fact. According to McDonald, and reported by Ted Bloecher in his book about the 1947 wave of UFO sightings, "Just a matter of days before this writing, I spoke on the telephone with Walter A. Minczewski, the U. S. Weather Bureau observer whose April, 1947, theodolite-tracking case is cited in the text. Minczewski emphasized that he had never reported it to other than his Weather Bureau superiors and hence was surprised to be called about it twenty years later. Yet his recollection of the details of the whitish disc-like object he had tracked one clear morning in Richmond, Virginia, was still distinct in his mind."

Later, Bloecher, in *The Report on the UFO Wave of 1947*, added some important details to the case. He wrote:

As early as the middle of April 1947, at the Weather Bureau in Richmond, Virginia, a U. S. Government meteorologist named Walter

James McDonald was a senior physicist at the Institute for Atmospheric Physics and a meteorology professor at the University of Arizona at Tucson.

A. Minczewski and his staff had released a pibal balloon and were tracking its east-to-west course at 15,000 feet when they noticed silver, ellipsoidal object just below it. Larger than the balloon, this object appeared to be flat on bottom, and when observed through the theodolite used to track the balloon, was seen to have a dome on its upper side. Minczewski and his assistants watched the object for fifteen seconds as it traveled rapidly in level flight on a westerly course, before disappearing from view. In the official report on file at the Air Force's Project Blue Book, at Wright-Patterson Field, in Dayton, Ohio, this sighting is listed as Unidentified.

The evidence, some of which was available in the government files, and some of which has now disappeared from those files, based on documentation seen by UFO researchers, suggests an effort to ignore any report made prior to Arnold. This way, all the reports made afterward could be chalked up to "hysteria" caused by Arnold. People were now seeing all sorts of strange things in the sky, not because they were there, but because of the publicity resulting from Arnold's sighting.

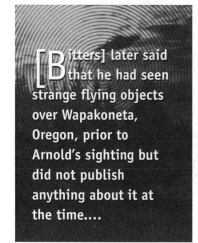

[Bitters] later said that he had seen strange flying objects over Wapakoneta, Oregon, prior to Arnold's sighting but did not publish anything about it at the time....

Since there was little official interest in these "aerial apparitions" in early 1947, McCoy and Deyarmond's unofficial investigation was not causing a stir. They would have had access to everything that came into the Air Technical Intelligence Center and they could have posed questions to intelligence officers and military attachés around the world. They could screen reports received for anything that interested them.

One of the best sources was pilot reports. When pilots saw something strange in the sky, they would communicate it to their fellow pilots and that information could make its way to the investigation at Wright Field. The Foo Fighter and the Ghost Rocket sightings would have suggested something going on, and they would be attempting to learn about it. With sightings moving into the United States, McCoy and Deyarmond would be even more interested.

Finding documentation of the sightings would have been difficult in early 1947. There were no newspaper reports and people were not talking about these things. No civilian agencies and certainly no newspapers were covering stories about flying saucers or flying disks. In fact, Richard L. Bitters, an editor at a large newspaper, the *Wapakoneta* [Ohio] *Daily News,* reported his sighting on July 1, 1947. He later said that he had seen strange flying objects over Wapakoneta, Ohio, prior to Arnold's sighting but did not publish anything about it at the time because, to him, it wasn't news until after the Arnold story made it into the national limelight.

The lone exception to this was a short article in the *Cedar Rapids Gazette* on June 23, 1947. A railroad engineer said that he had seen ten disk-shaped objects flying in a string formation. A careful search of the newspaper for that day and several that followed failed to verify that claim.

However, the story of a railroad engineer in Joliet, Illinois, published after the Arnold report, seems to be the genesis of this case. According to the article that did appear in the *Cedar Rapids Gazette*, "Flying Discs Seen By Railroad Man." The newspaper is dated June 28, 1947, and appears two days after the Arnold story.

The article said:

A railroad man said Friday [which is June 27, 1947 and eliminates the need for further information right there because the story appeared after Arnold] he saw "about nine" spinning discs speeding through the sky last Tuesday [June 24] the same day an Idaho flyer said he saw some flashing objects in the air.

Charles Kastl, 60, an employe [sic] of the Elgin, Joliet and Eastern railroad for 38 years, said he saw the discs about 1:50 P.M. (CST) as he was walking along the highway to work.

No other person in the Joliet area reported anything unusual.

Kastl said he saw a string of flat, circular objects going faster "than any plane I ever saw" about 10 to 12 miles east of Joliet [Illinois]. They were flying about 4,000 feet, he said.

"They appeared to be very high, and were going from north to south," he said. "I could see no connecting link between them, but they acted as though the leading disc had a motor in it to power the others, because when it flipped, the others would too. When it would right itself, the others would right themselves."

Kastl said he did not tell anyone but his wife about seeing the objects until Friday, "because I didn't think anything about it."

When he returned from a railroad run Friday, however, he learned that Kenneth Arnold, Boise, Idaho, pilot had reported seeing objects similar to the ones he claimed to have seen. Arnold said he saw objects over the Pacific Northwest.

Charles Preucil, head of the Joliet astronomical society, said there would be no natural cause for a display such as Kastl described.

Given the information in this article and given the descriptions given for the Cedar Rapids sighting, this must the source of the original claim. It did not happen in Cedar Rapids, nor did it happen on June 23. It seems that someone (Frank Edwards?) miscalculated the date of Tuesday, believing it to be the 23rd, and not realizing it was the 24th.

A second report, made by Dale Bays, a bus driver from Des Moines, also fit some of the information but that sighting is dated as June 29, 1947, which means it was made after Arnold. Bays said that he saw a single file line of "dirty white" round objects that were somewhere between circular and oval in shape. Bays thought they were 175 to 250 feet in diameter and twelve feet thick. He said they were at 1,200 feet and traveling about 300 miles an hour. The Air Force found the report to be unreliable.

The collection of such reports changed the day Kenneth Arnold made the report that began the blizzard. Over the next three or four weeks, hundreds of sightings were made and reported by the media.

Kenneth Arnold and his Nine Flying Objects

It was Kenneth Arnold's sighting on June 24, 1947, that set the whole thing off, at least in the mind of the public. Arnold, a businessman pilot, was flying his private plane at about 9,500 feet when a bright flash of light caught his eye. In the distance, near Mount Rainier, Washington, he saw nine objects that he first thought might be other aircraft, flying at about the same altitude and at an estimated speed of more than 1,500 miles per hour. As he watched them, however, he realized that they were not something conventional.

When Arnold landed in Yakima, Washington, he told reporters that the objects moved with a motion similar to saucers skipping across the water. The shape, however, according to drawings that Arnold completed for the Army within days of the sighting, showed objects that were heel shaped. In later drawings, Arnold elaborated, drawing objects that were crescent shaped, with a scalloped trailing edge.

An artist's depiction of the nine UFOs that Arnold reported seeing while flying his small aircraft in 1947.

Arnold's sighting didn't gain front page status immediately. Newspaper stories about the sighting appeared a day or two later, and the tale was regarded as an oddity. Arnold later claimed that he thought he had seen some sort of new jet aircraft.

According to the government files, however, Arnold wasn't the only person in the area to see strange objects in the sky that day. Fred Johnson, listed as a prospector, also reported sighting five or six disk-shaped craft as they flew over the Cascade Mountains. Johnson said the objects were round, with a slight tail and about thirty feet in diameter. They were not flying in any sort of formation and as they banked in a turn, the sunlight flashed off them. As the objects approached, Johnson noticed that his compass began to spin wildly, and when they finally vanished in the distance, the compass returned to normal.

After learning of the Arnold sighting, Johnson wrote to the Air Force on August 20, 1947, saying:

> Saw in the portland [sic] paper a short time ago in regards to an article in regards to the so called flying disc having any basis in fact. I can say am a prospector and was in the Mt Adams district on June 24th the day Kenneth Arnold of Boise Idaho claims he saw a formation of flying disc [sic]. And i [sic] saw the same flying objects at about the same time. Having a telescope with me at the time i [sic] can asure [sic] you there are real and noting like them I ever saw before they did not pass verry [sic] high over where I was standing at the time. plolby [sic] 1000 ft. they were Round about 30 foot in diameter tapering sharply to a point in the head and in an oval shape. with [sic] a bright top surface. I did not hear any noise as you would from a plane. But there was an object in the tail end looked like a big hand of a clock shifting from side to side like a big magnet. There [sic] speed was far as I know seemed to be greater than anything I ever saw. Last view I got of the objects they were standing on edge Banking in a cloud.

The letter is signed: "Yours Respectfully, Fred Johnson."

Johnson was eventually interviewed by the FBI, whose report contained essentially the same information that was in the letter Johnson had sent to the Army. The FBI report, found in government files, ended by saying, "Informant appeared to be a very reliable individual who advised that he had been a prospector in the states of Montana, Washington, and Oregon for the past forty years."

Johnson's report is important because it corroborates what Arnold reported and comes from an independent source. Of course, the problem is that Johnson did not contact anyone about his sighting until after all the publicity about Arnold's sighting.

Regardless of the possible corroboration and his aviation experience, the Air Force eventually decided that Arnold had been fooled by a mirage, and, in the end, that was how they labeled the case. In 1947, as members of the Army Air Forces and various intelligence communities were attempting to learn what was happening, Arnold's sighting was listed as an unknown.

The Investigations Begin ... Sort Of

As of June 1947, there was no official investigation of the flying saucers. Though McCoy and Deyarmond may have provided some direction from Wright Field, all investigations were handled by the local bases and local units. For example, the Fourth Air Force, at Hamilton Army Air Field, California, investigated the Arnold sighting, but there was no coordinated effort into which the flood of new information could be directed. It was all hit or miss.

The officers at Fourth Air Force sent to interview Arnold were Lieutenant Frank M. Brown and Captain William L. Davidson. They developed a respect for Arnold and viewed him as an honest man who had seen something extraordinary. At the end of their meeting, Brown and Davidson asked Arnold to give them a call if he had any questions. Little did they know that Arnold would eventually ask for their help, dragging them into what has been called the dirtiest hoax in UFO history.

Collaborating with Ray Palmer, Kenneth Arnold published his *The Coming of the Saucers* in 1952.

Arnold's sighting had drawn the attention of Ray Palmer, a magazine editor in Chicago. Palmer had been editor of the science fiction magazine *Amazing Stories* at one time, and he had rebuilt its circulation with the story of an underground world of advanced technology, responsible for many of the problems faced by humans on the surface. Known as the Shaver Mystery, Palmer's story featured robotic beings, who tormented the human race from inside the Earth. Palmer promoted the story, may even have written parts of it himself, and insisted that the story was true. Coincidentally, he published an installment of the Shaver Mystery in the June 1947 issue of *Amazing Stories*.

When Arnold's story burst into the public arena in late June 1947, Palmer viewed it as proof that the Shaver Mystery was real. As far as Palmer was concerned, the flying saucers were craft from the inner Earth civilization in the Shaver story. Palmer contacted Arnold to learn more about his sighting, but Arnold wasn't interested in discussing it with the editor, nor was he interested in writing anything about his sighting for publication in the magazine. Palmer then offered Arnold a fee for his story. Arnold merely sent him a copy of the report he had forwarded to the Army Air Force.

A few days later, Palmer called again, but this time he wanted Arnold to investigate another sighting, this one from Washington state. Although Arnold was reluctant and had no experience as an investigator, Palmer offered him $200 to follow up on the story, and Arnold eventually agreed to investigate.

The basics of the Washington story were not all that incredible. A harbor patrolman named Harold Dahl said that on June 21, he was out near Maury Island on a small boat with his son and their dog. They saw six doughnut-shaped objects, one of which seemed to be in trouble. It leaked some liquid metal that fell on the boat, injuring Dahl's son and killing the dog. Dahl was able to recover some of this metal.

In a slightly different version of the story, told sometime later by the witnesses to other investigators, the sixth object touched down on Maury Island. It then disintegrated, leaving behind a residue, which Dahl was able to collect. In either case, the Maury Island sighting was important because of the physical evidence associated with it.

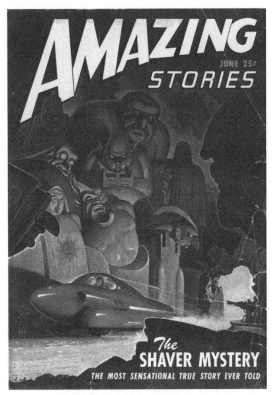

The tale of the Shaver Mystery was recounted in the June 1947 issue of *Amazing Stories*.

At this point, Dahl hadn't told anyone about the sighting or the physical evidence. Dahl also told Palmer that a dark-suited, somewhat bizarre looking stranger told him all about the sighting, as if he had seen everything, or had, at the very least, known exactly what had happened. This stranger said that it would be best for Dahl to forget about what he had seen and not mention it to anyone else.

Dahl ignored the advice and told his immediate supervisor, Fred Crisman about the sighting. Crisman was able to recover some of the strange metal himself, and it was Crisman who wrote to Palmer, telling him the whole story. Palmer, in turn, contacted Arnold, asking him to investigate.

When Arnold arrived and talked to Dahl and Crisman, he realized that he was out of his depth. He called Captain E. J. Smith, a United Airlines pilot who had seen several flying disks while on a flight in the Pacific Northwest. Smith's sighting, according to the government files, remains as "Unidentified."

Even with Smith's help, Arnold still was unsure how to proceed. According to the government files, Arnold then called Frank Brown, believing that something very strange was going on. Ed Ruppelt wrote in his book:

> For the Air Force the story started on July 31, 1947, when Lieutenant
> Frank Brown, an intelligence agent at Hamilton AFB, California, re-

Ray Palmer, who was the editor of *Amazing Stories* and later *Fate Magazine,* did a lot to publicize the testimonies of UFO eyewitness in the 1930s, '40s, and '50s.

ceived a long-distance phone call. The caller was the man whom I'll call Simpson [Kenneth Arnold] who had met Brown when Brown investigated an earlier UFO sighting … He [Arnold] had just talked to two Tacoma Harbor patrolmen. One of them had seen six UFOs.…

Brown and Davidson arrived at Arnold's hotel about five that evening. Once Arnold showed them some of the recovered metal, both officers recognized it for what it was, that is, worthless slag, and that lead them to the conclusion that it was a hoax.

There is another interesting point to all this which needs to be remembered. While Brown and Davidson were in the hotel room with Arnold and Smith, Arnold asked what the Army had learned about the flying saucers. According to George Earley, a UFO investigator living in Oregon and who has studied this case in-depth, Davidson drew a picture of a flying saucer. He told Arnold it was based on one of several pictures that the Army had received.

Earley reported that Brown agreed with Davidson's rendering of the flying saucer, saying, "It came from Phoenix, Arizona the other day. We have the prints at Hamilton Field, but the original negatives were flown to Washington, D.C."

This is a reference to the photographs taken by William Rhodes in Arizona on July 7, 1947. The Fourth Air Force was involved in that investigation as well, according to the government files. The object photographed was similar to that seen by Arnold, including a cockpit centered on the heel-shaped craft. According to the government files, the pictures would eventually be written off as a hoax, based not on the photographic evidence but on the unconventional lifestyle of Rhodes, whose abrasive personality rubbed most of the investigators the wrong way.

As Brown and Davidson were leaving Arnold's room, he insisted that they take a sample of the metal with them. Neither Brown nor Davidson wanted to, but they didn't want to embarrass Arnold or Smith, according to Ruppelt. They took the metal and thanked Arnold for all his help. They drove back out to the airfield to claim their aircraft for the return flight to California.

Not long after takeoff, the engine on the left wing caught fire. Brown, according to the government files and the accident investigation, left the cockpit to assist their two passengers, Woodrow D. Matthews and Sergeant Elmer L. Taff, into their parachutes. After the two bailed out, Brown apparently returned to the cockpit to help Davidson. Earley theorized Brown and Davidson believed they could save the aircraft because the B-25 could be flown on a single engine and they were not carrying a heavy load. Unfortunately, the engine hadn't just failed, it was also on fire.

Taff later told the investigators that he saw the left wing burn off. It smashed into the tail, spinning the aircraft out of control. Neither pilot was able to get out and both were killed in the accident.

The government files, and Ed Ruppelt, suggested that the Air Force thought about prosecuting Dahl and Crisman in the deaths of the two officers. Both men had admitted that the rocks given to Arnold, and later to Brown and Davidson, were nothing more than useless slag. The whole story was a hoax that got out of hand when Crisman wrote to Palmer. Crisman was willing to say almost anything that Palmer wanted him to say to advance the story and see his name in print.

Kenneth Arnold, shown here, gained the trust of Fourth Air Force officers Lieutenant Frank M. Brown and Captain William L. Davidson, whom he would lead into what has been called one of the biggest UFO hoaxes in history.

The Rhodes Photographs

The government file on these photographs is quite large, and the investigation that began in July 1947 continued for several years. What is interesting is that the FBI was involved early on, but the role of the Army in the investigation was concealed.

Rhodes, who seemed to be unemployed in July 1947, held a number of patents and was also listed as the Chief of Staff of the Panoramic Research Laboratory. The lab was apparently located in his backyard, but given his background and the fact that he had done some high level work for the Navy (and would later assist in the development of equipment for the Kitt Peak Observatory) a little bit of self-promotion seemed harmless.

According to the government files, Rhodes was walking toward his lab when he heard what sounded like the "whoosh" of a P-80 Shooting Star, one of the new jets. He grabbed his camera and ran back outside to take a photograph. Rhodes told reporter Robert C. Hanika that he had sighted an object along the side of his camera and took one photograph.

Rhodes advanced the film but didn't take a second picture. He only had one frame left and hoped that the object would come closer. When he realized that it was moving away, Rhodes took the second photograph.

Although the Air Force spent years investigating the sighting, they eventually labelled it a hoax.

Although the Air Force spent years investigating the sighting, they eventually labelled it a hoax. Their reasoning was based more on Rhodes' unconventional lifestyle and his abrasive nature, which annoyed military investigators and certainly didn't help with the evaluation of the case.

Interestingly, according to the government files, the Army's role in the investigation was concealed when they interviewed Rhodes. A document in the government files notes, "It should be stated that at the time of the interview with [name redacted, but clearly is Rhodes] Mr. BROWER identified himself as an agent of the Federal Bureau of Investigation and he exhibited his credentials. However, pursuant to a request from Mr. FUGATE [who was an Army counterintelligence corps agent], he was introduced only as a representative of the United States government. His exact official connection was not made known to Mr. [again, name redacted, but it is Rhodes]."

In another interesting aside to this case, there is a reference to this investigation in the Grudge Report, which includes synopses of cases written by various experts called in to assist with the investigations. Dr. J. Allen Hynek, who was the consultant in astronomy, wrote about "Incident #40—Phoenix, Arizona—July 7, 1947":

> This case is especially important because of the photographic evidence and because of the similarity of these photographs to the drawings by Kenneth Arnold (incident #17). The two incidents are separated by slightly more than two weeks, and, of course, they occurred in different locations. It is, however, perhaps more than coincidence that these two best-attested, entirely independent cases should agree so closely concerning the shape of the object and its maneuverability.

It is evident from other documentation in the government files that Fourth Air Force headquarters, located at Hamilton Field, California, the same base where Brown and Davidson served, ran part of the investigation. They would have had access to the Rhodes' photographs and would have been able to describe them to Arnold.

Given this early connection, and the obvious similarity between the Arnold drawings and the Rhodes photograph, it appears that investigators wanted to keep information about both sightings secret. If they could bury the Rhodes photograph under a cloud of controversy and slam them as a hoax, it would be easy to dismiss them. The problem is that there is no good link between what Arnold had said and what the photographs showed. In other words, Rhodes couldn't have created the hoax based on descriptions given by Arnold because those descriptions had been skewed by the press. Following today's logic, that flying saucers are the result of Arnold's poor description or the press grabbing a term that sounded good but did nothing to illustrate what he had seen, the Rhodes photographs should have shown a saucer.

That Early Confusion

The information and testimony seems to suggest that when the sightings began in the United States, although they were not publicized until Arnold, the investigation was already in progress. Since it was being conducted out of T-2 at Wright Field, General Nathan Twining, while not involved in the day-to-day activities, would have known about it. As the number of sightings and newspaper reports increased, the importance of the investigation was growing, and a disconnect developed among the various agencies providing quotes to newspapers. On July 3, 1947, for example, Major Paul Gaynor, apparently speaking for the Army Air Forces said that their preliminary investigation of the "flying disks" had been dropped due to a lack of evidence.

On the very same day, Dave Johnson, a reporter for the *Idaho Evening Statesman,* got a statement from Twining, which said that the top secret research they were conducting had not been able to duplicate the performance of the flying disks. Twining added that they had not produced any technology that would be considered comparable to what had been observed. He confirmed that a "reputable scientist" had seen one of the flying disks and that his report was being analyzed. While Twining did not say that the investigation was continuing, it is clear from later information found in government files that it was.

Gaynor and Twining's conflicting statements demonstrate a level of confusion inside the military during the summer of 1947. The one investigation that was in progress was housed in a single office in the T-2 facility and very few knew about it. That was about to change. Too many sightings were being made, too many of them were being reported in the newspapers, and there were too many questions being asked.

What was about to happen was that someone, who decided that they needed to make an assessment of the situation, was about to take action. A brigadier general, George F. Schulgen, was about to gather the best cases that he knew about and forward them to Wright Field, the Air Materiel Command, and General Twining for an analysis. It would change the course of the investigation.

General Nathan Twining launched Project Sign in 1947; in 1953 he would replace Hoyt Vandenberg as chief of staff.

The Estimate of the Situation

Captain Edward Ruppelt, one-time chief of Project Blue Book alerted the world to the existence of an official "Estimate of the Situation" discussing UFOs. Ruppelt, in his book, *The Report on Unidentified Flying Objects*, noted, "In intelligence, if you have something to say about some vital problem you write a report that is known as an 'Estimate of the Situation.' A few days after the DC-3 was buzzed [a reference to the Chiles-Whitted UFO sighting], the people at the Air Technical Intelligence Center (ATIC) decided that the time had arrived to make an Estimate of the Situation. The situation was the UFO's [sic]; the estimate was that they were interplanetary!"

Although the sighting that sparked the analysis had occurred only a few days earlier, the genesis of the Estimate went back to the summer of 1947. At this time, according to Ruppelt, the Pentagon was in a panic over the sudden appearance of the flying saucers. "As 1947 drew to a close, the Air Force's Project Sign had outgrown its initial panic and had settled down to a routine operation."

When the UFOs first appeared that summer, there was panic because, according to the government files, newspaper reports, and military officers, nobody knew exactly what was happening. Theories were floated on an almost daily basis and some of them were just plain silly. A scientist suggested that the flying saucers were simply spots before the eyes. As people left dark movie theaters and went into bright sunlight, before their eyes adjusted, they saw floating images. The scientist seemed unaware that such a problem would likely create black spots and not silver disks.

Other ideas had some merit, and were based on the observations of military and civilian pilots, highly educated individuals, and scientists assigned to some of the most highly classified projects in existence at the time. One of those theories spoken of quietly, but with some support, was the belief that some of the saucers were interplanetary spacecraft.

Those whose responsibility it was to determine the nature of the saucers wondered if the saucers were a highly classified research project, which meant that only a few people at the very top of the chain of command would have access to the information. Army Brigadier General George Schulgen and FBI Special Agent S. W. Reynolds believed that it was a waste of time, money, and

THE REPORT ON UNIDENTIFIED FLYING OBJECTS

Edward J. Ruppelt

Former Head of the United States Air Force Project Blue Book
Investigating Flying Saucers

The Report on Unidentified Flying Objects **was published in 1956. The author explains such sightings as the Lubbock Lights and the UFOs over Washington, D.C.**

personnel to investigate something that would eventually lead to a classified project, one they would not be allowed to truly investigate.

LTC George Garrett also believed that nothing useful would be found by an additional Air Force investigation. Garrett and Schulgen decided that the answer was above their pay grade and wanted to pass the buck back up the chain of command. They were quite certain that once they assembled their information in an intelligence Estimate of the Situation, they would be asked to stop investigating since those at the top already knew what the flying saucers were.

Nonetheless, Garrett began his work on the Estimate in the beginning of July, 1947. He selected sixteen flying saucer reports that seemed to demonstrate the truly unusual nature of the phenomenon, and then provided his analysis of the collected data.

Garrett's "Estimate of the Situation"

The first case Garrett mentioned preceded the Kenneth Arnold sighting by over a month. Many believe this sighting "launched" the UFO phenomena as we know it today. This sighting, from Manitou Springs, Colorado, happened sometime between 12:15 and 1:15 P.M. on May 19, 1947, and involved a silver object that remained motionless. The three witnesses got a good look at it before the object made a number of aerobatic maneuvers before disappearing at incredible speed. The sighting report mentioned that the object had been observed through optical instruments and remained in sight for over two minutes, meaning they had time to study it carefully. This sighting does not appear in the Project Blue Book files, though Garrett used it to support his conclusions at the end of this study.

The second report included in Garrett's study was from Oklahoma City on May 22, 1947. There are few details available about this sighting in the government files other than it was made by a businessman pilot who saw the object or light from the ground and not the cockpit.

The third case used by Garrett came from Greenfield, Massachusetts on June 22, 1947. According to the government files:

> Edward L. de Rose said ... there appeared across his line of vision a "brilliant, small, round-shaped, silvery white object" moving in a northwest-

erly direction as fast as or probably faster than a speeding plane at an estimated altitude of 1,000 feet or more. The object stayed in view for eight or ten seconds until obscured by a cloud bank. It reflected the sunlight strongly as though it were of polished aluminum or silver.... He said it did not resemble any weather balloon he had ever seen and that "I can assure you it was very real."

According to the information available, this case had been secretly investigated by the FBI, and given Special Agent Reynolds' participation with Schulgen and Garrett, it is not difficult to believe that the FBI was involved.

Next was the report that got everyone talking about flying saucers. This was Kenneth Arnold's sighting of June 24. In 1947, as Garrett was putting together his Estimate, this sighting was still considered an unknown by those who had investigated it and talked to Arnold.

Garrett's next sighting involved multiple witnesses and pilots. The government files available show that two Air Force (at the time Army Air Forces) pilots and two intelligence officers saw a bright light zigzagging in the night sky over Maxwell Air Force Base on June 28, 1947. The sighting lasted for about five minutes.

> • • • two Air Force (at the time Army Air Forces) pilots and two intelligence officers saw a bright light zigzagging in the night sky over Maxwell Air Force Base on June 28, 1947.

Ruppelt reported it this way:

That night [June 28, 1947] at nine-twenty, four Air Force officers, two pilots and two intelligence officers from Maxwell AFB in Montgomery, Alabama, saw a bright light traveling across the sky. It was first seen just above the horizon, and as it traversed toward the observers it "zigzagged," with bursts of high speed. When it was directly overhead it made a sharp 90-degree turn and was lost from view as it traveled south.

The eventual conclusion was that the object sighted was a balloon. Although it seems that four officers, including the intelligence officers, would have been able to identify a balloon, this was the accepted explanation. It would also seem that the maneuvers of the object would rule out a balloon, regardless of how strong the winds aloft were blowing.

Garrett's next case was witnessed by three scientists at White Sands, New Mexico. The object was silver in color and no external details were reported. There was the possibility of a slight vapor trail, but none of the three were sure how it disappeared, suggesting that the angle changed and they lost sight of it.

Civilian pilots were responsible for the next sighting that Garrett quoted. Captain E. J. Smith was piloting a United Airlines plane when one of the flying saucers appeared, coming at the plane. When the first officer, Ralph Stevens, reached down to blink the landing lights, Smith asked what he was doing. Stevens responded that another plane was coming at them, but as it closed, both pilots realized that it wasn't another aircraft, but a flying disk.

Chiles–Whitted: The Rest of the Story

When Chiles and Whitted first made their UFO report, it was suggested that they had seen a fireball. Of course, that didn't explain the detail of their drawings, including the cigar shape of the double row of square windows. It was the drawings that convinced many that they had seen something that was extraordinary and probably extraterrestrial.

On March 3, 1968, there was a series of UFO reports in the Midwestern United States. These described a cigar-shaped craft with lighted windows. Skeptics, including Philip Klass, UFO researchers, and the Air Force identified the UFO as the reentry of one of the Zond 4 booster rockets. The spacecraft had been placed in orbit the night before, so this sighting was of a spacecraft or rather part of one, but not one that was extraterrestrial.

Klass suggested in his book, *UFOs Explained,* that this was also the conclusion regarding the Chiles–Whitted sighting of July 24, 1948. Chiles and Whitted were the pilot and co-pilot of an airliner who reported they had seen what they first thought was some kind of jet aircraft, but later described it as a cigar-shaped object with lighted windows. Originally it was concluded that they had seen a meteor, but that explanation was rejected once the pilots clarified that their aircraft had been rocked by the passing UFO. It was a short sighting but one that originally baffled the Air Force investigators. Later, or maybe eventually, it was identified as a "Fireball."

Many weren't happy with the explanations offered by Klass and the Air Force, but now there are videos available of meteor falls, which appear to resemble some kind of craft with lighted windows, especially as the meteor begins to break up. Given the coincidence of the Zond 4 reentry, with the drawings and descriptions of the Chiles–Whitted sighting, it appears that these cases can be marked as solved, as Klass and the Air Force has suggested.

The Zond 4 illustrations, reentry, and descriptions by Chiles and Whitted suggest they probably saw a meteor as it approached them, before it broke up. Given

Ufologists James Moseley (left) and Philip Klass are shown here at a CSICOP conference in Buffalo, New York, in 1983.

that this was 1948 and extremely early in the morning, there simply weren't any other witnesses awake to see the object, though there were some ground reports.

The illustrations made by them seem to match those drawn to reflect the Zond 4. This case can be removed from the lists of the unsolved.

They could not make out a real shape but did say the craft was flat on the bottom, very thin, and seemed to be irregular on the top. The object appeared to be at the same altitude as the airplane and followed them for ten to fifteen minutes.

Moments later, four more objects appeared on the left of the aircraft. Smith was quoted in the newspaper as saying, "We couldn't tell what the exact shape was except to notice that they definitely were larger than our plane (a DC-4), fairly smooth on the bottom and rough on top."

Although the case was thoroughly investigated, the Air Force found no explanation for the occurence. In the government files, including Project Blue Book, it is still carried as "Unidentified."

The next case cited was reported by three airmen on a B-25, near Clay Center, Kansas, who saw a silver-colored object pacing their aircraft. One of the witnesses was the pilot, who said that a bright flash drew his attention to the object, which was thirty to fifty feet in diameter and very bright. The object appeared to be pacing the aircraft at 210 miles an hour. When they turned toward it, the object seemed to accelerate to high speed and disappeared. The Air Force would later suggest that the sighting was caused by a reflection on the windshield.

Garrett next reported that on July 6, 1947, Captain James H. Burniston, while at Fairfield-Suisun Army Air Base, saw one of the flying disks. According to the government files:

> He observed an object traveling in a southeasterly direction at an estimated height of 10,000 feet or more and at a speed in excess of that of any aircraft he had ever seen. The object was in his view for approximately sixty seconds during which time it travelled over three-quarters of the visible sky. Burniston could distinguish no definite color or shape. It appeared to roll from side to side three times during his observation and one side reflected strongly from its surface while the other side gave no reflection. He estimates the size to be about that of a C-54 and states that between the time the top of the object was visible and the time it rolled over … the bottom became very difficult to see and almost disappeared.

Although the next two reports seem to be related, Garrett broke them into two separate incidents, one from Koshkonong, Wisconsin, and the second from

East Troy, Wisconsin. In the government files, they are listed on the same "Project Card," which supplies very little information. Both sightings lasted under a minute, and in both cases the witnesses were members of the Civil Air Patrol, a civilian volunteer organization and an official auxiliary of the Air Force. The first of the sightings was reported at 11:45 (CST) in the morning and the second at 2:30 (CST) in the afternoon. Both were made on July 7, 1947.

The government files about this sighting said, "Saucer descended vertically edgewise through clouds, stopped at 4000' and assumed horizontal position and proceeded in horizontal flight from a horizontal position for 15 seconds covering 25 miles, again stopped, and disappeared."

Both these cases, which were reported by military and civilians, including pilots, were marked "Insufficient information for proper analysis." This begs the question of what Garrett thought was so important about them that he included them in his analysis, or what information Garrett may have had in 1947 that was left out of the government files. It wouldn't be the first time that information in the government files had been altered.

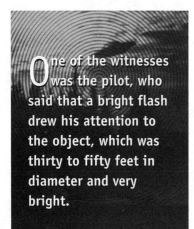

One of the witnesses was the pilot, who said that a bright flash drew his attention to the object, which was thirty to fifty feet in diameter and very bright.

Following his theory of who might make the best witnesses, the next case involved an Army Air Corps National Guard pilot flying near Mt. Baldy, California on July 8, 1947. The flat object, reflecting light, was about the size of a fighter. The pilot said that he gave chase, attempting to keep the object in sight but was unable to do so.

A police officer, among others, in Grand Falls, Newfoundland, reported an egg-shaped object with a barrel-like leading edge about thirty minutes before midnight on July 9, 1947, in the next case reported by Garrett. There were four objects that had a phosphorescent glow.

Next on the list there was a series of sightings in Newfoundland, which happened the following day. In his report, Garrett included the sighting that took place about four in the afternoon, and was seen by a "TWA Representative and a PAA Representative [who was identified as a Mr. Leidy] on the ground. The object was "circular in shape, like a wagon wheel," and was bluish-black with a fifteen foot long trail. The object "seemed to cut clouds open as it passed thru [sic]. Trail was like beam seen after a high-powered landing light is switched off."

The case took on added importance because there were color photographs of the disk as it cut through the clouds. Dr. Michael Swords reported in the *Journal of UFO Studies*:

> The bluish-black trail seems to indicate ordinary combustion from a turbo-jet engine, athodyd [ramjet] motor, or some combination of these types of power plants. The absence of noise and apparent dissolving of the clouds to form a clear path indicates a relatively large mass flow of a rectangular cross section containing a considerable amount of heat.

A Cessna 182, part of the Civil Air Patrol, is shown here with a U.S. Air Force fighter jet. The Civil Air Patrol serves as a non-combat auxiliary to the Air Force.

In the original analysis, T-2, part of the intelligence function at Wright-Patterson, excluded meteors or fireballs as a possible explanation. Later, as Blue Book officers became more interested in solutions than facts, the case was written off as a meteor sighting.

This was an important case and provides a hint as to what Garrett and the others thought in 1947. They believed that the answer rested in terrestrial technology, or in other words, this was something of Soviet manufacture. While the sighting itself is interesting because of the photographs, it was important because it seemed to point to the Soviets rather than aliens.

The final case Garrett cited in his report was from Elmendorf Field in Anchorage, Alaska. On July 12, 1947, a major in the Army Air Forces said that he observed an object that resembled a grayish balloon as it followed the contours of the mountains, some five miles away. The major said that the object paralleled the course of a C-47 that was landing on the airfield.

Garrett's report comprised of the sixteen reports discussed above and two that were added later. It is likely that he drew on these specific cases because he, along with Schulgen, believed they most accurately described the objects seen, the maneuvers they performed, and would most likely lead to the conclusion that these sightings were of a classified project in development at that time. They expected that they would be asked to quit because of the classified nature of the project. The answer they received from Air Materiel Command and Lieutenant General Nathan F. Twining was not at all what they had expected.

The Phenomenon Was Very Real

On September 24, 1947, Schulgen, Garrett, and the others received the written response from Twining's staff, whose analysis of the situation was based wholly on the information supplied by Garrett, through Schulgen.

It appears that Twining's staff did not duplicate the reports used by Garrett. Instead, they reached their conclusions based on information supplied directly to them. The reports Twining's staff used, for the most part, came from pilots, both military and civilian, including airline pilots. They came from scientists, police, and aviation personnel who should have been able to recognize aircraft in the air. The reports were selected because they were from multiple witnesses; one in particular was likely selected because it included photographs. These were some of the best reports that had been received, beginning with the May reports that did not make it into the Project Blue Book files.

The priority level of the new project also suggested that Twining wanted his answers quickly because he was under pressure from above to end the panic.

This response, then, from Twining's AMC staff was telling Garrett and his team that the phenomenon was "something real and not visionary or fictitious." Not only that, Twining was telling them that his command didn't know what the flying disks were and that they needed to be investigated.

If the flying disks were a U.S. project, then the last thing anyone at the higher levels of the chain of command would have wanted would be an official investigation. Any investigation would be a threat to the security of the project. To end such an investigation, one of those on the inside of the secret would have to drop a hint to someone on the outside. If, for example, it was such a secret project that General Twining and the AMC were outside the loop, then another general, on the inside, could call Twining to tell him to drop the investigation. He wouldn't have to spill any details of the secret project, only tell Twining that it was something he didn't need to worry about and that the answer did not involve the Soviets or anything else that could threaten national security. Twining would then end his inquiries, secure in the knowledge that the solution to the mystery was already known to someone inside the U.S. military and the government.

That didn't happen. Instead, Twining suggested that a priority project, with a rating of 2a, be created to investigate the flying saucers. He wanted information found and reported to his office. The priority level of the new project also suggested that Twining wanted his answers quickly because he was under pressure from above to end the panic.

At that point it seems that the gathering of intelligence data by the Army Air Forces, as conducted by the military in 1947, was disorganized, inefficient, and confused. A review of the documents available in the government files showed that interviews conducted with key witnesses, such as Kenneth Arnold, were not completed until weeks after their sightings, and even then, not all the questions were asked. To make things worse, the critical corroboration of the Arnold sighting by Fred Johnson was probably overlooked. Later, when Air Force policy changed, some of these sightings, thought of as so mysterious in 1947, would be labeled with some sort of possible explanation and then forgotten.

Swords, commenting on this, wrote, "What explains this confident display of mediocrity? Although we are apparently not dealing with genius here, neither should we assume complete stupidity. This report was not put together with any greater intensity because the authors did not feel that it was necessary. They did not think that UFOs were any great mystery. It was obvious to them that UFOs were mechanical, aerial devices. Who owned the devices was still up in the air (so to speak), but the indications were fairly clear: despite assurances to the contrary, they must be our own. 'Lack of topside inquiries' [meaning, of course, those higher up in the chain of command] made this the only reasonable conclusion in their eyes."

These men, who hadn't exactly shined during their investigation, had no burning passion to find the answers because they were convinced the answers already existed at the very top. Their estimate, according to Swords, was little more than a plea to those higher up in the chain of command asking, "Can we please quit this nonsense."

At this point, Alfred Loedding, a civilian engineer and scientist who had been assigned to T-2, and who had an interest in the flying saucers, got involved with the investigation. Given the structure of the organization, and according to both government files and the research conducted by Michael Hall and Wendy Connors, it seems that Colonel Howard McCoy, with Loedding's assistance, drafted the Twining memo for the general's review. They suggest that Loedding, along with Dr. Charles Carroll, a math and missile expert, were "laying the ground work for an official investigation."

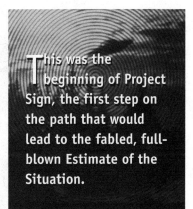

This was the beginning of Project Sign, the first step on the path that would lead to the fabled, full-blown Estimate of the Situation.

This was the beginning of Project Sign, the first step on the path that would lead to the fabled, full-blown Estimate of the Situation. According to Ed Ruppelt, the 2A priority was the second highest possible. Only the top people at ATIC were assigned to the new project. This was a serious project, designed to obtain specific answers to specific questions, and do so in a fairly quick manner.

The mission of Project Sign was to determine the nature of the flying saucers. According to Ruppelt, there were two schools of thought. One believed that the Soviets, using their captured German scientists, had developed the flying disks. ATIC technical analysts searched for data on the German projects in captured documents, both in the United States and in Germany.

It was clear that the second school of thought—that is, that the UFOs were not manufactured on Earth—began to take hold. No evidence was found that the Soviets had made some sort of technological breakthrough. Even if they had, it seemed unlikely that they would be flying their new craft over the United States. If one crashed, the Soviets would have just handed their breakthrough to the U.S. government. This is probably the inspiration for the paragraph that laments the lack of crash-recovered debris, which is a reference to the lack of this sort of information in the material provided by Garrett.

The ploy to end the investigations didn't work. It resulted in the creation of Project Sign, with funding that would allow the investigations to continue. It meant that those at the top were interested in answers and they didn't have them. It meant that things would continue.

The Real "Estimate of the Situation"

Project Sign began, semi-officially, with the beginning of the New Year, 1948. On January 7, 1948, Captain Thomas Mantell, leading a flight of F-51 fighters, encountered a UFO over Kentucky. Their original mission had been simply to move the aircraft from one airfield to another, but as they approached Fort Knox, Kentucky, they were asked to investigate a strange object that had been sighted overhead. Three of the aircraft turned toward the UFO, but the fourth, low on fuel, requested permission to land.

One of the most famous UFO encounters came in 1948, when Captain Thomas Mantell, leading a squadron of F-51s, saw one over the state of Kentucky. His wingmen witnessed the object, too.

Mantell and his wingmen saw the object and began climbing toward it. Mantell was convinced that it was huge, metallic, and moving away from him at about half his speed. He told his wingmen that he would climb to 25,000 feet, circle for ten minutes, and if he got no closer to the object, he would break off pursuit. He trimmed his aircraft to climb and then apparently lost consciousness due to a lack of oxygen at such high altitude. The plane continued to climb, finally stalled and fell into a power dive. At about 19,000 feet, the aircraft began to break up because of the external stresses. Mantell was killed in the crash.

The Air Force had a dilemma. One of its pilots, a National Guard pilot to be sure, but an Air Force pilot nonetheless, had been killed chasing a UFO. Not only that, there were literally dozens of witnesses who had seen the UFO as it drifted over southern Kentucky, including high-ranking officers who were in the airfield control tower and who provided detailed descriptions of the object. They had to act.

The Air Force decided that Mantell and the others had been fooled by Venus. They explained that Venus is bright enough to be seen in the daylight if you know where to look. It wasn't a very good explanation, but it was one that didn't involve an alien spacecraft. Michael Hall and Wendy Connors wrote, "The Sign team used Venus as a cover to explain away what at the time was an extensively publicized and long-investigated incident. Project Sign team members thought they might be forced to admit a far more shocking conclusion, but not before they had time to develop the ETH."

Much later, according to the government files, the Mantell sighting was identified as a Sky-hook balloon. Given the information in the files and the descriptions by those who saw it, this seems to be a solid solution. But the important point here is that in 1948, those at Project Sign believed it was an alien craft and that Mantell had died chasing it. They wished to study the phenomenon quietly and carefully so they allowed the wrong solution to be publicized until they had a chance to understand what was happening.

An artist's depiction of Mantell's UFO encounter.

The real problem came on July 24, 1948, when two pilots, Clarence Chiles and John B. Whitted reported that a cigar-shaped craft had buzzed their aircraft. They were flying a commercial DC-3 at about 5,000 feet, on a bright, cloudless, and star-filled night. Twenty miles southwest of Montgomery, Alabama, they spotted, slightly above and to the right of their craft, what they thought was one of the new jet aircraft. Within seconds the object was close enough that they could see its torpedo-shape and a double row of square windows.

Chiles called the attention of his co-pilot to the object saying, "Look, here comes a new Army jet job." The object approached in a slight dive, deflected a little to the left and passed the plane on the right, almost level to the flight path, according to the report in the government files. After passing, it pulled up sharply and disappeared into a cloud.

Questioned within hours of the event by Air Force investigators, both men said that they believed the object was about a hundred feet long. Whitted said, "The fuselage appeared to be about three times the circumference of a B-29 fuselage. The windows were very large and seemed square. They were white with light which seemed to be caused by some type of combustion. I estimate we watched the object for at least five seconds and not more than ten seconds. We heard no noise nor did we feel any turbulence from the object. It seemed to be at about 5500 feet."

Chiles, in a statement dated August 3, 1948, wrote, "It was clear there were no wings present, that it was powered by some jet or other type of power shooting flame from the rear some fifty feet ... Underneath the ship there was a blue glow of light."

Apparently all the passengers were asleep (or on the wrong side of the aircraft) with the exception of Clarence L. McKelvie. Chiles wrote, "After talking to the only passenger awake at the time, he saw only the trail of fire as it passed and pulled into the clouds."

Within hours of the sighting, the pilots were interviewed on radio station WCON in Atlanta, Georgia. They were also interviewed by William Key, a newspaper reporter. At some point during the interviews, someone suggested they had been startled by a meteor, but both men rejected the idea. They had seen many meteors during their night flights and were aware of what they looked like and how they performed.

There were, at the time, some other observations. In the newspaper article written by Albert Riley, he quoted the pilots as saying, "It's prop-wash or jet-wash rocked our DC-3."

In another newspaper article that is part of the Blue Book government files, Chiles was again quoted as saying, "... both reported they could feel the UFO's backwash rock their DC-3."

But a search of the government files that are part of Blue Book reveals that Chiles said, in a statement he signed on August 3, 1948, "There was no prop wash or rough air felt as it passed."

In a statement taken by military officers and available in the government files in the days that followed the sighting, Whitted said, "We heard no noise nor did we feel any turbulence from the object."

Dr. J Allen Hynek, the scientific consultant to the Air Force's Project Blue Book at the time, was asked for his assessment of the case. He could find no "astronomical explanation" if the case was accepted at face value. In other words, Hynek was saying that if the testimony of Chiles and Whitted was accepted, and there was some sort of prop wash or turbulence associated with the event, then it couldn't be explained. He wrote, "[The] sheer improbability of the facts as stated ... makes it necessary to see whether any other explanation, even though far-fetched, can be considered."

That, of course, was not the end of it. There was a ground-based witness near Robins Air Force Base, Georgia, who had spotted an object an hour earlier. According to Captain Robert Sneider, the object was heading in the direction of Montgomery. Sneider was convinced that these objects, such as that seen by Chiles and Whitted, were from outer space. With that, he decided it was time to write an Estimate of the Situation.

Hall and Connors reported that Loedding was one of the advocates of this idea, and despite encountering some resistance, the entire Sign

Clarence Chiles (left) and John B. Whitted reported a cigar-shaped UFO that flew very close to the DC-3 they were flying near Montgomery, Alabama.

team was beginning to push their theories in Washington, D.C. The document was prepared in Dayton, Ohio, using the government files and resources available and sent forward through the chain of command.

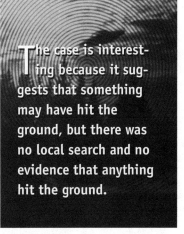

Ed Ruppelt and Dewey Fournet, the Pentagon's UFO resource, both said they had seen the document and that it was rather thick, printed on legal-sized paper and had a black cover. Stamped across the front were the words, "Top Secret."

According to Ruppelt, in his original manuscript, "It [the Estimate of the Situation] concluded that UFO's were interplanetary. As documented proof, many unexplained sightings were quoted."

The case is interesting because it suggests that something may have hit the ground, but there was no local search and no evidence that anything hit the ground.

There isn't much available about the contents in the government files today. A partial list of cases has been deduced from the information available from those who saw it. The Arnold sighting was used again. Another sighting detailed in the report came from the Lake Meade area. The government file said:

On 14 July 1947, 1st Lt Eric B Armstrong, O-2059709, 170th AAF Base Unit, Ferry Division, Brooks Field, San Antonio, Texas was interviewed and the following information was obtained: Lt. Armstrong departed Williams Field, Arizona at 1400 CST on 28 June in a P-51 for Portland, Oregon, by way of Medford, Oregon. At approximately 1515 CST on a course of 300 degrees, and a ground speed of 285, altitude 10,000 feet, approximately thirty miles northwest of Lake Meade, Nevada Lt. Armstrong sighting five or six white, circular objects at four o'clock, altitude approximately 6,000 feet, courses approximately 120 degrees and an estimated speed of 285 MPH. Lt. Armstrong said the objects were flying very smoothly and in a close formation. The estimated size of the white objects were approximately 36 inches in diameter. Lt. Armstrong stated that he is sure the white objects were not birds, since the rate of closure was very fast. Lt. Armstrong was certain that the white objects were not jets or conventional type aircraft since he has flown both types.

Another sighting was reported by a pilot of an F-80 flying near the Grand Canyon on June 30, 1947. According to the government files, he saw two round objects falling straight down at an inconceivable speed. One followed the other by seconds. The pilot, William McGinty, said the objects were circular. He thought they were a light gray in color, eight feet in diameter, and that they should have hit the ground some twenty-five miles south of the South Rim of the Grand Canyon.

The case is interesting because it suggests that something may have hit the ground, but there was no local search and no evidence that anything hit the ground. Sometime after the Estimate was created, the Air Force wrote the case off as a meteor sighting. The description, at least partially, sounds as if "Astro, meteor" would make sense, but in 1947 that wasn't the conclusion. The real question is why there was no attempt to find the object.

A clue about the kinds of cases and the witnesses to the objects used in the EOTS came from a series of sightings at and around Muroc Air Force Base beginning on July 7 and ending the next day. Major J. C. Wise, a test pilot, reported:

> On 7 July 1947, at approximately 10:10, while running up the XP-84 on the ground, I noticed everyone looking up in the air. Off to the north about 10,000 to 12,000 feet altitude was an object I assumed at first to be a weather balloon, but after looking at it for a while I noticed that it was oscillating in a forward whirling movement without losing altitude. It was travelling about 200 to 225 MPH, and heading from west to east.
>
> The object was yellowish-white in color and I would estimate that it was a sphere about 5 to 10 feet in diameter.

The next day there were several additional sightings in the area. Just before ten, four witnesses, "... all observed two silver disc like or spherical objects. All the witnesses estimated the altitude at about 8000 feet, and the speed between 300 and 400 MPH."

According to calculations in the government files, the objects were in sight for about thirty minutes. The witnesses had enough time to get a good look at them, but even with that, the Air Materiel Command eventually claimed they had been research balloons.

Then, at 11:50 A.M. on July 8, Captain John Paul Strepp said that he saw a single object for about 90 seconds. He said that it was silver and resembled a parachute canopy and then "assumed a more ovular shape." He thought it had two projections on the upper surface that might have been fins. They crossed one another, suggesting to Strepp that the object might have been rotating. It was moving slower than an airplane and he thought it was about fifty feet in diameter.

About noon, the same day, the commanding officer at Muroc, Colonel Gilkey, saw a single object that he thought might be paper blowing in the wind. He didn't report anything to the base intelligence officer, Captain Harry D. Black until August 11.

About the same time, Major Richard R. Shoop saw what he thought was a thin, metallic object some five to eight miles from his position on the ground. It was aluminum colored and had what was described as an "unconventional shape." He watched it for eight minutes as "The object moved from an intermediate altitude in an oscillating fashion, almost to the surface of the ground and then started climbing again."

Other, similar sightings from around the United States were mentioned, such as a sighting on September 23, 1948, at the AEC's Los Alamos Laboratory. There were a number of witnesses who saw a flat, circular object, high in the sky. It was little more than a speck seen in the distance.

The common thread in all these cases was that there were often multiple witnesses, all of whom were technically trained, including pilots, technicians, or scientists. They were familiar with the aircraft in the Air Force inventory, had

An aerial view of Los Alamos National Laboratory in New Mexico, a facility that conducts research on nuclear weapons and other technology of relevance to national security. In 1948 several witnesses there observed a flat, circular object in the sky.

worked or tested experimental aircraft, or had experience as fighter pilots, which meant they had been trained to make snap judgments.

Those at Sign in Dayton, putting together the Estimate, had decided among themselves that the most likely solution was that these objects were evidence of alien visitation. They accepted, at face value, the testimony of the witnesses, believed them to be accurate in their estimations of distance, size, and speed, and that each report seemed to substantiate all the others. They believed that, in the aggregate, it added up to something extraterrestrial, though their thinking was more interplanetary than interstellar.

With their work completed, EOTS began to work its way up the chain of command. Swords suggested, "Still, with the pro-ETH Wright-Patterson intelligence group on the one side, an anti-ETH Pentagon Intelligence Requirements Office on the other, and open-minded collections officers and the powerful Research and Development chief (General Donald Putt) in between, Cabell didn't want to decide this on his own. He handed the Estimate further upstairs to Vandenberg himself."

Vandenberg, then, according to Ruppelt "batted it back down." It appears that Vandenberg was not impressed with the quality of the evidence for alien visitation or the leap of logic contained in the documentation presented to him.

A review of the material presented to Vandenberg, combined with the information supplied by Ruppelt and Fournet about what cases were reviewed, and a search of the government records, shows that the evidence was indeed thin. Without some sort of physical evidence, the only conclusion that could be drawn was that the case was unproven, and Vandenberg found the Estimate unacceptable.

Fallout from the Failed "Estimate"

As Chief of Staff of the Air Force, Vandenberg, was the highest ranking Air Force officer at that time. He had just told his subordinates that he did not want to see anything that suggested these unidentified objects were extraterrestrial. His attitude and response was clear to those at Wright-Patterson and at Project Sign.

> Ruppelt noted that everything was subsequently evaluated on the premise that UFOs couldn't exist as alien spacecraft.

Loedding, with two others from Sign, traveled to Washington to argue the case for the extraterrestrial. They made no headway. In fact, Loedding, who had once been at the top of his game, was suddenly crippled in his career. He was out at Sign, and he was reduced to working on other projects. It appeared that he was being phased out at Wright-Patterson. According to Hall and Connors, while all of Loedding's evaluations until 1948 had been excellent, after the rejection of the Estimate, his evaluations began to decline. He finally resigned in early 1951.

Ruppelt, who wrote his book about all of this a few years later, wrote in a chapter titled "The Dark Ages," that the name of the project, Sign, was changed to "Grudge." The mandate to investigate UFOs was still in place, with the assumption that standard intelligence procedures would be used to complete the task. However, Ruppelt noted that everything was subsequently evaluated on the premise that UFOs couldn't exist as alien spacecraft. He wrote:

> New people took over Project Grudge. ATIC's top intelligence specialists, who had been so eager to work on Project Sign, were no longer working on Project Grudge. Some of them had drastically and hurriedly changed their minds about UFO's when they thought that the Pentagon was no longer sympathetic to the UFO cause.... Other members of Project Sign had been "purged."....

> With the new name and the new personnel came the new objective, get rid of the UFO's. It was never specified this in writing but it didn't take much effort to see that this was the goal of Project Grudge. This unwritten goal was reflected in every memo, report and directive.

Reviewing the government files today, that attitude is evident. If a witness said the object looked like a balloon, then suddenly it was a balloon. If it might have been a natural phenomenon, then it became that phenomenon. Although there is no written evidence reflecting this approach, the government files reveal that it existed. In April 1962, for example, Colonel Edward H. Wynn, the Deputy for Science and Components wrote, "Probable causes for sightings based on limited information should be accepted."

The real damage of the Estimate put together by those who favored the extraterrestrial was that it turned everything around. When word came from the highest uniformed authority in the Air Force that UFOs were not alien spacecraft, only those who were not worried about their careers or who were too naïve to interpret the direction of the investigation failed to understand what was happening. From that point on, with the exception of a short period when Ruppelt was the chief of Blue Book, there was an investigation in name only. The Air Force wanted out of the UFO business and although it would take another twenty years, the process had been started. UFOs became the third rail.

The Final Irony

Ruppelt, in *The Report on Unidentified Flying Objects*, wrote, "The Estimate died a quick death. Some months later it was declassified and relegated to the incinerator. A few copies, one of which I saw, were kept as mementos of the golden days of UFO's."

The implication here is that the document was ordered declassified and then ordered to be burned. If that is the case, it makes no sense. Once a document is declassified, there is no need to burn it. There should be nothing in such a document that it would harm national security; there is no classified information in it, so why burn it?

Could it be that Vandenberg thought that by declassifying the Estimate before ordering the destruction would mean that it would make its way into the public arena? If the document was as weak as the cases seem to indicate, then the best thing for the Air Force would have been for it to show up in the hands of a reporter or two and let the public learn the true nature of the evidence. It would ensure that they would quickly tire of UFOs.

> The implication here is that the document was ordered declassified and then ordered to be burned.

If that had been his plan, it failed. There were no real leaks about what was in the Estimate until Ruppelt wrote about it in the mid-1950s. As late as 1960, the Air Force was denying that it had ever existed. Lieutenant Colonel Lawrence Tacker, the official spokesman on UFOs at that time, said that the document only existed in the imagination of "avid saucer believers." He failed to mention the Air Force officers who also believed it had existed.

Projects Sign, Saucer, and Grudge

The history of the official investigations is confusing and that may have been done on purpose. If the news media was confused, they would be unable to ask precise questions and they could be led away from the truth. It is clear from the government records that the military was not forthcoming with information about the flying disks.

The classified project, as suggested by Twining in his September 23, 1947, letter, known inside the Air Materiel Command by the code name Sign, officially began in early 1948. The unofficial project had begun a year earlier, but now all the information collected in 1947 could be folded into Sign. As shown in the government files, most of those reports made it into the Project Sign records.

As noted earlier, there were a number of important cases, some of which were discussed by those in T-2 at Wright Field as they consolidated information about the strange aerial phenomena. These include most of the cases that were reported prior to May, including the attempted intercept over England and the Weather Bureau reports in April. There are also Ghost Rocket reports that have since disappeared from the government files.

Although there was no official project in 1947, there was the unofficial investigation by McCoy and Deyarmond at T-2. When Twining suggested they needed a priority project, the unofficial investigation became official. Most of the information collected during that time, during 1947, was folded into Project Sign, but there are gaps in the information, the biggest of them being the Roswell UFO crash case.

Government records reveal that a few sightings made prior to Arnold were reported in a way that was recognized by the military. After Arnold, there was an explosion of UFO sightings, which seemed to peak on the July 4 weekend. According to Ted Bloecher in the *Report on the UFO Wave of 1947*:

Doubtless, most other readers will be as stunned as I was to realize that already in the first two weeks after Kenneth Arnold's Mt. Rainier report of June 24, 1947, press reports of other American sightings of highly unconventional aerial objects numbered not the dozen or so that most of us might recall, but many hundreds. Since Bloecher is careful to concede that his own searching cannot possibly have gleaned every last report from the 1947 press files, we can safely round upwards his collection of about 800 reports to an estimate that at least some thousand sightings of unidentified objects probably occurred within the United States in midsummer 1947, the bulk of these coming within a rather sharply defined wavecrest centered on about July 7. [From the introduction written by Dr. James F. McDonald.]

Bloecher, in his research found that there were many sightings made prior to the Arnold report. Some of them, as have been noted, made it into the official government files. None of them were reported in the newspapers prior to Arnold, but many were reported within a couple of days after. One of those cases, as reported by Bloecher is:

Another case in the Air Force Blue Book files occurred on May 19th, sometime between twelve thirty and one P.M., at Manitou Springs, Colorado. Seven employees of the Pikes Peak Railway, including Navy veteran Dean A. Hauser, mechanics Ted Weigand and Marion Hisshouse, and T. J. Smith and L. D. Jamison, were having lunch when Weigand noticed a

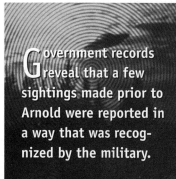

Government records reveal that a few sightings made prior to Arnold were reported in a way that was recognized by the military.

bright, silver-colored object approaching rapidly from the northeast. It stopped almost directly overhead and the group of men watched it perform wild gyrations for a number of minutes. Hauser said that the object, after having approached in a straight line, "began to move erratically in wide circles. All this time it reflected light, like metal, but intermittently, as though the angle of reflection might be changing from time to time." It was difficult to get a clear idea of its shape, and even viewing it through binoculars did not appear to "bring it any closer." They estimated its height at one thousand feet. For twenty minutes they watched it climb, dive, reverse its flight course, and finally move off into the wind in a westerly direction. "It disappeared in a straight line in the west-north-west in a clear blue sky," Hauser reported. At no time did anyone hear any noise. An account of the sighting appeared in the *Denver Post* of June 28. The next day the *Post* reported that the witnesses had been interviewed by representatives of the 15th Air Force headquarters and the results of the investigation would be sent on to Washington. The results, perhaps unknown to the witnesses even to this day, were "possible birds."

Bloecher also documents that there were several other sightings in June 1947 that didn't make it into the government files. According to him, one of the best was:

Dr. Colden R. Battey's sighting in the last week of May. Dr. Battey, a physician in Augusta, Georgia, had been fishing ten miles off St. Helena Sound, near Beaufort, South Carolina. At about eleven o'clock that morning he noticed a formation of four disc-like objects flying overhead in a southeasterly direction at a terrific rate of speed. The discs appeared to be spinning on their axes and were at an estimated altitude of about 20,000 feet. They were silvery and appeared "highly polished," and on their undersides, Dr. Battey could see a "circular rim, or projection, about one-quarter of the way from the edges." No sound was heard as they flew overhead. The formation sped out of view in less than twenty seconds. Dr. Battey's report of the sighting did not appear in print until July 6th, when the *Augusta Chronicle* gave it prominent front-page coverage. INS sent it out on the wires, where it was picked up by numerous newspapers around the country.

Beginning with the pre-Arnold sighting, Bloecher then documents the many sightings made afterward. There were literally hundreds of them, from every part of the country. By gathering reports from newspapers around the country, Bloecher showed that the number of sightings grew nearly geometrically from Arnold on June 24 to July 4, 1947.

This theory is corroborated by Michael Swords and Robert Powell, in *UFOs and the Government*:

> Sometime between June 25 and July 4, the Air Force [though in the historical context of the time, it was still the Army Air Forces] began to pay attention. On the 27th of June there was a cluster of seven sightings in New Mexico. Most of these concerned a silver or aluminum "streak" or a flash in the sky. One pilot described a ball of fiery blue, which moved 2000 feet *below* his plane, and then disintegrated. Despite the oddness of the report, the commander at White Sands Proving Ground announced that all the observations were of one of more meteors.

The White Sands Proving Ground (renamed the White Sands Missile Range in 1960) is near where unidentified objects were spotted between June 25 and July 4 by Air Force pilots. However, the commander there dismissed the sightings as meteors.

This was the same time period when the military or the government did not seem to know what was happening. There were many reports and statements from officials that turned out to be wrong or contradictory. As noted earlier, on July 3, 1947, Major Paul Gaynor said that a preliminary investigation of the flying disks, flying saucers, had been dropped for a lack of evidence.

And, of course, on July 3, the *Idaho Evening Statesman* reporter Dave Johnson said that Twining had told him that officials were looking into the "matter of the flying disks." He said that even the top secret research they were conducting couldn't match the technology reported for the flying saucers.

On the same day both Brigadier General Roger Ramey and his chief intelligence officer, Colonel Alfred Kalberer, made statements about the flying saucers. Ramey said he thought they were mirages, that is heat, radiating off hot surfaces, and Kalberer thought they were just Buck Rogers stuff, meaning they were more science fiction than anything else.

All of this happened the July 4 weekend. During that three-day weekend, there were dozens of solid reports from around the country. On the west coast, military units flew airborne alerts searching for flying saucers while other organizations remained on the ground, ready to respond. All this activity would pale for three hours on July 8, 1947, when it was announced that the Army had captured a flying saucer.

The Roswell Case, Briefly

It is clear from the public record that the Roswell crash was national news for about twenty-four hours. The military, in this case, the 509th Bomb Group at the Roswell Army Air Field, recovered the debris and announced the retrieval to the media on July 8, 1947. The story went out over the news service wires after Colonel William Blanchard, commander of the 509th, told First Lieutenant Walter Haut to issue a press release about the find to the four media outlets, two radio stations and two newspapers, in Roswell. The release went out to the national press over the news wire either by Frank Joyce or George Walsh or by both of them.

According to a newspaper story written in 1947, there are exact times for the Roswell sighting. *The Daily Illini* reported the first of the stories on the Associated Press (AP) wire appeared at 4:26 P.M. on the east coast. That would mean that the stories went out from Albuquerque, sometime prior to 2:26 P.M.

The Associated Press version, as it appeared in a number of west coast newspapers said:

> The many rumors regarding the flying disc became a reality yesterday when the intelligence office of the 509th Bomb Group of the Eighth Air Force, Roswell Army Air Field, was fortunate enough to gain possession of a disc through the cooperation of one of the local ranchers and the sheriff's office of Chavez County.

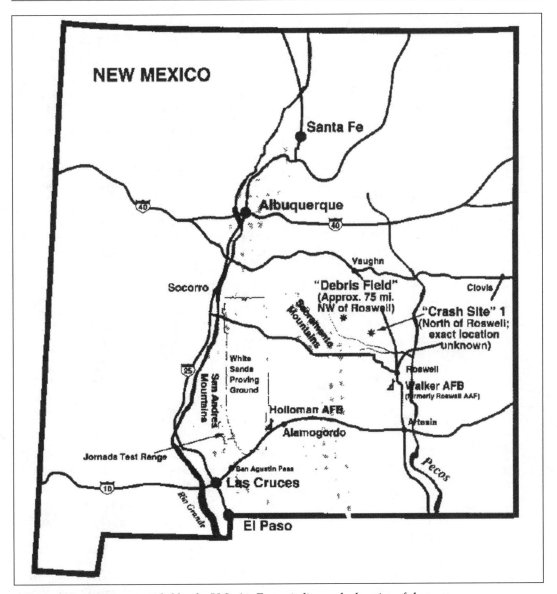

A map of New Mexico, provided by the U.S. Air Force, indicates the location of the two Roswell crash sites.

The flying object landed on a ranch near Roswell sometime last week. Not having phone facilities, the rancher stored the disc until such time as he was able to contact the sheriff's office, who in turn notified Major Jesse A. Marcel of the 509th Bomb Group Intelligence Office.

Action was immediately taken and the disc was picked up at the rancher's home. It was inspected at the Roswell Army Air Field and subsequently loaned by Major Marcel to higher headquarters.

At 4:30 P.M. (EST), there is the first "add" to the AP story, which mentioned "Lt. Warren Haught [Walter Haut]," who was described as the public information officer at Roswell Field. This new information suggested that the object had been found "last week" and that it had been sent onto "higher headquarters."

The original United Press bulletin, which went out fifteen minutes later, at 4:41 P.M. (EST), according to newspaper sources, said:

Roswell, N.M.—The army air forces here today announced a flying disc had been found on a ranch near Roswell and is in army possession.

The Intelligence office reports that it gained possession of the 'Dis:' [sic] through the cooperation of a Roswell rancher and Sheriff George Wilson [sic] of Roswell.

The disc landed on a ranch near Roswell sometime last week. Not having phone facilities, the rancher, whose name has not yet been obtained, stored the disc until such time as he was able to contact the Roswell sheriff's office.

The sheriff's office notified a major of the 509th Intelligence Office.

Action was taken immediately and the disc was picked up at the rancher's home and taken to the Roswell Air Base. Following examination, the disc was flown by intelligence officers in a superfortress (B-29) to an undisclosed "Higher Headquarters."

The air base has refused to give details of construction of the disc or its appearance.

Residents near the ranch on which the disc was found reported seeing a strange blue light several days ago about three o'clock in the morning.

At 4:55 P.M. (EST) on the east coast, 2:55 P.M. (MST) in New Mexico, the location of the discovery, that is New Mexico, was released. This bulletin, described as a "95", which is just below bulletin in importance, was repeated at 5:08 (EST) and a minute later, at 5:09, was followed by another repeat of the story that said the information came from a radio reporter. The identity of the reporter was not revealed.

At 5:10 P.M. (EST) or 3:10 P.M. (MST), there was a message addressed to the newspaper editors to let them know that the Associated Press had now gone to work on the story. This fact becomes important when the information from Jason Kellihan is added. Kellihan had, at one time, been the editor of the *Roswell Morning Dispatch*, but in July 1947, worked for the Associated Press in Albuquerque.

According to the *Daily Illini*, "One minute later, at 5:11 [P.M. EST], the third add [additional information] to the bulletin announced, 'The war department in Washington had nothing to say immediately about the reported find.' That meant the AP was on the job investigating."

At 5:53 P.M. (EST), 4:53 P.M. (CST), there was another bulletin with a Washington dateline, but it was a statement by Ramey, which had to originate in Fort Worth, and it said the disk had been sent to Wright Field. What is critical here is the use of the past tense. The story didn't say it would be forwarded, but that it had already been sent.

At 6:02 P.M. (EST, 5:02 P.M. CST), the AP put together the whole story and started the transmission of the "First Lead Disk." This story, datelined Albuquerque said, "The army air forces has gained possession of a flying disk, Lt. Warren Haught [Walter Haut], public information officer at Roswell army airfield announced today." That new lead was to be integrated into the stories that had already been transmitted.

Dallas Morning News reporters called out to the Fort Worth Army Air Field, according to them, at 5:30 P.M. (CST, 6:30 EST) and interviewed Major E. M. Kirton, an intelligence officer at Eighth Air Force Headquarters. Kalberer, who had earlier described the flying saucers as Buck Rogers stuff, was Kirton's immediate superior. Kirton told reporters that "there is nothing to it … It was a rawin high altitude sounding device." Kirton said that the identification was final and there was no reason to send it on to Wright Field for confirmation. He confirmed that the material had been flown to Fort Worth on a B-29.

A sign posted by the military warns unauthorized personnel to stay clear of the Area 51 site.

Warrant Officer Irving Newton said that he was alone in the weather office when he received a call ordering him to General Ramey's office. When Newton arrived, around 6:00 P.M. (CST, 7:00 EST), a colonel or a lieutenant colonel briefed him. Newton didn't remember who it was, only that he was told that "These officers from Roswell think they found a flying saucer, but the general thinks it's a weather balloon. He wants you to take a look at it."

At 7:15 P.M. (EST, 6:15 CST), there was a bulletin that said General Ramey would make a statement on national radio. WBAP, a Dallas radio station, had arranged for the national hook up for Ramey over the NBC radio network.

The FBI entered the picture just two minutes later, at 6:17 P.M. (CST, 7:17 EST) with one of the few government files available on the Roswell crash. The FBI office in Dallas sent a message about the story to the FBI office in Cincinnati. Sent to the director, J. Edgar Hoover and to the SAC (Special Agent in Charge), the message was titled, "Flying Disc, Information Concerning." The text said:

> Major Curtan [sic, Edwin Kirton], Headquarters Eighth Air Force, telephonically advised this office that an object purporting to be a flying disc was recovered near Roswell, New Mexico, this date [July 8, 1947]. The disc was hexagonal in shape and was suspended from a balloon by cable, which baloon [sic] was approximately twenty feet in diameter. Major Cur-

tan further advised that the object found resembles a high altitude weather balloon with a radar reflector, but that telephonic conversation between their office and Wright Field had not borne out this belief. Disc and balloon being transported to Wright Field by special plane for examin [sic]. Information provided this office because of national interest in case and fact that National Broadcasting Company, Associated Press, and others attempting to break the story of location of the disc today. Major Curtan advised would request Wright Field to advise Cincinnati office results of examination. No further investigation being conducted.

Before much more was reported over the wire, a new lead was transmitted. It said, "Fort Worth—Roswell's celebrated 'flying disk' was rudely stripped of its glamor by a Fort Worth army airfield weather officer who late today identified the object as a 'weather balloon.'"

Thomas DuBose, who would eventually retire as a brigadier general, and who was in Ramey's office did talk about the press conference and the debris on the floor of Ramey's office. He said, "... actually it was a cover story, the balloon part of it for the remnants that were taken from this location and Al Clark took it to Washington.... That part of it was in fact a cover story that we were told to give to the public and the news and that was it."

DuBose elaborated on this. He said, "That [balloon cover story] was the direction we were told. We were told this is the story that is to be given to the press and that is it.... I don't know whether it was [Major General Clements] McMullen or Kalberer or who, somebody cooked up the idea as a cover story we'll use this weather balloon."

DuBose's confirmation of a cover up seems to add to the suspicions that had arisen given the timing of various press stories. The timing of statements, such as that given by Kirton to the *Dallas Morning News*, suggest that the weather balloon identification had been made before Newton arrived at Ramey's office.

The photographs all show the remains of a rawin radar target in a very degraded state, and the blackened neoprene rubber of the balloon itself can be seen. However, Newton reported to various investigators and Air Force officers investigating the case in the 1990s that Marcel attempted to convince him that some of the elements were strange. It seems that Marcel had not been fooled. According to Johnny Mann, a reporter for WWL-TV in New Orleans, he had interviewed Marcel in the early 1980s about what he had seen and what he had done in 1947.

General Roger Ramey and future general Thomas DuBose examine some of the debris from the UFO wreckage. It would be officially declared material from a weather balloon.

He showed Marcel the photographs taken in Ramey's office and said, "Jesse, I've got to tell you that looks like a balloon."

Marcel, according to Mann, said, "That's not the stuff that I brought from Roswell."

By 10:00 P.M. (CST, 11:00 P.M. EST), the story was virtually over. Ramey had not appeared on NBC, but at 10:00 he was quoted on ABC's "Headline Edition," and the weather balloon story entered the public consciousness. The newspapers were reporting the error on the part of the officers in Roswell. The *Las Vegas Review Journal* reported:

The excitement ran through this cycle:

1. Lieutenant Warren Haught [Walter Haut], public relations officer at the Roswell base, released a statement in the name of Colonel William Blanchard, base commander. It said that an object described as a "flying disk" was found on the nearby Foster ranch three weeks ago by W. W. Brazel and had been sent to "higher officials" for examination.

2. Brigadier General Roger B. Ramey, commander of the 8th air force, said at Fort Worth that he believed the object was the "remnant of a weather balloon and radar reflector," and was "nothing to be excited about." He allowed photographers to take a picture of it. It was announced that the object would be sent to Wright Field, Dayton, Ohio, for examination by experts.

3. Later, Warrant Officer Irving Newton, Stessonville, Wisconsin, weather officer at Fort Worth, examined the object and said definitely that it was nothing but a badly smashed target used to determine the direction and velocity of high altitude winds.

4. Lieutenant Haught reportedly told reporters that he had been "shut up by two blistering phone calls from Washington."

5. Efforts to contact Colonel Blanchard brought the information that "he is now on leave."

6. Major Jesse A. Marcel, intelligence officer of the 509th bombardment group, reportedly told Brazel, the finder of the object, that it "has nothing to do with army or navy so far as I can tell."

7. Brazel told reporters that he had found weather balloon equipment before but had seen nothing that resembled his latest find.

Colonel William Blanchard was the base commander at Roswell when the UFO incident occurred in 1947.

Those who saw the object said it had a flowered paper tape around it bearing the initials "D. P."

While this story was winding down, with the principals unavailable for comment (Brazel was being held by the military, Marcel was either in Fort Worth or enroute back to Roswell, and Blanchard was on leave), reporters were unable to gather any additional information. Sheriff Wilcox would say little. It was reported, "Wilcox said he did not see the object but was told by Brazell [sic] it was 'about three feet across.' The sheriff declined to elaborate. 'I'm working with those fellows at the base,' he said."

In the years that followed, many of the military officers were interviewed about what they had seen and what they had done. With but a single exception, they confirmed that the craft they had seen was extraterrestrial, some of them said they had seen bodies associated with the crash, and many others mentioned the herculean efforts to keep people from talking about it, even decades later.

Robert Hastings interviewed Chester Lytle, a respected scientist. Lytle had been a friend of William Blanchard. According to Lytle, Blanchard confirmed there had been a crash and alien bodies had been recovered. Hastings, in his book *UFOs and Nukes* wrote:

> Suddenly, the general [Blanchard] mentioned the Roswell Incident. Lytle, who held Top Secret clearances relating to his work with the AEC, was informed by Blanchard that a crashed alien spacecraft had indeed been recovered in July 1947. The general said that four dead humanoid beings had been aboard.

> Startled by Lytle's unexpected admission, I [Hastings] asked, "Blanchard actually told you that the Roswell object was an alien spacecraft?" Lytle replied emphatically, "Oh, absolutely!"

The information about the crash would have been transmitted up the chain of command from New Mexico, through Fort Worth and Roger Ramey, and onto the Strategic Command Headquarters, then in Washington, D.C., Given the situation, that information would have been transmitted to Wright Field, where the laboratories and scientists were located who would have been able to exploit the find.

The World on July 9, 1947

According to Bloecher, the wave peaked on July 7, 1947, with the number of reports dropping off on July 8. In the Project Blue Book files, the number of sightings on July 7 is nine and on July 8, merely three. But, most of the reporting was taken up by the Roswell case, and that case appears nowhere in these government files.

At about this time, meaning around the beginning of July 1947, the Pentagon began to organize an investigation into the flying disk problem. The chief of the Army Air Forces Intelligence Collection Division, Colonel Robert Taylor gave the mission of consolidating the information to his assistant Lieutenant Colonel George Garrett. Garrett then linked up with FBI agent S. W. Reynolds. The trouble here, as it becomes clear from the government records, was that there was no real communication between the Pentagon investigation and what was happening at Wright Field in Ohio.

At this point, there was now an official investigation in Washington, D.C., and the unofficial investigation that McCoy and Deyarmond had started in late December 1946. It is unclear from the government files who ordered that earlier investigation, but the later one grew out of the number of reports being received through intelligence channels and newspapers. The military was now admitting that they were investigating the flying disks.

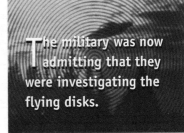

The military was now admitting that they were investigating the flying disks.

Michael Swords and Robert Powell, in *UFO and Government*, note that "Around mid-August, Colonel Garrett and FBI liaison S. W. Reynolds ... felt they had gotten somewhat of a handle on the matter. But they were extremely puzzled. The cases they were reviewing indicated an unusual aerial technology of at least one type, and, through the first weeks of July there had been intense pressure exerted down the chain of command ... to get an explanation. But by late July and into August, that pressure had suddenly evaporated."

The sudden change in attitude is documented in the newspapers. According to the Associated Press, in a story that appeared in newspapers around the country on July 9, 1947, the Army and the Navy "... began a concentrated campaign to stop the rumors [of flying saucers whizzing through the sky]."

Not only did the officers of the Pentagon investigation, which, while not hidden, certainly wasn't announced, realize that those at the top were no longer pressing for answers, but also that information was given to the press. A subject that had been of pressing national security implications was suddenly relegated to the back burner. To top it off, there was a campaign to stop the stories now considered to be little more than rumors.

This new lack of concern, evident in the government files, apparently didn't apply to those working on the investigation in other locations. As noted earlier, Brigadier General Schulgen sent a request to Wright Field, asking for an analysis of some of the more spectacular or more reliable sightings. Those who had been working on this for months were now called on to examine some of the evidence. All this was resolved in September when Twining's letter about the flying disks was sent. He wanted to continue the investigation.

But Twining, of course, didn't examine the cases sent to Wright Field, nor did he write the response to Schulgen. Looking at this from a military perspective, when Schulgen's request landed at Twining's office, he would regard it as an intelligence matter and would have passed it along to the officers in T-2 for a response. They would then make the required study, draft a proposed response and sent it to Twining for review and approval. When the final draft was finished, it would be sent to Schulgen.

The important point here is that the man who was responsibile for drafting the response would have been Howard McCoy. Again, he might have given it to someone else to study, though given the security levels of the investigations in place at the time, he may have completed the staff study himself. McCoy would have been the man to coordinate all this with Twining.

Other than McCoy or Deyarmond, the person who might have ended up with the ultimate responsibility for drafting the response would have been Alfred Loedding. Because of his experiences and his background, Loedding would have been quite sympathetic to the idea of alien visitation. Loedding would later have a hand in the first Estimate of the Situation, which concluded that some of the sightings were of extraterrestrial craft, though in 1948, they would have been called "interplanetary."

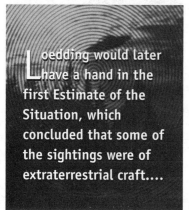

Loedding would later have a hand in the first Estimate of the Situation, which concluded that some of the sightings were of extraterrestrial craft....

Project Sign, then, which was an outgrowth of Twining's letter and had its origins, not in that letter, but with McCoy's and Deyarmond's unofficial investigation, begun months earlier. Now suddenly, with Arnold and all, a push was on for an official investigation. McCoy and Deyarmond must have understood the implications as they prepared to launch that "new" investigation at the beginning of 1948.

There are some problems, such as the disappearance of some of the better cases. As noted, many of the Ghost Rocket cases collected in 1946 and much of the information provided by the attachés in the embassies in Scandinavian countries, including the data shared by the Swedish military, didn't make it to Project Sign. The Richmond weather bureau sightings from April 1947 didn't make it into the government files, either.

To make matters worse, some of the sightings that did make it into the files contained little or no information, while others were noted, but marked as "Case Missing." In other words, sightings and information that should have been passed along to Project Sign, were not. This was classified information so that it was more carefully controlled than letters and documents without any security classifications. It means that the information, while known to some at Project Sign, was not officially passed along to it.

Project Saucer

The official investigation announced to the press was called Project Saucer. The real code name was Project Sign, and although classified in nature, there was no real reason to mislead the public about the code name. It would seem that Project Saucer then, was just the public name for the real thing.

But there seems to have been a Project Saucer. Although the documentation is sketchy about when the name, Project Saucer, was first used, this was the unofficial investigation that McCoy and Deyarmond had set up in December 1946. To those on the inside, Project Saucer was now the cover for that unofficial investigation.

The discrepancy between the two names suggests that there were two investigations taking place at Wright Field. The unofficial Project Saucer, and the new, official Project Sign. The men running both investigations were McCoy and Deyarmond. Sign had a military officer assigned to it, Captain Robert R. Sneider and, of course, Alfred Loedding. They could do their jobs without knowing that Saucer actually existed, but it was a hidden, more highly classified investigation.

The dual investigation presented some interesting problems. If the debris recovered outside Roswell was truly alien in nature, you would expect those at Wright Field, working in T-2, to know this. However, if there was a closed investigation, meaning one that was more highly classified than the other, it could mean that some of those would know about the Roswell debris but others would not. McCoy and Deyarmond, operating in the highly classified and highly re-

A copy of the July 9, 1947, issue of the *Roswell Daily Record* bears the headline announcing the extraordinary news of the UFO discovery.

stricted Project Saucer, would have access to everything, but Sneider and Loedding, now working on the less classified and more open Project Sign, would not.

This creates an interesting problem. On the one hand, McCoy knew about the recovered debris, but on the other, he did not. This means that when discussing the flying disks with Deyarmond or their immediate superior, General Twining, McCoy, and Deyarmond could discuss the Roswell debris, but when talking with Sneider and Loedding, they would be required to pretend that nothing like the Roswell case had happened.

There is some evidence for this split personality in the UFO investigations. First, there is no mention of the Roswell case in the Project Blue Book files, except for a short, three paragraph story about the case included in the newspaper clippings gathered for this project. The middle paragraph mentions that the officers at Roswell had received a blistering rebuke for the press release stating they had recovered a flying saucer in the region.

As mentioned, this story dominated the press for a short period. Newspapers from coast to coast carried the story. Cases that had much more restricted press coverage were found in the Blue Book files, and that does include cases that were quickly found to be hoaxes.

For example, on July 7, 1947, a flying disk was recovered in Shreveport, Louisiana. This was a small thing, just little more than a foot or a foot and a half in diameter. It seemed to crash into the street and was quickly recovered. Both Army investigators and the FBI were involved in the tale. But it was found to be a hoax. One man said that he had created the disk using parts from an overhead lighting system and a few wires. He said that he wanted to fool his boss. The story made its way into the Project Sign files.

This suggests that the Roswell case would not have been left out of Project Sign because it was "identified" as a balloon. It means that there was another reason for leaving it out, such as the fact that it was covered in the other, more highly classified investigation. If Roswell was alien, then it was too highly classified to be reported to Project Sign.

There is another interesting point as well. As mentioned earlier, on July 9, both the Army and the Navy began their attempts to "stop the rumors" dealing with the flying saucers. This begs the question, "Why suddenly on July 9 did the military care about the flying saucers?" Prior to that point, they had admitted confusion, had offered multiple explanations, and denied that they had anything in their aviation inventories that would explain the sightings, and that there were no secret projects that might have given rise to the reports.

Such a change in policy had to have been precipitated by something. On July 8, the military didn't seem to care that people were seeing flying saucers, they didn't care that these sightings were being reported, almost daily, on the front pages of newspapers across the country. Then, on July 9, the policy changed. Why?

Something was recovered near Roswell, and the military and the government no longer wanted people talking about flying saucers. They wanted the problem buried and began to work toward that end. They had the data diverted to the highly classified project that was already in place and then pretended that it had never happened.

Project Saucer, then, became the public name of the UFO investigation and Project Sign was the classified name. This might seem counterintuitive, but it would seem that the name, Project Saucer, in its public guise, was an outgrowth of the media putting a name to the then unnamed project. To civilians, it seemed natural that the investigation would be called Project Saucer.

The government files about this now rest under the golf course at Wright-Patterson Air Force Base, according to Wendy Connors. Much of the classified material was destroyed in accordance with military regulations, that is, properly disposed of once its usefulness had been concluded.

Project Sign

The Air Force investigation into the flying disks officially began on January 22, 1948, just two weeks after Thomas Mantell was killed chasing a saucer. The consensus among UFO researchers today is that Mantell had been chasing what was then a classified Navy balloon experiment. These "skyhook" balloons were huge and had a metallic sheen. In 1948 they were not well known, and it would explain Mantell's belief that he was chasing something else.

With one pilot dead, the pressure was on to get some answers. In 1948, the Air Force didn't know about skyhook and began to issue a series of answers for this and other cases. It seemed, based on the evidence in the government files that they didn't much care what the answer was, as long as they had one. Claiming that Mantell had attempted to chase Venus was ridiculous on the surface, but it answered the case. Had they shown some patience, investigated carefully, they would have found an answer and no one would have been able to put forward all the other explanations.

At this point, meaning January 1948, Sign had the resources it needed to investigate. If a case was determined to be important, investigators would be dispatched from Wright Field. If it seemed to be a routine case, then an investigator,

The October 15, 1958, issue of the *Saucerian Bulletin* features a story by Trevor James in which he speculates that Mantell's plane was destroyed by a UFO.

probably the local intelligence officer, would be sent. In all cases, the witnesses would fill out a standard reporting form and the information would then be filed away at Project Sign.

It should be noted that while McCoy and Deyarmond had access to all the sighting reports, those at Project Sign did not. It is clear from the government records, and according to what Dr. J. Allen Hynek would later say, that not all the sighting reports made it to Sign. The project records show a number of missing cases. These are obvious ones that reached Sign, but the files were later removed for any number of reasons.

One of those cases took place in Rehoboth Beach, Delaware, on June 2, 1947. Oddly, there is some information about this in the government files, apparently created by the FBI. According to the government file:

> The attached newspaper clipping appeared in the "Morning News" of Wilmington, Delaware, July 8, 1947. It reports that a FORREST WENYON ... an aircraft pilot, had disclosed that in the past ten months he had twice seen flying discs which he was reported to have described as "flying mayonnaise jars." He was reported to have seen the first flying disc during September, 1946, and to have noted another such object on June 2, 1947.

> Mr. WENYON was quoted as having called the Federal Bureau of Investigation and was advised that the Bureau was not interested, whereupon he notified Eastern Airlines and the Civil Aeronautic Authority of the objects he had seen. Both agencies are reported to have accepted the information stating they would investigate. The clipping further stated that Mr. WENYON had received no answer from either agency.

> The clipping was submitted to me by the resident agents' officer at Wilmington together with the advice that no agent in Wilmington had been contacted by Mr. WENYON. I directed Mr. WENYON to be interviewed to determine the full facts.

> Mr. WENYON was interviewed and it was determined that his correct name is HORACE P. WENYON. Mr. WENYON advised that he had been an airplane pilot approximated thirty years. He stated that in September of 1946, while flying at an altitude of 1,000 feet, two or three miles south of Rehoboth Beach, Delaware, he noticed a projectile approximately fifteen inches in diameter which crossed his course at right angles and was moving in a west-to-east direction. According to Mr. WENYON, several jets of flame were spurting from the object and it was traveling at a very high rate of speed, 1,000 to 1,200 miles per hour. He stated that in October of 1946, he observed a similar projectile while flying over Rehoboth Beach at 1,400 feet. This was also traveling from west to east.

> Mr. WENYON stated that there is little question in his mind but that what he saw was some sort of rocket being tested. He stated that he wished to call the matter to the attention of the appropriate authority inasmuch as he thought that the series of airplane crashes that have occurred recently might in part be explained by what he had observed. He stated that he

had reported the information to the Civil Aeronautics Authority and had been interviewed by a reporter from the Wilmington "Morning News."

This wasn't the end of it, however. Another document in the government files, also from the FBI, revealed:

Mr. WENYON stated that what he had seen traveled at such a high rate of speed that it was very difficult to describe it, but the description "flying mayonnaise jars" was concocted by the newspaper reporter.

This information has not been brought to the attention of any Army sources in view of the fact that only a preliminary inquiry was conducted on the basis of a new article which sets forth essentially the facts obtained from Mr. WENYON.

No further action in his matter is contemplated by this office unless advised otherwise by the Bureau.

It is obvious from the government files that this case was developed sometime later. The project card concluded that this sighting was of a missile. The analysis said, "A 'mayonnaise jar'-shaped object heading north was sighted by [the] observer. The observer was a civilian pilot with 30 yrs exp. Estimated speed of object was 1000–1200 mph. This is the second such object this observer has seen. Previous one Sep. 46."

In the AMC analysis, it was suggested that what Wenyon had seen was a "Bumble Bee Ramjet." The size matches, but the problem is that the "flying mayonnaise jar" description seems to be the result of a reporter filling in a detail with which the witness disagreed. In fact, was it not for the small diameter of the object as described, the explanation probably wouldn't fit.

According to Mr. WENYON, several jets of flame were spurting from the object and it was traveling at a very high rate of speed, 1,000 to 1,200 miles per hour.

There is an additional problem here. The project card from the government files said the object was traveling north, but Wenyon said the object was traveling west to east. The point is that the card was created sometime later and it was based on poor information.

The inability to control information and stop the disappearance of cases from the government files was a problem in 1947 and into 1948. At a conference of the Scientific Advisory Board held in March, 1948, Howard McCoy said:

We have a new project—Project Sign—which may surprise you as a development from the so-called mass hysteria of the past summer when we had all the unidentified flying objects or discs. This can't be laughed off. We have over 300 reports which haven't been publicized in the papers from very competent personnel, in many instances—men as capable as Dr. X. D. Wood, and practically all Air Force, Airline people with broad experience. We are running down every report. I can't tell you how much we would give to have one of those crash in an area so that we could recover whatever they are.

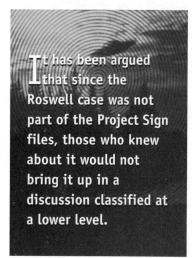

It has been argued that since the Roswell case was not part of the Project Sign files, those who knew about it would not bring it up in a discussion classified at a lower level.

There are two interesting statements here. First, according to the government files, there were only 127 cases logged in from the beginning of the UFO wave in June 1947 through March 1948. That accounts for less than half of what McCoy mentioned.

Second, the stunning statement that they wished one would crash so they could examine the debris. This would seem to suggest that there had been no crash near Roswell. It has been argued that since the Roswell case was not part of the Project Sign files, those who knew about it would not bring it up in a discussion classified at a lower level. It seems to be an odd thing for McCoy to say, but then, he wasn't talking about what was held in the other, more highly classified investigation of the flying saucers. He was talking about what was held in the Project Sign files and there was no real physical evidence in those files other than some hoaxes.

The EOTS Fallout

During the summer of 1948, it was decided that some sort of document needed to be prepared. This was the Estimate of the Situation. After it had been vetted several times, and after General Vandenberg rejected it, the attitude at Sign changed. They didn't want to find evidence that would contradict the Chief of Staff so they didn't look very hard. After the horror of the Estimate of the Situation, the attitude at Sign changed. While they were once convinced that alien visitation was the answer, now they were dead set against it. There was no alien visitation and all cases could be answered in the mundane. They began winding down, investigating with little enthusiasm and eventually wrote a final report entitled, "The Findings of Project Sign."

This report clarified the motivation behind Project Sign, identified the main players, and outlined the results of their research. In the "Summary," they wrote that the data were "derived from reports of 243 domestic and thirty (30) foreign incidents. Data from these incidents is being summarized, reproduced and distributed to agencies and individuals cooperating in the analysis and evaluation.... The data obtained in reports received are studied in relation to many factors such as guided missile research activity, weather and other atmospheric sounding balloon launchings, commercial and military aircraft flights, flights of migratory birds, and other considerations, to determine possible explanations for sightings."

They wanted to make the situation crystal clear and wrote, "Based on the possibility that the objects are really unidentified and unconventional types of aircraft a technical analysis is made of some of the reports to determine the aerodynamic, propulsion, and control features that would be required for the objects to perform as described in the reports. The objects sighted have been grouped into four classifications according to configuration:

1. Flying disks, i.e., very low aspect ratio aircraft.
2. Torpedo or cigar shaped bodies with no wings or fins visible in flight.
3. Spherical or balloon-shaped objects.
4. Balls of light.

They continued their analysis, writing:

Approximately twenty percent of the incidents have been identified as conventional aerial objects to the satisfaction of personnel assigned to Project "Sign" in this Command. It is expected that a study of the incidents in relation to weather and other atmospheric sounding balloons will provide solutions for an equivalent number.... Elimination of incidents with reasonably satisfactory explanations will clarify the problem presented by a project of this nature.

The possibility that some of the incidents may represent technical developments far in advance of knowledge available to engineers and scientists of this country has been considered. No facts are available to personnel at this Command that will permit an objective assessment of this possibility. All information so far presented on the possible existence of space ships from another planet or of aircraft propelled by an advanced type of atomic power plant have been largely conjecture.

Reviewing the reports on UFOs, they seem to come in four different varieties, including glowing balls of light, spherical objects, cigar-shaped objects, and disks like those pictured here.

They then provided a number of recommendations for the project, writing: "Future activity on this project should be carried on at the minimum level necessary to record, summarize, and evaluate the data received on future reports and to complete the specialized investigations now in progress." They then add a phrase that too many UFO researchers have overlooked in the past. They write: "When and if a sufficient number of incidents are solved to indicate that these sightings do not represent a threat to the security of the nation, the assignment of special project status to the activity could be terminated."

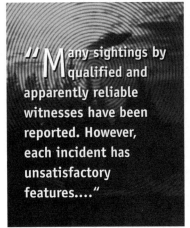

"Many sightings by qualified and apparently reliable witnesses have been reported. However, each incident has unsatisfactory features...."

As government files reveal, this theme would be repeated in one official UFO investigation after another for the next several decades. Each of the investigations, from Sign forward, had national security as its main concern. If national security wasn't threatened, then the question of reality of the flying saucers became unimportant. And, as time passed, it became obvious to all those investigators, both military and civilian, that there was no threat to the nation.

The conclusions of the report are quite interesting. "No definite and conclusive evidence is yet available that would prove or disprove the existence of these unidentified objects as real aircraft of unknown and unconventional configuration. It is unlikely that positive proof of their existence will be obtained without examination of the remains of crashed objects. Proof of the nonexistence is equally impossible to obtain unless a reasonable and convincing explanation is determined for each incident."

According to this government file, "Many sightings by qualified and apparently reliable witnesses have been reported. However, each incident has unsatisfactory features, such as shortness of time under observation, distance from observer, vagueness of description or photographs, inconsistencies between individual observers, and lack of descriptive data, that prevents conclusions being drawn."

This, then, becomes the catch all myth about UFO sighting reports. According to the reports, there were no good photographs, eyewitness testimony was unreliable and of short duration, and the sightings were of nothing more spectacular than a fuzzy object, seen for an instant in the far distance.

In a counterintuitive statement, they make a plea to continue the project. This had nothing to do with research into phenomenon or an attempt to identify what is being seen. Instead, according to the government files, "Evaluation of reports of unidentified objects is a necessary activity of military intelligence agencies. Such sightings are inevitable, and under wartime conditions rapid and convincing solutions of such occurrences are necessary to maintain morale of military and civilian personnel. In this respect, it is considered that the establishment of procedures and training of personnel is in itself worth the effort expended on this project."

About a year earlier, according to the government files, the personnel assigned to Sign had concluded that flying saucers were extraterrestrial. Now, using the same cases and the same evidence, those who survived at ATIC claimed there was nothing to the UFO phenomenon. More importantly, they said there was no threat to national security, but that the project should be continued for training purposes. They saw it as a cheap way of providing "real world" experience to their investigators.

Attached as "Appendix D" was a report that seemed to have been inspired by Brigadier General Putt. In a letter found in the government files (which is basically Appendix D to the overall report), Dr. James E. Lipp, an aeronautical engineer and a division head at the Rand Corporation, speculated about the extraterrestrial hypothesis.

It is clear from his letter that Lipp believes that the craft, if alien, were from inside the Solar System. He pointed specifically to Mars, ignoring Venus. Astronomical thought in 1947 was that both Venus and Mars might support intelligent life, though most believed Mars the more likely candidate. Heavy cloud cover prevented observation of the Venus' surface.

People used to believe that aliens could be visiting us from Mars, but it is now clear that, while Mars may have once had water on its survace, it is now a barren world.

In today's world, with probes having landed on both planets, it is clear that neither supports any type of intelligent life. If flying saucers are real, then they come from outside the Solar System.

In the text of his letter, however, Lipp made a point that has been noted since by various members of the UFO community:

> One other hypothesis needs to be discussed. It is that the Martians have kept a long-term routine watch on Earth and have been alarmed by the sight of out A-bomb shots as evidence that we are warlike and on the threshold of space travel. (Venus is eliminated here because her cloudy atmosphere would make such a survey impractical). The first flying objects were sighted in the Spring of 1947, after a total of 5 atomic bomb explosions, i.e., Alamogordo, Hiroshima, Nagasaki, Crossroads A and Crossroads B. Of these, the first two were in positions to be seen from Mars, the third was very doubtful (at the edge of the Earth's disc in daylight) and the last two were on the wrong side of Earth.

Lipp then explained why he didn't believe this to be significant, suggesting it would mean a long-term surveillance of the Earth. While astronomers study Mars, it is not with the intensity suggested if they had seen the atomic blasts and then began a close survey. He wrote, "The weakest point in the hypothesis is that a continual, defensive watch of Earth for long periods of time (possibly thousands of years) would be dull sport...."

It was Lipp's suggestion that atomic research somehow caused the flying saucers to appear. While the theory is interesting, it is also wrong. Although many in the UFO community, and many of those at Project Sign, wanted to believe that the UFOs first appeared on June 24, 1947, historical evidence shows this not the case. The Foo Fighters of the Second World War can be regarded as the first manifestation of the flying disks, and the Ghost Rockets over Scandinavia also have no cohesive explanation. The sightings reported in 1947 seem to be a continuation of those events, though the government records and the attitudes at Sign seem to suggest otherwise. It was a point they did not wish to examine.

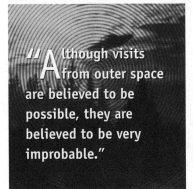

"Although visits from outer space are believed to be possible, they are believed to be very improbable."

The other consideration was that once the planets in the Solar System were eliminated as the home worlds of the space travelers, the objects had to have originated from a source outside of the Solar System. The distances were just too vast, according to Lipp and other thinkers at the time. Light travels only so fast, and even if the beings in another solar system could detect the atomic detonations on our planet, it would take more than four years for the light to reach them. That is, if they happen to live on a planet orbiting the closest star.

Lipp concluded, "Although visits from outer space are believed to be possible, they are believed to be very improbable. In particular, the actions attributed to the 'flying objects' reported during 1947 and 1948 seem inconsistent with the requirements for space travel."

Lipp's letter, in the government files, suggested that the extraterrestrial hypothesis was being considered by some inside Project Sign, ATIC, and the Air Force. However, it also suggests how opinions had changed after the Estimate of the Situation had been "batted" back down.

A Project Sign report prepared in February 1949 recommended that:

Future activity on this project should be carried on at the minimum level necessary to record, summarize, and evaluate the data received on future reports and to complete the specialized investigations now in progress. When and if sufficient number of incidents are solved to indicate that these sightings do not represent a threat to the security of the nation, the assignment of special project status to the activity could be terminated. Future investigations of reports would then be handled on a routine basis like any other intelligence work....

Reporting agencies should be impressed with the necessity for getting more factual evidence on sightings.... Personnel sighting such objects should engage the assistance of others, when possible, to get more definite data....

No definite and conclusive evidence is yet available that would prove or disprove the existence of these unidentified objects as real aircraft of unknown and unconventional configuration. It is unlikely that positive proof of their existence will be obtained without examination of the remains of crashed objects....

Even when it seems that everyone in the Air Force, from the top on down, believes that the flying saucer project should be reduced in scope, if not eliminated altogether, it continues at a high priority. In the Sign report of February 1949, there is a page that notes the title of the project is now Grudge, by authority of "Hq, USAF, Deputy Chief of Staff, Materiel, Washington 25, D.C., dated 30 Dec. 1947." The project retained its 2A priority, and the purpose was "To collect, collate, evaluate, and interpret data obtained relative to the sighting of unidentified flying objects in the atmosphere which may have importance on the national security, and to control and effect distribution of all objective information as requested to interested governmental agencies and contractors."

The project was not closed down, the investigations didn't end, but the name was changed, and work continued on the project while leaving the impression that there was nothing going on and nothing left to do.

The Green Fireballs and Project Twinkle

Project Blue Book files and subsequent reports on Project Twinkle cite Ellen Peterson's sighting of a green object crossing the sky in Phoenix on October 24, 1948, as the first green fireball sighting. In November 1948, a number of people in Albuquerque reported seeing flashes or streaks of green low on the eastern horizon. On December 20, 1948, another sighting was reported by four observers, two each at separate locations, of a bright light falling slowly toward the ground.

Peterson sent a letter about her sighting to Dr. J. Hugh Pruett, a professor of astronomy at the University of Oregon. Pruett eventually forwarded the information to Dr. Lincoln La Paz at the University of New Mexico in Albuquerque.

In the letter, dated November 3, 1948, Peterson wrote, "On October 24ᵗʰ I noticed a very strange star or fireball in the Eastern sky. It was green and my first impression was that it was a plane. It moved very slowly South and slightly North as if it wasn't certain of which way to go.... It took at least 75 minutes to cross over Phoenix. The star seemed to be drawn to other stars, and when it came close to them, it would become very bright.... Everytime the star would light up and leave the other star, it would be dimmer. Finally, we could hardly see it. When I thought it had completely disappeared, it suddenly became very bright and fell apart."

This sighting would be of no importance, except that it was the first mention of a green object and fireball in the same communication. In the Project Blue Book files, the Air Force reported, "This incident as described is not amenable to any astronomical explanation. The object took 75 minutes to cross the sky. The witness is not a very critical observer (... there could be no possible connection between the object's brightness and its apparent distance from a star).... The object could have been a lighted balloon; speed and maneuvers check."

In the world of Air Force investigation that meant it was a balloon. The official explanation is "balloon," but the evidence for that seems thin. Had the original letter not ended up with La Paz, there probably would be no sign of the case at all.

Ed Ruppelt, who was the chief of Project Blue Book in the early 1950s, reported in his book, "The green fireballs streaked into UFO history late in November 1948, when people around Albuquerque, New Mexico, began to report seeing mysterious 'green flares' at night. The first reports mentioned only a

The official explanation is "balloon," but the evidence for that seems thin.

'green streak in the sky,' low on the horizon. From the description the Air Force Intelligence people at Kirkland AFB in Albuquerque and the Project Sign people at ATIC wrote the objects off as flares."

These sightings began to evolve. Another report found in the government files about the green fireballs came early in November. Colonel William P. Hayes reported, "On November 3 or 4 1948 at approximately 2150 hours, I observed a ball of light, reddish white in color, 1 foot in diameter, falling vertically. The ball burst 100–300 feet from the ground in a spray of reddish color which extinguished before reaching the ground.... The location is approximately 10 miles east of Vaughn, New Mexico, on Highway 60."

About three weeks later, Hayes had another sighting in about the same place. The description of the light or object was the same as that seen earlier and it reacted in the same way. Hayes thought it might be some sort of secret experiment but the Air Force wrote it off, again, as "flares."

The December 5, 1948, Event

These sightings, all found in the government files that deal with the green fireballs, would have gone virtually unnoticed had it not been for a multiple-witness sighting of something more than a streak of light in the distance. On December 5, 1948, a brilliant green object flashed by a military C-47 transport enroute from Lowry AFB in Denver to Williams AFB in Chandler, Arizona. The pilot of the military aircraft, Captain William Goade, reported that he, along with his crew, including Major Roger Carter, had seen a green flash just west of Las Vegas, New Mexico. They believed, at that time, they had seen a meteor.

But, twenty-two minutes later, at 2127 hours (or 9:37 P.M.) they decided it was something else. Goade said he had seen an intense green light rise from the east slope of Sandia Peak. It climbed to about 500 feet and looked like the "flare" he had seen before. That would seem to rule out a meteor as the answer.

At 11:00 P.M., the pilot of a Pioneer Airlines flight that was making its way from Tucumcari to Las Vegas to Albuquerque and then onto Santa Fe and Alamogordo, said that he had seen a green "light" just west of Las Vegas, New Mexico. When the plane landed at Albuquerque the crew was interviewed by the Control Tower crew. Captain van Lloyd said that he had seen a pale green light that seemed to be headed straight at him, so he jerked the aircraft to avoid a collision. The light and its tail then curved down and away, disappearing a few seconds later.

The same evening, another report came in, this one from a civilian named Harold M. Wright, who had been driving along Highway 60 near Blanca, Colorado (east of Alamosa, CO), when he spotted a green fireball. According to the

Sandia Peak, near Albuquerque and the Rio Grande valley, where Air Force pilots Captain William Goade and Major Roger Carter reported seeing a strange green light that they thought might be a meteor.

report in the Project Blue Book file, "[It was] moving horizontally and westerly, at a very fast rate of speed, it once more appeared to be a bright green. Wright stated that the 'fireball' seemed closer and more brilliant than previously."

The comment referred to a sighting by Wright made on September 12, 1948. Wright was with a teacher from the Moffat, Colorado high school who was identified only as Mr. Funk. Wright said that the object "appeared to be a bright green falling star."

But that wasn't Wright's last sighting. On December 12, while near Monte Vista, he saw another object he described as a bright green falling star. He was with Charles Elliott. Wright was unable to give precise details about the size, shape, or location, but the Air Force investigator noted, "Wright was above-average in intelligence and that the 'fireball' was not a figment of his imagination."

Wright, like Colonel Hayes, was a repeater, meaning he saw the lights, the green fireballs, on more than one occasion. That might have been enough for the Air Force to discount his sightings, except that there were other witnesses to his sightings, and many of those who reported the fireballs saw them multiple times.

None of the sightings were too spectacular except for one fact. The lights, objects, or fireballs, were all traveling through an area where a number of secret research facilities and bases, working on highly classified missions, were located. Lt. Col. Doyle Rees, who was the commander of the 17th District of the Air Force Office of Special Investigation, decided that these reports required additional investigation.

Rees assigned two officers, Captain Melvin E. Neef and Captain John Stahl, to interview those at every agency or operation who might know something about the lights. They wanted to be sure that the lights were not part of a classified project. When that failed to produce results, Neef and Stahl decided they needed to check the terrain. Both were pilots and they took a T-7 out of Kirtland early one evening.

According to the government files, available through the National Archives, Stahl reported:

> At an estimated altitude of 2,000 feet higher than the airplane … a brilliant green light was observed coming toward the airplane at a rapid rate of speed from approximately 30 degrees to the left of course, from 60 degrees ENE, to 240 degrees WSW. The object was similar in appearance to a burning green flare of common use in the Air Forces. However, the light was much more intense and the object appeared to be considerably larger than a normal flare. No estimate can be made of the distance or the size of the object since no other object was visible upon which to base a comparison. The object was definitely larger and more brilliant than a shooting star, meteor or flare. The trajectory of the object when first sighted was almost flat and parallel to the earth. The phenomenon lasted approximately two seconds at the end of which the object seemed to burn out. The trajectory then dropped off rapidly and a trail of glowing fragments reddish orange in color was observed falling toward the ground. The fragments were visible less than a second before disappearing. The phenomenon was of such intensity as to be visible from the very moment it ignited and was observed a split second later.

The description sounds like that of a meteor, and if it was approaching the aircraft, it would have seemed larger than it was. Military pilots with combat experience would have been aware of this. Tracers fired by enemy gunners often looked larger and closer than they actually were.

To make matters worse, on December 6 Joseph Toulouse, a security officer with the Atomic Energy Security Service, saw a "greenish flare" on the Sandia Base at Kirtland. He said the light was about one-third the size of the moon, was visible for three seconds before it arced downward and vanished. Given the nature of the base and the highly classified work being done there, Rees thought there was a possibility that some sort of sabotage or espionage was going on.

Lincoln La Paz, Meteorite Expert Enters the Investigation

Now there was some confirmation of the events, with two of the intelligence officers spotting a green fireball themselves and the report from the security officer at Sandia. But there was also the possibility, however remote, that the green fireballs were meteors. On December 9, Neef contacted Dr. Lincoln La Paz, one of the foremost experts on meteors at that time. As a bonus, La Paz already held a top secret clearance and had been consulted by the Air Force on other matters relating to unidentified flying objects.

Neef said, during a March 1949 classified meeting called "Conference on Aerial Phenomena:

It all started back in December, 1948, when we first received some reports from some airline pilots that these green fireballs were sighted. At this stage we had no idea what to do with it or what it was. We approached Dr. La Paz who has been assisting us, gratis, since that date. Almost over two months now that he has been assisting us, so in order to have you get the facts as they are to a scientist.

La Paz began to study the green fireballs. On December 12, 1948, La Paz, along with several companions, was driving near Bernal, New Mexico, when they spotted one of the green fireballs heading from east to west, low on the horizon. The others, identified in the Blue Book government files, were Major C. L. Phillips, an Air Force–CAP liaison officer, Lieutenant Allan Clark with the New Mexico Wing of the CAP, an additional person identified as an intelligence officer, and Inspectors Jeffers and McGuigan, AEC Security Service at Los Alamos.

La Paz, having been introduced at the March conference by Neef, then went on to describe the December 12 event for the others there. He said:

> It is the only one of the incidents that I am in a position to vouch for on the basis of experience ... was not a conventional meteorite fall. It was the so-called Starvation Peak incident [Bernal, New Mexico] on the night of December 12, 1948. Time of observation around 9:02 P.M., plus or minus thirty seconds. The fireball appeared in full intensity instantly—there was no increase in light. Its color, estimated to be somewhere about wave length 5200 angstroms, was a hue green, or yellow green such as I have never observed in meteor falls before. The path was as nearly horizontal as one could determine by visual observation. We have a photograph which might be some liters of departure from horizontal. The trajectory was traverse at, I am inclined to believe, constant angular velocity. Just before the end of the path there was the very slightest drooping of the path, that is the green fireball broke into fragments, still bright green.

La Paz was asked questions and told the others that on December 12, he had been on an investigation into the sightings from the week before and was, therefore, somewhat prepared. He had a stop watch and a transit, which he used to make various measurements so that he was not relying solely on his perceptions.

The sightings continued after December 12. What is interesting is that many of them were made by those who were tasked Air Force Office of Special Investigations (AFOSI) and the Atomic Energy Security Service, saw the green fireballs. Inspector William D. Wilson, who was with Inspector Buford G. Truett, both of the AESS, saw something. In an official report, the incident was described this way:

// The fireball appeared in full intensity instantly— there was no increase in light."

> At 2054 [hours], 20 Dec 48, we saw the object described below making a path thru the sky. It was travelling in an almost flat trajectory and its decline formed an angle with the horizon of approximately 20 [degrees]. The angle of elevation from our point of observation was approximately thirty

Roswell UFO Crash—January 30, 1949

There have been persistent rumors for decades that on January 30, 1949, a UFO crashed south of Walker Air Force, New Mexico. A search team was sent out that included Dr. Lincoln La Paz, Master Sergeant Lewis "Bill" Rickett of the AFOSI detachment stationed in Roswell, Sergeant Raymond P. Platt, who worked in the control tower at the field, and several other, unidentified airmen. There were also some unidentified civilians with them who might have been FBI.

Platt, whose name does not surface in the Air Force files about the January 30 event, said that what he saw was very slow moving and that it was very bright. It was traveling from north to south and was east of Roswell and Walker AFB, out toward the Bottomless Lakes. Platt said that he saw it explode into six or seven pieces.

Rickett said that La Paz and the airmen talked to ranchers, talked to people in towns, talked to anyone who had seen anything. They had a caravan of four vehicles.

According to the records available, if the object had held a straight line, and the information about the height of the object was accurate, then La Paz calculated that it should have come down near Lamesa, Texas, south of Lubbock. Searches of the area failed to find any sort of debris.

Rumors, however, suggested that a craft was found, badly damaged, as well as a single alien creature, who had survived the crash. According to Linda Moulton Howe, she was shown a document in the offices of the AFOSI in Albuquerque that confirmed the information. She said that the alien was taken to a safe house at Los Alamos. It was small, gray and humanoid. It was befriended by an Air Force officer and it lived until June 18, 1952.

While there is little doubt that Howe was shown a briefing that contained the information described above, it is also clear that the document was riddled with inaccuracies.

[degrees]. The object was moving at a very fast rate of speed and disappeared behind the mountain directly northeast of Ft. Eagle. Total time of visibility was about one and one-half seconds.

Description:

An intense blue-white light about the size of a basketball. As the object traversed the sky, there was a faint trail of light behind it and two objects about the size of a baseball separated from the main body. These objects were the same color and intensity of the main body, and trailed directly in its path at even intervals of distance equal to approximately three times the diameter of the main body. The size of the main body was approximately one quarter the size of the moon.

Although this report is part of the green fireball files, it seems to describe a bright meteor that broke up as it fell. The report is important because it is contained in the government files and suggests the importance of this small part of the overall UFO investigation taking place in late 1948 and early 1949.

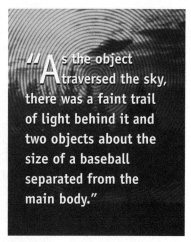

"As the object traversed the sky, there was a faint trail of light behind it and two objects about the size of a baseball separated from the main body."

A similar report by Inspector John D. Hardie was made just days later. He wrote, "At approximately 0431, this date [December 28, 1948], while looking east from Station 108 towards Station 101 I noticed high in the sky what appeared to be a falling star, white in color, descending in a vertical path. My attention remained with the object when I noticed the rate of descent seemed to be slower than that of a falling star. After watching it lose altitude for several seconds, I saw it suddenly disappear with a greenish-tinged flash which momentarily illuminated a small cloud between the object and myself."

This all resulted in a report dated December 29, 1948, by Major Godsoe, an intelligence officer at the Fourth Army Headquarters. The first few paragraphs contain the most interesting information. Godsoe wrote:

> Since the initial report of unidentified objects, described as flares or moving lights in the vicinity of Las Vegas, New Mexico, on 5 December 1948, there have been 23 reports from observers up to and including 28 December 1948. Of these reports 21 have been in New Mexico and 1 in Oregon....

> The appearance of the lights are of a definite pattern. All have been of an intense white or greenish white. The trajectory or path of flight has been north to east or west to east. Altitude has been reported from 3000 to 20,000 feet above the terrain, which in this area is 5000 to 7000 feet above sea level. Speed has been undetermined except that it seems to be about the supersonic range....

> It is of interest to note that at least two of the objects have been sighted over the Los Alamos AEC project. One person who observed one of the objects at Los Alamos has stated that it looked exactly the same as V2 Rockets he had seen over England during the war.

All that was interesting, and the letters being passed around at the time suggested that the various intelligence agencies, those in charge of the secret research projects, and the military were stumped by the sightings. They were doing everything they could think of to identify the green fireballs, but everything was about to change.

January 30, 1949—The Second Roswell Crash?

On February 11, 1949, Paul L. Ryan, in the AFOSI 17th District at Kirtland AFB in Albuquerque wrote a report about "Aerial Phenomena, that had been observed on January 30. He wrote, "Mr. Charles Naffziger, Administrative Supervisor, advised that a peculiar light or aerial phenomena had been observed at 1755 hours, 30 January 1949, in the vicinity of Walker AFB, Roswell, New Mexico, and that Sgt. Edward P. McCrary, a tower control operator of Walker AFB be contacted."

The next day, January 31, several of those at Roswell were interviewed about the sighting. The official report said:

> … a blue-green light resembling a flare was observed travelling on a horizontal line. This light came out of the North headed South at an estimated altitude of 2,000 feet, moving slowly, and disappeared in the vicinity of SE Walker Air Force Base. To some observers, this phenomenon disappeared in its entirety while other statements mention a disappearance as a disintegration into a shower of smaller lighted fragments such as a shower of sparks. The only sound accompanying this object was heard by Sgt. McCrary, who described it as a high pitched whining noise similar to a blowtorch. All of these observers sighting this light from a position west of it while facing east.

One of those men, Sergeant Raymond D. Platt was interviewed more than forty years later. He provided a little more detail, saying that he, "didn't believe it was a flying saucer. He believed it to be a meteor." In 1949 he was "interrogated by base personnel, the CIC and the FBI."

He said the object was flying very slow, was very bright, and it exploded into six or seven pieces. It was travelling at a very shallow angle, going from north to south and was bright white and blue in color. It burned out after it exploded, which is why he lost sight of it.

The front gate of Walker AFB, circa 1950s, is located just a couple miles from Roswell.

There were other reports of this object from other areas around Roswell. In Alamogordo, Major James C. Petersen said that he had sighted a single, bright green object looking to the east. He said it was a bright green fireball of flame, travelling in a southerly direction, without evidence of smoke or trail of any kind. He lost sight of it when it seemed "to fizzle out."

Also in Alamogordo, Wilfred T. Martin, a technician for the Boeing Aircraft Company, said that about six in the evening, he saw a single green fireball to the east and travelling to the south. He saw no signs of an exhaust; he watched for about ten seconds and said that it did not explode.

Martin was with Sergeant Maurice C. Anthon at the time, who was also interviewed about the sighting. He said, "I observed an object that appeared to be travelling diagonally across in front of me.... Its distance seemed very close and appeared to be travelling very slowly.... Gentle downward glide, bright burning (green and yellowish light) a fizzling out and then a bright burning, and then appeared to die out. This could have been the effects of its passing beyond my view."

Using the information gathered from more than 100 witnesses, Dr. Lincoln La Paz set out in an attempt to find where the object came down on earth....

PFC Ira W. Vail, assigned to the weather detachment at Holloman AFB in Alamogordo, told investigators that he had "seen a green ball of flame with a trail of some kind in an Easterly direction. Vail described the object as traveling in a Southerly direction and added that the object was visible for approximately six seconds. Vail described the object as bright green and disappeared without exploding."

South of Alamogordo, near the White Sands National Monument, two women identified in the official report as Mrs. Edgar J. Bethart and Mrs. Robert R. Johns, reported they had seen an object just a few minutes before six on January 30. They described a bright, burning green object that seemed to glide gently downward and "fizzle out with the light becoming less intense and finally disappearing altogether."

There were other similar reports coming from other parts of New Mexico and west Texas. The track of the object, or the green fireball, could be plotted based on the observations of the witnesses, and the investigators took many of the witnesses back to the places where they had seen the fireball in order to get accurate measurements suggesting height and direction. Using the information gathered from more than 100 witnesses, Dr. Lincoln La Paz set out in an attempt to find where the object came down on earth, if it was an ordinary meteor.

According to the report, "Special Agent [Lewis] Rickett [a member of the Counter Intelligence Corps stationed in Roswell] continued the search throughout Southeast New Mexico and West Texas from 1400 hours, 2 February 1949, to 2400 hours 8 February 1949, in the company of Dr. Lincoln La Paz of the University of New Mexico. All information obtained during this part of the investigation was retained by Dr. La Paz and will be incorporated into his report."

A verbal report of that activity was made to the Scientific Advisory Board Conference of February 16, 1949. La Paz said:

> In the case of the January 30th fall, due to the fact that there had been a large number of military personnel alerted, we were able to obtain observations within a minute after the fall occurred and pursued the investigation over a distance of 1,000 miles—in Texas mud primarily—in some ten days' time interviewing literally hundreds of people, we saw not one substantial account of noise produced by the meteorite fall....

> These lines are drawn [on a map of observers' sightings, giving direction of the object from the observer and the direction of travel] from the points of observation. The center ... of the points of appearance is somewhere Southwest of Amarillo or South-southwest of Amarillo. The disappearance point is in the vicinity of Lubbock, Texas.

They then get into a discussion of noise associated with meteor falls, but with the January 30 fall, they have very few reports of sound. In Roswell, however, there were five men together and they all reported hearing a whirring or whistling sound, similar to a blowtorch.

La Paz then said:

> One more thing in connection with the noises. In every other meteorite fall, any one meteorite fall that I have investigated—that covers many years—I have never yet found an occasion of a detonating fireball, without meteorites coming down, in which there was not some evidence of alarm of animals. Chickens will fly around to try to get under cover. Dogs will howl and try to get into the house. Horses will run away. In the case of the Texas fall, in spite of the tremendous area in which the light was observed, we found not a single case in which the animals were disturbed. We knew of the case of a farmer in sunny Texas, a pond with five-inch layer of ice, who reported that a meteorite had fallen through the ice on that pond. Captain Neef here put on a pair of rubber boots and very thoroughly searched the pond without finding a meteorite. Even in that case there was no evidence of alarm by animals.

La Paz explained that his plots suggested that the meteorite, if that is what it was, should have struck the ground near Lamesa, Texas, south of Lubbock. Working with a team, including military men such as Rickett, Platt, and Neef, they searched the area for several days without results. La Paz was puzzled because in other cases describing large, bright meteorites, he had had great success in recovering fragments.

La Paz mentioned a meteor fall on February 18, 1948, in Kansas. He said, "The time [of] that fall ... the rumor got around somehow in Northern Kansas and Southern Kansas that it was a Russian bomb, and it was aimed at the geographical center of the United States.... Apparently a great many people gave credence to that rumor and were delighted when we finally recovered meteorites up there."

In other words, using the techniques that had worked in the past, such as interviewing the witnesses and getting their directions of flight, La Paz and his crews were able to follow the meteorite fall to its impact location. This wasn't the only time that La Paz successfully tracked down the remnants of a meteoric impact. His methods had been tested over time.

Toward the end of the Advisory Board conference, La Paz was asked about the locations of the sightings. They were only being reported over the southwest, and most of the sightings were made in New Mexico. Some believed that this was an unusual circumstance. Why would people in New Mexico or the desert southwest see these green meteors if they weren't being seen by others around the country.

In fact, one of the participants, Dr. Holloway of the University of California, asked, "How much interest would the military have if they found out these things were landing all over the country, Canada, Hawaii...."

La Paz then said, "Most of them [others interested in meteors such as the President of the American Meteor Society] ... I think that if anyone at UCLA Institute of Geophysics had been observing, it would have gotten to Kaplan's ears [Joseph Kaplan at UCLA]."

La Paz goes on to say that they have had clear skies over the southwest in the previous weeks. He was not suggesting that this was a reason that the green fireballs seemed to be seen only in that area. It was just an observation about the weather conditions.

[T]he rumor got around somehow in Northern Kansas and Southern Kansas that it was a Russian bomb, and it was aimed at the geographical center of the United States...."

Commander Mandelkorn, representing the Naval interests, asked, "Well, wouldn't the phenomena of this nature have been reported to the Society, no matter where they occurred?"

La Paz responded that a thorough examination of the records had revealed just a single case of a fireball in which the observers mentioned a green color, but not the green that was mentioned by so many other observers in New Mexico.

He also said that the observing conditions around the country were such that if green fireballs were falling in those regions, then they would have been seen. He said, "To my knowledge ... these were nothing out of the normal in the East, and in the South, shall we say as far up as White Sands."

Toward the end of the conference, La Paz explained that the green fireballs seemed to be regional in nature, that the sound associated with them was unlike the sound reported in other meteor falls, and that La Paz had been unable to find any fragments, even when he had more than a hundred witnesses to the event. He said, "You see why I'm puzzled ... Nothing like this, to my knowledge, has ever been observed in the case of meteorite drops."

Doyle Rees prepared a transcript of the meeting and with a cover letter dated March 29, 1949, and forwarded it to the commanding general at the Air Materiel Command. The letter gave away little, other than to warn that "There are numerous errors in the minutes, due to the fact that they were transcribed from a recording of the conference. The combination of a jack hammer outside the window and the number of persons speaking made accurate transcription impossible."

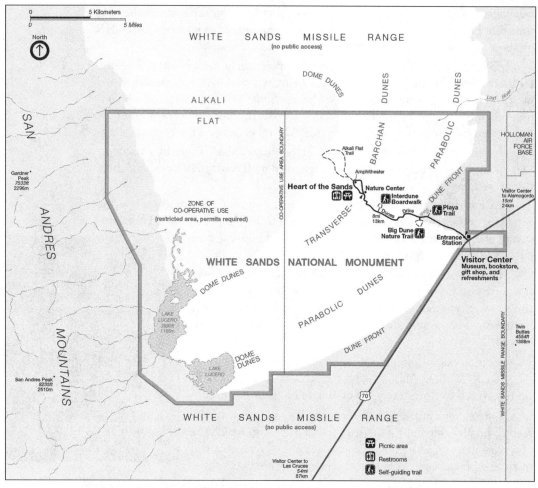

A map showing the White Sands National Monument and surrounding area, including the restricted zone to the west and Holloman AFB to the east.

He didn't ask for help or guidance, and said that the investigation would continue. There was no real response from AMC about the reports of the fireballs, or the effort by AFOSI to investigate them.

On April 23, Captain Roger Groseclose and Lieutenant Howard Smith were sent from AMC in Ohio to Kirtland. On April 24, there was a meeting attended by Neef, La Paz, Jack Boling, and Godsoe in an AFOSI office. Godsoe suggested that the AFOSI was wasting its time investigating the fireballs because AMC was ungrateful for the effort. The AMC officers shot back that it wasn't the business of Army officers to worry about fireballs.

That argument escalated and Godsoe stormed out of the room, which left La Paz exposed. The AMC officers had a list of complaints, including the fact that La Paz had sent them raw data rather than his finished analyses. This seemed to annoy La Paz, who said he had been working on the project as a volunteer and that he had to return to his regular job. Any further request for his assistance had better come with a contract.

Not all of the meeting was quite so acrimonious. Everyone agreed with Godsoe's recommendations that a network of observation posts with cameras, surveyor's transits, and trained observers was needed. There should be another search, both on the ground and in the air, for fragments from the green fireballs. All this was necessary because it seemed that the fireballs were seen only in a limited area of the southwest, and they were seen over some of the most sensitive installations in the country.

Continued Sightings

Had the green fireballs evaporated at that point, nothing would have been done about them. They would have been regarded as an anomaly and probably written off as meteors. But the sightings continued, and while few were as spectacular as the January 20 fall, other sightings fit into the category of "green fireball."

On February 27, 1949, Lieutenant H. E. Dey, in an official report, wrote, "I was returning from station 101 to station 100. While on the straight strip of road adjacent to the airstrip I happened to glance toward the north at which time I observed a greenish colored light moving across the northern sky toward the east. It was visible for approximately two seconds. It did not appear to travel beyond my range of vision, but suddenly disappeared as I was watching it. It did not leave a trail in the sky nor did it appear to have a tail like a meteor."

On March 3, D. M. Rickard, who was a sergeant with the Atomic Energy Security Service reported, "I was sitting in a chair facing East and talking to Lt. Buckley. A bright green light fell almost straight down, East-North-East of Station 101. This light was bright all the time that I observed same."

From Albuquerque, on April 30, an observer reported a "round blue-green object. It was very bright and heading West. It simply went out after about two seconds."

Even with continued sightings and La Paz's stated reasons about why the green fireballs were not natural, in Washington, the conclusion was that these were not meteors but some sort of "auroral effect." La Paz acknowledged that the distances were so far from the magnetic poles that their rapid, horizontal motion was difficult to explain. Air Force intelligence "tentatively accepted" the explanation and Air Force Headquarters began a review of the reports.

On June 2, again at Los Alamos, "Observers saw a 'ball of light' descending East to North. Had a long unbroken trail same width of object. Green color." According to the information, it was only in sight for about one second.

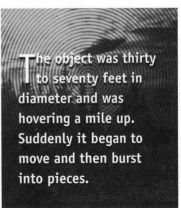

The object was thirty to seventy feet in diameter and was hovering a mile up. Suddenly it began to move and then burst into pieces.

While not a green fireball, there was an interesting sighting from Camp Hood, Texas, on June 6 that deserves mention because of all the "aerial phenomena" activity in the area. Four officers, at two separate locations, sighted a bright yellow or orange light at the same time. Lieutenants Virgil Williams and Marvin L. Jones were at one site and Lieutenants Bernard G. Raftery and Alfred H. Jones were at the other. Given that they had proper directions and equipment, triangulation, of a sort, could be done. The object was thirty to seventy feet in diameter and was hovering a mile up. Suddenly it began to move and then burst into pieces. The sighting lasted for three minutes and the government files suggested "Object could have been a balloon bursting."

A few days later, on June 11, there was another sighting. According to the government file, "Object appeared as a star or light. Object green, then red at end of flight, with short red tail. Appeared to climb then fell almost straight down."

On June 20, at Los Alamos, it was reported that "Object was round, turning green to orange before vanishing. Object went through 90 deg [sic] of arc and disappeared as though it was extinguished." This sighting lasted for three seconds.

These, and more than a dozen additional sightings were reported in New Mexico, many from around the secret laboratories at Los Alamos, which worried the security people. All were eventually written off as "Astro (METEOR)." But that answer was applied later, when the Air Force began to push for solutions to sightings. In fact, on September 1, 1949, Colonel John W. Schweizer, of Air Force intelligence wrote, "… reports that fall in the 'fireball' category will no longer be included in Hq. Air Materiel Command and Directorate of Intelligence, Hq. USAF, investigative activity on unidentified aerial incidents."

Early in 1949, the green fireballs had alarmed those responsible for the security of the secret installations, but by the middle of the year, they seemed to be of no consequence. They weren't paying much attention to the reports, even though La Paz had suggested the fireballs might be some kind of controlled craft or probe.

On July 24, one of the green fireballs was seen falling near Socorro, New Mexico. The next morning, Dr. W. D. Crozier of the New Mexico School of Mines collected dust samples from around the campus in Socorro. Crozier relayed his findings to La Paz, who wrote to Rees on August 17, 1949: "These collections, to Dr. Crozier's evident surprise, were found to contain not only the first copper particles he had found in air dust collections, but these particles were of unusually large size—up to 100 microns in maximum dimensions."

It wasn't quite that simple, of course. Crozier thought that the copper might have come from the roofs and the gutters of the buildings on campus. If the copper was found away from the campus, then the finding would be significant, but when the copper turned up far from the campus, Crozier seemed to be unimpressed, calling the results, "unimpressive."

La Paz, again, disagreed. He wrote to Rees, "I wish to emphasize most emphatically that if future more detailed work shows that the numerous copper particles found by Dr. Crozier and Mr. [Ben] Seely [Crozier's assistant] are indeed floating down from green fireballs, then the fireballs are not conventional meteorites. Copper is one of [the] rarest of the elements found in meteorites ... In fact, I know of no case in which even the tiniest particle of copper has been reported in a dust collection supposedly of meteoritic origin."

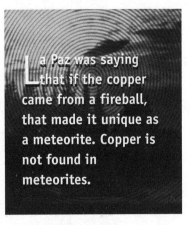

La Paz was saying that if the copper came from a fireball, that made it unique as a meteorite. Copper is not found in meteorites.

To understand this, it is important to note that Crozier had been collecting the dust samples over a period of time. So when the copper appeared in the samples after the July 24 fireball, it could be suggested that the particles were from the fireball. When copper was found over a large area, it added to the belief. La Paz was saying that if the copper came from a fireball, that made it unique as a meteorite. Copper is not found in meteorites. Therefore, the fireballs were not meteorites and deserved further investigation.

Project Twinkle

Although those in Washington seemed to have answered the questions about the green fireballs to their own satisfaction, those in New Mexico weren't happy. Sightings of the fireballs continued, though now, according to Rees, they seemed to be falling vertically and he noticed that there were more reports on the weekends, especially on Sunday. It was also around this time, summer 1949, that Joseph Kaplan met with Norris Bradbury, who had been at the February conference. Bradbury thought that a classified scientific study of these aerial phenomena should be made and suggested convening a conference to discuss it.

Kaplan suggested to the AFOIN director, General Charles P. Cabell, that they should attempt a scientific study of the green fireballs, but Cabell did not have the budget to support it. Kaplan, during a visit with the AMC's Cambridge Research Laboratories in Boston tried to learn what could be done to facilitate the research. Finally, on September 14, 1949, the Air Force Chief of Staff, General Hoyt S. Vandenberg, ordered the then commander of AMC, Lieutenant General Benjamin Chidlaw, to evaluate the sightings in New Mexico and Texas.

The meeting that Kaplan wanted was held on October 16, 1949, and included representatives of AFOSI, the Air Materiel Command, the AESS, the Fourth Army, the FBI, and representatives from Los Alamos including Edward Teller. Unlike other conferences about UFOs, in this case everyone agreed there was a real phenomenon out there. They just couldn't agree on what it was.

Kaplan took his plan to AFSAB, and after review by the Defense Department's Research and Development Board, it was approved. On February 21, 1950, Project Twinkle began with an outpost manned by two observers who scanned the sky. They had a theodolite, a telescope, and a camera. As Ed Ruppelt noted, "If two or more of the cameras photograph the same object, it is possible to obtain a very accurate measurement of the photographed object's altitude, speed and size."

General Charles Cabell was director of AFOIN at the time of the fireball sightings in New Mexico. He was asked to order a study on the phenomenon, but refused because it was not in the AFOIN budget.

Ruppelt then wrote, "Project Twinkle was a bust. Absolutely nothing was photographed. Of the three cameras that were planned for the project, only one was available."

It had been noted by the *Houston Chronicle*, "Others who have written on this subject have intimated they were conferring with officials in the inner sanctum. This book, which may well become the bible of the UFO devotees, makes it clear that Ruppelt is the inner sanctum." But it is not clear if Ruppelt was aware of everything that was happening, especially those projects that were not directly part of Blue Book.

The Project Twinkle Final Report, written by P. H. Wyckoff, Chief, Atmospheric Physics Laboratory, notes, "Some photographic activity occurred on 27 April and 24 May [1950], but simultaneous sightings by both cameras were not made."

In the government files, there is very little information about these two cases. The April 27 case has no project card. There is a letter dated May 31, 1950, that says:

Per request of Dr. A. C. Mirarchi, during a recent visit to this base [Holloman], the following information is submitted.

Sightings were made on 27 April and 24 May 1950 of aerial phenomena during morning daylight hours at this station. The sightings were made by LAND-AIR, Inc., personnel while engaged in tracking regular projects with Askania Phototheodolites. It has been reported that objects are sighted in some number, as many as eight have been visible at one time. The individuals making these sightings are professional observers. Therefore, I would rate their reliability superior. In both cases photos were taken with Aaskanias.

The Holloman AF Base Data Reduction Unit analyzed the 27 April pictures and made a report, a copy of which I am enclosing with the film for your information. It was believed that triangulation could be effected from pictures taken on 24 May because pictures were taken from two stations. The films were rapidly processed and examined by Data Reduction. However, it was determined that sightings were made on two different objects and triangulation could not be effected. A report from Data Reduction and the films from the sighting are enclosed.

The same letter appears in the May 24 file, but there is a project card for it, and it says, "Photos taken by two stations on Videon Camera. Two different objects and triangulation could not be effected [sic]. Photos sent to Dr. Mirarchi at Cambridge. File incomplete."

It should also be noted that letter lists several enclosures, only one of which appeared in the government file:

Objects observed following MX776A test of 27 April 1950.

2nd Lt. [name redacted] EHOSIR 15 May 50

1. According to conversation between Col. Baynes and Capt. Bryant, the following information is submitted directly to Lt. Albert.

2. Film from station P10 was read, resulting in azimuth and elevation angles being recorded on four objects. In addition, size of image on film was recorded.

3. From this information, together with a single azimuth from station M7, the following conclusions were drawn:

    a) The objects were at an altitude of approximately 150,000 ft.

    b) The objects were over the Holloman range between the base and Tularosa Peak.

    c) The objects were approximately 30 feet in diameter.

    d) The objects were traveling at an undeterminable, yet high speed.

(signed)
Wilbur L. Mitchell
Mathematician
Data Reduction Unit

The other enclosures included a number of films of the objects. Both files were labeled as "Insufficient Data." That label was used when the officers at Blue Book didn't want to call a case "Unidentified," but were required to put some kind of label on it.

What this means is that either Ruppelt paid no attention to the final report on Project Twinkle, which mentions these two cases, or he knew about them and for some reason ignored them. No matter which explanation is correct, Ruppelt was wrong when he suggested that "Project Twinkle was a bust. Absolutely nothing was photographed. Of the three cameras that were planned for the project, only one was available." The evidence in the government files suggests otherwise.

[T]he final report on Project Twinkle was less a scientific document than it was a public relations tool.

In fact, the final report on Project Twinkle was less a scientific document than it was a public relations tool. It was created to explain the green fireballs as a mundane occurrence and ignore the data recovered during the various studies, investigations, and searches.

Elterman, the author of the report that in early 1950, the Geophysics Research Division had been told to investigate "peculiar light phenomena" and that Project Twinkle was established to do so. Like Ruppelt, Elterman wrote, "The gist of the findings is essentially negative.... There has been no indication that even the somewhat strange observations often called 'Green Fireballs' are anything but natural phenomena."

He broke the report down in what he labeled "Contractual periods," the first from April 1, 1950 to September 15, 1950. In addition to the sightings on April 27 and May 24, he noted that "On 31 August 1950, the phenomena were again observed after a V-2 launching. Although much film was expended, proper triangulation was not effected [sic], so that again no information was acquired."

Although they had the photographic theodolites, the "grating cameras" functioned only periodically and the military personnel who operated them had been reassigned because of the Korean War. He was offering excuses for the failure.

He did note that the "phenomena activity over Holloman AFB 150 miles south of Vaughn, N. Mexico during the latter part of August 1950 was considered sufficiently significant so that the contract with Land-Air (Askania cameras only) was extended for six months."

And when the extended contract expired, so did the research. Elterman wrote, "In summary, the results during this period were negative."

Also important was a note in the "Post Contractual Inquiry," that the 17th OSI [Office of Special Investigations] District, now under Colonel Cox, had been "diligent" in forwarding copies of their reports to Elterman and his group until March 15, 1951, but after that "little attention was being given this matter. Most of the reports originated from personnel at Los Alamos."

In an attempt to prove there was nothing strange going on in New Mexico, Elterman wrote:

> Mr. D. Guildenberg, who is an assistant to Major Doty and an active amateur astronomer, commented that he has been spending several hours at his telescope almost every night for the past few years and never once observed an unexplainable object; that on one occasion, an excited acquaintance was pacified when a "strange object" showed up as an eagle in the telescope; that Clyde Tombaugh, discoverer of the planet Pluto and now engaged in activities at White Sands, never observed an unexplainable aerial object despite his continuous and extensive observations of the sky....

The problem with this statement is that it is not true. While Guildenberg might not have ever seen anything he couldn't explain, La Paz, who was called into the investigation, did see a green fireball. La Paz was a leading expert on meteors and he didn't think what he saw was a meteor, and he was unsure of the nature of it.

Even worse, Clyde Tombaugh had seen something unexplainable on August 20, 1949. It is listed as case 536 in the Blue Book index, but it is not clear when the information was gathered. Although it predates Elterman's report, the data may not have been added until later. And even if it was present, there is no indication that Elterman would have known about it. The strange thing is that he would mention Tombaugh in the report.

To be fair to Elterman, he did note that "On 28 August 1951, the subject was discussed with Dr. Lincoln La Paz, who expressed disbelief in all aerial phenomena except for the green fireballs. The red fireball occasionally reported he believed was the visual after-effect of the green. Their recent origin (1947) and peculiar trajectories did not permit, according to Dr. La Paz, them to be classified as natural phenomena.... Dr. La Paz expressed the opinion that the fireballs may be of our own military origin, but if not, they are a matter of serious concern."

The conclusions are interesting in that Wyckoff suggests that many of the sightings can be explained as mundane objects, such as balloons, or as natural phenomena. He noted, interestingly, that photographs had been taken on thirty-five nights when observations were made, but none "of the photographs revealed the presence of unusual sky phenomena."

Under recommendations, Elterman wrote:

No further fiscal expenditure be made pursuing the problem. This opinion is prompted partly by the fruitless expenditure during the past year, the uncertainty of existence of unexplainable aerial objects, and by the inactive position currently taken by Holloman AFB as indicated by the "stand-by status" of the project. The arrangements by HAFB for continued vigilance by Land-Air, the weather station as well as the briefing of pilots on the problem in part relieves the need for a systematic instrumentation program.

This illustration depicts the incident in 1949, when astronomer Clyde Tombaugh reported seeing UFOs near Las Cruces, New Mexico.

Within the next few months, Dr. Whipple will have completed the installation of two 18-inch Schmidt cameras for meteor studies. The cameras will be stationed about 20 miles apart in the vicinity of Las Cruces, New Mexico. Since these studies will be sponsored by the GRD, arrangements can be made for examining the film for evidence of aerial object phenomena.

And with that, Project Twinkle faded away. It was caught in the crossfire between those who thought the green fireballs were meteors and those who thought they were not. La Paz, the real expert in this, rejected the idea of natural phenomena because of the limited geographic area in which the fireballs were seen, their sudden appearance in 1948, the lack of success in recovering any fragments from them, and their subsequent disappearance.

Although a satisfactory solution for the fireballs was never found, those cases that made their way into the Project Blue Book files were all labeled as "Astro (Meteor)." And while that might be true for some of them, many of the sightings were not of meteors and the gathered evidence seems to prove it.

Holloman AFB, circa 1944. The base is about six miles from Alamogordo, New Mexico.

There is a final note of importance. On February 19, 1952, Albert E. Lombard, Jr. sent a letter to the Directorate of Intelligence, and to the attention of Colonel John G. Erickson, about the declassification of the Project Twinkle report and the activities surrounding it. Lombard wrote, "The Scientific Advisory Board Secretariat has suggested that this project [Twinkle] not be declassified for a variety of reasons, chief among which is that *no scientific explanation for any of the 'fireballs' and other phenomena was revealed by the report* [emphasis added] and that some reputable scientists still believe that the observed phenomena are man made."

In the end, when all the government files on this subject are examined, it is clear that the question of the green fireballs was never resolved. They stopped falling, people stopped seeing them, and no one cared anymore. They became little more than a footnote in the history of UFO research. Clearly they deserved more than that.

Clyde Tombaugh's UFO Sighting

For most of his life, Dr. Clyde Tombaugh was the only living man to have discovered a new planet. Tombaugh was also among the few astronomers who had seen something in the sky that he couldn't identify. According to a document he signed on August 7, 1957, he had seen what he termed "An Unusual Aerial Phenomenon." He wrote:

> I saw the object about eleven o'clock one night in August, 1949 [The actual date, according to government files is August 20, 1949] from the backyard of my home in Las Cruces, New Mexico. I happened to be looking at zenith, admiring the beautiful transparent sky of stars, when suddenly I spied a geometrical group of faint bluish-green rectangles of light similar to the "Lubbock lights." My wife and her mother were sitting in the yard with me and they saw them also. The group moved south-southeasterly, the individual rectangles became fore-shortened, their space of formation smaller (at first about one degree across) and the intensity duller, fading from view at about 35 degrees above the horizon. Total time of visibility was about three seconds. I was too flabbergasted to count the number of rectangles of light, or to note some other features I wondered about later. There was no sound. I have done thousands of hours of night sky watching, but never saw a sight so strange as this. The rectangles of light were of low luminosity; had there been a full moon in the sky, I am sure they would not have been visible.

Astronomer Clyde Tombaugh, best known for discovering Pluto, was also witness to a UFO in 1949.

He would later add an addendum to the sighting. In a letter to Richard Hall on September 10, 1957, Tombaugh wrote,

> Regarding the solidity of the phenomenon I saw: My wife thought she saw a faint connecting glow across the structure. The illuminated rectangles I saw did maintain an exact fixed position with respect to each other, which would tend to support the impression of solidity. I doubt that the phenomenon was any terrestrial reflection, because in that case some similarity to it should have appeared many times.

What is most interesting here is that this sighting came in the middle of the green fireball investigation and while the rectangles are not fireballs, the green color fits into the pattern of the other such sightings in New Mexico.

Blue Book Special Report 13

As Project Grudge evolved into Project Blue Book, the Air Force produced a dozen special reports beginning in November 1951. Originally, these status reports, as they were called, were to be issued monthly, and for a number of months they were. But as time passed and the emphasis of the investigation changed, the reports were issued infrequently and eventually ended with Blue Book Special Report No. 14.

Lieutenant (later captain) Ed Ruppelt, who was assigned to Project Grudge in late 1951 with orders to revitalize the UFO project, made many significant changes to the UFO project once he took over. One of these was the reorganization of Grudge so that an emphasis was placed on investigation. In the months before he took over, Ruppelt had observed the attitude of officers at the highest levels and he felt that the investigations had been allowed to deteriorate as long as a ready solution was available.

Ruppelt wrote in Status Report No 1, issued on November 30, 1951, and distributed to several of the Air Force intelligence functions:

> This report is the first of a series of monthly status reports of Project Grudge. Each report will be written on or near the last day of the month and will contain a list of all incidents reported during the month covered by the report. The reports that are considered to be outstanding will also be summarized in the appendices of the report so that more details can be presented. The overall status will also be presented.

Ruppelt wrote that much of the work they had accomplished thus far included a reorganization of Project Grudge, a review of the old Project Sign and Grudge files, and an attempt to cross-index the information. He wrote, "It is contemplated that all of the sightings of unconventional flying objects will soon be cross-indexed according to size, color, location, etc., so that as much statistical data as possible will be available."

He also wrote about consulting with other agencies, such as the weather bureau and flight service, which should have included the Federal Aviation Administration (FAA) and the OSI. In fact, the first status report contained a lot of information that would be considered "housekeeping," meaning it documented who had responsibility for various aspects of the investigation, how the investigation

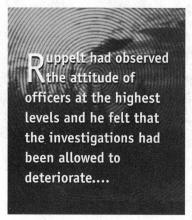

Ruppelt had observed the attitude of officers at the highest levels and he felt that the investigations had been allowed to deteriorate....

would be conducted, and even that it would be necessary to remind other commands and organizations of their responsibilities in reporting sightings to ATIC.

The second part of the report was labeled, "Reports of Specific Incidents," which was to be a summary of all the incidents that had been reported or were being investigated during the period covered by the report. Ruppelt's plan was, in the future, to include in his monthly reports, all the new sightings for that month and to update information on sightings that had been reported earlier but were still being investigated. Ruppelt also wrote that it would become the policy of "Project Grudge to concentrate on those incidents that appear to have originated from high grade sources, such as pilots, technically trained people, etc. The only exception to this will be where a number of sightings occur in a certain area at about the same time."

That turned out to be an interesting notation. The very first report covered under this new format was listed in a table on the following page as having come from Lubbock, Texas, on the night of August 25, 1951. This sighting, or series of sightings, would become known as the Lubbock Lights.

The Lubbock Lights

The first people to report seeing the lights were four professors from Texas Technical College (later known as Texas Tech). At about 9:10 P.M., they were sitting outside, looking for meteors when they saw a "group of lights pass overhead from N to S. The lights had about the same intensity as a bright star but were larger in area.... The pattern of the lights was almost a perfect semi-circle containing from 20 to 30 individual lights."

Later that evening, the lights reappeared, and over the course of about three weeks, the men saw the lights about a dozen times. They were unable to immediately identify the lights and were puzzled by the incident. Although unidentified in the Status Report, their positions and education were mentioned, including the fact that all of them held doctoral degrees.

The men have since been identified as W. L. Ducker, A. G. Oberg, and W. I. Robinson. The fourth man's identity was not revealed in the government documents but he was Dr. E. L. George. Ducker called the local newspaper, the *Lubbock Avalanche*, to tell them about the sighting. Jay Harris, the managing editor wasn't interested at first, but Ducker convinced him of the story's importance. Harris finally agreed to print something, but only if he could identify the group. Ducker wasn't thrilled with that idea and said that he would have to check with the public relations department at the college. Eventually Ducker called Harris and told him to run the story.

Although it is not mentioned in the Status Reports, other government files, including those housed at the National Archives, show that others saw the first pass of the lights. These included Mrs. Earl Medlock, Mrs. F. A. Rogers, Mrs. R. A. Rogers (noted in the files that their names were given in the convention of the times) and Professor Carl Henninger.

In Brownsfield, Texas, near Lubbock, Joe Bryant said that he had also seen strange lights on August 25. He was sitting in his backyard when he said there was "kind of a glow, a little bigger than a star." A short time later, a second group appeared but neither group was in any sort of a formation.

There was a third flight, but instead of flying over, as they had before, now the lights dropped lower and circled the house. Bryant could see the objects quite clearly and when one of them "chirped," he recognized them as plovers. When he read about the professors' sightings the next day, he realized he would have been as fooled as they were, had he not seen them close by.

The professors, being scientifically trained, and having observed multiple flights, thought there might be a chance the lights would return. They decided to create a baseline, place observers at each end, and attempt to determine the altitude, size and speed of the lights. On nights that the teams were deployed, the lights did appear and those at the center of the base, the scene of the first observations, did see the lights. Those at the ends did not. It meant the lights were lower, slower, and smaller than originally thought.

There were some observations that had been made. There seemed to be no sound associated with the lights. They flew from north to south the majority of the

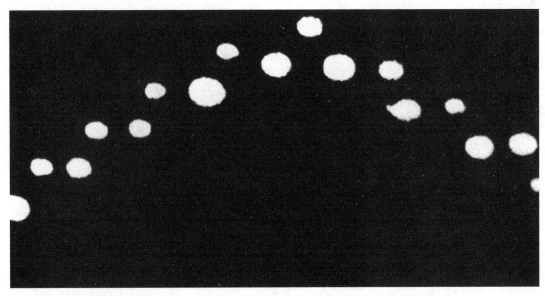

An image taken of the odd formation of lights that appeared over Lubbock, Texas, in August 1951.

time. There were two to three flights a night and the period between each flight was about an hour and ten minutes. The objects were blue-white and there were twenty to thirty lights in each formation. In the case of the professors, the first two flights observed were in a semi-circle formation, but later flights had no order to the formations.

Things changed on August 31, 1951, when Carl Hart Jr., a freshman at Texas Tech saw the lights as they flew over his house. Hart was an amateur photographer and took five pictures of two of the formations. What he saw and photographed matched what the professors saw, except that these lights were in "V" formation.

Hart, because he had photographs, became an important witness in the case. He was interrogated several times. The government file reported:

> The photographer who claims to have photographed the object was interrogated. Every effort was made to find a flaw in the photographer's account of the incident but the results were negative. The college professors did not believe the photographs were authentic as they had never observed a V-shaped group of lights. They were not sure, however, whether or not they had observed the same objects that were photographed. Since the interrogation, two discrepancies in the photos have been found and the photographer is being reinterrogated by the O.S.I. [sic].

The investigation continued, with Ruppelt making a trip to Lubbock in early November. In Status Report No. 2, dated December 31, 1951, Ruppelt again described the situation in Lubbock, especially the investigation that surrounded the photographs. Now Ruppelt wrote:

> The photographer [Hart] was interrogated, in conjunction with the OSI, in regard to the photographs of the objects. His account of the incident seemed logical, and there were no obvious indications of hoax. The photographer had previously been interrogated by the Lubbock newspaper [William Hams, the newspaper's chief photographer] and the photos inspected by Associated Press and *Life* Magazine representatives. It was their opinion that the photos were not obviously a hoax.

Although there was a government investigation in process, the newspaper conducted their own. Harris, who had interviewed Ducker the first night, and Hams feared some kind of a hoax. Harris called Hart a number of times and bluntly accused him of a hoax.

Hart, of course, denied that he had faked anything. He didn't care what Harris thought and he didn't care about payment for the pictures either. Eventually the newspaper paid him ten dollars, but that was about the only payment he ever received. He had failed to have them copyrighted.

He said, "Advice from a friend and professional journalist at the time was that if [I] copyrighted them, somebody's going to think [I] faked them and [was] trying to make money out of them. I was interested in the part of it [proving them to be authentic] and didn't do it [copyright them]."

Appendix I

LUBBOCK, TEXAS – 25 August 1951

The first of a series of sightings related to this incident occurred the evening of 25 August 1951 at approximately 2110 CST. Four Texas Technical College professors were sitting in the backyard of one of the professor's homes observing meteorites in conjunction with a study of micrometeorites being carried out by the college. At 2110 they observed a group of lights pass overhead from N to S. The lights had about the same intensity as a bright star but were larger in area. The altitude was not determined but they traveled at a high rate of speed. The pattern of the lights was almost a perfect semicircle containing from 20 to 30 individual lights. Later in the evening a similar incident was observed and during a period of about three weeks a total of approximately twelve (12) such flights were observed by these men.

The group of men included:

a. The Head of the Petroleum Engineering Department
b. Professor of Geology, has Ph.D.
c. Professor of Physics, has Ph.D.
d. Professor of Chemical Engineering, has Ph.D.

Besides the above four men the following have observed the incidents:

a. Professor of Mathematics, has Ph.D.
b. Graduate student working on Ph.D.

In addition, a Professor of Astronomy was consulted on the incident, but he did not observe any of these flights.

The above mentioned men took a personal interest in the phenomena and undertook a study of the objects. Attempts were made to obtain an altitude measurement by laying out a measured base line perpendicular to the usual flight path of the object and placing angle measuring devices at the end of the base line, however, all their attempts failed because the objects did not appear on the nights the observers were waiting for them.

From the series of observations, the following facts were obtained:

a. The angular velocity of the object was very nearly 30° of arc per second.

b. There was no sound that could be attributed to the object.

c. The flight path of the object was from N to S in the majority of the flights.

d. There were two or three flights per evening.

e. The period between flights was about one hour and 10 minutes.

A page from the declassified Lubbock report, dated August 25, 1951. It describes what was seen and lists several witnesses, five of whom held Ph.D.s.

Hams decided to see if he could duplicate the pictures. He thought that the experiment might reveal how Hart may have faked them. Hams used a Speed Graphic camera and went to the roof of the newspaper building in downtown Lubbock. Hams didn't see anything, other than a flight of migratory birds that were barely visible in the glow of the streetlights below. They were in a ragged "V" formation, dark against a darker sky. Hams was surprised they were so quiet because ducks and geese typically made all sorts of noise.

Hams took pictures, but the image was so weak that it was nearly impossible to see and not bright, like the pictures that Hart had taken. He tried it another time and failed again. Hams could not duplicate the pictures Hart had taken.

Other government files showed that Ruppelt, along with Lieutenant John Farley and AFOSI Special Agent Howard Bossert, interviewed Hart a number of times. During the September 20, 1951 visit, Bossert and Farley asked for the negatives but Hart could only find four of the five. The negatives were sent to Wright-Patterson AFB for analysis.

The report, "WCEFP-2-4, Physics Branch Sensitometry Unit," dated November 29, revealed nothing about the photographs other than the objects seemed to be individual lights rather than lights on a larger, darker object. They also determined that if the objects had been at 5,000 feet, they would have been 310 feet in diameter, though there was nothing on the negatives to suggest altitude or size.

Although Ruppelt had hinted in the earlier Status Report that they had discovered some internal inconsistencies, or problems with Hart's story, nothing found by the lab suggested a hoax. The sequence in which the objects were photographed was corroborated by examination of the negatives. Hart's story was not inconsistent.

Then, on December 2, 1951, Hart was again questioned by the military. This time, according to the documentation in the government files, Hart was told by the Air Force officers exactly what his rights were under the Constitution of the United States, including an explanation about the Fifth Amendment. This was the equivalent to giving him a Miranda warning and was undoubtedly a tactic of intimidation.

Hart was interviewed in private and then asked to give a written statement, which outlined how he had taken the photographs, the fact that he had only four of the five negatives, and that he was telling the truth as best he could. In other words, he was sticking to his story regardless of the tactics employed against him.

In fact, according to the government files, this was not the first time that Hart had been warned about the consequences of a hoax. Both the editor and the chief photographer at the newspaper told Hart they were about to put the pictures on the wire, which meant a national audience. The AP would not take kindly to having a hoax perpetrated on them. If the pictures were a hoax, now was the time to say so and end the story from expanding any further. Hart insisted that he had not faked anything.

On February 1, 1993, UFO investigator Kevin Randle had an opportunity to interview Hart in Lubbock, Texas. Randle knew that many of the young men who had faked UFO photographs eventually came clean, sometimes admitting the hoax decades later. Randle asked Hart what he had photographed, and Hart told him the same thing that he had told so many others over the years when he was asked if he knew what he had photographed. He said, "I really don't."

The Air Force interviewed dozens of witnesses and it is clear from the government files that some of those witnesses saw birds, either the plover, or some other migratory bird. It is also clear from those documents, though there are contradictory notations in them, that the original sightings are of birds and that the Hart photographs are not of birds. That didn't stop the Air Force from closing the case, writing the sightings off as birds.

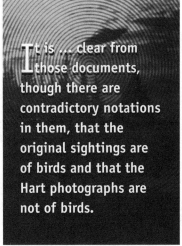

It is ... clear from those documents, though there are contradictory notations in them, that the original sightings are of birds and that the Hart photographs are not of birds.

On January 19, 1956, the *Avalanche Journal* reported "'Lubbock Lights' Puzzle Solved, Chief Air Force Prober Claims." Ruppelt, in his book, *The Report on Unidentified Flying Objects*," reported that he knew the solution. He had thought they were birds reflecting the streetlights, but they weren't the lights. He had another explanation.

In a chapter titled "The Lubbock Lights, Unabridged," Ruppelt wrote:

It is very unfortunate that I can't divulge exactly the way the answer was found because it is an interesting story of how a scientist set up complete instrumentation to track down the lights and how he spent several months testing theory after theory until he finally hit on the answer. Telling the story would lead to his identity and, in exchange for his story, I promised the man complete anonymity. But he fully convinced me that he had the answer, and after having heard hundreds of explanations, I don't convince easily.

With the most important phase of the Lubbock Lights "solved"—the sightings by the professors—the other phases become only good UFO reports.

But an explanation that isn't offered, by a scientist who isn't identified, is no explanation at all. Long after his death, Ruppelt's personal papers eventually made their way into the hands of UFO researchers and his long-concealed explanation was finally revealed. The first sightings, according to Ruppelt, were the result of fireflies.

Ducker told the newspaper, "We have never speculated as to the identity of what we saw. Thank God, we didn't! We still don't know what we saw and we still are not speculating." This seemed to rule out the bird explanation being offered at the time.

Then on March 20, 1969, the Lubbock newspaper reported again on the Lubbock Lights, noting that it had been eighteen years since the sightings. At that time, Ducker told the newspaper, "The lights have been a matter of considerable embarrassment over the years.... I want no further involvement in it...."

Hart told the reporter that, "The most plausible explanation is that they were a natural phenomena [sic]." But he offered no suggestion of what that phenomenon might be.

The explanations that have been offered until now do not fully explain the photographs. The birds didn't reflect the light with sufficient intensity that they could be photographed. Fireflies would have been too dim, were the wrong color, and they don't fly in formation. The case should have remained "Unidentified."

The Albuquerque Sighting

In those same Status Reports, another sighting has a certain relevance to the Lubbock Lights. At 9:58 MST (or about an hour and a half after the first of the Lubbock sightings) on August 25, 1951, a security guard at the Sandia Base and his wife saw "what they described to be a flying wing type aircraft similar to the Northrop Fly-Wing Bomber (B-49) pass over their backyard." They thought it was flying low, no more than a thousand feet over them. The color was not apparent because it was near twilight but there did seem to be stripes along the wings. There were "Six to eight pairs of soft flowing [sic, glowing] lights ... on the trailing edge of the wing."

The sighting was included in the report based on the rules established for the reports. The witness held a "Q" clearance, which meant that his background had been thoroughly investigated before he was hired. The "Q" clearance was meant for staff who dealt in some fashion with atomic energy. The government file reported, "... it is assumed that he apparently is mentally stable."

The report said, "It is interesting to note that a very similar sighting took place in Lubbock, Texas. The exact time and date of the sighing could not be determined due to the fact that the observer believed she had seen an illusion of some type and did not report the incident. The only date that could be given was "late in August or early September."

In the government files, however, the time and date are given precisely, and the case is labeled as "Unidentified." Given that the description generally matches the first sightings by the professors and the pictures taken by Hart a few days later, it creates an interesting series. It also suggests something about the investigations by the Air Force. The obscure sighting is "Unidentified," but the one that resulted in all the publicity is labeled "birds."

The Washington Nationals

Over the next few months, Ruppelt and his staff produced their monthly Status Reports. Some of them were quite thin, dealing with a handful of sightings. Status Report No. 7 was issued in May, 1952, but No. 8 didn't appear until the following December. The officer in charge explained:

> This report is the eighth of a series of Status Reports of Project Blue Book [the code name had been changed early in 1952]. Normally each report is written on or near the last of the month. This procedure has not been followed during the months of June, July, August, September and Octo-

A 1942 aerial shot of Sandia AFB near Albuquerque, New Mexico.

ber due to an extremely heavy workload caused by an increase in reports. The procedure for listing all reported sightings will also be eliminated in this report since 886 reports were received during the period covered by this report and compiling such a list would not be feasible at this time.

Ruppelt was referring to the summer when thousands of people reported seeing flying saucers and on two consecutive weekends in July, radar operators at Washington's National Airport reported UFOs on their radar screens, while pilots, both military and civilian, were watching the objects in the sky. In one case, during an attempted intercept by Air Force fighters, the situation got "real hairy."

Officially, and according to the government files, the sightings began at twenty minutes to midnight on July 20, 1952, when two radars at the Air Routing and Traffic Control Center (ARTC) at National Airport picked up eight targets near Andrews Air Force Base.

These objects were traveling too fast to be airplanes. First they moved along at only a hundred miles an hour but would accelerate to fantastic speeds. One of the

An aerial shot of Washington National Airport, where eight UFOs were detected in 1952; they were also observed at nearby Andrews AFB.

objects was tracked, according to the calculations made at the Center, at 7,000 miles an hour.

One of the controllers at the ARTC called for a senior controller, Harry C. Barnes, who in turn called the National Airport control tower. They had unidentified targets on their scopes, as did the controllers at Andrews Air Force Base. All three locations had eliminated a mechanical malfunction as the cause, and with the objects showing up on other scopes in other locations, there was no longer any question of their reality. The performance of the blips ruled out airplanes. All the men in the control tower that night, including Barnes, were sure they were looking at solid objects based on their years of experience with radar. If weather was the explanation, the targets would have varied from scope to scope, but apparently they did not.

According to the government files, about two in the morning on July 20, the Radar Officer, Captain Harold C. Way, at Andrews Approach Control learned that the ARTC had a target east of Andrews. He went outside and saw a strange light which he didn't believe to be a star. Later, however, he went back out, and this time decided that he was looking at a star. It is unclear if the second object was the same as the first.

The ARTC again told the controllers at Andrews that they still had the targets on their scopes. There is conflicting data in the government files because some reports suggest that the Andrews radar showed nothing, while other reports, also in the government files, claim they did.

The sightings lasted through the night, and during that time, the crews of several airliners also reported seeing the lights right where the radars showed them to be. Tower operators also saw them, and jet fighters were brought in for attempted intercepts. Associated Press stories written hours after the sightings claimed that no intercepts had been attempted that night, but those stories were inaccurate. Documents in the Project Blue Book files, as well as eye witnesses, confirm the attempted intercepts.

Typical of the sightings were those made by Captain Casey Pierman on Capital Airlines Flight 807. Pierman was on a flight between Washington and Martinsburg, West Virginia, at 1:15 A.M. on July 20, when he and the rest of his crew saw seven objects flash across the sky. Pierman said, "They were like falling stars without trails."

Capital Airline officials said that National Airport radar picked up the objects and asked Pierman to keep an eye on them. Shortly after takeoff, Pierman radioed that he had the objects in sight. He was flying at 180 to 200 mph, and reported the objects were traveling at tremendous speed. Official Air Force records in the government files confirm this.

> [P]ierman] was flying at 180 to 200 mph, and reported the objects were traveling at tremendous speed. Official Air Force records in the government files confirm this.

Another Capital Airlines pilot, Captain Howard Dermott, on Capital Flight 610, reported a single light following him from Herndon, Virginia, to within four miles of National Airport. Both the ARTC and the National Tower confirmed that an unidentified target followed the aircraft to within four miles of landing. At about the same time, Air Force radar at Andrews AFB was tracking eight additional unknown objects as they flew over the Washington area.

One of the most persuasive sightings came early in the morning, when one of the ARTC controllers called the Andrews Air Force Base control tower to tell them that there was a target south of the tower, over the Andrews Radio range station. The tower operators looked to the south where a "huge fiery-orange sphere" was hovering. This again was explained by the Air Force as a star.

Just before daylight, about four in the morning, after repeated requests from the ARTC, an F-94 interceptor arrived on the scene, but it was too little, too late. All the targets were gone. Although the flight crew made a short search of the local area, they found nothing unusual and returned to their base quickly.

During that night, the three radar facilities only once reported a target that was seen by all three facilities. There were, however, a number of times when the ARTC radar and the Washington National tower radars had simultaneous contact. It also seems that the radars were displaying the same targets observed by the crews of the two Capital Airlines flights. What it boils down to is that multiple radars and multiple eyewitnesses observed and reported objects in the sky over Washington, and this is confirmed in the government files.

Ruppelt, in *The Report on Unidentified Flying Objects*, wrote that during the week following the first round sightings at Washington National Airport, he spoke to Captain Roy James, a radar expert based at Wright-Patterson. James suggested that the sightings sounded as if the radar targets had been caused by weather. Later, Ruppelt wrote, "But Captain James has a powerful dislike for UFO's—especially on Saturday night."

The Washington Nationals—Round Two

The Saturday night on which James professed his dislike for UFOs was the second time, a week later and almost to the hour, the UFOs visited Washington National Airport. About 10:30 P.M. the same radar operators who had been on duty the week before once again spotted several slow moving targets. This time

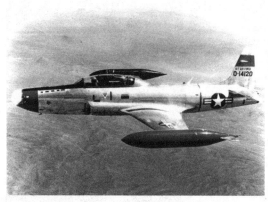

An F-94 interceptor like this one was dispatched to the scene after repeated requests from the ARTC to check out the UFOs.

the controllers carefully marked each of the unidentified objects so they could follow their progress. When they were all marked, they called the Andrews AFB radar facility. The unidentified targets were on their scope too.

An hour later, with targets being tracked continually, the controllers called for interceptors. Al Chop, the Pentagon spokesman for the UFO project, told UFO investigator Kevin Randle that he was in communication with the main basement command post at the Pentagon during the sightings. Chop requested that interceptors be sent. As a civilian, he could only suggest a course of action and then wait for the flag officer (general or admiral) in command at the Pentagon to make the official decision.

As happened the week before, there was a delay, but by midnight, two F-94s were on station over Washington. At that point, Chop asked the reporters who had assembled to observe to leave the radar room at National Airport because classified radio and intercept procedures would be in operation. Ruppelt in his book, commented, "I knew this was absurd because any radio ham worth his salt could build equipment and listen in on any intercept. The real reason for the press dismissal, I learned, was that not a few people in the radar room were positive that this night would be the big night in UFO history—the night when a pilot would close in on and get a good look at a UFO—and they didn't want the press to be in on it."

A second major witness talked to Randle later. Major Dewey Fournet, the Pentagon liaison between the UFO project in Dayton and the intelligence community in Washington, was also at National Airport along with Naval Lieutenant Holcomb, an electronics specialist assigned to the Air Force Directorate of Intelligence.

With Fournet and Holcomb in attendance, as well as the controllers at various facilities using radars, the F-94s arrived. The UFOs vanished from the scopes immediately. The jets were vectored to the last known position of the UFOs, but even though visibility in the area was unrestricted, the pilots could see nothing. The fighters made a systematic search of the area, but they were unable to find anything. Nothing showed on the radar either, and the pilots returned to their base.

Chop told Randle, "The minute the first two interceptors appeared on our scope all our unknowns disappeared. It was like they just wiped them all off. All our other flights, all the known flights were still on the scope … We watched these two planes leave. When they were out of our range, immediately we got our UFOs back."

Later, Air Force officers would learn that as the fighters appeared over Washington, people in the area of Langley Air Force Base, Virginia spotted weird lights in the sky. According to the government files, an F-94, in the area on a routine mission, was diverted to search for the light. The pilot saw a light and turned toward it, but it disappeared "like somebody turning off a light bulb."

The pilot continued the intercept and managed to get a radar lock on the now unlighted and unseen target. That was broken by the object as it sped away. The fighter continued the pursuit, obtaining two more radar locks on the object, but each time the locks were broken.

Back at Washington National, Air Defense Command was alerted again and once more fighters were sent out. This time the pilots were able to see the objects, vectored toward them by the air traffic controllers. But they could not close on the lights. The pilots saw no external details, other than observing lights where the radar suggested that something should be visible.

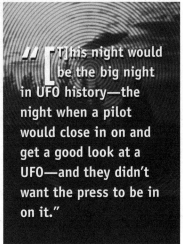

"[T]his night would be the big night in UFO history—the night when a pilot would close in on and get a good look at a UFO—and they didn't want the press to be in on it."

After several minutes of failure to close on a target, one of the lights was spotted lopping along. A fighter piloted by Lieutenant William Patterson turned, kicked in the afterburner and tried to catch the object. It disappeared before Patterson could see much of anything.

Interviewed the next day, Patterson said, "I tried to make contact with the bogies below one thousand feet, but they [the controllers] vectored us around. I saw several bright lights. I was at my maximum speed, but even then I had no closing speed. I ceased chasing them because I saw no chance of overtaking them. I was vectored into new objects. Later I chased a single bright light which I estimated about ten miles away. I lost visual contact with it...."

Al Chop remembered this intercept, as did Dewey Fournet. Chop said, "The flight controllers had directed him to them [the unknowns]. We had a little cluster of them. Five or six of them and he suddenly reports that he sees some lights.... He said they are very brilliant blue-white lights. He was going to try to close in to get a better look ... he flew into the area where they were clustered and he reported they were all around him."

Chop said that he, along with the others in the radar room, watched the intercept on the radar scope. They could see on the radar what the pilot was telling them.

Patterson had to break off the intercept, though there were still lights in the sky and objects on the scope. According to Chop, the pilot radioed that he was running low on fuel and turned around so that he could head back to his base.

Chop said the last of the objects disappeared from the scope about the time the sun came up. Ruppelt later quizzed Fournet about the activities that night. According to Ruppelt, Fournet and Holcomb, the radar expert, were convinced the targets were solid, metallic objects. Fournet told Ruppelt that there were weather-related targets on the scopes, but the controllers were ignoring them. Everyone was convinced that the targets were real.

Major General John A. Samford, chief of air intelligence, held a press conference to explain the sightings in Washington, D.C., but lack of information made it look as if the military was hiding something.

The situation was a repeat of the week before. Headlines around the world on Tuesday, July 29, told the whole story. In a banner headline that was more appropriate in a science fiction movie, *The Cedar Rapids Gazette* declared, "Saucers Swarm over Capital."

At 4:00 P.M., in Washington, D.C., Major General John A. Samford, chief of air intelligence, held a press conference. Of that conference, Ruppelt wrote, "General Samford made an honest attempt to straighten out the Washington National Sightings, but the cards were stacked against him. He had to hedge on many answers to questions from the press because he didn't know the answers. This hedging gave the impression that he was trying to cover up something more than just the fact his people fouled up in not fully investigating the sightings. Then he brought in Captain Roy James from ATIC to handle all the queries about radar. James didn't do any better because he'd just arrived in Washington that morning and didn't know very much more about the sightings than he'd read in the papers. Major Dewey Fournet and Lieutenant Holcomb, who had been at the airport during the sightings, who had observed all that had happened, were extremely conspicuous by their absence," as was the Pentagon spokesman on UFOs, Al Chop.

Major General John A. Samford, Chief of Air Intelligence, held a press conference. Of that conference, Ruppelt wrote, "General Samford made an honest attempt to straighten out the Washington National Sightings, but the cards were stacked against him. He had to hedge on many answers to questions from the press because he didn't know the answers."

Ruppelt notes that the press decided that Samford's suggestion that the sightings were weather related was the final answer. Ruppelt reported in 1956 that the sightings were still classified as unknowns in the Project Blue Book files.

Ruppelt wrote, "Some people said, 'Weather targets,' but the chances of a weather target's making a 180-degree turn just as an airplane turns into it, giving a radar lock-on, then changing speed to stay just out of the range of the airplane's radar, and then slowing down when the airplane leaves is as close to nil as you can get."

The series of sightings, on two separate nights, over the national capital, had to be explained by the military. After all, if flying saucers can flash through the sky at will, what good is an Air Force charged with keeping our skies free of the "enemy"? So the answer began to evolve, from it "sounds like a temperature inversion" to "it definitely was some kind of temperature inversion."

The Condon Committee and the Washington Nationals

When the University of Colorado assumed the task of investigating UFO sightings through a grant from the Air Force, the Washington National sightings were one of the few "classic" reports that demanded further attention. According to the final report of the Condon Committee, as it appears in the government files, "One of the earliest of our field trips (December 1966) was made to Washington, D.C., to interview separately two air traffic control operators who had been involved in the great UFO flap there in the summer of 1952. Fourteen years later, these two men were still quite annoyed at the newspaper publicity they had received, because it had tended to ridicule their reports. Our conclusion from this trip was that these men were telling in 1966 stories that were thoroughly consistent with the main points of their stories in 1952."

The University of Colorado scientists wrote, "There are a tremendous number of reports of UFOs observed on these two nights. In most of the instances visual observers, especially in scrambled aircraft, were unable to see targets indicated on ground radar, or to make airborne radar contact."

This is a strange observation because Michael Wertheimer, who conducted the preliminary investigation in over a day and half in December, 1966, for the Condon Committee, learned the truth. He spoke to Barnes, Andrews AFB tower operator Monte Banning, as well as other personnel who were on duty that night at both National Airport and Andrews. Writing of the sightings on July 20, Tad Foster of the Condon Committee noted, "Thus, Pierman, Dermott and Patterson [airline pilots and the interceptor pilot] each observed a visible light, and verbally described its position and/or motion which in turn correlated with the blip on the radar screen."

The official Condon Committee report also seems to be at odds with what Ruppelt and others reported, including those who were on the scene in July 1952 and what is available in the government files. Interceptor pilots did see the lights and onboard radars did lock onto solid objects. In one case, the ARTC radar returns vanished as the interceptors arrived on the scene, and once the fighters left, the objects returned. According to Ruppelt, the objects seemed to respond to the interceptor aircraft. Al Chop reported this as well. Weather-related phenomenon would not be adversely affected by the appearance of the fighters.

The University of Colorado report includes a number of eyewitness statements, including one from "A USAF Captain [undoubtedly Captain Harold C. Way] at Andrews AFB radar center." The unidentified captain reported:

> At about 0200 EST Washington Center advised that their radar had a target five miles east of Andrews Field. Andrews tower reported seeing a light, which changed color, and said it was moving towards Andrews. I went outside as no target appeared on Andrews radar and saw a light as reported by the tower. It was between 10 degrees and 15 degrees above the horizon and seemed to change color, from red to orange to green and red again. It seemed to float, but at times to dip suddenly and appear to lose

Dr. Edward Condon was a nuclear physicist who had worked on the Manhattan Project. He directed the Condon Committee from 1966 to 1968.

altitude. It did not have the appearance of any star I have ever observed before. At the time of the observation there was a star due east of my position. Its brilliance was approximately the same as the object and it appeared at about the same angle, 10 degrees to 15 degrees above the horizon. The star did not change color or have any apparent movement. I estimated the object to be between three and four miles east of Andrews Field at approximately 2,000 ft. During the next hour very few reports were received from Washington Center. [According to Washington Center's account, however, the 0200 EST object was seen on radar to pass over Andrews and fade out to the southwest of Andrews—G.D.T. (parenthetical statement in original government files)] At approximately 0300 EST I again went outside to look at the object. At this time both the star and the object had increased elevation had increased elevation by about 10 degrees. [The azimuth would have also increased about 10 degrees, so that the observed change was apparently equal to the sidereal rate, 15 degrees of right ascension per hour—G.D.T. (parenthetical statement in original)] The object had ceased to have any apparent movement, but still appeared to be changing color. On the basis of the second observation, I believe the unidentified object was a star.

Ruppelt, reporting on this, would write that the Andrews personnel had been pressured into altering their reports. The unidentifieds, on second thought, were definitely confirmed as being stars in the government files though there was no real justification for the alteration.

The University of Colorado study concluded, "The atmospheric conditions during the period ... in the Washington, D.C., area, was conducive to anomalous propagation of radar signals.... The unidentified radar returns obtained during the incidents were most likely the result of anomalous propagation (AP).... The visual objects were, with one or two possible exceptions, identifiable most probably as meteors and scintilling stars."

In Appendix L to the final (Condon) report, Loren W. Crow, a certified consulting meteorologist, wrote:

> It is the author's opinion that hot, humid air prevailed on both nights in both Washington and Norfolk. The general weather would have been considered fair weather by the trained observers at the various airports

and they may not have reported all the scattered clouds which actually existed. It would have been considered an "easy shift." Visibilities remained above six miles at all times. The horizontal movement of scattered clouds, plus formation and dissipation of some few low clouds, both could have been seen at various times by ground observers whose eyes were well adjusted to the darkened sky. Anomalous propagation could have been observed on weather radar units during both nights at both locations. The echoes due to anomalous propagation would have had horizontal motion similar to clouds.

Interestingly, the two Pentagon personnel Randle interviewed later, Major Dewey Fournet and Al Chop, disagreed with the weather-related explanation. Both were sure, based on their observations in the radar room, that the returns showed solid objects. Both were listening to Holcomb, the acknowledged expert in radar who was also present in the room. In fact, Chop said that he was unimpressed with the analysis made by a man from over a thousand miles away and fifteen years after the fact.

In 1952, the sightings over Washington National were classified in the government files

Scientific Study of Unidentified Flying Objects

The complete report on the study conducted by the University of Colorado under research contract number F44620-67-C-0035 with the U.S. Air Force

Dr. Edward U. Condon
University of Colorado, Project Director

Introduction by
Walter Sullivan
of
The New York Times

The official Condon Committee report, published in 1969, concluded that UFO research would likely never discover anything of importance.

as unidentified. Those in the various radar rooms reported the objects they saw were solid and metallic, not the sort of returns caused by temperature inversions. Pilots ordered to intercept spotted objects were able to obtain radar locks, albeit temporarily. Airline pilots saw the lights and reported them to the radar facilities.

Equally interesting is that these sightings, which fit the criterion set up for the Status Reports (multiple, qualified witnesses; radar data; and performance by the UFOs that suggested a technology ahead of what was available at the time) did not rate a mention in those reports. The first Status Report to be published after the Washington Nationals dealt more with administrative details, analysis of statistical information, and definitions of the terms used in the report.

Status Report No. 8

There is nothing particularly significant in Status Report No. 8, other than it broke the cycle of reports of one each month to one per quarter. As noted, Status Report No. 7 had been issued on May 31, 1952, and No. 8 came out on December 31, 1952.

In this report, the Air Force blames the increase in sightings on the publicity given UFOs by respected national magazines. According to the government files:

> A noticeable increase in reports started in Jun [sic] 52 and reached a peak on 28 Jul 52 when 43 reports were received ... Much of the increased volume of reports can be accredited [sic, attributed] to widespread publicity given by Life, Time, Look and many other magazines and newspapers. One noticeable characteristic of the reports is that in general the quality has improved, a factor which resulted from the distribution of Air Force Letter 200-5, Subject: "Reporting of Unidentified Flying Objects," and to widespread briefings given by Project Blue Book Briefing teams.

Such a conclusion is open to interpretation and there simply might be no causal relation. The chart provided in the government files seems to indicate that the first article, which provided a "solution" to the question of UFOs, resulted in a minor increase in the number of sightings. The *Life* magazine article seemed to precede a dip in sightings while the *Look* article preceded a mild increase.

While there is a slow increase in sightings, the first big jump comes nearly a month after the *Look* article, and everything seemed to peak with the news reports on the Washington National sightings. Interestingly, the overall peak comes just prior to the press conference held in Washington about the sightings there. The number of sightings dropped off sharply at that point, though the UFO reports were still circulating. The number being reported to the Air Force was down, which could be related to the press conference held by Major General John A. Samford. It was described as the largest Air Force press conference since the end of the Second World War.

According to the government files:

> On 29 Jul 52 a press conference was held in the Pentagon to answer the many questions that were being directed to the Air Force by the press. The conference was held by Major General John A. Samford, Director of Intelligence, USAF. Others participating were Major General Roger M. Ramey, Director of Operations, USAF, and officers of the Air Technical Intelligence Center.

In essence General Samford stated that to date there were no indications that any of the reported objects that could not be identified constitute a menace to the United States. However, the Air Force would continue to give the subject "adequate, but not frantic attention."

There is a special report, buried inside which is a survey of 44 astronomers regarding UFOs. It was conducted by an unnamed professional astronomer, but who was clearly Dr. J. Allen Hynek, the consultant to Project Blue Book. Of the professionals surveyed, five had "observed objects or phenomena they could not readily explain."

Eight astronomers from the group surveyed said they were very interested in UFOs, while seven said they were completely indifferent to them. Hynek noted,

"The great majority were neither hostile nor overly interested...." Their concern seemed to be the reaction by their fellow astronomers or the new media to the idea that an astronomer had seen a UFO. They seemed to think that one headline suggesting an astronomer had seen a UFO would brand that astronomer "as questionable among his colleagues."

The end of the report contained a summary of some of the reports that had been received between the end of May and the end of October, 1952. Typical of these is a report from Los Alamos, New Mexico on July 29. According to the government file:

> At approximately 0949 MST on 29 July 1952, several pilots and guards from Los Alamos observed an UFO. The object was flying straight and level at high speed north of the Los Alamos landing field. The object, which was a shiny metallic color, was observed for 30 minutes with binoculars.
>
> Fighters in the Los Alamos area were diverted to the area of the sighting and visually vectored toward the object. The object disappeared but reap-

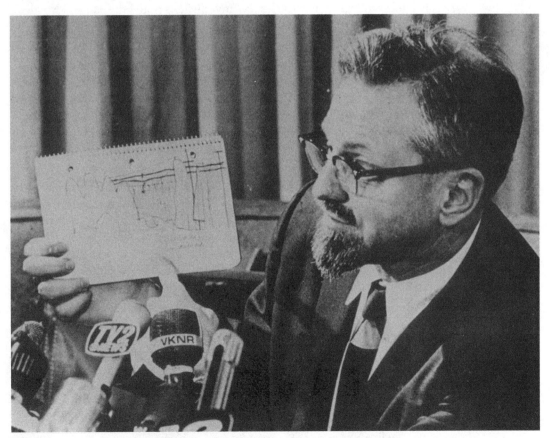

Dr. J. Allen Hynek was the founder and head of the Center for UFO Studies in 1973. Before that, he seerved as a consultant to government investigations into UFOs.

peared in front of the flights, and a 360 degree turn. The fighters did not observe the object. The aircraft were at 40,000' left vapor trail, but the object did not.

They classified this as an "unknown," but noted that "there is hardly enough data to evaluate the report."

The other reports were equally uninteresting. What was missing, of course, was any mention of the Washington National sightings, which, because of the multiple witnesses and radar observations available, were the most interesting. The Air Force, however, had decided that weather related phenomena were the most likely answer and because of this, the sightings were ignored in this Status Report.

Status Report No. 13 (aka Special Report 14)

While Status Report No. 12, dated September 30, 1953 was the last to be published, there was a Special Report No. 14 available in May 1955, which was finally published in October 1955. UFO investigators noted the gap and wondered about Status Report No. 13. What happened to it? Did it contain some kind of special, highly classified information that had been ignored in the earlier reports and that was unnecessary in the statistical analysis that made up Special Report No. 14?

Like the Estimate of the Situation that Ruppelt mentioned in his book, Special Report No. 13 was not seen by many. It was just a rumor based on speculation; that is, until a witness surfaced, a man who had seen the report, who had been required by his job to study it, and prepare an analysis of it. Bill English, would, in the late 1980s, tell a few people what he had seen and what he knew about this document.

William "Bill" English said that he was a former Special Forces captain who had served in Southeast Asia and who had been assigned to work with the Royal Air Force at one point. He said that he had led a team into Laos to recover the bodies from a B-52 that had crashed during the Vietnam War. Radio reports alleged to have come from the pilots, saying that they were under attack by a UFO. The aircraft was intact, sitting in the jungle, but the bodies had been badly mutilated. The suggestion was that the mutilations have been carried out by alien creatures.

According to the information provided by English, he received a terminal assignment in Germany, where he was honorably discharged in 1973. He, along with his wife, a teacher, remained in Germany until she was sent on to RAF Chicksands. English accompanied her and there ran into his former commanding officer, who offered him a job. He remained in that job until July 1976.

As part of his new job, English apparently had the opportunity to review the more than 600 pages of Blue Book Special Report No. 13. It had arrived in a diplomatic pouch. He said that it was an eight-by-eleven-inch document with a gray cover with a date of 1953. It was stamped in red ink, "Top Secret, Need to Know Only, Cryto Clearance 14 Required."

The table of contents provided more information about the nature of the document. It said:

Part 1. On Design of Generators to Accomplish Strain Free Molecular Translation.

Chapter 1: Design Criterion for a Simple Generator and Control System Referring to Equation 17 Appendix A.

Chapter 2: Reports of UFO Encounters, Classifications, "Close Encounters of the 1st Kind," subtitle: Sightings and Witnesses.

Chapter 3: Military Encounters with UFOs

Part 2. The Generation of Space Time Discontinuums, Closed, Opened and Folded.

Chapter 1: Continuation of Einstein's Theory of Relativity to Final Conclusion.

Chapter 2: Close Encounters of the 2nd Kind, subtitle UFO Sightings Witnessed in Close Proximity.

Chapter 3: Military Reports Concerning Sightings on Radar and Electronic Surveillance of UFOs.

Subsection 2: Analysis Report, J. Allen Hynek, Lt. Col. Robert Friend.

Appendix—Continued on for about five pages. Opening page consisted of the findings as written by Lt. Col. Friend and His Analysis.

Part 3. On the Generation of Temporary Pseudo Acceleration Locas.

Chapter 1: Possible Applications of Einstein's Theory of Relativity at Conclusion.

Chapter 2: Close Encounters of the 3rd Kind, subtitle, UFO Encounters and Extraterrestrial Life Forms Witnessed and Personal Encounters. Subtitle: Colonies, Relocations Thereof.

English then said that he had to stress the point that this version had been annotated. There were inserts added after the report had been initially printed, which was a very neat way of explaining how a rating system that hadn't existed in 1953 had been included in the document.

According to English, it was clear to him that those who had reported genuine Close Encounters of the Third Kind (CE3) were moved in the middle of the night and relocated to sites in the Midwest and the Northwest. He said that in many cases these people exhibited some sort of physical problem associated with their experiences. He did not explain why these people were moved and why their experiences did not leak into the mainstream. He did not explain what had happened to them.

English also told of some of the cases in the report. In one of them, from March 1956 (or three years after the report was written), Major William Cunningham and Staff Sergeant Jonathan P. Lovette, stationed at the White Sands Missile

It was just a rumor based on speculation. That is, until a witness surfaced, a man who had seen the report....

ranch, encountered a UFO early one morning. According to the report, they were down range, looking for missile debris when Lovette walked over a short sand dune. Cunningham heard him scream, as if in terror or agony, and thinking that Lovette had been bitten by a snake, ran to the top of the dune. He saw Lovette being dragged to a silver, disk-shaped object, which hovered some ten to fifteen feet in the air. Lovette was carried inside and the craft lifted off, disappearing quickly. Cunningham used the jeep's radio to report what he had seen and was told that there was a radar contact with the object.

Search parties were sent out but it was three days before Lovette's nude body was discovered. The body had been mutilated in ways that mimicked reports by ranchers about missing cattle that they had found. This was clearly an attempt to draw a parallel between this event and the animal mutilations that began to be reported in the 1970s. There was an additional note indicating that birds feeding on the body had died after ingesting the flesh.

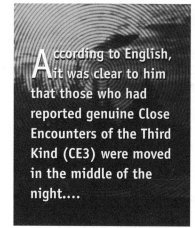

According to English, it was clear to him that those who had reported genuine Close Encounters of the Third Kind (CE3) were moved in the middle of the night....

According to English, there were a number of teams devoted to the recovery of crashed UFOs and collection of evidence from landings and sightings. Recovery Team Alpha was the primary team and they were based, again according to English, at Wright-Patterson Air Force Base.

This information conflicts with what was said by Brigadier General Arthur Exon, the base commander at Wright-Patterson in the 1960s. Exon told UFO investigator Don Schmitt, when asked if they [Air Force personnel sent out on UFO investigations] came from Wright-Pat, "they would come from Washington, D.C., and they'd ask for an airplane tomorrow morning and that would give the guys a chance to get there by commercial airline to meet them. The airplane would take off at such and such a time. Sometimes they'd be gone for three days and sometimes they'd be gone for a week."

Schmitt specifically asked if the men had been assigned to Wright-Patterson, and Exon said, "No."

This information from Exon, who would have known the truth, came after English had made his claims about Special Report 13. If the document was real, then the information in it should have been accurate. The team that Exon mentioned was not based in Ohio.

More important than the identity of the teams was a segment of the report that dealt with the alien creatures. These photographs were high quality and in color. The naked body was laid out on an autopsy table. It was about four feet tall, had a rounded cranium that was described as slightly enlarged, eyes that were almond shaped, slits for nostrils, a small mouth, and holes for ears. The creature was a bluish-gray.

English claimed that Hynek was involved in this report, providing a description that suggested the creature had come from what was termed a UFO capture.

Hynek, it was clear, did not see the creature, only the photographs of it, and he signed the report, again, according to English.

Other claims from this report were that there were seventeen different alien species involved in the UFO sightings. They were referred to as ALFs or Alien Life Forms. One of the captured or recovered UFOs, flown by two Air Force pilots, reached the upper atmosphere but then exploded.

The reality of all this is based on the credibility of the witness. No one other than English has made claims to having seen the report. If English served in the Special Forces as an officer, as he said, that would certainly say something about his character. He certainly could have led a team into Laos to recover the remains from the B-52 incident he described, and if he was who he said he was, military records would exist to verify his claims of military service.

Military records are simple to check. There is a huge repository in St. Louis that houses the military records of nearly all who have served, whether the term of service lasted just two or three years or for more than twenty or thirty. According to these files, William S. English served as an enlisted man for just over five years and was discharged as PFC or E-3 in 1974. There is no indication that he had any Special Forces training, or any of the years of training necessary for the Special Forces, no record of overseas service, and no awards or decorations other than the National Defense Service Medal, which is given to everyone who served in the military during a specified time in relation to hostile activities. Conspicuous by its absence is a Good Conduct Medal, awarded to enlisted soldiers for three years of unblemished service. English's relatively low rank at discharge and the lack of the Good Conduct Medal suggest that his service was not without a few problems. Of course, those records are protected by the Privacy Act of 1974.

The argument usually made is that the records have been altered to ruin English's credibility as a witness. The problem with this theory is that it would be impossible to find every single bit of evidence and alter it. Military officers have their names published in an index that is then distributed to various libraries. In order to alter the index, every single book would need to be located, destroyed, and then reprinted, and not just for a single year. Their names appear in documents at training sites, on promotion orders which often contain the names of others promoted at the same time, in yearbooks, and on

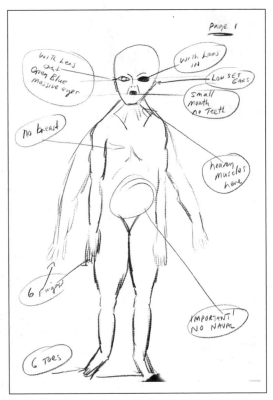

A drawing by filmmaker Spyros Melaris shows his concept of what an Alien Life Form (ALF) would look like.

awards and decorations, many of which are published as general orders and are in the hands of tens of thousands of military personnel. A soldier should have dozens of documents to prove the point. As it stands, English has offered nothing to support his claims and the latest information is that he has dropped out of sight.

The Real Special Report No. 13

UFO researcher Brad Sparks, among many others, believes that, in the beginning, there was a Special Report No. 13. It was part of Project Stork, which was the Battelle study of data accumulated by the Air Force. The history of the study, the timing of its inception, and the attitude that it created might help to understand the real nature of the mythical Special Report No. 13.

> English has offered nothing to support his claims and the latest information is that he has dropped out of sight.

Not long after Ruppelt took over Project Grudge, which, of course, evolved into Project Blue Book, he, along with Colonel S. H. Kirkland, a member of ATIC, met with the staff at the Battelle Memorial Institute. This was a think tank in Columbus, Ohio, and asked them for assistance with the changes in the Air Force investigation of UFOs. Battelle agreed. The study would have two parts. One part would focus on estimating the value of reliable eyewitness testimony, such as how much a person can be expected to see and accurately remember. The second was a statistical analysis of UFO reports.

Project Stork was another classified study of the Soviet Union's technological warfare abilities by Battelle. The UFO study was incorporated into his ongoing research. There were five requirements, including providing consultants, improving the questionnaire, analyzing the existing reports, subscribing to a clipping service, and advising the sponsor monthly, or in this case, provide Blue Book with the information.

Interestingly, Ruppelt, in his book, mentioned the clipping service, which was implemented in either late 1951 or early 1952. According to the government files, the new "interrogation form" was published in the December 31, 1952 Blue Book Status Report No. 8. That was the first report that included any sort of statistical data, even though those data were quite raw and less than helpful.

The data used for Stork came from the military or completed copies of the questionnaire, which, again were indirectly from the military. There were 3,201 sightings from Projects Sign, Grudge, and Blue Book. The sightings were grouped into balloons, astronomical, light phenomenon, birds, clouds and dust, insufficient information, psychological, unknown, and other.

Once all the sightings had been categorized by a team member, another would do the same, but without knowing the original conclusion. If both agreed on the explanation, the report was considered solved. If they disagreed, the whole panel examined the case, or if both listed an event as "unknown," it was evaluated by everyone.

The statistical analysis completed by Stork personnel found, according to the government files, "no trends, patterns, or correlations," which meant that "the probability that any of the unknowns considered in this study are 'flying saucers' is concluded to be extremely small, since the most complete and reliable reports from the present data, when isolated and studied, conclusively failed to reveal even a rough model."

In other words, there was nothing in the data to suggest that any of the sightings, even the truly "unknown," led to a conclusion that some UFOs might be alien. The problem was that while the statistical analysis might have been over the heads of the general public or the reporters who wrote about it, others who did understand it studied it. According to this review, a third of the sightings labeled as "un-

The Battelle Memorial Institute in Columbus, Ohio, served as the think tank that assisted with the government investigation into UFOs.

known" were sightings with a high reliability. The analysis showed that there was little likelihood that the unknowns were similar to the knowns, which meant that some of them could be alien spacecraft, something the study authors refused to admit.

When others analyzed the data from the report, their conclusions differed from the ones supposedly drawn by the Battelle engineers and scientists. J. Allen Hynek wrote that the report "completely disregards the results of these tests almost brazenly, as if they did not exist." The results were incredible.

The document was published as Special Report No. 14, which is often considered to be one of the Status Reports that began 1951. The history seems to suggest that it was not part of the Status Reports, having begun about the same time as those were initiated. Although some of the suggestions, such as creating a new questionnaire, appear in the Status Reports, it doesn't seem as if Special Report No. 14 belongs in the sequence. It was something completed concurrently with those Status Reports.

However, there is one troubling question. Status Report No. 1 was dated November 30, 1951, and Status Report No. 2 was dated December 31, 1951. There is another document in the government files labeled as Special Report No. 1 and dated December 28, 1951. According to the document itself, "This is a special report on the investigation of the sighting of an unidentified aerial object. Special reports such as this will be made on outstanding incidents and in incidents where such a report is requested by higher authority."

This Special Report concerned a short series of sightings on September 10 and 11, 1951, over Fort Monmouth, New Jersey, and it included both visual sightings and radar sightings. The conclusions were:

The unidentified aircraft reported by the T-33 pilots was probably a balloon launched by the Evans Signal Laboratory a few minutes before the T-33 arrived in the area.

The 1110 EDST [sic] radar sighting on 10 September 1951 was not necessarily a high-speed aircraft. Its speed was judged only by the operator's inability to use aided tracking and this was possibly due to the operator being excited, and not the high speed of the aircraft.

The 1515 EDST radar sighting on 10 September 1951 was a weather balloon.

The 1050 EDST radar sighting on 11 September 1951 was a weather balloon.

The 1330 EDST radar sighting on 11 September 1951 remains unknown but it was very possible that it was due to anomalous propagation and/or the student radar operators' thoughts that there was a great deal of activity of unusual objects in the area.

The Special Report does contain solutions for this series of sightings. According to the report:

A. The unidentified aircraft reported by the T-33 pilots was probably a balloon launched by the Evans Signal Laboratory a few minutes before the T-33 arrived in the area.

B. The 1110 EDST radar sighting on 10 September 1951 was not necessarily a very high-speed aircraft. Its speed was judged only by the operator's inability to use aided tracking and this was possible due to the operator being excited, not the high speed of the aircraft.

C. The 1515 EDST radar sighting on 10 September 1951 was a weather balloon.

D. The 1050 EDST radar sighting on 11 September 1951 was a weather balloon.

E. The 1330 EDST radar sighting on 11 September remains unknown but it was very possible that it was due to anomalous propagation and/or the student radar operators' thoughts that there was a great deal of activity of unusual objects in the air.

When the Project Blue Book files were consolidated and declassified, all the sightings were explained. The probable and possible were dropped, and all the remaining sightings were explained away as weather balloons and anomalous propagation. There are no indications in the government files that the answers were changed from what was little more than speculation to make it appear as if the reports contained final, definitive answers.

It should be noted here that there were three different types of reports being issued. There were the Project Stork reports that covered the gathering of the statistical data, the Status Reports from Project Grudge and later Blue Book that provided data on some of the UFO sightings but not all, and the Special Reports that covered single reports that demanded additional investigation. All these projects and reports ran concurrently.

In the context of the situation, the answers offered in the reports are not of real importance here. The bigger issue is that neither Special Report No. 1 nor the Project Stork Reports are part of the Status Report system. This seems to have created some confusion. As it stands now, there is a Special Report No. 1, seven Project Stork Reports, and twelve Project Grudge/Blue Book Status reports. There is no evidence that a Status Report 13 existed. For some reason, the numbering jumps from 12 to 14. It is possible that a regular report 13 was scheduled to be issued before the completion of Blue Book Special Report 14.

In which case, Blue Book Status Report 13 is, in fact, Blue Book Special Report 14. In this context, Report 13 never existed.

But this leads to an interesting question. If the Status Reports stopped after 12, and there is a Special Report 1, what happened to reports 2 through 13?

The FBI Files

Within a couple of weeks of Kenneth Arnold's sighting near Mount Rainier, Washington, Army Air Forces requested that the FBI assist them in the investigation. The Army didn't want the FBI to investigate the UFO sightings, but instead investigate the people who were reporting them. In a letter dated July 10, 1947, with the topic of "Flying Discs," FBI agent E. G. Fitch wrote:

> General Schulgen indicated to Reynolds that the Air Corps has taken the attitude that every effort must be undertaken in order to run down and ascertain whether or not the flying disks are a fact, and, if so, to learn all about them. According to General Schulgen, the Air Corps Intelligence are utilizing all of their scientists in order to ascertain whether or not such phenomenon could in fact occur. He stated that this research is being conducted with the thought that the flying objects might be a celestial phenomenon and with the view that they might be a foreign body mechanically devised and controlled.

> General Schulgen also indicated to Reynolds that all Air Corps installations have been alerted to run out each reported sighting to obtain all possible data to assist in this research project. In passing, General Schulgen stated that an Air Corps pilot who believed that he saw one of these objects was thoroughly interrogated by General Schulgen and scientists, as well as a psychologist, and the pilot was adamant in his claim that he saw a flying disk.

> General Schulgen advised Reynolds that the possibility exists that the first reported sightings of the so-called flying disks are fallacious and prompted by individuals seeking personal publicity, or were reported for political reasons. He stated that if this was so, subsequent sightings might be the result of mass hysteria. He pointed out that the thought exists that the first reported sightings might have been by individuals of Communist sympathies with the view to causing hysteria and fear of a secret Russian weapon.

> General Schulgen indicated to Reynolds that he is desirous of having all the angles covered in this matter. He stated that reports of his scientists and findings of the various Air Corps installations will be available in his office. He advised that to complete the picture he desired the assistance of the Federal Bureau of Investigation in locating and questioning the individuals who first sighted the so-called flying disks in order to ascertain

whether their statements were prompted by personal desire for publicity or political reasons. General Schulgen assured Reynolds that there are no War Department or Navy Department research projects presently being conducted which could in any way be tied up with the flying disks. General Schulgen indicated to Reynolds that if the Bureau would cooperate with him in his matter, he would offer all the facilities of his office as to the results obtained in the effort to identify and run down this matter.

Reynolds advised General Schulgen that his request would be made known to the Bureau and an answer made available to him as soon as possible.

Reynolds also discussed this matter with Colonel L. R. Forney of MID. Colonel Forney indicated that it was his attitude that in as much as it has been established that the flying disks are not the result of any Army or Navy experiments, the matter is of interest to the FBI. He stated that he was of the opinion that the Bureau, if at all possible, should accede to General Schulgen's request.

It is clear from this letter that the Army, at the highest levels, did not know what the flying disks were, only that they weren't a product of anyone's secret experimentation inside the United States. Although it was possible that they were of Soviet manufacture, no one believed this explanation because the Soviets would not risk exposing the technology to the Americans if one of the objects crashed or was shot down. Any advantage held by the Soviets would be easily lost through reverse engineering.

It is clear from this letter that the Army, at the highest levels, did not know what the flying disks were....

It is interesting that Schulgen suggested that the sightings might be some sort of Soviet trick to create hysteria. There was no information that those reporting these objects had any real political agenda and it quickly became clear that such a theory was without merit.

Even with some of the outrageous claims in the letter, there were a number of comments on it that made sense. David Ladd, an assistant director at the FBI, recommended that they not become involved in the investigations. Even at that early stage, Ladd believed that there was nothing to the sightings. He wrote, "I would recommend that we advise the Army that the Bureau does not believe it should go into these investigations, it being noted that a great bulk of those alleged discs reported found have been pranks."

But Clyde Tolson, the number two man at the FBI, wrote on July 15, "I think we should do this."

And most important, J. Edgar Hoover wrote, "I would do it but before agreeing to it we must insist upon full access to discs recovered. For instance in the L.A. case the Army grabbed it & would not let us have it for cursory examination."

This document establishes two things. First, there was a real interest in finding out what the flying discs were, and who they belonged to, and second, that the government was taking all of this very seriously. The tone of the letter and its contents suggest that all available resources were being used. It also hints that there was a real sense of urgency by the U.S. government, especially the Army.

But it also says something else. Ladd thought that the reports, referring specifically to those of flying disc crashes, were made up of hoaxes and pranks. Looking at the newspaper reports and the government files of the time, this was a legitimate conclusion at that time.

Starting on July 6, 1947, or four days before the Fitch letter was written, there were a number of UFO crash reports in the press. Some of them received national attention while others were of more regional or local interest. But the Army, tasked with learning something about the flying discs, certainly would have been gathering information from around the country.

Clyde Tolson (left) is shown here with FBI director J. Edgar Hoover. He encouraged Hoover to have the FBI assist in UFO investigations.

On July 6, 1947, it was reported in the *San Diego Union* that John Kuder had seen a "luminous flying disc" circling about a half mile off Mission Beach. It then dipped into the ocean. There was a sudden ball of fire that faded out rapidly. While there are no indications that the military thought this sighting was a hoax, there was nothing in the government files about it, either.

One of the stories to receive national attention appeared on July 7. Vernon Baird, a pilot flying over the Tobacco Root Mountains in western Montana, claimed that he had seen a formation of "clamshell-shaped" objects. He was flying at 32,000 feet and at about 360 miles an hour when one of the craft that was pearl gray, with a Plexiglas dome on top, was caught in his prop wash and went spiraling to the ground.

With him was one witness, George Sutton, a professional photographer. Suttin did not do anything when the objects appeared, photographing nothing that would provide any corroboration for the story. The next day, J. J. Archer, Baird's boss, said that the whole thing was a hoax.

Finally, on July 7, Lloyd Bennett said that he heard something fall through the trees and found a small disk about six or seven inches in diameter and about an eighth of an inch thick. He said that he was going to notify the Army and claim the reward. Over the July 4 weekend there had been reports of three offers, by three separate and private organizations, of a thousand dollars each for answers to the flying disc mystery. All of the reward offers expired quickly and no one ever made a serious claim for any of them.

Each of these cases was vague, without any real detail, other than the fact that someone observed something in the distance. Importantly, none of them fit the note made by Hoover about the "La. case" when the "Army grabbed it" and didn't allow the FBI to take a look at it.

This report did make it into the government files, and it sparked something of a controversy with the Roswell UFO crash case, which was not mentioned in the government files until much later. It was the handwritten "La." which, given the sloppy nature of Hoover's handwriting, could be interpreted a number of ways including Sw, Sov or 2a.

According to the government files, on July 7, 1947, near Shreveport, Louisiana, a man named Harston said that he:

> … had heard the disc whirling through the air and had looked up in time to see it when it was approximately two hundred feet in the air and was coming over a sign board adjacent to the used car lot where he was standing … [Harston] stated that smoke and fire were coming from the disc and that it was traveling at a high rate of speed and that it fell into the street.

The following day, on July 8, 1947, Army investigators talked to another witness who told them that it was all a joke that he had played on his boss. He had made the disc from parts that included a florescent light and two condensers from electric fans. He said that he had thrown the disc so that it sailed over his boss' car but the man failed to see it and drove away. He said that he believed that anyone who saw the disc would know that it was harmless.

He had made the disc from parts that included a florescent light and two condensers from electric fans.

Interestingly, there is another document in the government files dated "10 July 47—Major Carlau … says the FBI advises this was a hoax." This suggests that the FBI had not been cut out of the investigation, making it difficult to ascertain what Hoover meant when he said that the Army had grabbed it and wouldn't let the FBI have it.

In fact, a document in the government files said, "FBI resident agent cma [meaning comma] Shreveport cma was informed and contacted FBI officer cma New Orleans cma by phone cma made initial report and later informed that office that discovery was a hoax and rendered complete report of investigation pd [period]."

The controversy over the interpretation of the notation by Hoover was cleared up by another document in the FBI files. On July 24, 1947, E. G. Fitch sent an "Office Memorandum" to D. M. Ladd. The note by Hoover was now typed and it said, "La." It is quite clear from the evidence that Hoover is referring to the Shreveport hoax of July 7.

In that same memo, the FBI was assured by Schulgen that they would be granted access to all the discs recovered and that, from time to time "make the results of the studies of his scientists available to the Bureau for the assistance of the FBI Field Officers."

The memo noted, "General Schulgen indicated to Mr. [name redacted, but is probably Reynolds] that here has been a decrease in the reported sightings of the discs which might be because of the fact that it has lost much of its publicity value."

The problem here, however, is that on July 9, 1947, the day after the announcement that a flying saucer had been recovered in Roswell, and after Brigadier General Roger Ramey's declaration in Fort Worth that it was just a weather balloon, both the Army and the Navy issued new instructions. Newspapers from all over the nation published a United Press story that announced, "Reports of flying saucers whizzing through the sky fell off sharply today as the Army and the Navy began a concentrated campaign to stop the rumors." Schulgen was apparently unaware of this.

The FBI Investigations Begin

While the FBI was negotiating with General Schulgen about the role they would play in UFO investigations, some of their agents were already involved with a photographic case from Phoenix, Arizona. On July 7, 1947, the Rhodes photographs were announced in a Phoenix newspaper.

As noted earlier, the government files reveal a long investigation into the Rhodes photographs, including evidence of assistance by the FBI and attempts by the government to smear his name. According to the government files, on July 14, 1947, Lynn C. Aldrich, a special agent in the Army's counterintelligence corps (CIC), wrote, "On 8 July 1947, this agent obtained pictures of [an] unidentifiable object...."

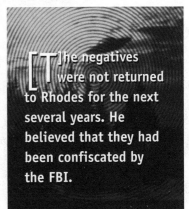

[T]he negatives were not returned to Rhodes for the next several years. He believed that they had been confiscated by the FBI.

Later, when Fugate asked for the negatives, Rhodes said that he would deliver them to the FBI. Rhodes apparently went to the FBI office on August 20, 1947, to provide the negatives. The FBI made it clear that they were acting on behalf of the Army and that the negatives would be sent on to the Fourth Army Headquarters.

To complicate matters, the negatives were not returned to Rhodes for the next several years. He believed that they had been confiscated by the FBI. On October 9, 1966, Dr. James McDonald seemed to confirm this when he wrote to Rhodes, "About all one can say is that the timing is (2–3 weeks after the FBI confiscation of your negatives) to make the story entirely plausible."

To be fair, it must be noted that the failure to return the negatives was most probably a mistake rather than an attempt to "confiscate" them by the government. However, when Rhodes asked for the negatives back in 1952, some five years later, the Air Force decided that "we have concluded that the photos were probably not authentic. It seems as if Mr. Rhodes attempted to get on the "picture selling band wagon" and if he can prove he sent the negatives to ATIC or to the Air Force and they were never returned, it may lead to a touchy situation."

The Hottel Memo

It happened again in 2012. Someone unfamiliar with the history of FBI investigations into UFO sightings and UFO crashes came across a memo dated March 22, 1950, and thought that it had not been seen before. The news media wondered if this was proof that something had crashed near Roswell, New Mexico, in 1947.

The Memorandum was written by Guy Hottel, the SAC (Special Agent in Charge) in Washington, and was sent to the Director, FBI, J. Edgar Hoover, with a subject line of "Flying saucers, information concerning." It said:

An investigator for the Air Forces [sic] stated that three so-called flying saucers had been recovered in New Mexico. They were described as being circular in shape with raised centers, approximately 50 feet in diameter. Each was occupied by three bodies of human shape but only 3 feet tall, dressed in metallic cloth of a very fine texture. Each body was bandaged in a manner similar to the blackout suits used by speed flyers and test pilots.

According to Mr. [redacted], informant, the saucers were found in New Mexico due to the fact that the Government has a very high-powered radar set-up in that area and it is believed the radar interferes with the controling [sic] mechanism of the saucers.

No further evaluation was attempted by SA [redacted] concerning the above.

This memo however, has nothing to do with the Roswell case, but refers to the Aztec, New Mexico, crash of March 25, 1948. The information about the three crashes, about the radar interference, and the bodies being tiny humans comes from Frank Scully's 1950 book, *Behind the Flying Saucers*. The book, and the information in it, was discredited by several investigations, including that by J. P. Cahn in 1952, Mike McClelland in 1976, and several others. Very few inside the UFO community

The Book Everyone Is Talking About

BEHIND THE FLYING SAUCERS

Frank Scully

Scully's claims in his 1950 book have been largely discredited.

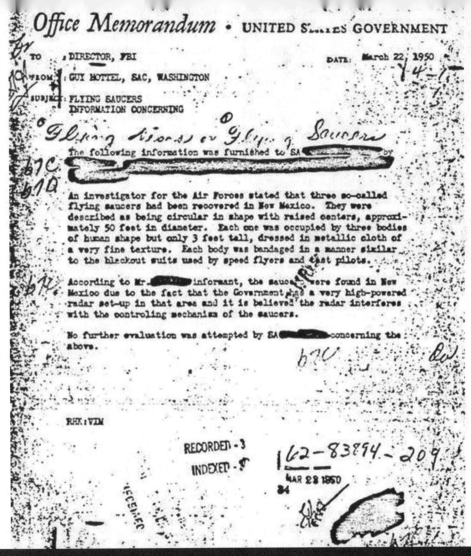

Office Memorandum • UNITED STATES GOVERNMENT

TO : DIRECTOR, FBI   DATE: March 22, 1950

FROM : GUY HOTTEL, SAC, WASHINGTON

SUBJECT: FLYING SAUCERS
         INFORMATION CONCERNING

"Flying Disos or Flying Saucers

The following information was furnished to SA ▓▓▓▓▓▓▓▓ by

An investigator for the Air Forces stated that three so-called
flying saucers had been recovered in New Mexico. They were
described as being circular in shape with raised centers, approximately 50 feet in diameter. Each one was occupied by three bodies
of human shape but only 3 feet tall, dressed in metallic cloth of
a very fine texture. Each body was bandaged in a manner similar
to the blackout suits used by speed flyers and test pilots.

According to Mr. ▓▓▓▓▓ informant, the saucers were found in New
Mexico due to the fact that the Government has a very high-powered
radar set-up in that area and it is believed the radar interferes
with the controling mechanism of the saucers.

No further evaluation was attempted by SA ▓▓▓▓▓ concerning the
above.

RHK:VLM

RECORDED - 3
INDEXED - 5

162-83894-209
MAR 23 1950
54

The Hottel memo is actually not about Roswell, but rather the Aztec, New Mexico, crash, and the information in it comes from Scully's discredited book.

believe that Aztec reflects a real UFO crash. Most believe it to be a hoax.

In a few years someone else, new to UFO investigation, will again find this

memo in the FBI files and believe he or she has discovered something new and important. At that time, we'll have to, once again, provide the information that this memo refers to a well-known hoax.

Journalist Drew Pearson (left) with President Lyndon Johnson. Rhodes went to Pearson to tell the columnist that the FBI had taken his negatives and would not return them.

Rhodes told columnist Drew Pearson that the FBI had borrowed his negatives and when he asked for their return, he was told that they were not available.

The FBI responded that they didn't have the negatives and that "in fact Rhodes knew full well that the FBI turned them over to Air Force Intelligence representatives, Hamilton Field, on 30 August 1947, with the understanding that he might never have them returned." This would be the Fourth Air Force, which had also investigated the Arnold sighting.

At this point in time, the FBI had a limited role in both the general investigation into the flying disks and the Rhodes case specifically. The physical evidence, in this case, the photographic negatives, had been passed on to the Army, then forwarded to ATIC in Dayton, Ohio. There, the photographs were examined, and though there was nothing in them to suggest hoax, it is clear from the government files that something about Rhodes offended the officers investigating the case. The truth was that Rhodes had a somewhat abrasive personality, but he was a smart man who held several patents and earned money from them. He did specialized scientific work and while he might have attempted to sell his photographs of the UFO in 1952, it is clear that in 1947 that thought had not occurred to him.

The FBI Policy on "Flying Discs"

After a number of memos were exchanged at the highest levels of the FBI, they developed a policy. According to a July 30, 1947 document:

> The Bureau, at the request of the Army Air Forces Intelligence, has agreed to cooperate in the investigation of flying discs. The Air Forces have confidently advised that it is possible to release three or more discs in odd numbers, attached together by a wire, from an airplane in high altitudes and that these discs would obtain tremendous speed in their descent and would descend to the earth in an arc. The Army Air Forces Intelligence has also indicated some concern that the reported sightings might have been made by subversive individuals for the purpose of creating mass hysteria.

> You should investigate each instance which is brought to your attention of a sighting of a flying disc in order to ascertain whether or not it is a bona fide sighting, an imaginary one, or a prank. You should also bear in

mind that individuals might report seeing flying discs for various reasons. It is conceivable that an individual might be desirous of seeking personal publicity, causing hysteria, or playing a prank.

The Bureau should be notified immediately of all reported sightings and the results of your inquiries. In instances where the report appears to have merit, the teletype should be followed by the letter to the Bureau containing in detail the results of your inquiries. The Army Air Forces have assured the Bureau complete cooperation in the matters and in any instances where they fail to make information available to you to make the recovered discs available for your examination, it should promptly be brought to the attention of the Bureau.

This spirit of cooperation didn't last very long. On September 3, 1947, there was a letter from the Air Defense Command Headquarters stationed at Mitchell Field in New York. This letter suggests the first rift between the FBI and the Army Air Forces.

The subject was the "Cooperation of FBI with AAF on Investigations of 'Flying Disc' Incidents" and was directed to the commanding generals of the various numbered Air Force commands. It said:

1. The Federal Bureau of Investigation has agreed to assist the Air Force Intelligence personnel in the investigation of "flying disc" incidents in order to quickly and effectively rule out what are pranks and to concentrate on what appears to be a genuine incident.

2. It was the original intent of the AC/AS-2 [Assistant Chief of Staff/Air Staff—Intelligence], Headquarters, Army Air Forces that whereas the ADC [Air Defense Command] Air Forces would interview responsible observers whose names would be furnished by the AAF, the FBI would investigate incidents of so-called "discs" being found on the ground. The services of the FBI were enlisted in order to relieve the numbered Air Forces of the task of tracking down all the many instances which turned out to be ash can covers, toilet seats, and whatnot.

3. It is requested that each A-2 informally coordinate and cooperate with the FBI, generally keeping the FBI informed of any proposed calls intelligence personnel will make on this subject. Very shortly, with the separation of the AAF from the War Department, a firm policy will be established to clarify the liaison arrangements between A-2's and FBI Special Agents. Presently, it is considered inadvisable to promulgate a formal interim policy—only to have it replaced in a month of so by another.

This was signed by Colonel R. H. Smith, the Assistant Chief of Staff for intelligence and was written by the command of Lieutenant General Stratmeyer.

What was interesting in the letter, other than the AAF attitude, were the references to "incidents of so-called 'discs' being found on the ground." During July 1947, there had been several of these reports. Those that had been reported in the press had been explained, for the most part. Shreveport was a hoax, the Montana crash was a hoax, and the Lloyd Bennett report, while probably not a hoax, was certainly not a recovered alien spacecraft.

In addition to those, on July 10 in Black River Falls, Wisconsin, Sigurd Hanson found a small flying saucer while he and two others were installing lights on the fairgrounds. He claimed to have found the object in some tall grass, but some believed that he had made it himself.

The saucer itself weighed about a pound and a half and was made of cardboard. It was fifteen inches in diameter and had a vertical fin that was topped by a propeller, which seemed to be connected to a small motor and powered by a photoelectric cell. There were scorch marks near the fin, suggesting there might have been a small rocket mounted there to power the craft, though no evidence of that was found.

What was interesting in the letter, other than the AAF attitude, were the references to "incidents of so-called 'discs' being found on the ground."

A 1997 newspaper article suggested they knew the name of the person who had created the "saucer." According to the article, he was still chuckling about it.

On July 11, 1947, a small saucer that was described as looking like cymbals was discovered and turned over to the FBI. The object was about thirty inches in diameter, was gold on one side and silver on the other. It had been anchored to the ground. Apparently the FBI sent it on to Fort Douglas where a "high-ranking officer" said that he could neither confirm nor deny that they had heard of the discovery.

Sometime in July 1947, the base commander at the Alamogordo Army Air Field ordered a master sergeant to print a special report about a crashed and recovered flying saucer. The commander, Colonel Paul F. Helmlek, is reported to have told the sergeant to print it himself and not show it to anyone else. Once the project was finished, according to the unidentified sergeant, Helmlek picked up everything about it and took it all away.

There was also the crash outside Roswell, New Mexico, but since that had received national attention, and was explained by the Army quickly, it doesn't seem to have made an impression on anyone at the time. The government files available for 1947 show but a single reference to the case, in the middle paragraph of a three-paragraph newspaper article. This explained that the officers at Roswell had received a "blistering rebuke" for their premature press release. It wasn't until 1978 that the true nature of the case was revealed.

✳

The FBI Response

The letter leaked to the FBI. It was supplied to the San Francisco office by the intelligence officers at Hamilton AAF. Dated September 19, 1947, the letter expressed Special Agent Harry M. Kimball's annoyance with those in New York:

It is my understanding from recent Bureau instructions that we are to assist the Air Force Intelligence personnel in the investigation of flying disc incidents. However, it will be noted from the attached letter that it is the Army interpretation that it was their intent that the Bureau would investigate those incidents of the so-called "discs" being found on the ground and apparently not only those observed in flight. Further, the attention of the Bureau is respectfully called to paragraph two of this letter and to the last sentence therein which states, "The services of the FBI were enlisted in order to relieve the numbered Air Forces of the task of tracking down all the many instances which turned out to be ash can covers, toilet seats, and whatnot."

In the first place, the instructions issued by the Army Air Forces in this letter appear to limit the type of investigations which the Bureau will be asked to handle and secondly it appears to me the wording of the last sentence in the second paragraph mentioned above is cloaked in entirely uncalled for language tending to indicate the Bureau will be asked to conduct investigations only in those cases which are not important and which are almost, in fact, ridiculous.

The thought has occurred to me the Bureau might desire to discuss this matter further with the Army Air Forces both as to the type of the investigations which we will conduct and also to object to the scurrilous wordage which, to say the least, is insulting to the Bureau in the last sentence of paragraph two.

In the event the Bureau decides to discuss the matter further with the Army Air Forces, it is recommended that no indication whatsoever be given indicating this letter was referred to me by Lieutenant Colonel Springer in as much as it would undoubtedly cause him serious embarrassment and would certainly cause the excellent personal relationship which exists between Lieutenant Colonel Springer and this office is endangered.

1. A number of letters in the government files discuss the "Cooperation" letter. On September 26, 1947, Assistant Director Ladd recommended that "the Bureau protest vigorously to the Assistant Chief of Air Staff. 2. It is also recommended that the Bureau discontinue all activity in this field and that the Bureau Field Offices be advised to discontinue all investigations and to refer all complaints received to the Air Forces."

The next day, Hoover wrote to Major General George MacDonald, who was the Assistant Chief, Air Staff. Hoover followed Ladd's suggestion, telling MacDonald that he "was advising the Field Divisions of the Federal Bureau of Investigation to discontinue all investigative activity regarding the reported sightings of flying discs, and am instructing them to refer all complaints received to the appropriate Air Force representative in their area."

And then, on October 1, 1947, according to the government files, the FBI ceased its cooperation with Bureau Bulletin

[O]n October 1, 1947, according to the government files, the FBI ceased its cooperation with Bureau Bulletin 59....

59: It said, "FLYING DISCS—Effective immediately, the Bureau has discontinued its investigative activities as outlined in Section B of the Bureau Bulletin No. 42, Series 1947, dated July 30, 1947 ... All future reports connected with flying discs should be referred to the Air Forces and no investigative action should be taken by Bureau Agents."

The FBI UFO Investigations

Even with the end of the cooperation, and the suggestion that UFO sightings be referred to the Air Force, the FBI maintained an interest in them. On January 31, 1949, there was a letter sent to the Director that referred to the Weekly Intelligence Conference of the G-2 [Army Intelligence], ONI [Office of Naval Intelligence], OSI, and FBI, in the Fourth Army Area [which was along the west coast] in which they all discussed "Unidentified Aircraft" or "Unidentified Aerial Phenomena," which was called the "Flying Discs" or the "Flying Saucers." That document from the government files suggested that it was "well known that there have been, during the past two years, reports from various parts of the country of the sighting of unidentified aerial objects...." It then lists the information on several events including:

> In July 1948, an unidentified aircraft was "seen" by an Eastern Airlines Pilot and Co-pilot [Chiles and Whitted] and one or more passengers of the Eastern Airlines plane over Montgomery, Alabama. This aircraft was reported to be of an unconventional type without wings and resembled generally a "rocket ship" of the type depicted in the comic strips. It was reported to have windows; to have been larger than the Eastern Airlines plane, and to have been travelling at an estimated speed of 2700 miles an hour. It appeared out of a thunderhead ahead of the Eastern Airlines plane and immediately disappeared in another cloud narrowly missing a collision with the Eastern Airlines plane. No sound or air disturbance was noted in connection with the appearance. [See the Sidebar in the Estimate of the Situation, Chapter 3]....

> There have been day time sightings which are tentatively considered to possibly resemble the exhaust of some type of jet propelled object. Nighttime sightings have taken the form of lights usually described as brilliant green, similar to a green traffic signal or green neon light. [See Chapter 5: The Green Fireballs.] Some reports indicated that the light began and ended with a red or orange flash. Other reports have given the color as red, white, blue-white, and yellowish green. Trailing lights sometimes observed are said to be red. The spectrum analysis of one light indicates that it may be a copper compound of the type known to be used in rocket experiments and which completely disintegrated upon explosion, leaving no debris. It is noted that *no debris has ever been known to be located anywhere resulting from the unexplained phenomena* [Emphasis added]....

> In every case but one the shape of the objects has been reported as round in a point of light with a definite area to the light's source. One report

gives a diamond shape; another indicates that trailing lights are elongated. The size is usually compared to one-fourth the diameter of the full moon, and they have also been compared in size to a basketball with trailing lights the size of a baseball....

Some nine scientific reasons are stated to exist which indicated that the phenomena observed are not due to meteorites. The only conclusions reached thus far are that they are either hitherto unobserved natural phenomena or that they are man-made. No scientific experiments are known to exist in this country which could give rise to such phenomena.

It needs to be remembered that the document was created in 1949, and much of the information contained within had been superseded by newer and better information. As noted earlier, the Chiles–Whitted sighting was probably a fireball. But it is also clear that these various agencies, while suggesting that there was nothing to the flying saucers, or fighting among themselves about who to investigate with and what to investigate, were in fact taking the topic seriously.

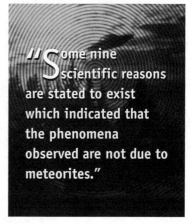

"Some nine scientific reasons are stated to exist which indicated that the phenomena observed are not due to meteorites."

It is important to note that there were several agencies involved, including the Army Air Forces, the Navy, and the FBI. The other important thing is to note that this was held in concert with the Fourth Army Area, but that this did not include Roswell. The comment about "no debris has ever been known to be located anywhere resulting from the unexplained phenomena," is interesting even though there were a number of cases in which physical evidence had been recovered. These just weren't in the Fourth Army Area.

The Investigation Continues (Sort Of)

J. Edgar Hoover was famous for attempting to expand his investigative empire and during his tenure, FBI jurisdiction seemed to expand beyond the borders of the United States. However, when it came to UFOs, once Hoover was convinced there might be nothing of importance there, FBI interest in them weakened.

Government files show a number of sightings over the Oak Ridge, Tennessee's Atomic Energy Commission's testing facilities. A summary of the sightings was found in the government files. Although there had been sightings reported there as early as June 1947, a series began on October 12, 1950 and ran through November 5, 1950. The following is based on both the FBI files and those of Project Blue Book:

At 2325 hours (11:25 P.M.) on October 12, the Knoxville Airport Radar Unit reported a series of unknown targets over the "Restricted Zone" at Oak Ridge.

At 2347 hours (11:47 P.M.) on October 12, a fighter was sent to investigate and made "three perfect intercepts" but could find nothing.

Control panel operators at the Y-12 Plant at the Oak Ridge facility, which was involved in the Manhattan Project to develop nuclear bombs. Was it a coincidence that UFOs were also spotted over Oak Ridge?

At midnight to about 0100 hours (1:00 A.M.) on October 13, or some thirteen minutes after the failed intercepts, there was additional radar targets spotted. There were no corresponding visual sightings.

Sometime after 1500 hours (3:00 P.M.) on October 15, a fighter made unsuccessful passes at a "good" radar target four miles from the East Boundary, identified as the Kerr Hollow Gate.

At 1520 hours (3:20 P.M.) on October 15, "SUBJECT" was seen at Kerr Hollow Gate by "Troopers Rymer and Zarzecki, Mr. Hightower, and Mr. Moneymaker.

From 1455 hours (2:55 P.M.) to 1530 hours (3:30 P.M.) on October 16, objects were seen by Troopers Isabell, Briggs, and Clark.

Also at 1520 hours on October 16, the radars at McGhee-Tyson Airport indicated unidentified targets.

From 1956 hours (7:56 P.M.) to 2004 hours (8:04 P.M.) on October 16, NEPA Guards Brown, Herron, and Davis reported peculiar sounds.

At 1655 hours (4:55 P.M.) on October 20, Larry Riordan sighted an object overhead. This sighting was detailed in a memorandum dated October 25.

At 1630 hours (4:30 P.M.) on October 23, Francis J. Miller sighted an object. At the same time Geiger counters in that same area had unexplained readings.

From 1855 hours (6:55 P.M.) to 1900 hours (7:00 P.M.), October 24, Major Dallveg and Mr. Fry made visual sightings. There were additional sightings made at the radar station. This series of sightings was detailed in the memorandum dated October 25.

From 1823 hours (6:23 P.M.) to 1920 hours (7:20 P.M.), October 24, several small targets were tracked by radar. This series of sightings was detailed in the memorandum dated October 25.

On October 26, Robert W. Lassell and five others sighted several objects near the Knoxville Airport.

From 1155 hours (11:55 A.M.) to 1200 hours (Noon) on November 5, Don Patrick made a sighting.

The FBI made no analysis of these sightings and the listing was just that, a list of sightings. It contained basic information about who had seen what, plus additional information that suggested instruments were involved in some of those sightings.

On October 25, 1950, the FBI provided some additional details on a few of these sightings. That memorandum said:

> At 1655 hours, on 20 October 1950, Mr. Larry P. Riordan, AEC Badge No. 522, Superintendent of Security at X-10 in the "Control Zone" at Oak Ridge, Tennessee, while enroute from X-10 to the Oak Ridge residential area, on Benton Valley Road, saw an object in the sky which appeared to be directly over the University of Tennessee Agricultural Research Farm. This object gave the general appearance of an aerial balloon which had lost its "basket." In other words, the object was generally round, appeared to come together at the bottom in wrinkles (rather indistinct), and something was hanging below. The balloon was described as being from eight to ten feet long; of a lead pipe or gunmetal color; and seemed to be approximately one-fourth (¼) mile from the observer, at thirty (30) degrees elevation.... Mr. Riordan is certain that the object was not a weather balloon but his first impression was that this object was an experimental "gab" being utilized by the University of Tennessee Agricultural Research Farm....

> At 1845 hours, on October 24, 1950, Mr. William B. Fry, Assistant Chief of Security, NEPA Division, Oak Ridge, Tennessee, while attending a Drive-in theater with his wife and child, at Oak Ridge, noticed an object in the sky North-Northwest of his position, at thirty (30) to forty (40) degree elevation. This object was moving gently in a horizontal plane, back and forth, within thirty (30) degrees of his line of sight. This object emitted a glow, varying in color from red to green, to blue-green, to blue, and to orange. The variations were checked on the vertical window post of Mr. Fry's vehicle and were witnessed by Mr. Fry's wife. The attention of another observer, the Projectionist at the Drive-in theater, was also called to the object and verification of this sighting was made. The object disappeared from his sight at 1920 hours.

> At 1855 hours, on October 24, 1950, an Air Force Major, Lawrence Ballweg, NEPA Division, Oak Ridge, Tennessee, also saw from his residence an object which he described similarly. The object disappeared from the sight of Mr. Ballweg at 1920 hours, which coincides with the time of disappearance of the object from Mr. Fry's sight....

> On 24 October 1950, at 1823 hours, several small, slow targets were seen on the Radar screen at the Knoxville Airport Radar Site. These targets appeared in the Southwest sector of the "Restricted Flying Zone" and over the city of Oak Ridge. These targets moved from the city area to and along the East boundary of the area. At 1826 hours, the fighter aircraft was "scrambled" and preceded to the area where it was vectored among the targets but the pilot reported no visual contact with said targets. At 1920 hours the targets disappeared from the Radar Screen and the fighter was vectored toward another target believed to be one of three (3) aircraft enroute from Andrews Field to Steward Field. (Note: 1920 hours is also the time that the object sighted by Mr. Fry and Major Ballweg disappeared from their view).

Other Government Files Concerning these Sightings

In an interesting discrepancy, the Project Blue Book files have additional information on some of these cases but not on all of them. Although the sightings were made at or near the Oak Ridge laboratories, which, of course brought in the FBI, they were of objects in the sky. Air Force fighters were scrambled in attempts to intercept and identify the objects. Only a few were investigated and all but one of the sightings was "identified" by the Air Force.

The index page from Project Blue Book for October 1950 provides limited information. From October 12 to October 16 there are five sightings. The radar sightings are written off as "radar peculiarities," the sighting on October 15 involving Moneymaker and Rymer is unidentified, and the others were either balloons or aircraft.

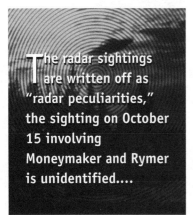

The radar sightings are written off as "radar peculiarities," the sighting on October 15 involving Moneymaker and Rymer is unidentified....

In a letter dated December 4, 1950, that referenced another letter, this one from the Headquarters of the Third Army, the answer for the radar sightings are provided. It said, "It appears that some form of unexplained radar phenomena has occurred at Oak Ridge which gives false targets on the screen.... It appears that the radar difficulties are due either to: a. Chemical impurities in the air, b. Radioactive particles, c. some form of radar phenomena."

These answers are of little use, ranging from explanations that include chemical impurities, radiation, or some form of radar phenomena that we don't understand and apparently haven't seen before. In other words, they did not have an answer and were throwing out explanations to see if one made any sense. In the end, without a real conclusion, they wrote the case off as "radar peculiarities." This, while not very helpful, does eliminate the case from the "unidentified" category list.

In another report in the government files, it was noted that, "The spurious radar echoes described in Inclosure [sic] 1 are believed to have been caused by atmospheric conditions. Atmospheric conditions causing spurious microwave echoes usually consist of rain, heavily water-laden clouds and ice-laden clouds."

They also noted that it was impossible to explain the visual sightings, which followed the pattern of reports of other incidents. In other words, they were using past explanations to solve the sightings in and around Oak Ridge. These included weather balloons, peculiar clouds, or aircraft seen through a layer of thin or broken clouds. Given all that, Colonel Harold A. Watkins believed that the visual sightings were not all that important.

There is another document in the government files which attempted to refine these conclusions. It said:

The trend of opinions seem to follow three patterns or thoughts. The first is that the objects are physical phenomenon which have a scientific explanation; the second is that the objects are experimental objects (from an undetermined source) guided by electronics; and the third is similar to the second except that an intended demoralization or harassment is involved. The fantastic is generally rejected.

In the end, no real solutions were offered. It is clear, looking back on this, that no experimental craft were linked to the sightings. After more than half a century, there are no experiments that would still be classified, and if the experimental aircraft explanation was accurate, it would be known to everyone today.

They have rejected the fantastic out of hand. They simply did not consider that the sightings might have been of alien spacecraft.

The telling phrase is the last one. They have rejected the fantastic out of hand. They simply did not consider that the sightings might have been of alien spacecraft. This is one of those fantastic explanations.

The unidentified sighting made by Rymer and Moneymaker was referenced in a document dated October 16. It said:

> Description of object seen by Atomic Energy Commission Security Patrol Trooper Edward D. Rymer; who approached the object as close to Fifty (50) feet, at about 1520 hours on 15 October 1950, is substantially as follows: When first seen at an estimated altitude of twelve (12) to fifteen (15) thousand feet, the object appeared to be an aircraft starting to "skywrite." The "streamer" left behind is estimated to be approximately one-fourth (¼) of a mile long. The object then started a controlled descent, almost vertical, at a slower speed than an aircraft would dive, and the "tail" followed the object. "It" then appeared to take the shape of a large bullet with a streamer, or ribbon, as thick as the bullet, trailing the path of the object but connected to it. The object then levelled [sic] off parallel to the horizon, decreased its speed, and passed within seventy (70) yards of Rymer and another observer whom Rymer had stopped (John Moneymaker). Rymer had reported via telephone that this object was a "falling object." As the object decreased its speed to less than a man's normal walk, Rymer attempted to approach the object, but when he got within fifty (50) of it, the object moved toward the Southeast at about six feet altitude above the terrain; made almost a mechanical maneuver to go over a nine (9) foot chain link cyclone fence; then another similar maneuver to pass over a willow tree and a telephone line; and finally gained altitude and speed and went over a hill about one mile distance.
>
> When Rymer was within fifty (50) feet of the object it appeared to be a two (2) by five (5) card (similar to the ones issued to vehicles entering the "Control Zone" at Oak Ridge) with a twenty (20) foot ribbon tail, the first two feet of which were easily visible and the last eighteen (18) feet of which was almost transparent and divided into several sections. The sections of the tail would pulsate a dim "glow" alternately. Through the entire length of the tail, was a black line which might be described as a "wire." The entire color was bluish-gray similar to the color of the top of a "wood

cooking range." The "body" of the object was gently moving up and down, and the tail waved in the breeze light a ribbon or a worm and followed the path of the "body" of the object. There was no breeze at the time! (Knoxville Airport reports a high breeze of eight (8) miles per hour). Further, from fifty (50) feet away, the object looked no bigger than it did from two hundred and ten (210) feet away; and when it disappeared over the hill, one (1) mile away, it still looked the same size that it had appeared at only fifty (50) feet, but the "body" was then "bladder" or "pear-shaped."

When questioned further, Rymer stated that the object had to change size from the time they first observed it until it came near the ground; and it had to get larger as it went over the hill or they would not have been able to see it at such distances.

Object appeared two more times within the next ten (10) minutes and Rymer was able to get two other observers to verify that they could see the same "thing."

The three observers, other than Rymer, were E. W. Hightower, Maxon Construction Corporation, Badge No. 6633; John Moneymaker, caretaker of small animals at the University of Tennessee Agricultural Research Farm, Oak Ridge; and Joe Zarzecki, Captain of the AEC Security Patrol, Oak Ridge, Tennessee. At no time were [there] any noises from this object.

It should be noted here that while there is no explanation for the sighting, it did have a high strangeness factor. Something that can shrink and expand seems to take the sighting out of the realm of alien visitation, but that same description also eliminates nearly everything else. Rymer was within fifty feet of it, and it was in sight long enough for him, and the other witnesses, to get a good look at it. That they couldn't identify it, and that they had an opportunity to observe it carefully is the likely reason that the Air Force labeled the case as "unidentified."

The FBI "Spies" on UFO Lecture

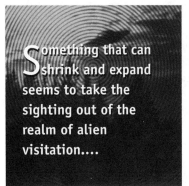

Something that can shrink and expand seems to take the sighting out of the realm of alien visitation....

There has always been the rumor that the government had sent representatives to various UFO lectures. Some speakers on the lecture circuit were so outrageous it would seem that no one in the government would care what they were saying. Such is not the case. Government files prove that agents from various departments attended these lectures and sent on reports to their higher headquarters.

In a Memorandum to the Director of the FBI dated May 4, 1960, and with the subject of "Flying Discs," an agent in Denver described his attendance of a lecture in Denver. According to the cover letter, the Special Agent, whose name was redacted, "attended this lecture on Sunday, 4/17/60, after hearing of its impending presentation over the radio. He recognized no one at this meeting and was known to no one at the meeting."

At the bottom of the document is the note, "PROPERTY OF FBI—This memorandum is loaned to you by the FBI, and neither it nor its contents are to be distributed outside the agency to which it is loaned." In other words, at one time the document was classified.

The lecture was held at the Phipps Auditorium in Denver and was attended, according to the government documents, by 250 people. The audience was "comprised of a majority of older individuals and also a majority of the audience was female."

The presentation began with a forty-five-minute movie "which included several shots of things purported to be flying saucers, and then a number of interviews with people from all walks of life regarding sightings they had made of such unidentified flying objects."

George Van Tassel (left) is seen here at flying saucer convention. He was an aircraft mechanic who, in 1953, said that he had been contacted by aliens from Venus.

From that point the speaker, whose name had been redacted, but who clearly was contactee George A. Van Tassel, told the audience and the FBI that he had been in the "flying game" for thirty years, referring to the fact that he had owned and operated the Giant Rock Airport near Landers, California. When that was identified in the FBI Memorandum, it provided the clue to the name of the lecturer.

According to the government files, the majority of the lecture "was devoted to explaining the occurrences in the Bible as they related to the space people."

Van Tassel explained that when Earth was created, all the animals were acclimated to a temperature of 105 degrees, but then there was a polar shift. The temperature changed to 98.5 degrees to sustain life. With the animals now gone, the space people returned with new animals now able to live in the new, non-tropical environment. This was, of course, Noah's Ark.

He continued with the other contactee message of the era, which was that the space people were worried about the atomic bomb. He said that the detonation of the bombs had upset the Earth's rotation and caused earthquakes. He claimed that various governments were aware of this and that they were in some kind of negotiations with the space people.

From the tone of the document, it seems that the FBI agent attempted to listen to the lecture and to report on what was said. According to the report, it was noted that "He also mentioned he was not advocating or asking for any action on the part of the audience because he said the evil was destroying itself."

Or, in other words, he was not advocating the overthrow of the government or any other subversive activity. This would, of course, be within the scope of FBI jurisdiction but then who believed a man who claimed to have ridden a flying saucer and who had met with a council of "discarnate" humans?

What this government file does show is that the FBI in 1960, years after it had rejected investigation of UFOs, was still investigating some aspects of them. And it proves that the claims that the FBI attended UFO lectures, no matter how outrageous the message, are true.

The Bureau Does Not Investigate UFO Sightings

In 1977, one of President Carter's staff, Jody Powell, asked about how the FBI handled UFOs. The FBI response said, "I advised him [Powell] that as far as the FBI is concerned there appears to be no conceivable jurisdiction for us to conduct any inquiries upon the receipt of information relating to a UFO sighting and, in absence of some investigation, be referred to the Department of the Air Force without any action being taken by the Bureau."

Although there is a history of FBI investigation of UFOs, much of it from 1947, but some of it extending into the 1960s, and the FBI was routinely copied on various reports about UFOs. The director denied that the FBI had ever inves-

Jody Powell (left) was on President Jimmy Carter's staff in 1977 when he queried the FBI about its involvement in UFO investigations. The FBI denied it had much to do with them and would refer such cases to the Air Force.

tigated UFOs. On September 1, 1989, the Director of the FBI at that time, William S. Sessions, wrote, "I have discussed your request with my colleagues, and I would first like to explain that the investigation of UFOs is not now nor has it ever been the responsibility of the FBI. The Department of the Air Force conducted investigations and studies of UFO reports from 1947 to 1969."

Sessions explained the Air Force position, that the official investigation ended in 1969 and that all the records were available at the National Archive in Washington, D.C., for review. Sessions even suggested that the Modern Military Branch would be able to answer any questions about UFOs.

Sessions also noted that NASA had been asked by President Carter to "look into the possibility of resuming UFO investigations in 1977. After studying all the facts available, it decided that nothing would be gained by further investigation, and the Department of the Air Force agreed with that decision."

This seems to be the official policy throughout the government. They all, including the Air Force, have adopted that attitude. The FBI has no reason or jurisdiction to investigate UFOs. Given the history of UFO investigations over the last half century, it is clear that the FBI has no desire to become entangled in UFO investigations. Sessions' 1989 letter simply underscores that position.

The Cisco Grove
Physical Evidence Case
and Other Alien Encounters

Skeptics, disbelievers, and debunkers like to say that there is no evidence to support the theory that alien creatures have visited the planet. They ignore, reject, or are unaware that the government files do contain examples of physical evidence that has been recovered. One of those cases took place in September 1964 and was reported to Project Blue Book.

The witness in this case, whose name was redacted in the government files, was first identified by Richard Hall in his 1988 book *Uninvited Visitors* as Donald Shrum. In September 1964, Shrum and two friends, Vince Alvarez and another, headed into the mountains in the Cisco Grove area of California to do some deer hunting with bow and arrow. They set up camp and then split up to go out on their own. Shrum, following a ridge line, lost his way. He realized that he would not be able to find his way back to the camp that night and decided to remain where he was.

Like many hunters who have found themselves alone in the wilderness at night, he decided that he would sleep in a tree. It raised him off the ground where the animals of the night scurried and slithered. Sitting in the tree, he noticed a white light that seemed to hover below the horizon, but in the distance. Believing it was a searchlight from a helicopter, possibly flown by rescuers or rangers, Shrum climbed down from his perch and started three fires on the large rocks near him. Standing among the fires, he hoped to draw the attention of whoever was piloting the aircraft, and apparently he was successful. The light turned and began flying toward him. Only after it neared did he realize that the light was not making a sound. That was when he began to get scared, according to the story he told later.

As light hovered between two trees some fifty or sixty yards away, Shrum realized that it was too small to be a helicopter. He could see three glowing, rectangular panels set on the vertical in a stepping-down pattern. The lights seemed to circle around until they were no more than fifty feet away. He realized that it was a UFO, threw his bow back up into the tree, and scrambled up after it. According to Shrum, "Something came out of the second [panel], and all I could see was a kind of flash. Something went straight down the hill … pretty fast." It fell down the hill, landing on a bush. Shrum believed that whatever had fallen was now on the ground, down the hill a short distance from him.

The eyes were large and dark and looked like welder's goggles.

There was a scrambling sound, a crashing that came from the bushes, and a humanoid figure emerged from the darkness. It wore a light-colored, silver or whitish uniform with bellows at the elbows and knees. The eyes were large and dark and looked like welder's goggles. It appeared to be doing something on the ground, and before long was joined by a second, similar creature. The two entities worked their way toward the tree and were soon standing at the base, looking up at him.

While the first object, or rather the lights, continued to hover, the thrashing noise began in another part of the forest. Along the ridge Shrum could see big glowing spots that reminded him of two flashlights hooked together, bouncing along. Finally he could see it was another being of some kind because the lights were bright enough for him to see the face. He described it as square and metallic, with a hinged mouth that hung open, reminding him of a ventriloquist's dummy. This alien was about five feet tall, just slightly taller than the humanoids that he had seen earlier at the base of his tree.

The metallic being, a robot of some kind, joined the two humanoids at the base of the tree and stood staring up at Shrum. Eventually the robot walked over to one of the fires, swept an arm through it and then walked back to the humanoids. It put its hand to its mouth and a white vapor came out, drifting upward, toward Shrum. He gasped for breath, and then momentarily lost consciousness, falling across his bow, which kept him in the tree.

When Shrum regained consciousness, just minutes later, he was sick to his stomach. Convinced that the beings wanted to capture him, Shrum decided he was going to fight. First he lit a book of matches and tossed it down. When the entities backed up, reacting to the fire, he set his hat on fire and threw it down. This forced them farther back, but when the fires began to die, the beings came forward again.

Now Shrum started lighting everything he could, throwing it down, hoping to set the ground cover on fire. He eventually burned everything in his pockets and the camouflage clothes he wore until he was left in a T-shirt, trousers, and his shoes. The fires kept the beings away from him for a few minutes.

With nothing left to do, Shrum picked up his bow. He said, "I tried shooting the robot with my bow, as he was the only one that was doing anything against me. The other two just stood and looked. The bow I've got has a velocity of a rifle at the range of twelve feet or so. So I just pulled it back as far as I could, and hit him the first time. It was just like a big arc flash. It just flashed up real bright. I only had three arrows with me, so that was all I shot. I shot him three times, and all three times it pushed him back a little bit, with just a big, bright flash.... He was right up against the rocks, so it didn't push him very far. And every time I shot, too, these others scattered a little bit...."

But Shrum had quickly run out of arrows. He mentioned in an interview with Ted Bloecher and Paul Cerny, published in *International UFO Reporter* in the winter of 1995, that, "I only had three arrows with me, so that was all I shot. I shot him three times and all three times it pushed him back a little bit, with just a big, bright flash."

In a minor discrepancy, Shrum told Steven Reichmuth that he had three arrows with him and shot two of them at the aliens. "One of the arrowheads struck the robot's chest area from a range of eight feet, knocking the robot on its proverbial 'metal ass.'"

Shrum returned later and was able to retrieve the two arrows he had shot. He gave one to the Air Force, which promised to return it but never did. The second was given to Cerny for analysis, but there was nothing unusual about it, at least in a metallurgical sense.

Either out of arrows or saving the last one, Shrum climbed higher in the tree and tied himself to the trunk near the top with his belt. The robot let loose with another cloud of vapor and the witness passed out again. When he came to, the two humanoids were trying to climb the tree. When one of them began to make some progress, Shrum shook the tree as violently as he could. The beings would scramble down, apparently unaware of what had happened.

This pattern went on for a period of time. The robotic creature would emit a mist; the witness would lose consciousness and then awaken to find the humanoids trying to climb the tree to reach him. He'd then shake the tree, and they'd get down.

Finally, Shrum began breaking branches from the tree to throw at them. He tossed the change in his pocket, his canteen, and anything else he could find, trying to distract them. The creatures picked up the canteen, examined it and dropped it. They grabbed the coins and apparently kept them, though it is surprising a hunter would have loose change in his pocket.

The pattern kept up thought the night, with Shrum once howling like a coyote, hoping the creatures would think there were more people around. Shrum did everything he could think of to keep the creatures from climbing toward him.

A second robot joined the group during the night, and just before dawn, stood face to face with the other robot. "Arc flashes" passed between them, lighting up the area. A fog was generated by the "conversation," which rose slowly. Shrum said he blacked out again and when he awakened, he was hanging by his belt but all the creatures, both metallic and humanoid, had disappeared.

The robot let loose with another cloud of vapor and the witness passed out again.

With the creatures gone, and no sign of the lights that seemed to have brought them, Shrum climbed down from the tree. He recovered the things he'd thrown in the night and found the arrows he'd shot at the robot. Only the coins from his pockets were missing.

Eventually, Shrum found his way back to camp. He later related his story to Paul Cerny, an NICAP UFO investigator.

The Investigations Begin

Judy Shrum, Donald Shrum's wife, after reading an article about UFOs written by Don Keyhoe, at the time the Director of NICAP, sent a letter to him. That information was sent on to NICAP investigator Paul Cerny, who did the most comprehensive work on this case.

According to that investigation, Vince Alvarez said:

I was the one that found Shrum as he was heading towards camp. The night had been very cold, and all he had on at the time ... was a thin cotton tee shirt and his pants. He was weak and exhausted.... I helped him to camp, fixed some soup for him and put him to sleep. He kept on saying that he would have been all right if they had left him alone. I didn't know what he meant so we let him sleep. He slept for about six hours. When he awoke, we asked him how he felt. He said fine. Then he said, "Turn on the radio ... there may be something on the news about the spaceship I saw." The news did say something about a light in the sky. I also saw the light as I was working my way thru the canyon to camp. (I got lost too that night.) We asked him what had happened to his clothes and then he told us his experiences....

There were a number of investigations of the case by both official organizations and private groups. APRO researchers were among the first to interview Shrum. According to Coral Lorenzen, writing in *Flying Saucer Occupants*, "We learned about this particular incident quite by chance through rumors in the Sacramento area, and notified Dr. James Harder, one of APRO's advisors."

Shrum read a copy of that report [the July/August 1966 issue of *The APRO Bulletin*] and noted many inaccuracies in it.

The first account of the witness' tale appeared in the July/August 1966 issue of *The APRO Bulletin*. Shrum read a copy of that report and noted many inaccuracies in it. For example, the *Bulletin* account placed the event in September 1963.

Several other sources also got the date wrong, with some suggesting the encounter happened on September 4, 1964. In a *MUFON Journal* article Steven Reichmuth suggested that the actual date was September 11.

Bloecher and Cerny, in their *IUR* article, wrote: "He [Shrum] was pretty sure that they were out in the area the first Friday after Labor Day, which, of course, would be the previous Monday.... Unfortunately, it confuses the issue. Labor Day was September 7, 1964, which would push the date of the sighting to Friday, September 11. This is too late, since the letter from astronomer Victor Killick to Mather Air Force Base is dated September 9."

To make things even worse, a letter found in the government files, written by Victor Killick, an astronomer consulted by the Shrum family, noted, "He [Shrum] told me that on Friday, Sept 5th, he and two companions went out for a deer hunt...." But the truth is that the event took place on the night of Friday, September 4, and the morning of Saturday, September 5. A year later, Shrum told Cerny he thought it was the Friday after Labor Day, but clearly it was the Friday before.

A day or so after the events, given the timeline that developed, would have been just prior to September 8. Shrum's mother-in-law, Beatrice Legg, phoned Killick and told him the extraordinary tale. The story didn't seem all that interesting to Killick, but he asked for additional details. At that point, Shrum was put on the phone and outlined what had happened. Killick decided that the story was interesting enough that he wanted to meet the man and arranged to interview Shrum on September 8.

Impressed with the story, and the sincerity of the witness, Killick wrote to Mather Air Force Base on September 9, telling officers there, "As far as my contact with them goes, these people all appear to be in good health and rational. The family believes the man's story. They told me that when he got home he was 'as pale as a sheet,' and badly shaken up. I did a little probing to try to find an ulterior motive without success."

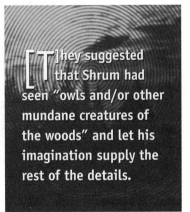

[T]hey suggested that Shrum had seen "owls and/or other mundane creatures of the woods" and let his imagination supply the rest of the details.

Killick's letter reported that he was asked if there had been any bright meteors that night, but Killick mentioned only one on the day before. He wrote, "I replied that we had a report of a brilliant meteor having passed over Los Angeles and which had exploded in the Sierra east of Vistula...."

On September 25, according to the tale, a colonel and a master sergeant from the intelligence office at McClellan Air Force Base interviewed the witness. In reality, it was a captain named McCloud and a Senior Master Sergeant R. Barnes (who has been incorrectly identified as a sergeant-major in some accounts), who conducted the interview. The real point is not the ranks of the individuals, but that someone with an official standing from the Air Force did, in fact, interview Shrum.

In their report for the government files, McCloud and Barnes wrote, "Mr. [name redacted in original but is, of course, Donald Shrum] is a local resident and ... married and recently employed at a local missile production plant. He appears stable and consistent in telling his story and believes that the [events] occurred as described."

During the taped interview, with a partial transcript available in the government files, Shrum had said, again, "I never heard a noise out there," but then the interview degenerated into a discussion of a physical that Shrum had about two weeks earlier. Shrum said, "I just worried about my own, I didn't know if I had contacted radioactivity."

Before McCloud and Barnes left, Shrum provided them with a map of the area and one of the arrowheads, which they promised to return. It should be noted that he never received the arrowhead back and that the Air Force forwarded it to the University of Colorado UFO project, that is, the Condon Committee, for analysis.

The Air Force eventually solved this case, at least to their satisfaction. According to the government files, after abandoning their attempts to convince Shrum he had either seen Japanese tourists or teenage pranksters, they suggested that Shrum had seen "owls and/or other mundane creatures of the woods" and let his imagination supply the rest of the details. It was, in effect, a retreat to the "Other, psychological" category.

Yet there seems to be evidence that the Air Force took a more active interest in the case than they let on. According to Shrum, about a month after the sighting, he, along with his brother and his two hunting companions returned to the scene of the stand-off. It appeared to them that someone had "raked over" the area. They found cigarette butts from many different brands scattered in the area. The suggestion was that these were Air Force personnel, but that seems unlikely. They would have "field stripped" the cigarette butts, meaning they would have destroyed the filters and rolled the remaining paper into tiny balls before disposing of them. Other than that, the area appeared to have been cleaned, although the site was remote and inaccessible.

Shrum had recovered two of his arrows in the morning after the fight, but out there now, he located the third. It was lying on top of some scrub brush. Confusion about the number of arrows recovered might be explained by the following—on the morning of September 5, he found two and sometime later he found the last. It also suggests that an Air Force search of the area, if there had been one, was less than thorough.

Paul Cerny, the NICAP field investigator who was brought in when Shrum's wife wrote to the organization's national headquarters, interviewed Shrum and his wife in July 1965. He was given the remaining two arrowheads. Analysis, however, revealed nothing. It had been hoped that metal from the robot might have become embedded on the arrowhead, but close examination failed to find anything. Cerny said that there had been a platinum colored smear on one of the blades, but it was possible that it had been worn off or dislodged during transit. At any rate, the lab doing the analysis could find nothing other than the expected metals.

Cerny, who stayed in contact with the Shrums long after the event was over, was impressed with Shrum's sincerity and sanity. In fact, in November 1995, Cerny added an "epilogue" to the case. In a boxed addition to an article in the *International UFO Reporter*, Cerny wrote, "Having just reviewed the case files on this fascinating and unusual encounter, there is absolutely no doubt in my mind that this incident is factual and authentic. I have spent considerable time and many visits with the main witness, and along with the testimony of the other witnesses, I can rule out any possibility of a hoax. This also includes the involvement of the USAF investigation team."

"The psychological effects on [Shrum] were extremely convincing and traumatic due to the aftereffects of his experience. Also noteworthy were the unusual detail, proximity, and reactions of the Alien Crew."

The most surprising thing in this case is the fact that the Air Force actually investigated it, given the circumstances of it. For the most part, and especially by this time in their official investigations, they stayed away from reports involving the occupants from the craft. In the 1960s, for example, almost no one had heard of alien abduction until the *New York Times* bestseller *The Interrupted Journey* was published. The book told the tale of Barney and Betty Hill who believed that they were abducted by the crew of a spaceship while driving home late at night. Although given a post hypnotic-like instruction to forget about the encounter, Betty Hill suffered from a series of nightmares that seemed to reveal what had happened.

> In the Barney and Betty Hill abduction case, Project Blue Book personnel nearly refused to acknowledge the abduction....

The Hills did remember seeing a bright light they believed to be a UFO and reported that to the Air Force. The Project Blue Book personnel nearly refused to acknowledge the abduction other than admit to a possible radar contact reported about the same time in about the same location. The government file noted that officers at Pease Air Force Base conducted the investigation, which consisted of a telephone call to Barney Hill, or rather, the results of a call from Hill. The entire government file is mostly made up of magazine articles and newspaper clippings concerning the case, but it offers little to advance any knowledge of the case or provide any real insights into it.

Kelly-Hopkinsville: A Somewhat Similar Case

In August 1955, the Sutton family in the Kelly-Hopkinsville area of southern Kentucky reported that their farm house had been attacked by small alien creatures during the night of August 21, 1955. The siege lasted through the night with the men shooting at the small beings with shotguns and rifles. Eventually the family fled the farm house and drove to the Sheriff's Office to tell the tale. According to the family, it all started about 7:00 P.M., when Billy Ray Taylor went out to the well. He ran back into the house to say that he had seen a flying saucer. He thought it had landed in a gully behind the house.

About 8:00 P.M. one of the dogs started barking and Billy Ray Taylor and Lucky Sutton went out to investigate. They saw a small figure approaching. It had glowing yellow eyes, silverish in color, and was about three and a half feet tall. It had an oversized head, floppy, pointed ears, and long arms that ended in talons and almost reached the ground.

The two men ran inside, one grabbing a .22 and the other a shotgun. When the figure got close, both fired. The creature, apparently struck, flipped over backwards and then ran to the side of the house. Not long after, another creature, or possibly the same one, appeared at a side window. J. C. Sutton shot at it and it reacted the same way as the other creature. When struck by bullets, it did a flip and ran off.

This continued throughout the night. One of the creatures climbed to the roof and was shot off. Each time the creatures were shot at, they would react, but it was as if they had been hit with a tennis ball and not bullets. Finally, the family abandoned the house and headed for the Sheriff's Office.

Because a UFO had been seen, and because the creatures were apparently alien, there were those who believed that Project Blue Book would be involved in the investigation. But, according to the government file, Project Blue Book did not investigate. They had no real interest in the sighting, although the Blue Book files contain documents that suggest one active duty officer, and possibly more, did some sort of investigation. This one was "unofficial."

Without any sort of physical evidence except the bullet holes in the house, or other proof that the Kelly-Hopkinsville tale was true, most people were quite skeptical. The media reflected that attitude. The Air Force issued a statement saying there was no basis for an investigation. In other words, the case was so unimportant that the Air Force wasn't going to waste its time or limited resources on a family of "hicks" who thought that alien beings had landed near their farm house and attacked them throughout the night.

Military personnel from Fort Campbell, Kentucky, did visit the house, however, and interviews with the Sutton family were conducted in 1955. An investigation by the Air Force eventually took place two years later. According to the government files, in August 1957, prior to the publication of a magazine article that would review the case, someone decided they should "investigate."

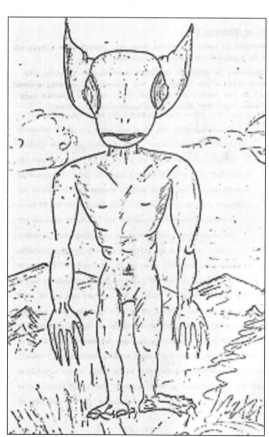

In a letter from the ATIC at Wright-Patterson to the commander of Campbell Air Force Base, available in the government files, Wallace W. Elwood wrote, "This Center requests any factual data, together with pertinent comments regarding an unusual incident reported to have taken place six miles north of Hopkinsville, Kentucky on subject date [21 August 1955]. Briefly, the incident involved an all night attack on a family named Sutton by goblin-like creatures reported to have emerged from a so-called 'flying saucer.'"

Later in the letter, Elwood wrote, "Lacking factual, confirming data, no credence can be given this almost fantastic report. As the incident has never been officially reported to the Air Force, it has not taken official cognizance of the matter."

And that sums up the Air Force and its investigation. If there is no official report, even if the Air Force is aware of the case, they have no obligation to investigate. Over the course of Project Blue Book, they collected information

A drawing showing one of the creatures that the Sutton family says they encountered in Kentucky.

from a variety of "unofficial" sources, but other than sticking it in a file folder and labeling this type of information, they did nothing with it.

Whatever the Air Force opinion or policy, the matter was assigned to First Lieutenant Charles N. Kirk, an Air Force officer at Campbell Air Force Base. Kirk spent about six weeks investigating the case before sending the material on to ATIC on October 1, 1957. He researched the story using the Hopkinsville newspaper from August 22, 1955, and September 11, 1955. He also had a letter from Captain Robert J. Hertell, a statement from Glennie Lankford [the matriarch of the Sutton family who had been present throughout the night], a statement given to Kirk by Major John E. Albert [who unofficially investigated the case in 1955], and a copy of an article written by Glennie Lankford. All that material was available in the government files.

Albert's statement provides some interesting information. Remember, the Air Force claimed that the case had not been officially reported, and therefore, the Air Force had not investigated. This sounds suspiciously like a police officer who, having witnessed a robbery in progress, then ignores it because it hadn't been reported to the station and he wasn't dispatched by headquarters. A police officer can't ignore the crime and it seems reasonable to assume that the Air Force shouldn't have ignored this case. The sighting was reported in the media, including on the radio the next morning. Newspapers from various locations around the country were also reporting what had happened. The Air Force officers at Blue Book or ATIC must have known that the sighting had been made, but they chose to ignore it. If the sighting wasn't reported through official channels, then it didn't exist. Since no one reported this case through official channels, the sighting never happened.

> " [T]he incident involved an all night attack on a family named Sutton by goblin-like creatures reported to have emerged from a so-called 'flying saucer.'"

Or is that the case? Lieutenant Kirk, in his report in 1957, sent a copy of the statement made by Major John E. Albert on September 26, 1957, on to ATIC. The very first paragraph seems to suggest that Campbell Air Force Base was notified, which should have, according to regulations in effect at that time (1955), been sufficient to record the sighting as being reported through official channels. The regulation is quite clear on the point, and regardless of whether everyone in the military believed the sighting to be a hoax, a hallucination, or the real thing, it should have been investigated.

That investigation probably would not have been conducted by ATIC and Project Blue Book staff, but by the 4602d Air Intelligence Service Squadron. The version of AFR 200-2 in effect at the time outlines the precise procedure for such an investigation. It should have been passed on to the 4602d. If that is the case, the investigation apparently disappeared there because there is no sign of it in other areas of the government files.

In the statement, Albert said:

On about August 22, 1955, about 8 A.M., I heard a news broadcast concerning an incident at Kelly Station, approximately six miles North of Hopkinsville. At the time I heard this news broadcast, I was at Gracey, Kentucky on my way to Campbell Air Force Base, where I am assigned for reserve training. I called the Air Base and asked them if they had heard anything about an alleged flying saucer report. They stated that they had not and it was suggested that as long as I was close to the area, that I should determine if there was anything to this report. I immediately drove to the scene at Kelly [for some reason the word was blacked out, but it seems reasonable to assume the work is Kelly] Station and located the home belonging to a Mrs. Glennie Lankford [again the name is blacked out], who is the one who first reported the incident. (A copy of Mrs. Lankford's statement is attached to this report).

Albert's statement, as found in the government files, continued:

Deputy Sheriff Batts was at the scene where this supposedly flying saucer had landed and he could not show any evidence that any object had landed in the vicinity. There was nothing to show that there was anything to prove this incident.

Mrs. Lankford was an impoverished widow woman who had grown up in this small community just outside of Hopkinsville, with very little education. She belonged to the Holy Roller Church and the night and evening of this occurrence, had gone to a religious meeting and she indicated that the members of the congregation and her two sons and their wives and some friends of her sons', were also at this religious meeting and were worked up into a frenzy, becoming emotionally unbalanced and that after the religious meeting, they had discussed this article which she had heard about over the radio and had [been] sent for them from the Kingdom Publishers, Fort Worth, Texas and they had sent her this article with a picture which appeared to be [of] a little man when it actually was a monkey, painted silver. This article had to be returned to Mrs. Lankford as she stated it was her property. However, a copy of the writing is attached to this statement and if it is necessary, a photograph can be obtained from the above mentioned publishers.

There are a number of problems with the first couple of paragraphs of Albert's statement, but they are trivial. As an example, it wasn't Glennie Lankford who first reported the incident, but the whole family, who had all traveled into town to alert the police.

The third paragraph, however, is filled with things that bear no resemblance to reality. Lankford was not a member of the Holy Rollers, but of the Trinity Pentecostal. Neither she nor any of the family had been to any religious services the night of the "attack." She couldn't have heard about any article on the radio because there was no radio in the farm house. And there was no evidence that Lankford ever sent anywhere for any kind of article about flying saucers and little creatures. In other words, Albert had written the case off almost before he began his "investigation" began because of his false impressions. It appears that he was only interested in facts that would allow him to debunk the case instead of trying to learn what really happened during the night. Remember, he had no official standing, he was not acting on orders, and he had just interjected himself into the case.

Further evidence of this is provided in the next paragraph of his statement. "It is my opinion that the report Mrs. Lankford or her son, Elmer Sutton, was caused by one of two reasons. Either they actually did see what they thought was a little man and at the time, there was a circus in the area and a monkey might have escaped, giving the appearance of a small man. Two, being emotionally upset, and discussing the article and showing pictures of this little monkey, that appeared like a man, their imaginations ran away with them and they really did believe what they saw, which they thought was a little man."

Albert had written the case off almost before he began his "investigation" began because of his false impressions.

It is interesting to note that Albert is not suggesting that the witnesses were engaged in inventing a hoax. Instead, with absolutely no evidence, Albert invented the tale of a monkey that fooled the people. It is hard to explain how the monkey was able to survive the shots fired at it by the terrified people in the house, especially if it was as close to the house as the witnesses suggested. In other words, with shotguns and rifles being fired at the little man, someone should have hit the animal and there should have been broken bits of monkey all over the farm land.

But Albert wasn't through with the little monkey theory. According to the government file, "The home that Mrs. Lankford lived in was in a very run down condition and there were about eight people sleeping in two rooms. The window that was pointed out to be the one that she saw the small silver shining object about two and a half feet tall, that had its hands on the screen looking in, was a very low window and a small monkey could put his hands on the top of it while standing on the ground."

The final sentence of Albert's account said, "It is felt that the report cannot be substantiated as far as any actual object appearing in the vicinity at that time." The report was then signed by Kirk, who was reviewing everything for the Air Force.

It is interesting that Albert and Kirk were both willing to ignore the report of the object because there was nothing to substantiate it, but they were willing to buy the monkey theory, even though there was nothing to substantiate it either. It is possible that Glennie Lankford may have inspired the little monkey theory with something she included in her handwritten statement, available in the government files, signed on August 22, 1955:

My name is Glennie Lankford age 50 and I live at Kelly Station, Hopkinsville, Route 6, Kentucky.

On Sunday night Aug 21, 55 about 10:30 P.M. I was walking through the hallway which is located in the middle of my house and I looked out the back door (south) and saw a bright silver object about two and a half feet tall appearing round. I became excited and did not look at it long enough to see if it had any eyes or move. I was about 15 or 20 feet from it. I fell backward, and then was carried into the bedroom.

My two sons, Elmer Sutton aged 25, and his wife Vera aged 29, J. C. Sutton aged 21, and his wife Aline aged 27, and their friends Billy Taylor aged 21, and his wife June, 18 were all in the house and saw this little man that looked like a monkey.

So the Air Force seized on Lankford's description and turned it into a possible answer, suggesting that the Suttons had been attacked by a horde of monkeys who were immune to shotguns and rifles. They postulated a non-existent circus for the monkeys to have escaped from. They overlooked the evidence of the case, dispatched someone to look into it unofficially, and then denied that they had investigated it at all. The best way to debunk something was to offer any solution, no matter how ridiculous that solution might be. To their way of thinking, any solution is better than no solution, and people would only remember that the case had been solved. They rarely remembered what that solution might have been.

"Unidentified" Aliens

On April 24, 1964, just months prior to the Cisco Grove sighting, Lonnie Zamora, a police officer in Socorro, New Mexico, spotted an object with two small humanoids near it. According to the government files, Zamora was chasing a speeder when he heard a loud roar and saw a flash of light in the southwestern sky. Fearing that a dynamite shed on the edge of town might have exploded, Zamora broke off the chase and headed in that direction.

As he approached a gully, he saw what he first thought was an overturned car. Zamora stopped his patrol car and saw, near the object, "two people in white coveralls...."

Government files recorded the whole story and Captain (later lieutenant colonel) Hector Quintanilla provided a perspective on this situation. As the chief of Blue Book at the time, he not only had access to all the government files but he was running the investigation. After describing the overall situation, Quintanilla wrote:

All hell broke loose on April 24, 1964, and I started smoking again. On that date at approximately 17:45 hours, at Socorro, New Mexico, police officer Lonnie Zamora was headed south chasing a speeding automobile when he suddenly heard a roar and saw a flame in the sky to the southwest. He decided to let the speeder go in favor of investigating the flame, because he knew there was a dynamite shack in the area and it might have blown up. He turned onto a gravel road that led by the shack.

As he was driving slowly along the road, Zamora saw above a steep hill just ahead a funnel-shaped flame, bluish and sort of orange. The base of the

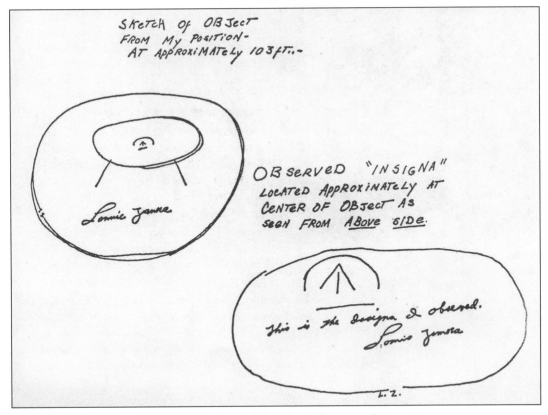

SKETCH OF OBJECT
FROM MY POSITION-
AT APPROXIMATELY 103 FT..-

OBSERVED "INSIGNA"
LOCATED APPROXIMATELY AT
CENTER OF OBJECT AS
SEEN FROM ABOVE SIDE.

Lonnie Zamora

This is the designa I observed.
Lonnie Zamora

I. 2.

Drawing made by police officer Lonnie Zamora of the "object" he saw in Socorro, including a closer detail of the insignia on it.

flame was hidden behind the hill, there was no smoke connected with the flame. He had trouble getting the car to the top of the hill because of loose gravel; he had to try three times before he made it. As he reached the top of the hill, he saw a shiny object to the south, this side of the dynamite shack, about 150 to 200 yards away.

It was off the road to the left in the arroyo, and at first glance it looked like a car turned over, but when he drove closer it appeared to be aluminum clay, not chrome, and oval-shaped like a football. Zamora drove about fifty feet along the hill crest, radioing back to the sheriff's office, "10-44 (accident), I'll be 10-6 (busy out of the car), checking a wreck down in the arroyo." From this point, seated in the car, he could not see the object over the edge of the hill. As he stopped the car, he was still talking on the radio, and while he was getting out he dropped his mike. He picked it up and put it back and started down towards the object.

Just then he heard a very loud roar, not exactly like a blast, but also not steady like a jet engine. It was of low frequency at first and then became higher. At the same time he saw a light blue flame, sort of orange at the

A photo of an imprint made by the alien craft that landed in Socorro.

bottom. Zamora believed the flame came from the underside of the object; he could see no smoke but he did see some dust in the vicinity. He panicked, thinking the object was going to blow up. The following is his report of what he experienced (with slight rearrangements for the sake of clarity).

"As soon as I saw flame and heard roar ... ran away from object but did turn head towards object. Object was in shape. It was smooth— no windows or doors. As roar started, it was still on the ground.

"Noted red lettering of some type like [redacted]. Insignia was about two and one half inches high and about two inches wide, I guess. Was in the middle of object, like [redacted]. Object still like aluminum white.

(Running), bumped leg on car back fender area. Car facing southwest ... fell by can [sic] and (sun) glasses fell off, kept running to north, with car between me and object ... rose to about level of car, about twenty to twenty-five feet, guess. Took I guess, about six seconds when object started to rise and I glanced back ... it appeared about directly over the place where it rose from.

"I was still running ... (then) about fifty feet from car. I ducked down, just over edge of hill ... I stopped because I did not hear the roar. I was scared of the roar, and I had planned to continue running down the hill. I turned around toward the object and at the same time put my head toward ground, covering my face with my arms ... when the roar stopped, heard a sharp tone whine and the whine lasted maybe a second. Then there was complete silence about the object.

"That's when I lifted up my head and saw the object going away from me ... in a southwestern direction.... It did not come any closer to me. It appeared to go in straight line and at same height—possibly ten to fifteen feet from ground, and it cleared the dynamite shack by about three feet. Shack about eight feet high. Object was traveling west fast. It seemed to rise up and take off immediately across country.

"I ran back to my car and as I ran back, I kept an eye on the object. I picked up my ... sunglasses, got into the car, and radioed to Nep Lopes, radio operator, to look out the window to see if he could see an object. He asked, 'What is it?' I answered, 'It looks like a balloon.' I don't know if he saw it. If Nep looked out his window, which faces north, he couldn't see it. I did not tell him at the moment which window to look out of.

"As I was calling Nep, I could still see object. The object seemed to lift up slowly, and to get small in the distance very fast. It seemed to just clear the Box Canyon or Mile Canyon Mountain. It disappeared as it went over the mountain. It had no flame whatsoever as it was traveling over the ground, and no smoke or noise.

"Feeling in good health. Last drink—two or three beers over a month ago. Noted no odors. Noted no sounds other than described. Gave direction to Nep Lopes at radio and to Sergeant Chaves (of New Mexico State Police at Socorro) to get there. Went down to where the object had been, and I noted the brush was burning in several places. I got my pen and drew a picture of the insignia on the object.

"Then Sgt. Chaves came up, asked me what the trouble was because I was sweating and he told me that I was white, very pale. I asked the Sgt. To see what I saw and that was the burning brush. Then Sgt. Chaves and I went down to the spot and Sgt. Chaves pointed out the tracks.

"When I first saw the object (when I thought it might be a car) I saw what appeared to be two legs of some type from the object to the ground. At the time, I didn't pay much attention to … the two legs. The two legs were at the bottom of the object, slanted outwards to the ground. The object might have been about three and a half feet from the ground at the time…."

Lonnie Zamora experienced an event which left quite an impression on him. He was a serious officer, a pillar of his church, and a man well versed in recognizing airborne vehicles in his area. He was puzzled by what he saw, and frankly, so am I. And yet, I've always had some doubt about this case, even though it is the best documented case on record. In spite of the fact that I conducted the most thorough investigation that was humanly possible, the vehicle or stimulus that scared Zamora to the point of panic has never been found.

During the course of the investigation and immediately thereafter, everything that was possible to verify was checked. The communications media must have been waiting for a case like this, because immediately after Zamora reported his sighting all hell broke loose. The telephone at my house was ringing off the hook. I went to my office so that I could direct the investigation from there and at the same time contact Kirtland, Holloman, and White Sands via our telephone communications system. As I walked into our building, and turned into the hallway towards my office, I could hear the telephone ringing, ringing, ringing. The operator informed me that I had ten or twelve calls waiting for me. I decided not to accept the calls until after I had talked with my UFO investigating officer at Kirtland. Major Connor was my primary investigator at Kirtland, but he was inexperienced.

A drawing showing what Zamora described, including the ship and two figures in white.

Fortunately, my chief analyst, Sgt. David Moody was on temporary duty at Kirtland. I asked Major Connor to get in touch with him and for Moody to get in touch with me regardless of the hour. It was hours before the investigation could be organized and on its way. A Geiger counter had to be found and the base photographer had to be called. The staff car, which had been provided for the investigation, had a flat tire midway between Albuquerque and Socorro. Socorro is located fifty-five miles south of Kirtland Air Force Base.

The Stallion Range Officer had already conducted a preliminary investigation and had also interviewed Zamora. This information was turned over to the Air Force investigators as soon as they began their interview with Zamora.

Connor and Moody kept in touch with me and provided me with good information, but there was nothing from which we could draw a definite conclusion or a decent evaluation. The news media was on SAFOI's back and SAFOI was on my back. I didn't have any idea as to what Zamora saw and reported, but by God, I was going to find it. Because of the pressure from the news media, I decided to send Dr. J. Allen Hynek, Project Blue Book consultant, to Kirtland to help with the investigation. I felt that Hynek could concentrate on Socorro while Connor and Moody could check all other activity at the other bases in New Mexico.

In the meantime, Marilyn Beumer Stancombe, my secretary, and I began checking for some sort of positive activity. Radiation had been checked by Connor and Moody and the readings were negative. I checked the Holloman AFB Balloon Control Center for balloon activity. All local weather stations and Air Force bases in New Mexico were checked for release of weather balloons. Helicopter activity was checked throughout the state. Government and private aircraft were checked. The reconnaissance division in the Pentagon was checked. I checked with the immigration division hoping they might help. Finally, I was at my wits end, so I told Marilyn, "Get me the White House Command Post." She looked at me with those beautiful blue eyes of hers like I was nuts. I said, "Yes, Marilyn, the White House Command Post."

She never asked me a question, she just started dialing. I was afraid she would ask me how she could reach them, but she didn't. It took her five or six calls, but she got me the Command Post. A Major General answered and I explained to him my situation. He was very sympathetic, but off hand he couldn't recall any type of activity in my area of interest. However, he'd check and call me back.

Fifteen minutes later the General called back and told me that the only activity which he had was some U-2 flights. That was no help, so I thanked him for his cooperation and put my thinking cap on again.

It took days for us to check all of these agencies and activities. I finally received Dr. Hynek's report; it was one of his typical reports which contained few technical details and added practically nothing to what had already

Only U-2 aircraft like this one were in flight around Kirtland Air Force Base at the time of Zamora's sighting.

been submitted by Connor and Moody. Actually, Hynek added very little to the investigation, however, his typical press interviews added more flame to the fire. The more press coverage the sightings got, the greater the number of sightings which were reported throughout New Mexico.

I was determined to solve the case and come hell or high water I was going to find the vehicle or the stimulus. I decided that it was imperative for me to talk to the Base Commander at Holloman AFB. I wanted to interview the Base Commander at length about special activities from his base. I needed help to pull this off, so I called Lt. Col. Maston Jacks at SAFOI. I told him what I wanted to do and he asked, "Do you think it will do any good?" I replied, "God damned it Maston, if there is an answer to this case it has to be in some hanger at Holloman." He went to work from his position at the Pentagon and the approval for my visit came through. Colonel Garman was the Base Commander during my visit. He was most cooperative and told me that I could go anywhere and visit any activity which interested me. I went from one end of the base to the other. I spent four days talking to everybody I could and spent almost a whole day with the down-range controllers at the White Sands Missile Range. I left Holloman dejected and convinced that the answer to Zamora's experience did not originate and terminate at that base.

On my way back to Wright-Patterson, I hit upon an idea. Why not a lunar landing vehicle? I knew that some research had been done at Wright-Pat-

This is the NASA lunar soft lander. Could the UFO have been a lander test? The only problem was the landers were not operational at that time.

terson; so as soon as I got back I asked for some briefings. The briefings were extremely informative, but the Lunar Landers were not operational in April 1964. I got the names of the companies that were doing research in this field and I started writing letters. The companies were most cooperative, but their answers were all negative.

It was now time for me to pass judgment on the case after a careful review of all the information at hand. I hate to use the word "judgment," but that is exactly what it boils down to. As President Truman used to say, "The buck stops here," and in the world of UFO's my desk was the end of the line. It was time for the Air Force to make a formal decision on the sighting of Socorro, New Mexico. I reviewed the Air Force Materials Laboratory Analysis of the soil samples which were gathered at the alleged landing area. Conclusion: no foreign residue. Laboratory analysis of the burned brush revealed no chemicals that could have been propellant residue. Radiation was normal for the alleged landing area and for the surrounding area. There was no unusual meteorological activity, no thunderstorms; the weather was windy, but clear. Although we made an extensive search for other witnesses, none could be located. There were no unidentified helicopters or aircraft in the area. Radar installations at Holloman AFB and at Albuquerque observed no unusual blips, but the down-range Holloman MTI (Moving Target Indicator) Radar, closest to Socorro, had been closed down for the day at 1600 hours. All the findings and conclusions were negative. The object was traveling at approximately 120 miles per hour when it disappeared over the mountains according to Zamora's best estimate.

I labeled the case "Unidentified" and the UFO buffs and hobby clubs had themselves a field day. According to them, here was proof that our beloved planet had been visited by an extraterrestrial vehicle. Although I labeled the case "Unidentified" I've never been satisfied with that classification.

Apparently, Zamora wasn't the only witness to the craft. The government files include information on additional witnesses. Opal Grinder, owner of a Socorro service station reported that a tourist had said something about jets flying very low over the town. That tourist has never been found and interviewed, so any description of the craft and the incident is second hand at best. It might have provided important corroboration for the case if the man and his family could have been located. As it is, it is simply an interesting anecdote with little value as evidence.

There are, however, two other witnesses who have been named and have been interviewed by reporters and UFO investigators. According to an article published in the Dubuque *Telegraph-Herald* on Wednesday, April 29, 1964, Paul Kries, who was twenty-four, and Larry Kratzer, who was twenty-six, were in Socorro the previous Friday when the object took off. They had been traveling along the highway.

Kratzer told the reporter, "We saw some brown dust, then black smoke—like rubber burning—then a fire. The smoke hid the shiny craft as it flew away."

Then they began to talk about things they couldn't have seen, but might have heard on the news or read in the newspapers. Remember, they were talking some five days later, after there had been a great deal published and broadcast about the sighting.

Kries said that federal agents had cordoned the area and that government sources had denied they had anything like the observed craft near Socorro. Kries said that there were four depressions, about twelve feet apart, left by the object. He also claimed that there was a large burned patch on the desert and that the exhaust had melted a pop bottle when it took off. None of these things are true.

> "We saw some brown dust, then black smoke—like rubber burning—then a fire. The smoke hid the shiny craft as it flew away."

Sometime later, an Iowa UFO researcher named Ralph DeGraw interviewed the two men, but he was not impressed with their story. He said that the account conflicted what Zamora had described and felt that their testimony was not trustworthy.

The descriptions offered by Kries and Kratzer of what was found on the landing site seemed to imply that they had been there and seen it. They suggest the area was cordoned, which was possible since there were police officers and police cars parked around the site. They talked about the landing traces left by the craft as it took off, implying they had seen that as well.

However, there is no evidence that any civilians were on the scene that night. Almost all the testimony that was offered by Zamora, Sergeant Sam Chavez of the New Mexico State Police, FBI agent Bynes, Army Captain Richard Holder, and whatever was filtered through Col. Eric Jonckheere seemed to suggest no civilian presence, though it is possible that some of the military men might have been in civilian clothes. The descriptions given by those who were on site is based on the documentation available in the government files and differs from what Kries and Kratzer said.

Their description of the landing marks were nothing new and could have been picked up by anyone who had watched the story unfold over the past couple of days. Kries and Kratzer didn't say anything about the sighting until a week or so had passed, with plenty of time to have seen and heard stories about what was seen.

While it would be nice to have additional witnesses to the case, there are many problems with Kries and Kratzer's testimony. Had they left it at having seen something in the sky as they drove by, it would be one thing, but they claimed to be at the landing site. And it is clear from the evidence found in the government files that neither of these men had walked the field.

In the end, the government file listed the case as an "unidentified." Quintanilla said that he didn't like that solution, or more properly the label he had applied to it, probably because it would delight those who believed that some UFOs represented alien visitation. As he said later, "Although I labeled the case 'Unidentified' I've never been satisfied with that classification."

Temple, Oklahoma, March 23, 1966

It has been claimed that the Socorro, New Mexico sighting is the only case involving occupants or creatures associated with a landed UFO labeled as unidentified in the Blue Book files. This is not true. Although it is somewhat hidden in the Project Blue Book files, there is another sighting that took place almost two years later. Hynek mentioned it in his book, *The Hynek UFO Report*, but he doesn't give a location and he dates it based on a newspaper clipping from the *Dallas Times Herald*.

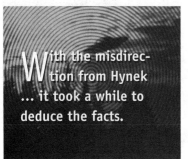

With the misdirection from Hynek ... it took a while to deduce the facts.

Hynek suggests the case is from the Wichita Falls, Texas, area and the witness, W. E. Laxson, was a civilian employee at Sheppard Air Force Base in Wichita Falls, but the government files list the case as Temple, Oklahoma. The newspaper clipping cited by Hynek is dated March 27, 1966, but the sighting occurred on March 23, 1966. With the misdirection from Hynek, probably a result of the classified nature of the case when he wrote his book, it took a while to deduce the facts.

Hynek, using the newspaper account, said there was nothing in the article that varied from what was in the government file. That file said:

> Observer [W. E. Eddie Laxson] was driving his car along the highway at approximately 0505, 23 March 1966, when he noticed an object parked on the road in front of him. He stopped the car and got out so as to get a better view of the object. The object was so parked that it blocked out a portion of the road curve sign. There were no sharp edges noted by the observer. The object had the appearance of a conventional aircraft (C-124) without wings or motors. There was a plexiglas [sic] bubble on top, similar to a B-26 canopy. As observer approached, he noticed a man wearing a baseball cap enter the object by steps from the bottom. After the man entered the object, it began to rise from the pavement and headed on a southeasterly direction at approximately 720 mph. The object had forward and aft lights that were very bright. As the object rose from the ground, a high speed drill type of sound was heard, plus a sound like that of welding rod when an arc is struck. Object was 75' long, nearly 8' from

top to bottom and about 12' wide. There were some type of supports up the bottom of the object.

After the object disappeared the witness got back into his car and drove approximately fifteen miles down the highway. At this time the original witness stopped and talked with another individual who had also stopped along the roadway to watch some lights over Red River which is approximately five or six miles to the southeast.

COMMENTS

Various organizations were contacted around the Temple [Oklahoma] area for a possible experimental or conventional aircraft. The observer stated that he thought the object was some type of Army or Air Force research aircraft. All attempts at such an explanation proved fruitless, since there were no aircraft in the area at the time of the sighting. Although there are numerous helicopters and other experimental in the area, none could be put in the area of Temple at approximately 0500, 23 March 1966. Because of this factor the case is listed as unidentified by the Air Force.

The second witness, who was not interviewed by the Air Force and who, according to the government file, did not fill out their long and involved form, was C. W. Anderson. Anderson confirmed for the newspaper that he had seen the craft as well. He told the reporter, "I know that people will say that Laxson is durned crazy. But that's what I saw."

Anderson said he thought the object had been following him down the road. He had watched it in his rearview mirror for several miles. The problem was that Anderson did not complete the Air Force form and nor did he see the pilot or crewman.

The drawing of the object made by Laxson resembled, roughly, the one that Lonnie Zamora had made of the craft he saw, which means it was sort of egg-shaped. Laxson's drawing was longer and was lying on its side. Like Zamora, Laxson said that he saw symbols on the object, but unlike Zamora, he recognized them. He told the reporter that, "On the side I made out … 'TLA' with the last two figures '38.'"

In a fit of honesty, the Air Force admitted they had no solution for the case. The description of the "alien" was more human than humanoid and he seemed to be dressed in conventional clothes right to the "mechanics" hat. Investigation revealed a second witness and that might have influenced the Air Force, especially since the two men had never met prior to the sighting. In the end, they labeled the case as "Unidentified."

Pittsburg, Kansas, August 25, 1952

In a review of the government records, another case, also labeled as "Unidentified" was found. This one took place in Pittsburg, Kansas. The case is

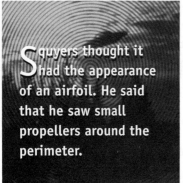

Squyers thought it had the appearance of an airfoil. He said that he saw small propellers around the perimeter.

single witness and has gone nearly unreported for more than sixty years. The information about it is found in the government files.

William Squyers was on his way to work along Highway 160, about eight miles from Pittsburg when, according to the information from the government files, he "sighted an unknown object hovering over a field...." It was about seventy feet in length and about twelve feet high. Squyers thought it had the appearance of an airfoil. He said that he saw small propellers around the perimeter. They were about a foot in diameter.

There were also a number of windows in the craft and through one of them, Squyers could see a man who seemed to be controlling the object. The man was facing forward, "to the edge of the object." The windows were described as blue, becoming darker as time passed.

This seems to be the type of sighting the Air Force would dismiss as "psychological," a polite way of saying that it was a hoax or there was something wrong with the witness. However, there was some physical evidence left behind. According to the government file:

> Object reported as hovering over an open field used for cattle grazing. General area under the exact location was pressed down and formed a round 60' diameter impression, with the grass in a recognizable concentric pattern. Loose grass lay over the top of the impression as if drawn in by suction when the object ascended vertically at a high speed. Vegetation and grass approximately 3 to 4' high. Area is extremely dry at present. Grass showed where Squyers had walked in to a fence and stopped. L. V. Baxter and D. Widner, local employees of KOMA, went to the place of sighting at 1135 CST with Squyers and confirmed his path to the fence and the 60' diameter impression in the tall grass. Robert E. Greene visited the site at 1600, 25 Aug 52, with source and reports that the vegetation was laid down in concentric circles but with the impression less distinct than reported by Widner and Baxter. Greene obtained grass and soil samples of the immediate area where the impression was made and also gathered control samples 200 yards removed from the site. He is sending some to the Air Technical Intelligence Center, Air Mail, Special Delivery.

Strangely, there seemed to be little interest in the pilot of the craft. Although the pilot is discussed at another point, there is no real addition to the information. Based on the descriptions, the alien was human enough to be indistinguishable from a human. Squyers did suggest that the occupant seemed to be frenzied in his activities inside the craft.

Although this case is essentially single witness, there was the physical evidence left by the craft. Baxter, Widner, Greene, and others did see the impressions in the ground left by the craft. Eventually this sort of evidence would become

Patterns like these, called crop circles, have been found all over the world. Many believe that the elaborate designs are caused by UFOs, but no one knows why they would make them.

known as a saucer nest, referring to the fact that the crushed vegetation left by a UFO on the ground had somewhat similar features in other parts of the country and other parts of the world. Ultimately, these impressions would be called crop circles. In this case, rather than an elaborate design, there was just a simple circle of crushed or flattened grass.

The soil samples taken by Greene were analyzed by the Air Force. In a short, one paragraph report, the technicians said they had found no radiation, burning, or stress of any kind. In other words, there was nothing in the samples to distinguish the ones taken from the landing area versus those taken 200 yards away.

There is one final aspect to the case that is mildly interesting. In a couple of the letters from the government files, there is a notation that reminds all of paragraph seven, a regulation that requires unidentified cases to be classified. Those who have information about the case are not allowed to discuss it with those who do not have the proper clearances.

J. Allen Hynek, writing in *The Hynek UFO Report,* provides a glimpse into the thinking at Blue Book at the time of this sighting. He wrote, "My skepticism was so great at that time that I was quite willing to dismiss it as a hallucination."

In other words, he was willing to reject the physical evidence that something had landed, he was willing to reject the observations of the three other men who had seen the depressions left in the grass because he didn't believe that such things were possible. In the 1970s Hynek modified that belief, stating that he thought the witnesses to such events, meaning UFO landings, sincerely believed they had a real experience, but that did not mean that a UFO had landed.

Even with that admitted bias, the case, which never received wide exposure, is another example where the witness said that he had seen the pilot of an unidentified craft, but the case was left as unidentified by the Air Force. In their zeal to label cases, this seems to be another one that they missed. They could have easily labeled it as "psychological" if it was not for the landing traces.

Labeling the Cases

Keeping with their tradition of labeling cases but not solving them, the Air Force officers decided that the Cisco Grove witness had psychological problems. There is no need to investigate if the witness is unreliable or has some kind of mental problem.

According to documents in the government files, in a letter dated October 2, 1964, Major Eric Jonckheere asked, "Did the interviewing officers feel that this occurance [sic] could have been attributed to an owl or other such birds or animals, coupled with an overactive imagination on the part of the witness?"

Can we say that we are surprised with the cavalier way they treated the evidence, such as obtaining the arrowhead, passing it along, and then losing it? Can we say that we're surprised with the way they handled the investigation considering the track record they had already established? Can we say that we're surprised with their conclusion, considering their belief that UFOs don't exist and if you see the creatures in one, then you must be psychologically disturbed?

In fact, the Pittsburg, Kansas, case has the same problem. Here was a case in which the object interacted with the environment. True, it was single witness, but the object left marks on the ground. Rather than send in someone to review the evidence carefully, the Air Force allowed samples to be gathered by a civilian. They may have provided some guidance, but if the Air Force was serious about investigating UFOs, it would have been infinitely better if an expert with proper training was sent to investigate.

Can we say that we're surprised with the way they handled the investigation considering the track record they had already established?

A military officer did gather some of the data for this case. Greene was apparently a second lieutenant in the Army Reserve, and he is the man who collected the samples, but there is no evidence to suggest that his military training had covered this type of recovery. Also, his membership in the Reserve meant that he filed his report with his own chain of command, and although it made its way to the Air Force, the report was delayed.

Zamora was a single witness, but there was physical evidence left behind, and the Air Force responded quickly. They gathered evidence and analyzed the situation, but found no answer that satisfied them.

There is the possibility that there were two other witnesses. They appeared after the fact, are not from the Socorro area, and their stories seemed to have been embellished with facts from news reports.

In fact, in all the cases, there was some physical evidence to be examined. The cases did not rest solely on the testimony of the witnesses. If there wasn't some kind of physical evidence, there was another witness to corroborate the sighting.

The Cisco Grove occupant report is just one more example of an opportunity that was missed. Or rather, one that seems to have been missed. There was some corroborative testimony from the other hunters, there was the damage to the arrows, and then there was the report that the area had been cleaned.

What we don't know is who had been out in the forest, cleaning the area in which the witness claimed to have seen the alien beings. Just who could have done that?

Belt, Montana, and the Minuteman Missile Crisis

Government files, including Project Blue Book, reveal that on March 24, 1967, near the small town of Belt, Montana, a truck driver named Ken Williams saw a domed object land in a canyon near the road. He was curious enough that he stopped, got out of his truck, and began to walk toward the object. The UFO then lifted off, flew further up the canyon and touched down again, now hidden from the highway by a ridge.

Williams, in a handwritten document filed with the National Investigations Committee on Aerial Phenomenon, told the whole story of what he had seen that night. In response to their request, on April 7, 1967, Williams wrote:

Gentlemen:

Object was first observed approximately 5 miles southeast of Belt, Montana. I was traveling North on Highway 87 enroute to Great Falls, Montana. Object was approximately 1 mile to my left and appeared to be about 5 or 6 hundred yards [1,500–1,800 feet] altitude. I would estimate its speed to vary from 40 to 50 miles per hour. I am judging this speed by the speed I was traveling as object seemed to be running evenly with me. Its appearance was that of a large doomed [sic] shaped light or that of a giant headlight. Upon climbing up the Belt Hill in my truck, I looked to my left and about ½ mile up a gully. I witnessed the object at about 200 yards [600 feet] in the air in a still position. I stopped my truck and the object dropped slowly to what appeared to me to be <u>within a very few feet from the ground</u>. [Underlining in original]. It was at this time that I felt something or someone was watching me. As a very bright effecting light emerged from the object it momentarily blinded me. This extremely bright light seemed to flare three times. Each time holding its brightness. By the third time the <u>light was so bright</u> [underlining in original] that it was nearly impossible to look directly at it. It was at this time that I drove my truck onto the top of the hill which was about another ½ mile. I stopped a car and asked the people [Don Knotts of Great Falls] if they would stop at a station at the foot of the hill and call the Highway Patrol. I went back down the hill and viewed the object for several more minutes. It was while watching it the second time that it rose and disappeared like a bolt of lightning. I went back to the top of the hill where my truck was parked and just as the Highway Patrolmen [sic] Bud Nader arrived the object appeared once again. About 2 miles away and traveling in a Northeast direction, whereas it stopped once again and <u>appeared to drop to the ground</u> [Underlining in the original.]. There are several deep gullys [sic] in the area where it appeared to drop out of sight. This was my last sighting of the object.

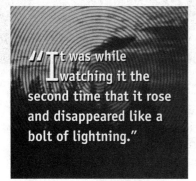

"It was while watching it the second time that it rose and disappeared like a bolt of lightning."

The government file on this case contains what was known as a Project Record Card, a 4" × 6" card that outlined the details of the case. While the case is labeled as "unidentified," it also noted that there was "(1 witness)," which they believed to be so important that it was underlined. But that isn't true and other documents in the government files prove it.

According to a letter written by Lieutenant Colonel Lewis D. Chase, and addressed to Edward Condon at the University of Colorado, there was at least one other witness. According to Chase, "Mr. Nader [sent by the Highway Patrol] reported that upon reaching the scene he observed an unusual light emanating from the area that the truck driver, Mr. Williams, claimed the object had landed a second time."

The Newspaper Accounts

The *Great Falls Leader* carried a series of articles about UFO sightings in the area at the time. Interestingly, some of what was printed in the newspaper was not found in the government files. Those who conducted the military investigation should have been aware of the other sightings, but there is no mention of them. It seems that as far as the Air Force was concerned, those sightings never happened.

Ron Rice, a staff writer on the newspaper said that there had been UFO sightings all over the state that day. He wrote, "Before midnight it was the Belt area; after 3 this morning, Malmstrom Air Force Base where one was picked up on the bottom of a Federal Aviation Agency radar scope which tracked it for a time before it disappeared in the direction of the Belt Mountains."

There were visual sightings as well. Airman Second Class (A2C) Richard Moore, a communicator-plotter said that he had seen something about five or ten miles from the base at 3:30 A.M. Airman Third Class (A3C) said that he had seen an object that appeared to be a bright light with orange lights on the bottom. This, according to Moore, was close to the ground and it was what the FAA radar had detected.

Moore also said that a sabotage alert team had located another object about 4:40 A.M. directly over Malmstrom. Moore said that he saw it as well, but it was more a point of light moving across the sky than anything else. He said it wasn't a satellite because it was zigzagging.

Another airman, Warren Mahoney, said that Moore had told him about the UFO at 3:10 A.M. and that at 3:42, he had received a call from the FAA that there was an object on their radar northwest of the base. Three minutes later it had turned, flying toward the southeast. At 4:26 A.M. it disappeared from the FAA radar.

Rice also mentioned that there had been a search of the canyon where Williams and Nader saw the UFO and they found some evidence, though it isn't clear exactly what they had found. Sheriff's deputies Keith Wolverton, Jim Cinker, and Harold Martin searched the ground for about two and a half hours and discovered some freshly broken twigs on bushes and branches of the trees. They thought it might have been cattle, but there were no cattle in the area. Martin was reported as saying, "Some of the trees are 25 feet high, and had limbs broken from them, and some bushes below them were broken. All were fresh breaks."

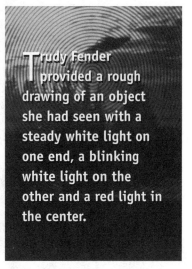

Trudy Fender provided a rough drawing of an object she had seen with a steady white light on one end, a blinking white light on the other and a red light in the center.

According to the *Great Falls Tribune*, Trudy Fender provided a rough drawing of an object she had seen with a steady white light on one end, a blinking white light on the other and a red light in the center. She had been waiting for her ride on March 26. The sighting isn't important because of her description of the object but because she saw something, and it refuted a theory that there had been no UFO sightings in Montana other than Williams sighting two days earlier.

The Government File

With all that was going on that night, with the news media alerted and with local law enforcement involved, there wasn't much that the Air Force could do other than respond. The government files, in a teletype message that was unclassified revealed, "Between hours of 2100 and 0400 MST numerous reports were received by Malmstrom AFB agencies of UFO sightings in the Great Falls, Montana area."

The message noted that "Reports of a UFO landing near Belt, Montana were received from several sources including deputies of Cascade County Sheriff's Office. Investigation is being conducted by Lt. Col. Lewis Chase.... The alleged landing site is under surveillance. However daylight is required for further search."

The investigation was apparently completed several days later and on April 8, 1967, Chase wrote a report that he sent on to Edward Condon at the University of Colorado who was leading the Air Force sponsored investigation into UFOs. After setting the scene, Lewis wrote:

> Numerous reports were being received by the dispatcher at Base Operations, plus questions from the public. At 2205 [10:05 P.M.], Lt. Col. Lewis D. Chase, Base UFO Investigating Officer, was notified by the Command

Malmstrom AFB in Cascade County, Montana, received numerous reports of UFO sightings in 1967.

Post of a reported landing. Sequence of events following notification were as follows:

2215—Check was made with Base Operations as to aircraft movement in the area. An outbound transient aircraft departed Great Falls enroute to Glasgow, Montana. Departure time was 2109 [9:09 P.M.]. All other aircraft were accounted for.

2230—Discussion with the Sheriff of Cascade County revealed that he had dispatched additional deputies to the area. Requested that he notify me of any significant findings. While talking to the sheriff, he contacted one of his mobile units. The man reporting said that they were at the scene and that there was no activity at the time. Requested the sheriff to forward any subsequent developments.

2330—I called the Sheriff of Cascade County for a status report. He put one of his deputies on the line (Ziener?) who had been at the scene and had interviewed the truck driver and highway patrolman. While on the phone, Sheriff Martin from Belt, Montana, called in from the scene. He discussed the possibility of manpower assistance from Malmstrom and/or helicopter support. Informed him that daylight would be the first possible helicopter support and that I would discuss the other manpower request with Colonel Klibbe.

2345—Discussion with Colonel Klibbe. He suggested that I go out and evaluate the situation and make my recommendations from there.

0030—Departed the base in radio equipped station wagon accompanied by Major John Grasser of the Helicopter Section, for an evaluation of the terrain for any possible helicopter survey at daylight, a driver, and the alert photographer.

0100—Arrived at the scene. Was met by Sheriff Martin, who repeated the previous reports. He had been on the scene continuously. A study of the terrain revealed the hopelessness of any ground survey at night. A tentative plan was agreed upon—the sheriff's office to conduct a ground search of the reported landing area on the morning of 25 March 1967, while concurrently a helicopter survey of the area would be performed by Malmstrom. (It had been reported by Major Grasser that a helicopter training flight was scheduled for 0730 Saturday morning. This procedure was later approved by 15th AF, provided no landing was made). Sightseers were in the area due to radio publicity and Martin reported some had gone on the ridges before he could stop them.

0215—Reported to Colonel Klibbe the tentative plan agreed upon with Sheriff Martin. He approved.

0230 to 0340—Numerous sightings reported.

0350—Discussed the make-up of a message with Captain Bradshaw, Wing Command Post, IAW [In Accordance With] AFR [Air Force Regulation] 80-17, to notify concerned agencies, including CSAF, of numerous sightings, plus the reported landing under investigation. Was concerned with resulting publicity and the need to notify other agencies prior to press releases. Message will merely state reported landing, that it is under investigation, that daylight hours are required to complete investigation, and that a subsequent report will be submitted. Preliminary message dispatched.

0800—Sheriff's ground search and Malmstrom aerial survey completed with negative results. Follow-up messages dispatched to interested agencies (AFR 80-17) stating negative results of the investigation.

The last part of the report confirmed that Chase had conducted the investigation and provided his contact information. In a teletype message sent later, he reported again that there had been negative results.

None of the newspaper articles appeared in the official government file, which is odd. Often the case files included many, if not all, the newspaper articles about the specific sighting. It could be, in this case, that the newspaper reports contradict some of the information contained in the official file. Although Chase wrote that his investigation was negative, the sheriff's deputies did report they had found some evidence at the scene. The problem is that the evidence wasn't sufficiently unusual and there were alternative explanations for it. Cattle certainly could have been responsible for some of it, though it is unlikely that cows could damage something twenty-five feet above the ground.

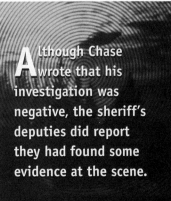

Although Chase wrote that his investigation was negative, the sheriff's deputies did report they had found some evidence at the scene.

All mentions of the radar reports are missing from the government files, as are the reports from Air Force personnel. Even if Chase was uninterested in most of the civilian sightings, it would seem that he would want to talk to the airman who saw something, if for no other reason than to explain the sightings. This is a hole in the investigation.

The radar sightings, with the corroborative visual reports would seem to be an important part of the case. The combination of the two would make it a stronger case, but Chase didn't follow up on it. The government files that are available suggest he did not explore the radar sightings, he did not request information from the FAA, and he didn't interview any of the radar operators. The newspaper files suggest that the information had been reported the next day and Chase should have known about it.

One thing that might have affected how the investigation was conducted was the mission of Malmstrom AFB, a minuteman missile base. Just days before, an entire flight of missiles had suddenly fallen into a "No-Go" situation, meaning they had been deactivated. This mission was a matter of national security and may have been the reason the Belt, Montana, sighting was so poorly investigated.

Echo Flight

Robert Salas and Jim Klotz were the first to tell the story of Echo Flight, which they did in an online article at cufon.org and later in their book, *Faded Giant*. Robert Hastings, in his *UFOs and Nukes*, provided additional information. The story began early on the morning of March 16, 1967, when two missile maintenance teams working on two different flights, widely scattered across the launch facility, said they had seen strange lights in the sky. A mobile security team confirmed this, saying they had seen the lights as well. All this was relayed to Colonel Don Crawford by Captain Eric Carlson and First Lieutenant Walt Figel per Salas's 1996 taped interview with Figel. Hastings was told virtually the same things during his interviews with Figel.

About 8:30 A.M., that same morning, as both Carlson and Figel were performing routine checks, the flight's missiles began to drop off line. Within seconds, though Figel later said it was minutes, all ten missiles were inoperable. This was a major national security issue and a point that later became important during a search of the government files.

Hastings wrote, "Immediately after the malfunctions at Echo, the launch officers ordered two separate Security Alert Teams to drive to each of the launch facilities where the UFOs had been sighted. Nevertheless, the maintenance and security personnel at each site reported seeing UFOs hovering near the missile silos."

He added that "some months after my book came out, in July 2008, I interviewed Figel on tape. He said one of the two SAT teams reported seeing the UFO over one of the silos. In 1996, he told Salas that both teams had seen it. A faded memory, it seems...."

But the story wasn't quite so mundane, as Hastings learned during his interviews with Figel. When Hastings talked to Figel, who retired as an Air Force Colonel on October 20, 2008, he was told that one of the guards had suggested the UFO had shut down the missiles. Figel thought the guard was joking. He told Hastings, "I was thinking he was yanking my chain more than anything else."

Hastings asked, "He seemed to be serious to you?"

And Figel responded, "He seemed to be serious but I wasn't taking him seriously."

Hastings wanted to know what the man had seen, and Figel said that it was just a large, round object that was directly over the launch facility.

To clarify the situation, Hastings and Figel discussed the security procedures. Figel said, "[When] the missiles dropped off alert, I started calling the maintenance people out there on the radio ... [I asked] 'What's going on?' ... And the guy says, 'We got a Channel 9 No-Go. It must be a UFO hovering over the site."

Robert Salas, shown here in 2013, was one of the first, along with Jim Klotz, to talk about Echo Flight.

Figel, of course, didn't believe him. He said that one of the two Strike Teams they had dispatched thought they had seen something over the site. They told Figel that a large object was hovering there.

All of this, of course, suggests that UFOs were somehow involved with the sudden shut down of the missile systems. Although the government files reject the idea, there is a great deal of eyewitness testimony to support this theory.

The maintenance teams were dispatched and once they had located the problem, they were able to bring the missiles back online, but the process was not simple and required hours of work on each missile. There was an extensive investigation that involved not only the Air Force but also the contractors who had designed and built the missiles.

According to the 341st Strategic Missile Wing Unit History, recovered through Freedom of Information:

> On 16 March 1967 at 0845, all sites in Echo (E) Flight, Malmstrom AFB, shutdown with No-Go indication of Channels 9 and 12 on Voice Reporting Signal Assemble (VRSA). All LF's in E Flight lost strategic alert nearly simultaneously. No other Wing I configuration lost strategic alert at that time.

> Guidance & Control channel 50 dump data was collected from E-7 facility and E-3 Facility and all 10 sites were then returned to strategic alert

without any LF equipment replacement. All 10 sites were reported to have been subject to a normal controlled shutdown....

The only possible means that could be identified by the team involved a situation in which a couple self test command occurred along with a partial reset within the coupler. This could feasibly cause a VRSA 9 and 12 indication. This was also quite remote for all 10 couplers would have to have been partially reset in the same manner....

In the researching of other possibilities, weather was ruled out as a contributing factor in the incident.

A check with Communications maintenance verified that there was no unusual activity with EWO-1 or EWO-2 at the time of the incident.

All of which, in the short term, did not explain why all the missiles went off line at virtually the same time. In a very technical part of the Unit History, it explains that a "30 micro sec Pulse ... was placed on the Self Test Command (STC) line.... Seven out of 10 separate applications of a single pulse would cause the system to shut down with a Channel 9 & 12 No-Go."

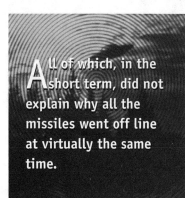

All of which, in the short term, did not explain why all the missiles went off line at virtually the same time.

Or, according to the government files, a randomly introduced electronic pulse which might be considered an EMP, and which shouldn't have affected the missile systems, had shut them down. The point of insertion was apparently the Launch Control Facility, but all those areas should have been shielded from such an occurrence.

The information about the Echo Flight was, quite naturally, communicated to the Condon Committee, and Dr. Roy Craig responded. Although not exactly part of the government files, Craig was working on a government contract for the Air Force when he made notes on his meeting with Lieutenant Colonel Chase at Malmstrom:

After Colonel Chase and I exchanged pleasantries in his office, I asked him about the Echo incident. The Colonel caught his breath, and expressed surprise that I knew of it. "I can't talk about that." ... If I needed to know the cause of this incident, I could arrange through official channels, to see their report after the completion of the investigation.... Although local newspapers carried stories of UFO sightings which would coincide in time with Echo, Colonel Chase had assured me that the incident had not involved a UFO ... I accepted the information as factual and turned review of Major Schraff's report (on the Echo incident) over to Bob Low [Dr. Robert Low, also a member of the Condon Committee], who had received security clearance to read secret information related to the UFO study ... Low, in turn, had to interface with his Air Force Liaison in Washington, Col. Hippler [Lieutenant Colonel Robert Hippler].... [Low wrote to Craig] "Roy, I called Hippler and he said he would try to get this, but he suspects it's going to be classified too high for us to look at. Says he thinks interference by pulses from nuclear explosions is probably involved."

It appears that a cause was found, or rather it seemed to have been found, but the ultimate source of the pulse was not identified. Hippler, speculating about the source of the pulse, came up with an electromagnetic pulse (EMP) from a nonexistent atomic blast. Because the pulse shut down all the missiles, the incident became a national security issue, which changed the level of the classification.

> "I witnessed a shimmering, reddish-orange object clear the main gate and in a sweeping motion pass quickly and silently pass by the windows."

Oddly, in the 341st SMW Unit History, it noted, "Rumors of Unidentified Objects (UFO) around the area of Echo Flight during the time of the fault were disproven. A Mobile Strike Team, which had checked all November Flight's LFs [Launch Facilities] on the morning of 16 March 67, were questioned and stated that no unusual activity or sightings were observed."

But that doesn't seem to be quite accurate. Hastings interviewed James Ortyl who had been assigned as an Air Policeman at Malmstrom. Ortyl said:

> I was an Airman 2nd Class [A2C] at the time. We were working the day-shift at Kilo Flight in March of 1967.... It was mid-morning and three or four Air Policemen were gathered in the launch control facility dispatch office. Airman Robert Pounders and I were facing the windows looking out to the yard and parking lot. The others were facing us. As we were conversing, I witnessed a shimmering, reddish-orange object clear the main gate and in a sweeping motion pass quickly and silently pass by the windows. It seemed to be within 30 yards of the building. Stunned, I looked at Pounders and asked, "Did you see that?!" He acknowledged that he had.

To be fair, Ortyl didn't know the exact date, but knew that it was near his birthday of March 17th. But then there is Craig's interview with Chase, which also moves in the direction of UFO sightings on the proper date. Craig's notes indicate that he had the names of some of those involved with the UFO sightings at the time of Echo's shut down, but he never contacted any of these witnesses.

Craig also had the name of Dan Renualdi, who, in March 1967, was a member of the Site Activation Task Force (SATAF). Renauldi said that he had been within a few feet of an object. A sergeant with the Air Force Technical Evaluation Team also said he had seen a flying saucer. There is no record of Craig talking to either of these men, nor are there any reports in the Project Blue Book files to suggest the sightings had been reported there. This violated the regulations in force at the time, although it could be argued there were contradictory regulations.

All this demonstrates is that there was another reported UFO around the time that Echo Flight had gone down, contrary to what the Unit History said. It does not prove that the UFOs had anything to do with the anomalous pulse.

Quite naturally, the Air Force wanted to know what had happened. The man who conducted the investigation for Boeing, the Defense Contractor for the missile systems, was Robert Kaminski. In a letter dated February 1, 1997, to Jim Klotz, he wrote:

At the time of the incident, I was an engineer in the MIP/CNP (Material Improvement Project/Controlled Numbered Problem) group.... The group was contacted by the Air Force so that Boeing could respond to specific Air Force Minuteman Missiles problems that occurred in the field....

I was handed the E-Flight CNP assignment when it arrived by the group supervisor. As the internal Boeing project engineer I arranged meetings necessary with management and technical personnel required to determine a course of action to be taken, in exploring why 10 missiles had suddenly fallen from alert status—green—to red, with no explanation for it. This was an unusual request and we had no prior similar incident or experience to this kind of anomaly....

"There were no significant failures, engineering data or findings that would come close to explain how ten missiles were knocked off alert."

Since this was a field site peculiar incident, a determination was made to send out an investigative team to survey the LCF and the LFs to determine what failures or related incidents could be found to explain the cause ... . After a week in the field the team returned and pooled their data. At the outset the team quickly noticed a lack of anything that would come close to explain why the event occurred. There were no significant failures, engineering data or findings that would come close to explain how ten missiles were knocked off alert. This indeed turned out to be a rare event and not encountered before. The use of backup power systems and other technical system circuit operational redundancy strongly suggests that this kind of event is virtually impossible once the system was up and running and on line with other LCF's and LF's interconnectivity....

The team met with me to report their findings and it was decided that the final report would have nothing significant in it to explain what happened at E-Flight. In other words there was no technical explanation that could explain the event.... Meanwhile I was contacted by our representative ... (Don Peterson) and told by him that the incident was reported as being a UFO event—That a UFO was seen by some Airmen over the LCF at the time E-Flight when down.

Subsequently, we were notified a few days later, that a stop work order was on the way from OOAMA to stop any further effort on this project. We stopped. We were also told that we were not to submit the final engineering report. This was most unusual since all of our work required review by the customer and the submittal of a final Engineering report to OOAMA....

However, as I recall nothing explained this anomaly at E-Flight.

Hastings, in a review of the material conducted in 2013, wrote, "Actually, the large round object sighted by the missile guard, and reported to launch officer Lt. Walter Figel, had been hovering over one of the Echo missile silos, not the launch control facility itself. Nevertheless, Boeing engineer Kaminski's revealing testimony essentially confirms Figel's account of a UFO presence during the incident."

Oscar Flight

In March 1967, Robert Salas was a Deputy Missile Combat Crew Commander (DMCCC) at Malmstrom AFB. When he first told his tale in 1995, he thought he had been assigned to Echo Flight, later he thought it might have been November Flight, but once he located his former commander, Fred Meiwald, he learned it was Oscar Flight. The story he told in 1995 was essentially the same as that about Echo Flight, that all ten missiles had gone off line within seconds of each other.

According to what Salas would report, while he was sixty feet underground in the capsule, he received a call from an NCO in the Launch Control Facility telling him that they had seen some UFOs nearby. They were just lights and no one was sure what they might be. But not long after that, the NCO reported that the object, later described as a red glow that was saucer shaped, was now over the gate. Before the NCO completed the report, he said that one of the men had been injured, apparently by the UFO. He hung up to go assist.

Salas said that he woke the commander and began to tell him about the UFO sightings. Within seconds, their missiles began to go off line. Later, there would be some question as to how many of the 10 missiles they lost. It might have been a few of them or it might have been all of them. In May, 2013, Salas said that he had believed all the missiles went offline, but his commander thought it was only five or six. In his first reports, Salas just split the difference.

In fact, Salas would say that once he mentioned what was happening outside, his commander, Meiwald, said that he had heard about a similar event the week before. Meiwald said an intrusion alarm went off the week before and a two-man security team was ordered to respond. As the team approached the site, they saw a UFO hovering over it. They raced back to the Launch Control Facility, shaken by what they had seen.

In a letter to Salas dated October 1, 1996, Meiwald wrote, "Topside security notified us the mobile team had reported observing the 'UFO' while responding … to the situation at an outlying LF…."

Hastings interviewed Meiwald in 2011 about the events at Oscar Flight. Meiwald said:

> … essentially, I was resting—whether or not I was sound sleep I don't recall—but I know Bob got me up because we had unusual indications on the consol [sic], plus we'd had a security violation and, uh, the response team that [inaudible] had gone out to investigate at one of the LFs. They reported unusual activity over there and—by that time I was up—and saw consol indications. [I] also directed that the strike team return to the LCF while maintaining radio contact on the way back. As they came back we did lose radio contact for a short period of time, however, the flight [security] leader—the person who was in charge at the time—recognized the team as it was approaching the LCF and opened the gate so that his troops could get in.

Meiwald didn't remember much, except confirming that they had seen something in the sky. Hastings asked him about the Flight Security Crew's description of a bright red oval-shaped object, but Meiwald said that he could only remember something about a bright object, confirming, at least, the UFO sighting.

Later, Meiwald said that he and Salas were called in for a debriefing by the AFOSI. He confirmed that they were asked to sign nondisclosure statements, but he didn't regard this as a big deal. That sort of thing apparently happened occasionally. At the Citizen Hearing in May 2013, Salas confirmed that they had been required to sign the nondisclosure statements. "It was then designated a highly classified incident," according to Salas.

The trouble at Oscar Flight was also reported by 1st Lieutenant Robert C. Jamison, who was Minuteman ICBM targeting officer at Malmstrom in March 1967. According to what he told Hastings and reported in *UFOs and Nukes*, he, Jamison, was tasked to assist in the restart of "an entire flight of ten Minuteman ICBMs which had simultaneously and inexplicably shut down immediately after a UFO was sighted in the vicinity...."

After a UFO was sighted in Montana, a number of Minuteman ICBMs shut down inexplicably, and silos like this one would not function.

More importantly, Jamison said that before he was sent into the field, he and his team were told to remain at Malmstrom until all UFO activity had ended, and then they received a "special briefing." They were told to report any UFO they saw in the area. If they saw something once they were at the missile silo, they were to enter the personnel hatch and wait until the UFO left. The Air Police guards, who were to accompany the team, would remain outside to watch the UFO.

While he was in a hangar waiting to go into the field, Jamison overheard a two-way radio conversation about a UFO on the ground. This is a clear reference to the Belt sighting and dates Jamison's recollections to March 24. Jamison said that one of the highest ranking officers on the base was on the scene of the landing. According to newspaper accounts and government files, this was probably Colonel Fred Klibbe.

The special briefing apparently was not just a one-time affair. Jamison said that for two weeks after the missile shut down, his team received a UFO briefing prior to heading into the field. This is something that would be repeated in other, similar events at other Air Force bases.

This seemed to be a repeat of the situation that happened just days earlier. Salas was later convinced that this incident happened on March 24, the same date as the Belt, Montana sightings.

Unlike the Echo Flight incident, there was no official record of this event. The Unit History doesn't mention it, and there is no documentation for it. It is as if it never happened and for that reason, there are some who think that this is a hoax. The only reason UFOs are mentioned in government files is because the news media was already involved with the Belt sightings and they couldn't be ignored. Had the media not been involved, neither the Echo Flight nor the Oscar Flight events would have leaked into the public arena.

The Bolender Memo

One of the criticisms of the stories of UFOs near Echo and Oscar Flights is that there were no UFO sightings in the area other than that at Belt, Montana, on March 24. Although there were newspaper reports of sightings earlier, and while it is clear from the testimony that Air Force personnel were seeing lights and objects on March 16, Air Force investigators simply ignored the sightings. The logical government files that may contain those reports are from Project Blue Book.

There is evidence that not all UFO sightings made it to Project Blue Book, even though the regulations seemed to require that they do. Dr. J. Allen Hynek, who was a scientific consultant to Project Blue Book for many years, often said that the really good cases didn't make it into the Blue Book files. He suspected another reporting system, but he couldn't prove its existence.

Hints about this other investigation came from Brigadier General Arthur Exon, who was the base commander at Wright-Patterson Air Force Base in the mid-1960s. Exon said that while he was base commander he would periodically receive a telephone call ordering him to prepare an aircraft for a mission outside the local Wright-Patterson area.

Exon himself described this in a May 19, 1991, recorded interview. He said, "I know that while I was there ... I had charge of all of the administrative airplanes and had to sign priority airplanes to the members who would go out and investigate reported sightings ... I remember several out in Wyoming and Montana and that area in the '60s, '64 and '65 ... I knew there were certain teams of people; they're representing headquarters USAF as well as the organizations there at Wright-Pat, FTD [Foreign Technology Division] and so on ... When a crew came back it was their own business. Nobody asked any questions...."

> "I always thought they were part of that unholy crew in Washington that started keeping the lid on this thing."

He expanded on this, saying, "The way this happened to me is that I would get a call and say that the crew or team was leaving ... there was such and such a time and they wanted an airplane and pilots to take X number of people to wherever.... They might be gone two or three days or might be gone a week. They would come back and that would be the end of it."

Asked about the overall control of these teams, Exon said, "I always thought they were part of that unholy crew in Washington that started keeping the lid on this thing."

Everything said to this point suggested that the operation was run through FTD, the parent organization to Blue Book at Wright-Patterson. But in an interview conducted about a month later, on June 18, 1991, Exon clarified what he had meant.

Asked if these teams of eight to fifteen people were stationed at Wright-Patterson, he said, "They were, they would come from Washington, D.C. They'd ask for an airplane tomorrow morning and that would give the guys a chance to get there [Wright-Patterson] by commercial airline.... Sometimes they'd be gone for three days and sometimes they would be gone for a week. I know they went to Montana and Wyoming and the northwest states a number of times in a year and a half.... They went to Arizona once or twice."

He also said, "Our contact was a man, a telephone number. He'd call and he'd set the airplane up. I just knew there was an investigative team."

What all this boils down to is an attempt to cover the activity. The team, whoever they were, would fly into Dayton, Ohio, on commercial air and then drive out to the base. If a reporter attempted to trace the movements of the team after it had been deployed, the trail led back to Wright-Patterson. After that it just disappeared.

This team, or these teams, were made up of eight to fifteen individuals at a time when Project Blue Book was composed of two Air Force Officers, an NCO, and a secretary. They were stationed at Wright-Patterson, but these other teams were assigned somewhere else, and there is no reason to assume that all members of a team were assigned to the same base. They would come together as needed.

On October 20, 1969, Brigadier General C. H. Bolender provided the documentation to prove that there was another investigation. In paragraph four of his memo, Bolender wrote, "As early as 1953, the Robertson Panel concluded 'that the evidence presented on Unidentified Flying Objects shows no indication that these phenomena constitute a direct physical threat to national security' ... In spite of this finding, the Air Force continued to maintain a special reporting system. There is still, however, no evidence that Project Blue Book reports have served any intelligence function. Moreover, reports of unidentified flying objects which could affect national security are made in accordance with JANAP 146 [Joint Army, Navy, Air Force Publication] or Air Force Manual 55 11, and are not part of the Blue Book system."

[T]he suspicions of Hynek and Exon were confirmed by this document from the government files.

In other words, the suspicions of Hynek and Exon were confirmed by this document from the government files. This organization dealt with matters of national security and the sightings at Malmstrom because the missile shut down was a matter of national security. Those sightings and the information collected about them would not be part of the Blue Book system and therefore would not be in the files. That they are missing is the significant point.

The Counterclaims

As with many other UFO incidents, there are a small number of people who are outraged by the thought that a UFO had been seen and interacted with the environment. In this case, the outrage came from James Carlson, son of Captain Eric Carlson, the Echo Flight MCCC on March 16, 1967. Carlson has carved out quite a presence on the Internet suggesting that Hastings and Salas were somewhat less than accurate.

But given all the information available, the number of men identified as being members of either Echo or Oscar Flight, and given the documentation that is available in the government files, some conclusions can be drawn. The situation can be better understood today, and looked at through neutral eyes.

James Carlson is of the opinion that nothing UFO-related happened that day. He said that his father told him about the events, but said that there was no need to speak to others. In fact, Carlson apparently wrote to Billy Cox, blogging as Devoid at the *Herald Tribune* (article at http://devoid.blogs.heraldtribune.com/10647/nukes-debate-gets-personal/), "I didn't question Walt Figel because his response is already part of the record. It wasn't necessary. My father was the commander at Echo Flight, and I questioned him ... my father would never lie to me about something like that."

Yet, according to Hastings, he interviewed Eric Carlson on October 6, 2008, and was told that the elder Carlson "himself had previously received reports from

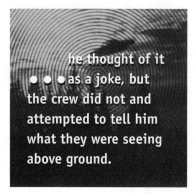

he thought of it ● ● ●as a joke, but the crew did not and attempted to tell him what they were seeing above ground.

missile security guards of UFOs during other missile alerts … but that he didn't take them seriously."

While this statement is not a direct refutation of what the son was saying, it does speak to the idea that UFOs had been reported and that Eric Carlson didn't believe them. In fact, he added, "You take an 18-year-old kid and stick him out there for days, with nothing but TV dinners, and they have a tendency to see things."

Carlson noted that the 341st SMW Unit History didn't mention any UFO sightings. It did say only that "Rumors of Unidentified Flying Objects (UFOs) around the area of Echo Flight during the time of the default were disproven."

But there is nothing in the Unit History to explain how they had been disproven, nor why, if the UFOs hadn't been sighted, they would even bother to mention this.

In reality, however, Figel mentioned the maintenance crew talking about UFOs. There are suggestions that the security teams saw lights and UFOs. In other words, the rumors weren't disproven, merely ignored, which isn't quite the same thing.

More importantly, any UFO sightings at the time, especially if linked to the failure of the missiles, would be a matter of national security. They would not have been reported through the same channels as other UFO reports. That none of these reports were filed with Project Blue Book, as regulations required (unless it was a matter of national security), is interesting.

In a similar vein, Carlson said that Figel had not believed the UFO story and thought it was a joke. He quotes Figel as saying, "I thought it was a joke." But the line is taken out of context. True, Figel did think that the maintenance crew was joking, but it is also true that Figel said they sounded sincere. In other words, he thought of it as a joke, but the crew did not and attempted to tell him what they were seeing above ground.

So Carlson didn't see any UFOs, but he talks of others, above ground, seeing them and reporting them. He seems to reject the idea that any UFO was seen on March 16, and that UFOs had anything to do with the shut down, contrary to what his deputy, sitting in the capsule next to him, had to say about this.

Carlson makes a big deal about the fact that Figel didn't attend the press conference held at the National Press Club by Hastings and Salas, wondering why he was excluded. Figel wasn't excluded, he did not attend the press conference because he didn't want to get in the middle of an argument between Hastings and Eric Carlson. Once the acrimony between the parties became known, Figel severed his communications with all. Figel had been invited, he just never responded to the invitation.

These sorts of arguments can become quite tedious, especially when one side takes statements out of context, doesn't provide full disclosure on all that witnesses said, and is driven by an agenda that leads to a very narrow and extremely hostile point of view. It is clear, based on the government files, that all ten Minuteman missiles of Echo flight failed in a matter of minutes, possibly seconds. There were reports of UFOs in the area, and both Captain Eric Carlson and 1st Lt. Figel knew of it. That Figel thought it was a joke does not mean that it didn't happen.

It is strange that there is no documentation for a similar failure at Oscar Flight just days later, but there are UFO sightings in the government files. There are other witnesses to this event than Robert Salas, and while their stories don't completely agree, the differences are minor. They are the sort of thing that is to be expected when someone is relying on memories from decades before.

More UFO Intrusions

If Robert Salas had been the only officer to talk of UFO involvement in minuteman missiles dropping off line, the tale could be ignored. But his commander confirmed it and the missiles in Echo Flight, on the same base, had been affected just days prior to Salas' experiences as documented in the government files. Other officers in other locations have also reported the same thing.

Dr. J. Allen Hynek, one-time consultant to Project Blue Book, in an article published in the December 17, 1966, issue of the *Saturday Evening Post*, wrote:

> On August 25, 1966, an Air Force officer [Captain Val Smith] in charge of a missile crew in North Dakota suddenly found that his radio transmission was being interrupted by static. At the time he was sheltered in a concrete capsule 60 feet below the ground. While he was trying to clear up the problem, other Air Force personnel on the surface reported seeing a UFO—an unidentified flying object high in the sky. It had a bright red light, and it appeared to be alternately climbing and descending. Simultaneously, a radar crew on the ground picked up the UFO at 100,000 feet.... When the UFO climbed, the static stopped.... The UFO began to swoop and dive. It then appeared to land ten to fifteen miles south of the area. Missile-site control sent a strike team ... to check. When the team was about ten miles from the landing site, static disrupted radio contact with them. Five to eight miles later the glow diminished, and the UFO took off. Another UFO was visually sighted and confirmed by radar....

Robert Hastings, in *UFOs and Nukes*, provided additional detail about the sighting. He quoted an article from the *Christian Science Monitor* in which Raymond Fowler, who worked for Sylvania Corporation, was interviewed. That article, published on December 5, 1973, said:

> Specifically, Mr. Fowler says he talked with an Air Force officer who had been in one of the subterranean Launch Control Facilities of a North Dakota Minuteman site on [sic] August 1966, when radar operators picked up a UFO maneuvering over the base at 100,000 feet. The officer declared that the LCF's sophisticated radio equipment, that enables it to receive firing instructions from coordinating centers and transmit them to the silo Launch Facilities [LFs] was blocked out by static when the UFO hovered

directly over it. Mr. Fowler recalls the officer saying that he could conceive of "nothing on earth" that could cause the equipment to malfunction from such an altitude, emphasizing that it was working perfectly before the object appeared overhead and after it left.

Asked to comment on Mr. Fowler's allegations, an Air Force spokesman in Washington declared that SAC, that operates the site, "could find nothing in its unit histories to confirm the presence of unidentified flying objects over it or indeed malfunctions in its equipment on the date mentioned."

Rather than search the unit histories, the Air Force spokesman should have reviewed another area of the government files. Project Blue Book contains information about this case. Major Chester A. Shaw, Base Director of Operations, wrote:

> Capt Smith [no first name given, but is Val Smith] (Missile Combat Crew Commander) on duty at Missile Site (Mike Flt) sixty (60) feet underground indicated that radio transmission was being interrupted by static, this static was accompanied by the UFO coming close to the Missile Site (Mike Flt). When UFO climbed, static stopped. The UFO appeared to be S.E. of MIKE 6, range undetermined. At 0512Z, UFO climbed for altitude after hovering for fifteen minutes. South Radar base gave altitude as 100,000 feet, N.W. of Minot AFB, NDak [sic]. At this time a strike team reported UFO descending, checked with Radar Site they also verified this. The UFO then began to swoop and dive. It then appeared to land 10 to 15 miles south of MIKE 6. "MIKE 6" Missile Site Control sent a strike team to check. When the team was about 10 miles from the landing site, static disrupted [sic] radio contact with them. Five (5) to eight (8) minutes later, the glow diminished and the UFO took off. Another UFO was visually sighted and confirmed by radar. The one that was first sighted passed beneath the second. Radar also confirmed this. The first, made for altitude toward the North and the second seemed to disappear with the glow of red. A3C [Airman Third Class] SEDOVIC at the South Radar base confirmed this also. At 0619Z, two and one half (2½) hours after first sighting, an F-106 interceptor was sent up. No contact or sighting was established. The Control Tower asked the Aircraft Commander of a KC-135 which was flying in the local area to check the area. He reported nothing. The Radar Site picked up an echo on radar which on checking was the KC-135. No other sightings. At 0645Z discontinued search for UFO.

On October 12, 1966, Colonel Jerome J. Jones sent a short letter to then Major Hector Quintanilla at Project Blue Book stating that his office had no explanation for the sightings but that it was possible a ball lightning was the culprit. He mentioned that an editor of *Aviation Week,* Philip Klass, had written an article on UFOs suggesting that ball lightning "might well cause static sufficient to interrupt communications—but not for 3½ hours."

Jones also thought this would be an ideal case with which to "inaugurate the $300,000 [that figure eventually became more than half a million dollars] contract with the University of Colorado."

Subsystems in the Electronics Directorate, which investigated the case, pointed out that there was no reasonable explanation for the sighting. He mentioned Philip Klass' theory of ionization of the atmosphere as an explanation for the UFO sightings. Klass was quickly debunked by atmospheric scientists who realized that the phenomenon that Klass cited was quite short lived and much smaller than the descriptions given by the witnesses. As of October 12, 1966, several weeks after the sightings, no reasonable explanation for the sighting had been found.

On January 4, 1967, First Lieutenant Roger D. Meyer, who was a Missile Security Operations Officer with the 862nd Combat Defense Squadron, answered a letter sent by Hynek. He wrote:

A3C [John M.] Turner was taken to the scene of the original sighting (M-6) by the undersigned [Meyer]. He indicated the following, (0 degrees is true north, 90 degrees true east, 180 degrees true south, and 270 degrees true west; degrees were extrapolated from the direction in which the subjects pointed by the undersigned).

Philip Julian Klass, who passed away in 2005, was an engineer and journalist who became one of the most famous critics of ufology.

He observed two objects. The first was a multi-colored object, which will be described in more detail. He did not observe the second object until after the strike team arrived and he described it as "the white light." The first object (the one which generated his report via radio) was very high and located most of the time approximately 40 degrees. However, it did move between approximately 0 degrees and 55 degrees. When A3C Turner was asked by the undersigned how he could be sure that he was pointing in the right direction he knew he was pointing in the right direction because the night he observed the object he used the "back side of the fence" as a reference point. The back fence is on the north side of the site.

He noticed the second object after the strike team arrived and pointed it out to him. He called it the "white light" and stated that it was very close to the horizon at approximately 100 degrees. Attachment #1 is a drawing made by A3C Turner of the first object. It represents the image of the object as it passed in front of some clouds. Light seemed to come from the back side of the object and reflect off the clouds and thus formed a silhouette. One last point made by A3C Turner was the fact that shortly after the strike team arrived, as he was trying to watch both the "white light" and the first object, he lost track of the first object.

A2C Holiday, the strike force leader, was also interviewed by the undersigned at M-6 during the hours of darkness. He provided the following information. As he and his rider (A3C Aldrich) approached the sight they were watching a "white" light very close to the horizon at approximately 80 to 100 degrees. Upon arrival at the site A3C Turner pointed out an "unusually bright" object at approximately 20 degrees which was very high. After looking at it for a few moments Airman Holiday turned his attention to the "white light." He observed the "white light" for some time. After a while he looked back to the north to find the unusually bright object" that A3C Turner had pointed out to him, but he could not find it.

A3C Aldrich, the strike team rider, was also interviewed at M-6 by the undersigned during the hours of darkness. The information he provided was as follows. He did not see the first object although he did hear the other personnel (A3C Turner, A3C [Michael D.] Mueller and A2C Holiday) mention it. He kept his attention on a white object at approximately 100 degrees which was very close to the horizon. He further stated that the object he was watching moved between approximately 75 and 110 degrees. The object also disappeared at various times for approximately 30 seconds at a time.

Attachment #2 is a transcript of the sequence of events recorded in the log book at south base (radar base). Attachment #3 represents a pattern of courses flown by the intercept plane as observed by the radar observer, SSgt Angel Camacho. Sgt Camacho further stated that the "object" was on his radar scope continuously from the time he picked up until he was relieved at approximately 0900Z (3 AM Central Standard time). The extract from the log book is also in Zulu time, which is equal to Central Standard Time plus six hours. Sgt Camacho stated that the object in question was "by itself" on his scope in that no other aircraft, ground clutter, or random "noise" bits were within 20–30 miles of the object on his scope except during the period when the fighter was in the area. The object did not disappear from his scope when the intercept plane flew it's [sic] pattern. The undersigned spoke to Capt Burg, 5th Fighter Interception Squadron, who piloted the intercept plane. He advised that he flew intercept courses at, as he remembers it, 1000', 2000', 3000', 4000', and 5000'. Capt Burg further stated that he made no visual contact and that his plane's radar equipment and infrared detection equipment recorded no contact. If you wish to have a sequence of events between the intercept plane and the control station (Great Falls Air Defense Sector) it will be necessary for you to write Col Duncan C. Myers, Director of Operations, Great Falls Air Defense Sector, Malstrom AFB, Montana 59402. The undersigned was unable to secure this particular sequence of events.

This letter, found in the government files, which may have been used as the basis of the Condon Committee investigation, left out some significant points. First and foremost is that there is no mention of the radio interference at the LCF, nor was any interference experienced by the strike team. Ignoring this point ensured that the case was no longer strictly a matter of national security, since it could be argued that radio static was not the same as the missiles going off line. It would also explain why the sighting report ended up in the Project Blue Book files. General Bolender made it clear that UFO sightings that were a matter of national security were not part of the Blue Book system.

The Condon Committee also seemed to ignore radar contacts that suggested the object was 100,000 feet above the ground. They rely, instead, on the height finding radar that put the object somewhere between one thousand and five thousand feet. Nowhere in their report do they mention the report of the high altitude.

It is clear from the information published by the Condon Committee that their investigation consisted of Hynek's letter to Minot AFB and assigning a first lieutenant at the base to the task of investigating. Although Hynek's letter with his questions is not in the government file, it is fairly clear that he was asking for specific information.

Their conclusion was that the case was difficult to evaluate because of the number of people and objects involved, as well as the vagueness and inconsistencies of the testimony. The Condon Committee decided that the descriptions of the first object were possibly based on a sighting of Capella, a very bright star which was in the general direction and azimuth of the area under question. They speculate that a sleepy guard on a lonely post might have a distorted impression of what he had seen, though they had no evidence that the man was sleepy or that the post lonely.

They do note that whatever the original object was, it was not the object seen by the radar because about the time the radar object was acquired, the visual object disappeared. Hynek and Low wrote, "Thus, what was ostensibly a single sighting was probably three; and there is much in the situation to suggest that the later two— radar target and white lights—were commonplace phenomena that were endowed with significance by the excitement generated by the first report. The weight of the evidence suggests that the original object was Capella, dancing and twinkling near the horizon; the evidence is not sufficient to justify any definite conclusion."

In the end, the original solution, ball lightning, was quickly rejected. Although those involved with the investigation were unable to provide a solution, it was eventually listed as a possible aircraft by the Air Force. This was later changed to aircraft without the qualifier.

Both the Condon Committee and the Air Force seemed to forget about the original electromagnetic effects, and that the radar tracks, as described by the radar operators, and visual sightings do correspond. Hynek, in his magazine article at the end of 1967, used this case to argue that something truly unusual was happening. It is even more important when it is remembered that there was interference with the radio communications and that this was not an isolated event.

Another from Minot

In May 2013, at the Citizen Hearing on Disclosure, retired Air Force captain David D. Schindele added another dimension to this case as well as the cases

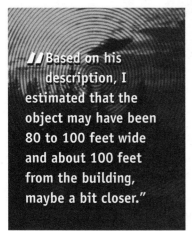

> **" Based on his description, I estimated that the object may have been 80 to 100 feet wide and about 100 feet from the building, maybe a bit closer."**

under consideration from other locations. He said that he had been involved in an incident while he was stationed at Minot AFB in 1966. He was off duty when the UFO sightings were reported, and he didn't see anything himself, but what is important is the aftermath of those sightings and how they affected him.

According to what Schindele said in the Washington for the Citizen Hearing, he had been aware of a UFO sighting about three miles west of Mohall, North Dakota:

> ... I drove to the airbase to attend the morning Predeparture Briefing at [455th Strategic Missile] Wing Headquarters, where all 15 missile crews would normally meet each day prior to "pulling alert duty" at their respective Launch Control Facilities. During the briefing, it was mentioned that some missiles at November Flight had gone "off alert" during the night, but no further information was provided. I immediately connected this to the news item that I had heard earlier in the morning regarding a possible UFO sighting near the town of Mohall.

So here, another source from a different base, was in essence saying the same thing. The missiles had been disabled, but they didn't give any additional information to the missile crews. Schindele said that those around him, at that briefing, were aware of the UFO sighting and they were all speculating about the possibility about the UFO and the missile failure.

Schindele said that when they arrived at the Launch Control Facility, their normal procedure was to inspect the grounds and the building, but on this morning he went in to debrief the security personnel. The site manager, a tech sergeant, asked if he had been briefed on what had happened and when Schindele said he hadn't, the sergeant told him about the sighting. According to Schindele:

> We then proceeded toward the windows on the west side of the day room where he described to me the large object with flashing lights that had been hovering just outside the fence that night, and he spread his arms out in front of him to indicate its size. Based on his description, I estimated that the object may have been 80 to 100 feet wide and about 100 feet from the building, maybe a bit closer....

> He then said that the object, while hovering close to the ground, then glided to the right toward the North end of the building out of sight. The object then came into view from the security section of the facility, and hovered just behind and slightly to the right of the main gate, concealed partly by the large garage located within the fenced area to the right of the gate....

> Security personnel confirmed everything that the Site Manager had related to me. My commander and I then proceeded to take the elevator down to the Launch Control Center to relieve the two man officer crew below. After entering the capsule, our eyes were immediately transfixed on the Launch Control Console, which showed that all missiles were off alert and unlaunchable.

The outgoing crew briefed us on the wild events that transpired overnight, and indicated that the missiles malfunctioned at the time the object was hovering directly above the capsule and next to the main gate. We speculated on the possibility of an EMF pulse that might have created the situation. We had no doubt, however, that the 10 outlying nuclear tipped missiles of November Flight had been compromised, tampered with, and put out of commission by the object that had paid a visit. Normally, it was quite unusual to have even one missile down....

As had happened at Malstrom, an entire flight of Minuteman missiles had been rendered useless by an outside force. True, they were brought back online but everyone realized the gravity of the situation. If an outside influence, whatever it might be, could take down a flight of missiles, it could take down the entire wing and the U.S. missile strategy would become useless.

Schindele also told the panel at the Citizen Hearing in 2013 that when he tried to get additional information from the Flight Security Controller, the controller said that he had been instructed not to discuss the situation. "That was when my commander told me that he had received a call while I was on a schedule rest break below ground, and he was told that we were never to discuss the incident. When I asked where the directive came from, he said the OSI."

Schindele said there were more than a dozen people involved in the incident and although neither he nor his commander had been there at the time of the encounter, they were required to deal with the aftermath. He said that besides the staff at the LCF, there were others involved, including the maintenance people who had to retarget and realign the missiles. Salas had said the same thing.

Schindele said, "Everyone had been silenced. The incident was never discussed and I never heard a word of any other incident from people I associated with. I never spoke a word about my incident for almost 40 years."

Like Salas, if Schindele was a standalone witness, his testimony could be ignored. He said say that he had run across others who knew of such events, two of whom had gone public, but others did not. Schindele said, "They fear losing their Air Force pensions or losing their personal integrity in keeping a secret, or of being ridiculed ... [T]here is the late Captain Val Smith of my squadron who was mentioned in official documents released via the Freedom of Information Act. He was interviewed by the late Dr. Allen Hynek ... who wrote an article in the *Saturday Evening Post* ... which described the incident that Smith was involved with on 25 August 1966."

F. E. Warren AFB, Cheyenne, Wyoming

If the stories about UFO sightings over missile sites are true, you would expect there to be many of them. The problem is that such things are normally classified and those involved are warned about revealing classified information. But more and more, tales of UFOs and missiles are coming to light.

Frances E. Warren Air Force Base near Cheyenne, Wyoming. The NCO there ignored reports of UFOs, not taking them seriously and not logging them.

Another example is the testimony of former Air Force captain Bruce Fenstermacher, who provided information to the Citizen Hearing in May 2013. He was a Minuteman III combat Crew Commander assigned to the 400th Strategic Missile Squadron at F.E. Warren AFB from 1974 until 1977.

Fenstermacher said that they were monitoring the VHF radio communications between the security NCO on the ground and the Security Alert Team who were doing the routine checks on the missile silos. At about two in the morning, the security NCO asked the SAT to pull over to look around. He wanted to know what the SAT could see. They spotted a light in the sky that was a pulsating white, with other colors visible between the pulsations.

Fenstermacher said, "I got on the direct line to the FSC and asked him what was going on. His reply was that right above the LCF there was a silent object with a very bright pulsating light. Between the pulsations he could see a blue light and a red light. I asked for specifics and he said that it was shaped like a fat cigar and was about 80 to 100 feet above him and appeared to be 40 to 50 feet long.... While we were talking he reported that it was slowly and quietly moving away to the east."

They ordered the SAT to head to the Launch Facility where the object was hovering. It took them some time to respond but they headed out. The object had moved farther east and Fenstermacher ordered them to that location.

Fenstermacher in his testimony in front of the Citizen Hearing on Disclosure panel said:

> Shortly after the object went to the first LF we reported the incident to the SAC command post at F. E. Warren. The NCO that took the call laughed at the report and said to call him back when the thing "ate the SAT" and hung up. As well as logging all the activity in the official log, my deputy also started taking personal notes dealing with what transpired.
>
> At our hourly 400th SMS crew check in for flights Poppa, Quebec, Romeo, Sierra, and Tango [which are the designations of other missile sites] we told the other crew members about our object and received laughter and an attitude of general disbelief. Right after the group communication, the crew from Quebec called—they were the team we had dropped off on our way to Romeo—and stated that earlier that morning they had a similar object about a couple of their LFs. When asked what direction it was headed they said that it appeared to be heading towards our area.... We asked what happened when they reported the incident

and the answer was, "Are you crazy? We didn't report it. We would have been laughed at." ...

We contacted the F. E. Warren SAC Command Post a few more times and finally asked if this incident had been entered into the log. They said it had not. I asked for the officer in charge and stated that if they did not enter I would wake up the base commander and report it directly to him.... Shortly after that we got a call from a senior NCO at the Command Post asking for specific details about the incident....

Upon our return to the 400th SMS we discussed the incident with our flight commander. The next morning we were called in to the 400th SMS commander's office. He asked us about the incident and when he learned about our personal notes he asked to look at them. Once in his hands he tore them up and said we were never to talk about this again and required us to sign documents that seemed to say we would not talk about it. We reluctantly signed them.

At our next couple of departure meetings an officer in uniform (not a crew uniform and not someone we recognized) briefed all crews that this incident was classified and officially never happened and that no one should talk about it.

While it is clear from Fenstermacher's statement that the UFO did not interfere with the missiles in any fashion and there were no reports of electromagnetic effects, it is the reaction of his fellow Air Force officers and the command structure that is important here. The culture inside the Air Force suppressed any sharing of information about UFO activity simply by wrapping it in a cloak of ridicule.

This resulted in two things. It prevented the crews from talking to one another about UFOs and it destroyed the paper trail about the sightings. Fenstermacher said that his commander had destroyed the notes about the sighting and that the Command Post wasn't interested in logging the event until he pushed the issue, but there is no evidence that the events were logged. There was an attempt to keep the information out of the government files.

These cases are all quite strong, based as they are on multiple witnesses, the radar tracks reported in some of them, and the interaction of the UFOs with the environment in others. There is documentation in the government files, such as on-the-record interviews with many of the principals, including those given in May 2013 at the Citizen Hearing on Disclosure in Washington, D.C., but there is an interesting lack of sighting reports in the Project Blue Book files where they should have been. There is testimony that witnesses were told not to talk about the sightings and in some cases signed nondisclosure agreements with anonymous government officials to prevent them from discussing the information.

Someone went to great lengths to hide something that supposedly didn't exist and that was not a matter of national security. Now, finally, some of that information is leaking into the public arena because of the pioneering work by both Robert Hastings and Robert Salas, Finally there is some disclosure of these important cases.

JAL 1628

John J. Callahan, a division chief for the FAA's Accidents, Evaluations, and Investigations Division, told the retired congressional representatives at the Citizen Hearing on Disclosure on May 3, 2013, "You are about to read about an event that never happened." The CIA also told him that they had not been to the White House to listen to his briefing about the UFO sighting.

The incident that led to that White House briefing, and to that security warning, took place about a year earlier when a Japanese 747 cargo plane carrying a consignment of wine, enroute from Paris, France, to Tokyo, Japan, encountered a UFO over Alaska. Captain Kenju Terauchi, a veteran pilot with more than 10,000 hours of flight time, including experience as a fighter pilot, said that he saw, below him, two objects that he could not identify. They were small, the size of a DC-8, though later he would say that they were no more than eight feet in diameter. He believed, at first, these were military aircraft on some sort of mission or training flight. The lights seemed to be white, yellow, and amber, and he thought they might be the exhaust of another aircraft.

He, along with his fellow pilots, First Officer Takanori Tamefuji and Flight Engineer Yoshio Tsukuda, watched the lights for several minutes as they kept pace with their aircraft. They turned off the cockpit lights to eliminate any reflection on their windows and to enhance their visibility outside of the airplane. Terauchi made minor maneuvers for several minutes, including a slight course correction ordered by the Anchorage Air Route Traffic Control Center (AARTCC). He attempted to identify the lights and to satisfy himself that he wasn't being fooled by his own navigation and cockpit lights or other internal reflections.

Terauchi later wrote, "The strange phenomenon happened immediately after we began left rotation.... There was an unidentified light ahead of the rotation. We set the course toward Talkeetna and began level flight. Then we saw the lights that looked like aircraft lights, 30 degrees left front, 2000 feet below us, moving exactly in the same direction and with the same speed.... We ignored the lights, thinking probably they were special missioned aircraft or two fighters because we did not notice the lights while communication with the Anchorage Center or on prior visual inspection. However, the position of the lights had not changed ever [sic] after a few minutes and that called our attention."

Captain Kenju Terauchi shows a drawing of one of the two UFOs he and his crew observed while flying a cargo plane for Japan Airlines over Alaska on November 17, 1986.

As they completed a course correction nine minutes after he originally spotted the lights, at 5:10 P.M. local time, First Officer Tamefuji called Anchorage Flight Control to ask if they were tracking any other traffic in his area. Terauchi was told they were seeing aircraft lights and were again told there was no military aircraft in the area. The flight crew was also asked about clouds at their flight level and they said the only clouds visible were above them, thin and spotty, and near the mountains.

Terauchi thought that a photograph or two might help them identify the object later. He would report, "I asked to bring my camera bag ... and began to take a picture.... [T]he lights were moving strangely. I had ASA 100 film in my camera ... and had the auto-focus on.... [I] aimed at the object but the lens kept adjusting and never could set a focus. I changed auto-focus to manual and pressed the shutter but this time the shutter would not close."

When the aircraft began to vibrate, Terauchi gave up on the photographs and turned his attention to observing the lights. He wrote, "Most unexpectedly two spaceships stopped in front of our face, shooting off lights. The inside cockpit shined brightly and I felt warm in the face."

The co-pilot, Tamefuji, said that the lights were like "Christmas" lights with a "salmon" color. He said, "I remember red or orange and a white landing light, just like a landing light. And weak green, ah, blinking."

He also said that on seeing the lights, he first thought it was two small aircraft. The lights were strange because there were too many of them, and then said he had the impression they were from a larger than normal aircraft. He said, "I'm sure I saw something. It was clear enough to make me believe that there was oncoming traffic."

Terauchi provided a more detailed description of the lights. He said that a fire, "like from jet engines stopped and became a small circle of lights as they began to fly in level flight at the same speed as we were, showing numerous exhaust pipes.... The middle of the body of the ship sparked an occasionally [sic] stream of lights, like a charcoal fire, from right to left and from left to right. Its shape was square, flying 500 to 1000 feet in front of us, very slightly higher in altitude than us, its size about the same size as the body of a DC-8 jet, with numerous exhaust pipes."

Terauchi said that the objects moved suddenly, but that he and his crew never felt they were in danger. He said that it would be impossible for any man-made craft to maneuver in a similar fashion, appearing in front of a jet flying at nearly 600 miles an hour. He also noted that while the objects, or lights, were near his aircraft, communication with the Anchorage center was "extremely difficult." He said that communications resumed normally once the two objects moved away from them.

At 5:28, the return had disappeared from the radar scopes. Captain Terauchi and his crew were now watching lights that were to the left of his aircraft and below it. They were too far away to be tracked on the weather radar. Now that it was getting dark, they could see the stars and the two smaller UFOs were so far away that they couldn't be seen in the clutter of ground lights and stars overhead.

With the two smaller objects gone, the flight crew could now see a pale white light in the direction that the others had taken. They asked Anchorage if the object was visible on radar but were told that nothing unusual could be seen. Terauchi then set his weather radar on twenty miles and there it was, not a bright red object as other aircraft sometimes appeared, but as a large, green, round object that was only seven or eight miles away. Terauchi again asked if Anchorage had anything visible and was again told that they did not.

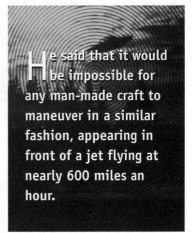

He said that it would be impossible for any man-made craft to maneuver in a similar fashion, appearing in front of a jet flying at nearly 600 miles an hour.

Anchorage, however, contacted the Elmendorf Regional Operational Control Center (ROCC) and asked if they had seen anything. The controller at ROCC told Anchorage that he could see an object on his radar that was not accompanied by a transponder code (in the lingo used, he was seeing some "surge primary return.") But when the ROCC controller suggested to Anchorage that this might be some sort of illusion, he was told that they also had the object and it was not "erroneous." The object was seen on two radar screens at two separate locations. ROCC also made it clear that there were no military aircraft in the area that could account for the object.

Looking behind them, the flight crew could still see a pale white light that, according to Terauchi, was "the silhouette of a giant spaceship." In his drawing, Terauchi rendered the spaceship as something that resembled a huge walnut. It was reflecting the lights off the ground, and Terauchi thought of it as a "mothership." This was the object he said was larger than two aircraft carriers.

Terauchi now wanted to evade the object and asked permission to make a 360 degree turn. Anchorage granted permission and the turn was initiated. The object seemed to remain in the same relative position with the aircraft throughout the turn. In other words, it was flying a very loose formation with the JAL cargo jet.

Again ROCC tracked the object behind the aircraft for a short period. ROCC asked if he wanted an interceptor scramble, but Terauchi said, "No." He later said that he was afraid that the pilot would be in danger. He would tell FAA investigators that

An F-16 flies over Eielsen AFB in Alaska, one of several locations in that state where UFOs were seen in 1948 by pilots of both commercial and military craft.

he remembered a fighter pilot in a "Mustang" had been killed chasing a UFO. This was a reference to the Thomas Mantell UFO case from January 1948, when a National Guard pilot, attempting to intercept a UFO, died when his plane crashed.

Terauchi said, "We had no fears so far but began to worry since we had no idea for their [the UFO] purpose. When the lights from Eielson Air Force Base and Fairbanks became clear and bright, two very bright lights appeared suddenly from the North from a belt of lights, perhaps four or five mountains away. The extremely bright lights reflected on the snow on the side of the mountains… We wondered if they were searching for something on the ground surface or to [attract] attention…"

They arrived on station above Eielson Air Force Base and Fairbanks, and nearly out of fuel, they checked behind them and saw that the huge, pale object was still behind them. They asked for a change of course, which was eventually granted. They checked again, and the object was still behind them. Terauchi believed they had to get away from the object. Anchorage Center told them to make a full 360 degree turn. They switched off the auto pilot. The maneuver failed. The object was still behind them.

Two other aircraft, a military C-130 and a United Airlines passenger jet, were also in the area. The United crew, having just taken off, was asked to search for the object, but all they could see was the JAL jet. The military aircraft saw nothing unusual. Captain Terauchi said that the object had disappeared about the time the United flight reached altitude, and by then, according to Terauchi, "There was nothing left but the light of the moon."

With the object now gone, and with the bright, smaller objects, also gone, the JAL plane started its descent into Anchorage. The ordeal was not over, though. When they landed in Anchorage, the crew was interviewed by the FAA, not about the UFO, but about the possibility of having violated FAA regulations by reporting the unidentified aircraft or "unusual traffic." Jack Wright, and later James Derry and Ronald Mickie, all from the FAA, interviewed the flight crew. Wright would record the interview for the government files and reported:

> I received a call from Dick Powers concerning a JAL flight which the Capt. had stated he was being followed or shadowed. I observed the aircraft land at 1820 hours [6:20 P.M.]. No other aircraft were noted. The B747 [Boeing 747] taxied into the international ramp area. I interviewed Capt. Terauchi and the crew of two [meaning the captain and two others]. The captain stated that this was the first time anything like this had happened to him. He stated that approximately five nm [nautical miles] after passing the Canadian/Alaskan border at 35,000 feet something appeared five to seven nm in front of the aircraft. At times the object would be to the captain's side [left side] of the aircraft. Never the other side. He referred to the dark side. After passing the Fairbanks area he requested to fly parallel to course and this was granted. When he turned to the right and flew parallel, the object was gone. (In all cases the weather radar was also used to identify the object and the five-to-seven nm [nautical miles] distance was taken from the radar display ...). They returned to course and the captain said, "There it was, as if it was waiting for me." At approximately the Talkeetna area the object took off to the east and was gone. A United flight departed from Anchorage and was requested to check if they could see anything but it was gone before United got there. Nothing different with the cargo except some expensive wine. The captain and crew were shook-up but professional. James Derry interviewed the crew at JAL operations. Capt. Terauchi had asked AARTCC if they were picking up two targets and was told, "just one." The total time was approximately 55 minutes. A new crew took the flight on to Tokyo. Capt. Terauchi and the crew were in Anchorage for days before any additional flights. James Derry requested that the tapes [recordings of the communications and data from the radars] and any other information be saved.

This provides a brief look at what was said in the hours after the encounter. It includes basic information about what was seen, but almost exclusively from the captain's perspective, not the other two crew members. This may be due to the fact that Terauchi spoke better English than his two crewmen and that he was the captain of the flight. He was the man in authority, the most experienced flyer of those on board, and the UFO seemed to have stayed on his side of the aircraft, giving him the better view.

The FAA team concluded their investigation. They viewed the incident, not as a UFO sighting, but as an intrusion of an unauthorized aircraft into controlled airspace. They were attempting to learn if FAA regulations had been violated, not by the JAL air crew, but by those other "aircraft" which seemed to be

Captain Thomas Mantell

Captain Thomas Mantell was a National Guard fighter pilot killed on January 7, 1948, during an active intercept mission of a UFO near Godman Army Air Field in Kentucky. Mantell was an experienced combat pilot who had earned the Distinguished Flying Cross during the Normandy invasion in 1944. During the war he had been a transport pilot and had been dropping paratroopers in June 1944. He had only recently transitioned into fighter aircraft and had only about 80 hours of flight time in them.

On January 7, he was leading a flight of four F-51 Mustangs on a ferry flight when they received a report from the Godman tower that there was a UFO in the area. Mantell was asked if his group could check it out. One of the pilots was low on fuel and landed at Standifort Field, but the other three began a pursuit.

The pilots had oxygen equipment with them, but it had not been recently serviced. Mantell, and his two wingmen climbed to about 22,000 feet, when one

A reconstruction of the Mantell incident when Captain Thomas Mantell of the National

of the pilots reported that he was dizzy. He and the other wingman broke off the intercept, but Mantell said he was going to climb to 25,000 feet and circle for ten minutes. If he was unable to identify the object or close on it, he was going to break off the pursuit.

Mantell had the object in sight and reported to the tower that, "It appears to be a metallic object, tremendous in size, directly ahead of me and slightly above."

But Mantell didn't have ten minutes left. He blacked out because of hypoxia, oxygen starvation, with his aircraft trimmed for a climb. It continued up until engine torque pulled it over and began a power dive. At about 20,000 feet, the plane began to break up and crashed moments later, killing Mantell. There is no evidence that Mantell regained consciousness or that he attempted to bail out.

Although he was chasing a UFO, and Captain Terauchi was correct in his memory of the sighting, the best evidence today is that Mantell was, in fact, chasing a high-altitude research balloon that was part of a classified project. Mantell's death was a tragic accident, caused by his attempt to identify the UFO, his bravery in continuing the chase to end his mission, and the misidentification of a terrestrial object. Many UFO investigators believe there is no evidence that the "UFO" in this case was responsible for Mantell's crash.

operating above 14,000 feet without benefit of flight plan or transponder, and which would be regarded as endangering the JAL jet.

In December 1986, all that changed. The information about the UFO and not the "intrusion" was being investigated by the Kyoda News Service in Japan, and they asked the FAA about the incident. The story appeared about December 29 [though the interview was December 24], and was picked up by the United Press International, according to Paul Steucke, of the FAA.

Callahan, in May 2013, said:

In early January 1987, I received a call from the Air Traffic Quality Control Branch in FAA's Alaskan regional office, requesting guidance on what to tell the media personnel who were overflowing the office. The media wanted information about the UFO....

[I asked], "What UFO? When did this take place? Why wasn't Washington Headquarters informed?"

"Hey.... Who believes in UFOs? I just need to know what to tell the media to get them out of here."

The answer to that question was easy. "Tell them it's under investigation. Then collect all the data—the voice tapes and computer data discs from both the air traffic facility and the military facility responsible for protecting the west coast area. Send the data overnight to the FAA Technical Center in Atlantic City, New Jersey...."

Walt Andrus, then the International Director of MUFON, called Steucke to ask about the sighting. He asked Steucke, "Someone has been sitting on this since November 17th. How did it leak out as far as you are concerned?"

Steucke replied, "Well, nobody was sitting on it. We just didn't do anything with it. We didn't put out a news release on it. We were not keeping it a secret. We just didn't announce it ... After about six weeks, I think someone in Japan, probably one of the crew members mentioned it enough times to family and friends...."

It was then that Jeff Berliner, with the UPI in Anchorage, learned of the report and called the FAA to ask questions. With all that going on, the FAA, on January 2, 1987, reopened the investigation. They again interviewed the pilot, Captain Terauchi, looked at the radar data from their flight operations center, and contacted the Air Force to find out what their personnel had observed.

Steucke explained it this way to Walt Andrus, "The reason we're exploring it is that it was a violation of air space. That may sound strange but that's what it was. The object of the inquiry, or collecting all the data and interviewing people, is to identify the object if possible. However, considering the type of data we have available, no one considers it realistic that we can identify the object."

On January 5, 1987, the *New York Times* published an Associated Press story about the new investigation. Steucke was quoted as saying, "We're looking at it to insure that somebody didn't violate airspace we control. We looked at it about six weeks ago but since then we've gotten a lot of public interest, so we went back and reinterviewed the pilot."

What no one seemed to ask was why it had taken six weeks for the FAA to investigate it. True, they had interviewed the flight crew and their employees on November 17, but that had been it. Apparently, at that point, they were satisfied that no regulations had been violated and they didn't know what the objects were. The overall sighting lasted for fifty minutes; the larger object had been seen by weather radar in the plane and by two radar units on the ground. Something had been in the sky, but since nothing had happened, no collision had taken place, and it hadn't disrupted flight services, either civilian or military, the FAA had no further interest in it. Now, after the Kyoda News Service and the United Press International had asked some questions, the FAA was going to reinvestigate.

Interestingly, it was Walt Andrus who uncovered, or at least first reported, one of the problems with the story. Although it appeared that two ground-based radars had detected the object, it turned out that there was only one source for the radar signal. Although the Air Force records for that night had been destroyed, radar data could be reconstructed based on the data collected by the FAA, so nothing was lost.

First, Andrus wrote that Don Berliner (no relation to Jeff Berliner), an aviation authority and UFO researcher, had interviewed Air Force officers about the sightings, and they confirmed that something had been detected by their radar. According to Berliner, through Andrus, Captain Robert Morris of the Alaska Air Command suggested the UFO was nothing more than "random clutter or weather interference."

Sergeant Jack Hokanson, another of the Air Force personnel interviewed by Andrus and Berliner, said, "We got out of the UFO business some time ago."

Which is, of course, irrelevant to the investigation. The situation was an intrusion by an unknown object that could have endangered civilian flight traffic, so the Air Force should have taken the sighting seriously, at least until they had identified the cause of the sighting. On November 17, they had both the eyewitness accounts and the radar track. Something was going on.

Andrus, during his interview with Steucke, learned that the military and FAA radar used the

Walt Andrus was the international director of MUFON when he interviewed Paul Steucke of the FAA about the JAL sighting. He would discover a number of problems with the reported facts in the case.

same base as a source of their radars. All the information came out of Fairbanks. There was no separate radar system. The difference was in the computer systems used. The FAA computer had finer filters on it, screening out some of the clutter that the Air Force radar displayed. In other words, the FAA radar had a cleaner screen. Similarly, there were reports that the North American Aerospace Defense Command (NORAD) had also tracked the object, but since NORAD also used the same Alaska source for their radars, in reality, there was only a single ground-based radar system supplying data about this sighting.

A Freedom of Information Act (FOIA) request to NORAD attempting to confirm that the radar had been monitored there, and to confirm that the FAA Special Agent and Captain Stevens at NORAD had conferred about the incident failed. On December 5, 2012, Major General Charles D. Luckey, in a letter to Kevin Randle, wrote, "After performing a search of our systems records, no responsive documents applicable to your request were found. If you have any further questions concerning your request, please do not hesitate to contact our FOIA Requester Service Center at the above address."

Steucke told Andrus, "The second thing is that the initial radar data that was received, in reviewing that data [the Air Force data] with ours, going backwards and regenerating the electronic data that we could see, which is a method we use all the time. What I call the secondary target, if you want to call it that, an unknown possible object did not come up on our radar when we regenerated it."

The loss of the Air Force data was not a serious issue because the radar data still existed and could be "regenerated." It meant that those looking at the data

John J. Callahan, a division chief for the FAA's Accidents, Evaluations, and Investigations Division, believed that the JAL encounter might be a real UFO sighting.

would be able to see exactly what the radar operators would have seen on November 17.

At the Citizen Hearing on Disclosure in May 2013, Callahan said, "The FAA had developed a computer program capable of re-creating the traffic on the controller's scope, called a plan view display (PVD). I instructed the FAA specialist to synchronize the voice tapes with the radar data. This way, we could hear everything the controller said and the pilot said while simultaneously watching the radar scope. This was as if you were standing behind the controller in Alaska, watching and hearing everything that was going on while the controller talked with the JAL pilot and crew. I video-taped the radar display as the event was played back on the scope."

In other words, they were able to recreate, exactly, the situation in Alaska on the night of the sighting. They could see everything that transpired in "real-time." They could watch the whole 31 minutes of the event as it unfolded.

Steucke did admit during his interview with Andrus that, "In reviewing the generated radar data.... The primary target which would be the JAL was very obvious and distinct. A secondary blip which was very intermittent and weak appeared in pattern every so often."

So, a ground radar did display something, but Steucke discounted it as unimportant, suggesting that it was a ghost image or a split image. That implied that the secondary target was a false return generated by the JAL jet and there was nothing in the sky near the aircraft. Callahan, in his testimony at the Citizen Hearing, didn't agree with that assessment.

There was also the image that had been displayed on the weather radar in the JAL jet. According to Terauchi, other aircraft, when "seen" by the weather radar, looked red. This object displayed as green and Terauchi wondered if the difference might suggest something about the construction of the craft. He wondered if it was made of metal different than that used in terrestrial built airplanes.

In effect, there were two separate radar systems that displayed the object, one on the ground and one in the air. Had Terauchi managed to photograph the objects, either the smaller ones that he saw first, or the later, larger one, the case would have been that much stronger. Attempts to photograph the lights, first by Terauchi, and later by the co-pilot, Tamefuji, failed. No photographic evidence was obtained.

There is an interesting problem that arises from this. Andrus, in his *MUFON UFO Journal* article, wrote, "As someone jokingly inquired, why weren't there any photographs made since nearly all Japanese visitors to the U.S.A. are observed carrying cameras? Apparently none of the crew members had a camera in his flight bag since no photographs were made."

In his later interviews, Terauchi said that he had tried to take pictures but couldn't get the camera to work properly. The question is, was this something that he added later to make his story more believable, or was it something that hadn't been mentioned earlier because no one had asked about it?

The Skeptical Argument

Before the FAA could publish their findings, and before all parts of the investigation had been completed, CSICOP (Committee for the Scientific Claims of the Paranormal, now known as CSI or Committee for Skeptical Inquiry) issued a press release claiming that they had solved the case. They wrote that according to a leading UFO investigator named Philip Klass, "at least one extraterrestrial object was involved—the planet Jupiter, and possibly another—Mars."

According to them, Jupiter was extremely bright and would have been about ten degrees above the horizon, on the left side of the aircraft. Mars would have been slightly lower and to the right of Jupiter.

The CSICOP (CSI) press release continued. "Although the very bright Jupiter, and the less bright Mars, had to be visible to JAL Capt. Kenju Terauchi, the pilot never once reported seeing either—only a UFO he described as being a 'white and yellow' light in his initial radio report to Federal Aviation Administration controllers at Anchorage."

The problem with the CSICOP (CSI) analysis was that it was made without the benefit of the drawings made by the pilot only hours after the event. While white and yellow lights had been reported, the drawings also showed two square-shaped objects that had several lights on them. And, of course, the two planets would not be able to follow the motions of the jet, which meant that at various

The Moon, Venus, and Jupiter are shown moving near the Very Large Telescope observatory in Chile. The Moon is rising through the three stills, while Venus is the bright "star" in the middle and Jupiter appears as if it is orbiting Venus. One explanation for reports of UFOs that many feel is absurd is that pilots are mistaking Venus for an alien ship.

JAL didn't want pilots who had hallucinations while flying for them and Terauchi was assigned a desk job in Japan.

times, the directions to the lights were not consistent with the relatively stationary planets.

In addition, there are the radar returns. If the ground base radar images are disregarded, there was still the contact made by the JAL's radar. Even without the confirmation of the ground based radars, that contact was sufficient to suggest that neither planet was the reason for the sighting. CSICOP was guilty of premature release.

Those obvious errors didn't stop their attempts to explain the sighting. In 1988, Klass revised the explanation, saying that the JAL crew had been confused by moonlight reflecting from the clouds and "turbulent ice crystals." Klass argued that the thin clouds, which had been reported above the JAL aircraft by the crew, had also caused the false radar echoes. Klass did not bother with the descriptions of the objects given by the crew, a proper review of the FAA audio tapes, or that the weather radar in the cockpit registered something other than weather.

Pilot Fallout

Although Terauchi remained on flight status for several months after he reported the sighting, he was eventually taken off. JAL didn't want pilots who had hallucinations while flying for them and Terauchi was assigned a desk job in Japan.

Dr. Richard Haines, who worked as a scientist at NASA-Ames Research Center at Moffett Field from 1964 to 1988, said:

> As I was leaving the Life Sciences building one day I met a Japanese gentleman standing, talking with a colleague. He was introduced as the Chief Medical Officer for Japan Airlines. One thing led to another and I had an opportunity to ask if he knew Captain Kenju Terauchi and about his sighting of unidentified aerial phenomena over Alaska. He said he did and was sorry to tell me that while Captain Terauchi was still with the airline, he was no longer flying. When I asked why this was, he replied to the effect that the airline looked carefully at all the data surrounding the sighting and did not want pilots who saw such things to be flying.

> I was surprised at hearing this. I then explained that I had personally interviewed Captain Terauchi very soon after the event and that I believed he was actually an exceptional pilot. He had complied with all FAA verbal (i.e., radio) reporting requirements (when others might not have under these circumstances). He had delivered his cargo safely, and he had kept his airplane under excellent control at all times in spite of the threat, distractions, and stresses that were present. The gentleman seemed surprised at my unexpected comments but then suggested that if I wanted to do so he would be pleased to receive anything in writing from me about this matter; then he gave me his business card.

Within days I had prepared a package of materials for Japan Airlines that outlined the above points. I also pointed out that my files already contained a number of other pilot sightings and near approaches made by very large unexplained phenomena/objects. In short, what Capt. Terauchi and his crew had seen was not all that unusual. My package was in the mail soon thereafter.

It was several years later that I learned through a third party that Captain Terauchi was flying again, for which I felt great relief. I don't know whether what I did made any difference in this case. All that really matters is that we do what we can to help others in their time of need.

Another FAA Report

On March 5, 1987, the FAA publicly announced the results of their new investigation. In their press release, they said that they "had been unable to confirm the event."

According to the press release, the event was unconfirmed because "a second radar target near the JAL flight at the time of the reported sighting was not another aircraft but rather a split radar return from the JAL Boeing 747."

NBC News picked up the story but didn't seem to understand it. As they reported it, the story was that Terauchi's co-pilot and flight engineer were not sure that they had seen a UFO. Thus, the story was reduced to a report by one pilot claiming a sighting, with no radar confirmation.

During an FAA interview, the co-pilot Tamefuji said that the [weather] radar echo was "just like other traffic, but, ah, I thought a little bit large." He said that he had seen many aircraft shown on the radar and in his opinion this looked similar to those other echoes.

But this wasn't what Callahan had experienced as he investigated the case. After he reviewed the playback on a controller's scope, videotaping the session, he received a "detailed" analysis of the incident. Callahan's brief for his boss, Harvey Safeer, who in turn alerted Donald D. Engen, the FAA Administrator, stated:

During the play back of the event I observed a primary radar target in the position reported by the Japanese pilot. The intermittent primary target stayed in close proximately to the B747 for approximately 31 minutes. Both the FAA controller and military NORAD controller reported observing the RADAR return of the "UFO" target on their "scopes." There was no noticeable weather in the area. "You can see into next Tuesday" was reported by a United pilot.

The UFO was painted as an extremely large primary target. As a result of the lacking run length identification the FAA computer system treated the UFO RADAR return as "weather" and transmitted it to the controller's PVD via a non-recorded

[Tamefuji] said that he had seen many aircraft shown on the radar and in his opinion this looked similar to those other echoes.

line. (All known aircraft are programmed in the FAA computer systems "Run Length" table.)

Callahan's analysis of the tape seemed to suggest that both radar operators were seeing a "real" target on their scopes. There was no weather phenomenon that would account for what was seen, and Callahan didn't seem to accept the other explanations being offered.

He also said that if the object had been either a Lear Jet or a military aircraft at the wrong altitude, the controllers would have known it. There were procedures in place to correct the situation of one aircraft violating another's air space, but as he said, "[There] are no procedures for UFOs."

Callahan said during that White House briefing that one of the scientists asked a number of questions about the capabilities of the radar, the frequencies, band width and the like.

At the Citizen Hearings in May 2013, Callahan expanded on the problems with UFOs and FAA radar. The radar system is set up to not recognize the UFO. If there is no transponder associated with a blip on the screen, then the blip is not recognized as anything of importance. A controller who sees such a blip near any aircraft might ask about other traffic in the area. Or, the controller might ignore the reading if there is no indication that the blip constitutes a threat to aerial navigation. In other words, if there is no discussion with recognized air traffic and there is no transponder code, the blip is ignored.

Callahan made it clear that all aircraft operating above 14,000 feet are required to have a transponder. There should be nothing above that altitude without one, and it should be broadcasting all the time. He also said that the FAA does not control UFOs.

Callahan said at the Citizen Hearing, "When I returned to the FAA headquarters, I gave Administrator Engen a quick briefing of the play back and showed him the video of the radar scope synchronized with the voice tapes. He watched the full half hour, and then set up a briefing with President Reagan's scientific staff, and told me my function was to give them a dog and pony show and hand this operation off to them, 'since the FAA can't communicate with unknown aircraft, we can't issue air traffic control instructions.'"

This briefing was arranged for members of Reagan's scientific staff and for the CIA. Callahan said, "At the CIA briefing they looked at the printouts and we played the video for the group."

There were thirty or forty people in the room and they talked for an hour and a half, while the scientists asked what Callahan thought were "very intelligent questions.... The FAA specialists we brought into the room were headquarters technical engineers—hardware and software specialists and they responded to the questions as if they were high school math coaches. They spit the answers right out; it was amazing to watch these FAA experts at work."

Ironically, when Callahan asked the hardware engineers what would cause a false echo, they replied that it was a software problem. But the software engineers blamed the problem on hardware. In other words, none of the engineers could identify a source for the image that appeared on the radars in the aircraft and on the ground.

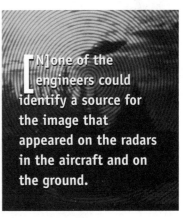

When the briefing ended, one of the people from the CIA said, "This event [the sighting] never happened. We [the CIA] were never here. We're confiscating all this data and you are all sworn to secrecy."

Callahan asked the CIA representative what he thought it might be. According to Callahan, the man said, "A UFO and this is the first time [we] have more than a minute of radar to go over. They, the president's team, are very excited to get their hands on this data."

[N]one of the engineers could identify a source for the image that appeared on the radars in the aircraft and on the ground.

Callahan thought they should issue a twix about the sighting, but the CIA man said, "No way. If we were to tell the American public there are UFO's they would panic."

According to Callahan, "And that was it. They took everything that was in the room, and in those days, computer printouts filled boxes and boxes. The FAA printouts were titled, 'UFO Incident at Anchorage, 11/18/86,' written out on the front cover. The printouts provided ample data for an automation specialist to be able to reproduce everything the controller saw and depict in on a chart."

Sometime after the briefing, Callahan has said numerous times and in numerous places, the detailed FAA report, "which included extensive interviews with the pilot and crew, the chart prepared at the Tech Center, and the facility voice tapes arrived at my office and were placed on a small table waiting for the CIA to request more data. The material stayed there until I retired two years later and I've had it ever since." He had much of it in Washington, D.C., in May 2013 for the Citizen Hearing on Disclosure.

The Other
Official Investigations

In the reported history of official UFO investigations, it has been a matter of faith that Projects Sign, Grudge, and Blue Book were the only operations. After the Robertson Panel made its recommendations in January 1953, the assumptions shifted subtley, quietly, and without fanfare. There was a new set of regulations and a change in the way UFO investigations were going to be handled. ATIC and Project Blue Book, who were the main action addressees on UFO related items of intelligence, were about to lose that distinctive status.

The process of creating an Air Intelligence Service Squadron (AISS) actually began in late 1951, according to government files. A project officer was appointed and a unit was created that would have a number of intelligence functions. The mission, classified as secret, was "to provide an organization within the Air Defense Command which will: a. Collect positive air intelligence information, by overt means, from: 1. Downed enemy air crews, 2. Enemy material, and 3. Bomb Damage Assessment as may be directed by Headquarters, United States Air Force."

Originally, the 4602nd AISS did not have a UFO mission. It was created during the Korean War with an eye on the possibility of a Third World War where the United States would be vulnerable to enemy attack. The huge oceans that had been barriers prior to the twentieth century would offer little protection against long-range bombers and it was anticipated that enemy flight crews would be a problem in such a war.

According to the government files, the early mission was training, which is to say, preparing to be activated. It was suggested that members of the unit learn parachuting, horseback riding, animal packing, skiing, mountain climbing, and various survival skills. The idea was that 4602nd members could parachute into rugged terrain and would be able to survive as they chased enemy flight crews.

There were additional documents in the government files about the creation of the 4602nd AISS. "The organizational data reflecting these changes was submitted to Director of Manpower and Organization, Air Defense Command (ADC), on 25 February 1952. This material requested an initial activation order be published authorizing a headquarters and three flights with a strength of 34 officers and 97 airmen for the period of 1 March to 1 June 1952."

This order was later modified to increase the strength on June 1, 1952. A few weeks before, the AISS was designated as the 4602ⁿᵈ AISS and was organized at Peterson Field, Colorado Springs, effective on March 1, 1952, per ADC General Order Number 20, dated 28 February, 1952. What all these dates from the government files indicate is that they were building a new unit, with a new mission, and the coordination was sometimes a little shaky.

About the time that the Robertson Panel was getting organized by the CIA to study the UFO question, the 4602ⁿᵈ AISS was finally getting up to authorized strength. New regulations, issued by the Air Defense Command on January 3, 1953, modified the mission of the 4602ⁿᵈ AISS, removing much of their Bomb Damage Assessment capability. According to the government files, Air Force Regulation 200-2, dated August 1953, tasked the 4602ⁿᵈ with the investigation of UFOs. According to the government files, all UFO reports would pass through the 4602ⁿᵈ AISS prior to transmission to ATIC.

What all these dates from the government files indicate is that they were building a new unit, with a new mission....

It is interesting to note that according to the government files, Ed Ruppelt, then chief of Project Blue Book, after briefing the members of the Robertson Panel, was on his way to Ent Air Force Base near Colorado Springs, the headquarters of the 4602ⁿᵈ. He was scheduled to arrive on January 24, 1953 to "present a one hour briefing at Officers Call." The trip was arranged by Major Vernon L. Sadowski on January 7, 1953, a week before the Robertson Panel began its meetings.

A rough draft of that briefing, found in the government files, provides a quick history of various official UFO investigations and then explains how the various classifications were made. At first the files were classified as top secret, but that mostly because they didn't know what they might find. There was a possibility that the investigations may have led to a highly classified, experimental project or they may have learned of Soviet intrusion into American airspace. Most of the information in the Blue Book files was classified as Restricted (Confidential) to protect the names of the witnesses. Some of the sightings and some of the information was classified secret.

Most of the briefing was about the day-to-day operation of the project and the normal run of statistics, but toward the end there were three examples of the reports they had received. One of those happened on May 13, 1952, and it reported:

> ... four amateur astronomers were making observations through a small telescope on a college campus. All of a [sic] sudden they noticed four oval shaped objects in a diamond-shape formation. The objects appeared nearly overhead and disappeared at an angle of 12 degrees above the horizon in about 3 seconds. The objects or lights were reddish brown in color and about the size of a half dollar, quarter turned, at arm's length.... Our evaluation of this was unknown. It could possibly have been ducks or geese reflecting light, except the observers pointed out that they had pur-

posely set up their telescope in an area that was completely dark so that there would be no ground lights to hinder their observations.

At some point between that briefing and the end of Project Blue Book, the status of the sighting was changed from unknown to "Poss Geese." This means that cases were to be solved and possible explanations were to be accepted.

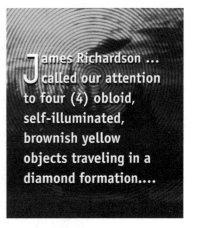

James Richardson ... called our attention to four (4) obloid, self-illuminated, brownish yellow objects traveling in a diamond formation....

The government files show that about 10:00 P.M., four amateur astronomers saw the objects in a diamond-shaped formation flash overhead. First Lieutenant Arthur S. Palmer was given the task of investigating the sighting, which took place in Greenville, South Carolina. Although the names have been redacted from the file, Palmer identified them as non-military. Two of the witnesses were described as responsible adults and the third as "a level-headed high school student." The fourth man was not identified.

Palmer gathered statements from all of them. The fourth witness whose name was redacted from the government files, told Palmer:

> On the night of May 13, 1952, at approximately 2233 EST, a group of amateur astronomers, of which I was one, gathered on the campus of Furman University located at Greenville, South Carolina. We were getting ready to call it an evening when James Richardson, one of the group, called our attention to four (4) obloid, self-illuminated, brownish yellow objects traveling in a diamond formation. These objects were in sight for about three (3) seconds traveling on a level course slightly arced to the left on a heading of about 300 degrees.
>
> I was unable to estimate the altitude or speed of these objects. They traveled directly overhead, making no sound, and rather wobbling in flight. Motion was similar to heavy winged birds in flight. It was a clear, quiet night, excellent for astronomy. There was a slight ground haze over the city, however, this did not extend to the Furman campus where it was perfectly clear.
>
> By way of further description, I would say the objects were similar to the "Lubbock Lights" as reported in Life Magazine. Approximate size would be that of a half dollar held at arms [sic] length and slightly turned.

In describing the objects to Palmer, another witnesses stated that there "were four objects, each the shape of the goose without neck or tail."

In his analysis for the report, Palmer wrote, "One observer was inclined to believe these were geese." He concluded that the case was "Unknown."

Another officer, probably in Ohio and reviewing the case, circled the "One" in "One observer," and wrote, "Two." He did the same thing under the conclusion, asking, "Why?"

There is nothing in the file that actually shows that any of the witnesses thought the objects were geese. One of them might have said that to Palmer. In two of the statements, the witness either mentioned the shape was similar to a goose without a head or tail while another described the motion as birds in flight. But there are not two witnesses who thought they were looking at geese.

The file does, however, reveal the evolution in the thinking of the Air Force officers associated with the investigation. In 1953, when the briefing was written, they had labeled the sightings as an "unknown," because they didn't have a good solution. Sometime later, another officer, reviewing the file and looking for any reason to remove it from the "unidentified" category, noted that two of the witnesses had mentioned birds and believed this to be the solution. The fact that they had used birds as a way to describe part of the sighting seemed to be lost on him. Birds had been mentioned, so birds it became.

The 4602nd in UFO Investigation

Ruppelt, in describing how the 4602nd entered into the UFO investigation business, seemed to think it was the result, not of manipulation at the top, but because of his pushing from the bottom. He wrote, "Project Blue Book got a badly needed shot in the arm when an unpublicized but highly important change took place: another intelligence agency began to take over all field investigations ... the orders had been to build it up—get more people—do what the [Robertson] panel recommended. But when I'd ask for more people, all I got was a polite 'So sorry.' ... I happened to be expounding my troubles one day at Air Defense Command Headquarters while I was briefing General Burgess, ADC's Director of Intelligence, and he told me about his 4602nd Air Intelligence Squadron, a specialized intelligence unit that had recently become operational. Maybe it could help...."

Ruppelt explained that he didn't expect much from Burgess. Ruppelt expected to write memos and letters and seal "it in a time capsule for preservation so that when the answer finally does come through the future generation that receives it will know how it all started."

> // Project Blue Book got a badly needed shot in the arm when an unpublicized but highly important change took place: another intelligence agency began to take over all field investigations...."

This time things were different. Ruppelt wrote, "But I underestimated the efficiency of the Air Defense Command. Inside of two weeks General Burgess had called General Garland, they'd discussed the problem, and I was back in Colorado Springs setting up a program with Colonel White's 4602nd."

In Ruppelt's book, he implies that all this happened late in the summer of 1953. Ruppelt's tour at Blue Book was scheduled to end in February 1953, and he departed for two months of temporary duty in Denver. He wrote, "When I came back to ATIC in July 1953 and took over another job, Lieutenant Olsson was just getting out of the Air Force and A1/c (Airman First Class) [Max] Futch was now it.... In a few days I again had Project Blue Book as an additional duty this time and I had orders to 'build it up.'"

In military terms, an additional duty is a job assigned to an officer for completion after his primary duty obligations have been fulfilled. It means that he does not devote as much time to the additional duty as he would to his regular duty because it is not a primary obligation. Many times, it is just something an officer does when time permits and often it is simply overlooked. Additional duties might be tax preparation officer, public information officer (in a lower level unit), or unit historian.

So, Ruppelt, at the end of the summer, was talking to General Burgess and within weeks, he was told that the 4602nd was available to investigate UFOs. Documentation in the government files, however, doesn't bear this out.

On March 5, 1953, months before Ruppelt met with General Burgess, a letter with the heading "Utilization of 4602nd AISS Personnel in Project Blue Book Field Investigations" is sent to the Commanding General of the Air Defense Command and to the attention of the director of intelligence at Ent Air Force Base. The plan of action, outlined in the letter was approved on March 23, 1953. In the letter it was noted, "During the recent conference attended by personnel of the 4602nd AISS and Project Blue Book the possibility of utilizing 4602nd AISS field units to obtain additional data on reports of Unidentified Flying Objects was discussed. It is believed by this Center that such a program would materially aid ATIC and give 4602nd AISS personnel valuable experience in field interrogations. It would also give them an opportunity to establish further liaison with other governmental agencies, such as CAA, other military units, etc., in their areas."

Now the U.S. Olympic Training Center, the former Ent AFB in Knob Hill, Colorado, received a memo in March 1953 that participating in Project Blue Book could give military personnel valuable interrogation experience.

The interesting statement here, as in many of the other documents relating to the 4602nd, is the idea that the field teams, by interrogating witnesses to UFO sightings, would gain valuable experience in interrogating people or, more accurately, enemy flight crews. In a peacetime environment, all they could do was interrogate "captured" Americans in simulations. According to Ruppelt, "Investigating UFO reports would supplement these problems [wartime simulations] and add a factor of realism that would be invaluable in their training."

All this happened while Ruppelt was on temporary duty and someone else was leading Project Blue Book. It would seem that some correspondence between the ADC and ATIC would have been on file at Blue Book. Ruppelt, when he returned to ATIC, should have been aware that negotiations between the 4602nd and ATIC were in progress. Yet his own book suggests he didn't understand that.

Upon publication of Air Force Regulation 200-2, in August 1953, a briefing about implementation of the regulation was held at Ent Air Force Base for members of the 4602nd. Publication of a regulation suggests that the changes had been in the planning stage for a long time. It suggests that the implementation of ADC regulation 24-3, published on January 3, 1953, was part of a larger plan. All of it was probably an outgrowth of the wave of sightings from the summer of 1952.

During the briefing, one of the officers asked, "What is the status of the 4602nd in regards to this new UFOB regulation?"

Government files reveal that Major BeBruler said, "I want to say that on this UFOB regulation that ADC will designate the 4602nd as the agency to discharge its responsibility for field and certain preliminary investigations. Secondly, there will be a criteria established as a guide to determine when the field units will conduct a detailed follow-up investigation and when they will not."

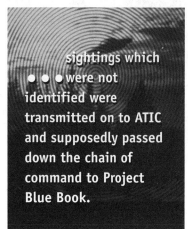

sightings which ● ● ● were not identified were transmitted on to ATIC and supposedly passed down the chain of command to Project Blue Book.

This marks an important shift in the UFO investigations. The Robertson Panel recommended no secrecy because they believed there was nothing to hide. They thought total openness would prove to the public that the panel had nothing to hide and interest in UFOs would end. Instead, Project Blue Book was stripped of its investigative function and became little more than a public relations clearing house, issuing periodic statements that didn't say much of anything. The real investigations were now conducted by the 4602nd AISS, an intelligence agency of which no one outside a limited circle inside the intelligence community knew. Public questions about UFOs went to Blue Book but no one asked the 4602nd what they were doing or what they knew. They operated outside the spotlight of the media.

Documentation available in the government files makes it clear that the investigative function after 1953 rested with the 4602nd. UFO sighting reports were transmitted electronically to the closest of the field units for investigation. Once the investigation was complete, sightings which were not identified were transmitted on to ATIC and supposedly passed down the chain of command to Project Blue Book.

It is also clear from the government files that the leadership of the 4602nd and the ADC was not happy with the task, regardless of the thought process that brought it about or the training it might provide. From the Commander's Call on June 22, 1953, came the following instructions:

> Investigation of unidentified flying objects is not presently part of the mission of this squadron. Field units are not authorized to make investigations of this type unless so directed or prior approval is obtained from Headquarters. If ATIC gets a report and feels that an investigation is necessary, they will notify this Headquarters and we in turn will then direct the proper field team to make the investigation.
>
> If you are asked by the D/I of your Division to make an investigation, let us know about it. If it is not going to involve much time, you can go ahead and make the investigation based on your own judgement [sic]. Don't let

this sort of thing get out of hand, but if it will assist you in your relationships with the D/I and you feel that you have the time, go ahead. Otherwise, notify this Headquarters for prior approval.

AFR 200-2, the regulation that covered the investigation of UFOs, was first published in August 1953. Its implementation seems to have lagged until August the following year. Reports available in the 4602nd Unit History, originally classified secret, show that there was some reluctance to take on the task of UFO investigation.

This is not to suggest that the 4602nd was operating to suppress UFO data, though that was the result. Based on the questions asked at the meetings, the men seemed more concerned with the logistical support available to them in order to complete their mission rather than hiding anything about their work. The regulations at squadron and flight levels had not yet been written.

// How can anyone suspect the Air Force takes UFOs seriously if the investigation consists of an officer, an NCO, an enlisted man or two, and a secretary?"

During the initial briefing held in 1954, Lieutenant Vaughn said, "General Carey is very vehement in his desire to see these reports before they are sent anywhere. What will be done about that? He has seen this AFR 200-2, but before they are sent in, he still wants to see them."

Colonel White answered, "I see no objection to that, if they don't get tied up. There is nothing in 200-2 that says that written reports (AF 112) should go to General Carey. Again this is in his division area of responsibility. General Carey is one of the sharpest officers in the Air Force today, and if he wants you to do something like this in his area, it, of course, should be done. The one arrangement that I would make is that you should hand carry the reports to him."

The question that must be asked, if this was indeed an attempt to circumvent AFR 200-2 by General Carey: Why should the reports be hand carried to him?

The simplest answer is that, since the UFO program was moving into his area of responsibility, General Carey wanted to be apprised of what was happening. Hand carrying the reports just expedited the process. There seems to be nothing underhanded or nefarious in the operations as they were being established by the 4602nd. They were tasked with a job and were attempting to carry it out to the best of their abilities.

What is notable here is the shift of investigative responsibility. Ruppelt complained that his tiny shop was overworked and undermanned, and a splendid compromise was found. It can be persuasively argued that military secrets are a necessity, and since Blue Book was well known by the beginning of 1953, the policy makes some sense. But it can also be argued that the policy is a result of a desire to mislead the public about the reality of the situation. The question frequently asked was, "How can anyone suspect the Air Force takes UFOs seriously if the investigation consists of an officer, an NCO, an enlisted man or two and a secretary?" The answer is, of course, not very.

Angel Hair

Although falls of Angel Hair, a wispy, gossamer-like substance, date as far back as the eighteenth century, it is its association with UFOs that has brought it to the attention of many. One of the original theories was that these were spider webs, or ballooning young spiders attempting to move on the wind to new locations.

In 1881 the *Scientific American* reported that in October of that year enormous spider webs coming from Lake Michigan "rained" down on cities in Wisconsin. Some of the strands were quite long but some were just specks. Although it was suggested that spiders were to blame for the material, they noted that no one had found any spiders associated with the material.

There were other such falls in the late nineteenth century. In one case, the strands of "silk" were reported to be between a mile and two miles long, while others were tiny. In all these cases, it was also noted that no spiders had been found. It seemed to be spider web without the spiders.

One of the first cases of a UFO sighting occured on September 26, 1948, when a man in Port Hope, Ontario, saw a series of objects that looked like stars moving across the sky. Using binoculars he saw that the objects, that continued to appear and disappear, were spherical, with the center brighter than the edges. Through the glasses he could also see what he described as three- or four-yard long spider webs associated with the UFOs, reflecting the light.

Reports of Angel Hair did make it into the government files. On October 14, 1954, in Roseville, California, silky material fell from the sky for about five hours. Samples were gathered and analysis by Colorado College, according to the government file, suggests that these were spider webs. The problem is that there was noth-

This is a sample of Angel Hair found in Japan. While some have said it is merely some type of spider silk, no spiders have ever been found near the substance.

(Continued from previous page)

ing in the file to actually support that conclusion and no reports of how the analysis was conducted or by whom.

A similar event occurred on October 22, 1954, near Marysville, Ohio. According to the government file, "Air filled with soft tufts that looked like cotton. Silvery. Landed in schoolyard and surrounding area." The conclusion was that it was spider gossamer. A conclusion based partially on the theory that similar falls have been identified in a similar fashion, though, again there were no reports of spiders.

The government files contained a page from Donald Menzel's *The World of Flying Saucers*. It said, "At afternoon recess the pupils of the Jerome Elementary School noticed a dazzlingly bright object in the sky. It disappeared, and for the next forty-five minutes both children and teachers watched white, cottonlike [sic] tufts floating slowly down to the ground. The material was in long strands, very fine and soft, could be stretched and rolled into a tiny ball, but quickly vanished to nothing and left a green stain on the hands....

Unfortunately, none of the material was preserved and no analysis possible.... Both the time and the weather were ideal for migrating spiders to take to the air."

But this analysis isn't quite accurate. According to a letter in the government files apparently written by Mrs. George Dittmar (conventions of the time usually identified a woman by her husband's name), "At a little past 3 P.M.... Mr. [name

redacted, but probably Rodney Warrick] called me to the upstairs fire escape of our school building. He asked me to look in the air and tell him what I thought about what I saw. The air as high and as far around as I could see was filled with the most beautiful soft white looking tufts, such resembling tufts of cotton, slowly floating to the ground.... As I looked he told me how the children ... called him to come out on the fire escape He [redacted, but undoubtedly Warrick] said he did so just in time to see a very shiny and silver looking cigar shaped object high in the air above, which seem for a split second to just hang and all in an instant take off at a terrific rate of speed, out of his view over the top of the school house ... while he was still standing there looking as the object disappeared, that he saw the white tufts floating down."

A teacher [name redacted but again was probably Mrs. George Dittmar] said that they collected some of the stuff, which was sticky to the touch. They could roll it into a small ball and that it very quickly seemed to "go to nothing." She then wrote, "In a short while our hands had a green stain on them." A strange response to a spider web, even if it had been created by tiny spiders riding the wind.

There is one other fact in the government files that is interesting. On November 4, 1954, Lieutenant Colonel Joseph A. Bloomer wrote to the woman whose name had been redacted. It was a standard let-

(Continued from previous page)

ter of thanks for reporting "your observation of certain unidentifiable aerial phenomena and further enclosed a piece of substance which you found."

There is nothing else in the government file and no analysis of the material the woman found and sent to the Air Force. Despite what Donald Menzel said, samples had been gathered and forwarded to the Air Force, but once again, the evidence disappeared from government control.

The *International UFO Reporter* in August 2008 also published an account of Dittmar's sighting. Bill Jones, then MUFON State Director for Ohio, interviewed Jack Pickering, an employee of the Battelle Memorial Institute in Columbus, Ohio. According to the article, a "woman known to both Jones and Pickering went to Marysville and secured a 'bottled sample' of angel hair from some unnamed woman there, almost certainly the school teacher [Dittmar]. She brought it back to Battelle, showed Pickering, and took it to a Battelle analyst to test unofficially.... Pickering wasn't involved with the test and doesn't know the results."

This just adds to the evidence that some of the Angel Hair was recovered and some of it was tested. It is unclear if the tests referred to by the Air Force are the ones conducted at Battelle, but that seems unlikely. It is more likely that tests at two institutions were conducted and the results of both tests have somehow disappeared over the decades.

That perception is not true. Investigation was continuing at a very high level with the addition of the 4602nd's intelligence teams. More information comes from the unit history (originally classified as Secret) and dated from 1 January to 30 June 1955. "The 4602d Air Intelligence Service Squadron continues to conduct all field investigations within the zone of the interior [meaning the United States] to determine the identity of any Unidentified Flying Objects." The unit history also noted, "The responsibility for UFOB investigation was placed on the Air Defense Command, with the publication of AFR 200-2, dated 12 August 1954."

These government files confirm what had been suspected. There was a secret study of UFOs conducted by the Air Force that was not part of the Blue Book System. Clearly ATIC was involved because regulations demanded it, but there is nothing to suggest that every report forwarded to ATIC made its way down to Blue Book.

The Attitude of the 4602nd AISS

If a unit is conducting investigations into some reported phenomenon, that unit should have an unbiased approach in order to ensure that preconceived notions do not influence the direction of the investigation. Documents in the government files suggest that the leadership of the 4602ⁿᵈ had ideas about the investigations into UFO sightings, and those opinions were not favorable.

In one of the briefings on "Unidentified Flying Objects (UFOB)," Captain J. Cybulski, wrote, "The primary reason for our participation in this program is to solve a very perplexing problem for the Air Force and the country as a whole … In all but a few cases a satisfactory solution has been reached and the Air Force feels that adequate, thorough investigative procedures can solve the small percentage of unsolved sightings."

In other words, Cybulski was repeating the Air Force line that the only reason there are any "unidentified" cases is because the information was incomplete and the investigation was not finished. He believed that a competent investigation would resolve the problem and wrote, "This is where we come into the picture."

Cybulski continued explaining the situation as he understood it. About his meeting with "an astronomer," likely J. Allen Hynek, Cybulski wrote:

> When I went to Dayton [Wright-Patterson AFB], the scientist and the astronomer they hired, were ready to quit. But before they were permitted to say anything I was introduced and told them what I was there for and what I was going to do. They threw their resignations away and decided to stay. Because as the astronomer said, "Put yourself in my position. I am being ridiculed by members of my profession for chasing these imaginary objects, and when I went into this, I went into it sincerely, because I thought that both the astronomical standpoint and also from the scientific value, I could disprove these things. In so doing I would be rendering my profession and my country some service. However, in the past, I have not been able to get support from the Air Force. It seems that we all think this is a hot subject, and they want to drop it. They don't want anything to do with it. No one wants to be quoted."

These statements, from the government files, that their astronomer entered the investigation to disprove "these things" are quite revealing. His bias was that there was no visitation, and instead of attempting to learn what really happened, he just wanted to prove his point of view. It is also interesting that he suggested his astronomical colleagues made fun of him for even undertaking the task, though if he found an answer, he would have rendered a valuable service. Or, if he could eliminate the idea of alien visitation, then his service was worth it. He didn't seem to think discovering alien visitation as real would have been a bigger service to the Air Force, or the scientific community.

Then, as if to prove he didn't have a complete grasp on the UFO situation, Cybulski wrote, "Then there are the cases, like that near Great Falls, Montana where a Warrant Office shot 40 feet of film. After you blow it up and look at it, you see it's a formation of high flying geese."

It is clear that he has confused two cases, and then doesn't give the explanation offered by the Robertson Panel for either of them. In 1950, Nick Mariana

Two stills from the footage of UFOs that Nick Mariana shot in 1950 show the strange lights moving above Great Falls, Montana.

shot footage of two objects as they crossed the sky over Great Falls, Montana. He was not in the military, but was a local businessman. The two objects on the film were little more than bright lights, but Mariana told investigators he had seen the objects before he began filming and they were disk shaped. The Air Force would eventually claim that the sighting was of two fighters thought to be in the area at the time. That answer was not universally accepted, even by those who were skeptical.

Mariana accused the Air Force of removing a number of frames from his film, stating that the missing frames showed the objects as disk shaped. The Air Force response, as outlined in the government files, was that they had removed a single frame because of damaged sprockets. Research by Barry Greenwood and others and documentation from 1950 showed that as much as six feet had been removed from the film before it was returned to Mariana. That would mean that the entire film has not been seen by any civilians since Mariana loaned it to the military in the early 1950s.

A Navy warrant officer, Delbert C. Newhouse, filmed a series of objects near Tremonton, Utah in July 1952. After sighting the objects, he stopped his car, got his 16 mm movie camera from the trunk and produced a short film. He said, and his wife agreed, that the objects passed over the car and they had an oval shape. They flew in no real formation. The Robertson Panel decided that these objects were sea gulls milling about on thermals. Naval investigators didn't agree, believing the objects were internally lit, and not reflecting the bright sunlight. That, of course, meant they were not birds of any kind.

This attitude about what they insisted on calling UFOB, continued. In a letter dated November 23, 1954, and signed by Colonel John C. White, it was noted, "In the majority of cases, provided the information concerning the sightings is sufficiently complete, the data will suggest that the sighting was probably some known object or natural phenomena [sic]."

Another document found in the government files that outlines more of the procedures, under the heading of "Investigation and Evaluation," said, "Sightings of less than ten seconds are almost completely worthless. Those under thirty seconds are likewise of little value. Such a short period of time will usually not suffice for reliable identification. No detail is possible under ordinary visual conditions."

There is something of value in this assessment. The problem is that most people are very poor at estimating the passage of time in these sorts of circumstances. To reject the sighting because the witness thought a short period had passed is not the best investigative technique.

Interestingly, in the same government files from the 4602nd it said, "Interval of time between the actual sighting and its reporting is of paramount importance. Observers will have a tendency to insert material and statements which have no value."

Experiments conducted over the last fifty years certainly bear this out. Other experiments show how flawed memory can be. The government document also said that "Vivid memory of UFOB is not too frequent." And there is no experimental evidence that supports this conclusion.

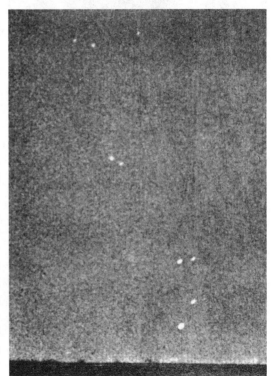

Attempting to explain the historical context, and after seeing how badly mangled the Montana Movie and the Tremonton Movie history was, the document said, "First recorded instance of genuine UFOBs occured [sic] in 1948 with the appearance of the 'Flying Saucer' in different parts of the United States. Rapid diffusion to all parts of the world, including the Soviet Union and its satellites."

This, coupled with the statement about the 40 feet of film by a warrant officer, demonstrates that those in the 4602nd were not paying attention to the history. They seem unaware of the Foo Fighters from World War II and the Ghost Rockets from Scandinavia in 1946. The people leading the discussions and preparing the documents were simply not aware of previous UFO research. If they were this ill-informed about the history of the UFOs, just how good were their investigations?

Also included in the government files, as part of the history of the UFOBs, is the rather

A still from the film taken by Navy warrant officer Delbert C. Newhouse in 1952, when he was driving near Tremonton, Utah.

bizarre statement, "Birth of new literary genre 'Science Fiction' which in most cases is entirely fictitious and unscientific [sic]. Manifestations of vigorous and expanding interest as a direct result of great technological advancements in airborne machinery during World War II."

To make it worse, the government file included this statement in what was called the "UFOB Summary" and written in this weird shorthand, "'Buck Rogers' Trauma. Emotional stimulus of speculation on the fantastic. Aberrated [sic] personality requiring this stimulus akin to the OUIJA Board and pseudo-metaphysics."

While these statements demonstrate a lack of understanding of science fiction, and seem unaware of the fact that the so-called "Golden Age" of science fiction happened in the 1930s, it had nothing to do with UFO sightings. However, this theory would surface in UFO research often. A publisher of a science fiction magazine, Ray Palmer, is often credited with "inventing" flying saucers but the truth is, as demonstrated in a study of the history of UFOs, that flying saucers were reported before he entered the picture.

UFO reports were sometimes written off as "Buck Rogers Trauma," named after the popular science fiction comic book and movie and radio serial.

What the officers of the 4602nd are saying is that those who see and report flying saucers have been adversely affected by these science fiction stories. It is a way of dismissing the witnesses without ever having talked with them or learned anything about them.

In fact, another document in the government files, part of the 4602nd Unit History covering September, 1955 reported:

> Considering the nationwide press release, by the Secretary of the Air Force, of the UFOB Summary and Study "and the statement that the Air Force ended its Project Blue Book," one would judge that the UFOB program had fulfilled its goal. This was especially true if one considered that the primary purpose of the program was to allay the hysteria by systematically squelching rumors and illusions. Reassuring the public mind that no tangible evidence … to support fears of an "invasion from outer space," or that "artificial technological advances and developments by the enemy" do not exist was imperative.

These statements suggest that the 4602nd, while taking their responsibilities seriously, didn't take the idea of UFOs seriously. They were instructing their personnel how to investigate, but not to forget that science fiction fans are somehow responsible for the UFO sightings.

Finally there is a policy statement that said, "In accordance with AFR 200-2 military personnel will restrict statements pertaining to UFOBs to [the] fact that UFOB was identified as a familiar object. If this is not the case only the statement that an investigation is being made by ATIC is authorized for release."

The Demise of the 4602ⁿᵈ AISS

In July, 1957 the 4602ⁿᵈ transferred its operations to AFCIN, which then assigned the duties to the 1006th AISS. A document in the government files shows that while the 4602ⁿᵈ had a large number of well-staffed field offices, when the UFO assignment was passed to the 1006th, both the number of field offices and the investigative staff at each location was reduced. The Air Force was not committing as many resources to the investigation as they had in the past.

The 1006th mirrored the attitude of the 4602ⁿᵈ. By the time the 1006th was tasked with UFO investigations, the Air Force was attempting to explain away all UFO sightings. This was quite evident in the investigation of a series of sightings on November 2, 1957, in Levelland, Texas.

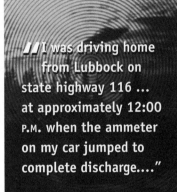

I was driving home from Lubbock on state highway 116 ... at approximately 12:00 P.M. when the ammeter on my car jumped to complete discharge...."

The object in question was spotted by witnesses in thirteen separate locations around Levelland, often either close to or on the ground. As it approached, car engines stalled, radios filled with static, and headlights dimmed.

Typical of the sightings was the one by Newell Wright, a nineteen-year-old college student at Texas Tech in Lubbock. He was nearing Levelland when he glanced at his dashboard ammeter. Wright (whose name was redacted from the Air Force report) told the Air Force investigator, Staff Sergeant Norman P. Barth of the 1006th AISS at Reese Air Force Base in nearby Lubbock:

I was driving home from Lubbock on state highway 116 [which is now state highway 114] at approximately 12:00 P.M. when the ammeter on my car jumped to complete discharge, then it returned to normal and my motor started cutting out like it was out of gas. After it had quit running, my lights went out. I got out of my car and tried in vain to find the trouble.

It was at this time that I saw this object, I got back into my car and tried to start it, but to no avail. After that I did nothing but stare at this object until it disappeared about 5 minutes later. I then resumed trying to start my car and succeeded with no more trouble than under normal circumstances.

Later in his interview with Barth, Wright would provide additional details. He said the object was oval shaped, and he thought it was about the size of a baseball held at arm's length. He estimated that the object was about seventy-five to a hundred feet long. Wright had the opportunity to get a very good look at the object, which wasn't all that far away and stayed on the ground for several minutes by his estimation. It wasn't a streak of light in the distance.

Donald Keyhoe was director of the National Investigations Committee on Aerial Phenomenon when the Levelland sightings occurred.

Wright made his report the next day. By that time, the news media was alerted and reports of the sightings in and around Levelland had been published and broadcast. It's possible that Wright did not actually see the object, but based his story on what he had read in the newspaper or heard on the radio, but there is no evidence to support that theory. Barth's evaluation of Wright said, "SOURCE seemed to the investigator to be very sincere about his sighting. He was appalled at the amount of publicity given him and was anxious to have the sighting resolved. He was unhesitating in his replies; however, during the course of further questioning, he admitted uncertainty in some of his answers. SOURCE can be considered usually reliable"

Donald Keyhoe, then director of the National Investigations Committee on Aerial Phenomenon, told reporters that there had been nine related sightings. The Air Force countered Keyhoe's statement and claimed that there were only three witnesses. Both were wrong because there were more people who saw the Levelland object, but this contradiction provides a glimpse of the prevalent Air Force attitude. Downplay the sightings, marginalize the witnesses, and claim that there is no national security implication.

The Levelland sightings are important because there were multiple witnesses, located in widely separated locations. These are some of the first sightings where the UFO interacted with the environment by stalling car engines and dimming headlights. The Air Force investigation lasted most of a day, though it seems Barth was assigned to Reese Air Force Base, about an hour away. He could have spent more time on the investigation, but by November 1957, the Air Force and the 1006th weren't overly concerned with proper investigative techniques, as the government files suggest. They were interested in solutions.

Electromagnetic Effects and Psychological Explanations

Levelland was not the only case from November 1957 in which electromagnetic effects were reported, nor was it the only such case investigated by the 1006th AISS. On November 23, 1957, at 6:30 AM, Air Force 1st Lieutenant Joseph F. Long, a pilot in the 321st Fighter-Interceptor Squadron at Paine Air Force Base, Washington, was about thirty miles from Tonopah, Nevada, when, according to the documents in the government files:

> ... the engine of his car suddenly stopped. Attempts to restart the engine were unsuccessful, and SOURCE [Long] got out of his car to inves-

tigate the trouble. Outside the car he heard a steady high-pitched whining noise which drew his attention to four (4) disc-shaped objects that were sitting on the ground about 300–400 yards to the right of the highway. These objects were totally unlike anything he had ever seen, and he attempted to get closer for a better look at them. He walked for several minutes until he was to within approximately fifty (50) feet from the nearest object. The objects appeared identical and about fifty (50) feet in diameter. They were disc-shaped, emitting their own source of light which caused them to glow brightly. They were equipped with a translucent dome in the center of the top which was obviously not of the same material as the rest of the craft. The entire body of the objects emitted the light, they did not seem to be dark on the underside. They were equipped with three (3) landing gears each that appeared hemispherical in shape, about two (2) feet in diameter, and some dark material. SOURCE estimated the height of the ob-

Paine AFB, located near Everett, Washington, was where Lieutenant Joseph F. Long was stationed when he was driving a car that apparently malfunctioned due to nearby UFO activity.

jects from the ground level to the top of the dome to be about ten (10) to fifteen (15) feet. The objects were equipped with a ring around the outside that was darker than the rest of the craft and was apparently rotating. When SOURCE got to within fifty (50) feet of the nearest object, the hum, which had been steady the air over since he first observed the objects, increased in pitch to a degree where it almost hurt his ears, and the objects lifted off the ground. The protruding gears were retracted immediately after take-off, the objects rose about fifty (50) feet into the air and proceeded slowly (about ten mph) to the north, across the highway, contoured over some small hills about half (½) mile away, and disappeared behind those hills. As the objects passed directly over SOURCE, he observed no evidence of any smoke, exhaust, trail, heat, disturbance of the ground or terrain, or any visible outlines of landing gear doors, or any other outlines or openings on the bottom. The total time of the sighting lasted about twenty (20) minutes. After the objects disappeared, SOURCE examined the place where he had first seen them on the ground. There was no evidence that any heat had been present, or that the ground had been disturbed in any other way than several very small impressions were very shallow and bowl-shaped, triangular in pattern (in equally sided triangles). SOURCE did not measure the distances between the impressions, but estimated it to be about eight (8) to ten (10) feet. After his investigation of the impressions, SOURCE returned to his car, and the engine started immediately and ran perfectly.

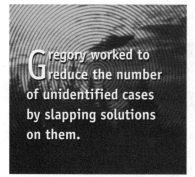

Gregory worked to reduce the number of unidentified cases by slapping solutions on them.

There was, of course, an investigation into Long's background. The details were reported at length in the government files. Captain G. T. Gregory was the chief of Project Blue Book at this time, and it appears that he was rabidly anti-alien and believed that all sightings had a terrestrial solution. During his time at Blue Book, Gregory worked to reduce the number of unidentified cases by slapping solutions on them. During his tenure, if someone suggested that a UFO looked like a balloon, then the sighting was classified as a balloon ... or if a witness suggested that the movement of a UFO resembled geese in flight, then the UFO became a bird.

The Long sighting was handled in a similar fashion. According to a document in the government files dated February 11, 1958 and entitled "Analyst's Comments Regarding Possible Reasons for Source Manufacturing Story", Gregory wrote:

> Officer has reserve status. Will be eligible for discharge in near future..... His academic training and education appears to be speech, *dramatics*, etc. for <u>TV</u> work....
>
> It is assumed that upon completion of his prescribed "Reserve Tour" he will associate himself with TV work—either as a writer, editor commentator, etc....
>
> If he has kept his thumb on TV's pulse, he knows the great public interest in "flying saucers" and "UFOs"—and the number of TV presentations on this subject....
>
> Interrogation brought out that he is familiar with names of prominent "saucer" and science fiction writers, authors which [sic] the average reader would not know. The arguments the SOURCE gave on page 11 of IR are almost word for word argument given by a number of these authors regarding "flying saucers" or their attempts to prove that they are not earth-made vehicles....
>
> SOURCE is therefore not considered to be unaware of the lucrative opportunity and the sensational interest in his suddenly appearing on a TV presentation as a commentator or observer (a la Kenneth Arnold), as a writer of a "flying saucer" eye-witness first person story, or as guest lecturer or star for Keyhoe, Davidson's or other TV programs. He cannot be totally unaware that there would be no better way to enter his chosen civilian profession than with the dramatic announcement that he is the only unimpeachable, completely reliable person, a qualified observer, an Air Force pilot to have seen and made an actually near contact with flying saucers—recently discharged from the service, etc. etc....
>
> Therefore there may be other motives for SOURCE manufacturing such a story, but on the basis of the above known facts, this is one motive that cannot be disregarded. Investigators broke a cardinal rule in handling this case ... : although they went to great lengths and pains to interrogate

SOURCE and obtain detailed statements and opinions, not a single check was made of all local facilities to determine if aircraft or operations were in the area at that time, as prescribed by par 5, AFR 200-2.

It is clear from Gregory's "analysis" that he has no respect for a "reserve officer," and that Long's college background, meaning his major area of study, suggests that Long might have invented the tale in order to find work in television after his discharge from the Air Force. Although Gregory writes about "known facts," much of it is supposition on his part and not at all based on what Long actually said to the "interrogators." According to Gregory, there were no "flying saucers" and anything that suggested otherwise had to be wrong. He postulates that Long will seek some kind of job in television and that Long likely hoped that this sighting would, if not secure a job outright, at least put him in touch with the right people as he recounted the case for the newspapers, magazines, books and television. There is, however, no evidence to support Gregory's theory.

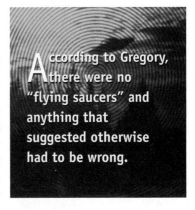

According to Gregory, there were no "flying saucers" and anything that suggested otherwise had to be wrong.

The case file, or rather the witness interrogation and statements were forwarded to a psychologist, who without speaking directly with Long, wrote that:

Officer had a background and studies in Speech and related subjects for TV work.

Was familiar with names of well-known science fiction and "flying saucer" writers.

Advanced the same classic arguments of "saucer" believers that the objects were space ships, i.e., did not resemble any design known to him, etc.

He is a reserve officer, with the possibility that he may complete his tour of duty with the Air Force in the very near future, and would probably enter into TV work.

He just completed the very rigid USAF Survival Course at Stead AF Base the day before; left immediately, and drove all night enroute to Las Vegas.

Checks show no UFO's or any report of unusual objects from radar, GOC, military and civil flight and other operations from that area. No reports from any other persons in the locality....

The case file was submitted to a well-known psychologist who had previously evaluated UFO sightings. His comments paralleled those of ATIC, but with recommendations that the officer be discreetly investigated with view of obtaining certain pertinent information to resolve the case. This would require the services of the OSI.

The damage and embarrassment to the Air Force would be incalculable, if, this officer allied himself with the host of "flying saucer" writers, experts, and others who barrage the Air Force with countless charges and accusations. In this instance, as matters now stand, the Air Force would have no effective rebuttal, or evidence to disprove any unfound charges.

They realized that they couldn't have an Air Force officer, even a reserve officer, say that he had seen a landed alien craft. There wasn't much they could do to stop him, but Long was only a lieutenant and would be off active duty soon. Rather than attempt to understand what he had seen, they decided that it was a hallucination because Long had just finished a rugged school and had been driving all night. These sorts of things happened all the time, the psychologist pointed out in his report.

Alternatively, Long was some kind of an opportunist who realized that his position as an Air Force officer would add a note of credibility to his tale of a landing flying saucer. He would be a hit on the lecture circuit. It meant that his story was a hoax, designed to gain attention of those in the small world of civilian UFO sightings and investigation. Besides, as they had been warned years earlier, he read science fiction and you simply couldn't trust anyone who admitted to that.

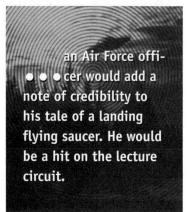

an Air Force officer would add a note of credibility to his tale of a landing flying saucer. He would be a hit on the lecture circuit.

Either way, Long's report was marginalized. The solution was an undefined psychological problem. If anyone asked the Air Force about the case or if someone found it, the case would be labeled as one that had psychological aspects to it. Not solved, but explained, at least, to the Air Force way of thinking.

The other problem with the case was the electromagnetic effect. Long reported that his car stalled, but when the UFOs were gone, the engine started again and ran perfectly. This was an aspect of the case that didn't seem to gain the notice of the investigators. Rather than look into it, they just ignored it, though the Levelland case some three weeks earlier had also highlighted this aspect of some UFO sightings. The Air Force wanted the case explained and according to the government files, ignored the interesting aspects of the sighting. It was explained and that made everyone, with the exception of Long, happy.

✳

The 1127th Field Activities Group

In July 1959, the investigation of UFOs passed from the 1006th AISS to the 1127th Field Activities Group that was based at Fort Belvoir, Virginia. There is nothing in the government files to suggest that the attitudes that had infected the previous investigations had changed. Air Force regulations still required that sightings be solved and that only those cases that had a solution, plausible or not, were released into the public mainstream. Project Blue Book was still considered the official repository of UFO information, and it maintained the public face, but the field investigations were handled by the 1127th FAG for the most part.

At about this same time, Air Force Regulation 200-2 underwent another revision. As before, the Air Force wanted the unidentified sightings reduced to the lowest possible number. Without actually requiring it, the Air Force was attempting to persuade its investigators to find a solution for every UFO sighting.

Even with the 1127th designated as the investigative arm of the Air Force UFO program, it did very few field investigations. Among those was a case from September 28, 1960, near Wichita Falls, Texas, and Sheppard Air Force Base. It was written off as a bolide, a very bright, daylight meteor, but the evidence in the government files, doesn't quite suggest that.

According to a document in the government files:

Something was reported as having hit the ground near Sheppard AFB. Was seen all over the area. Reports coming to ATIC with great frequency. the [sic] 1127th Group from Ft. Belvoir has been sent to the scene. First report to ATIC said it was seen in the early morning of 28 September and that a search would be started by Sheppard at daybreak.

In addition to personnel at Sheppard investigating, press is on scene also radio and TV. Nothing on the space track. ATIC has no positive information but does not believe it to be a *moon dust* [emphasis added] item [this is their vernacular for the refuse of any earth launched satellite]. People at Sheppard claim they know that it fell in a nearby area. ATIC believes that is meteoric.

A teletype message, available in the government files, said that the object had apparently been seen over the Texas and Oklahoma panhandles. There is also speculation that the object was either a meteor or a reentering satellite. The object is described as round, fairly large, and bluish to blue-white in color, changing to orange. In a teletype that is difficult to understand, it says, "Moon Dust sighted by LCL [local] police to have landed in FLD [field] ten miles SSW [south-southwest] Sheppard AFB, Texas at 28/1025Z [meaning September 28 at 0625 in Texas]. Search will begin at daybreak."

After an investigation that lasted about three weeks, Colonel Albert L. Betz summarized the case: "This report is on an Unidentified Flying Object (UFO) observed by many persons on 28 September 1960 at 4 A.M. (local time) in the vicinity West of Wichita Falls, Texas. Attached as inclosure [sic] is a sample of material which floated down from the sky into Wichita Falls at 0800 on the same day. Evaluation of the UFO: Probable meteorite. Evaluation of material: Possibly spider web, having no connection with the earlier sightings."

Typical of this group of sightings was one by a Wichita Falls police officer. According to the government file:

[Name redacted], Patrolman, Wichita Falls Police Department, Age 23, 18 months service with WFPD. RELIABILITY: Good. At 4:24 A.M. local, while cruising North at 5

A bolide (or meteor) burned up over Reno, Nevada, on April 22, 2012. Meteors like this are often blamed for being misreported as UFOs.

MPH on Fairway Boulevard just north of the Wichita Valley Railway track intersection, Patrolman [name redacted] observed through glass of the left rear window of his patrol car a bright blue-white light the size of a volley ball held at arm's length. The object was seen to turn yellow before falling behind the weeds along the roadside. Total time of the sighting was estimated at 2 seconds. [name redacted]'s window was open, but no sound was heard. Two newsmen [name redacted] and [name redacted] from the Wichita Falls Record News were in the patrol car and also witnessed the sighting. After reporting the incident by radio to Police Headquarters, they proceeded to a point SW of their position and joined Mr. [name redacted] in a search of the area, finding nothing to establish that an object had landed or crashed.

In the summary, there was also mention of material that had floated down from the sky. According to the government file as prepared by Captain Gregory Alexander:

MRS. [redacted], housewife … RELIABILITY: Good. At about 8:30 A.M. local, 28 Sep 60, Mrs. [redacted] observed from the balcony of her apartment a large quantity of billowing matter in long streaks flowing through the sky from SW to NE at an undetermined altitude. A smaller of the material appeared to break from the larger mass, taking the form of a bell with string-like streamers. Mrs. [redacted] watched while the material descended and observed a quantity falling to her front and back yards as well as on the apartment roof. She managed to catch a piece of the material about 3" X 2" before it hit the ground. The material had a rubber-like quality and upon contact with her hand, shrank to the size of a 25 cent piece. Mrs. [redacted] observed the material for approximately 45 minutes. Mrs. [redacted] stated she was unaware of the earlier sightings of the falling light when the material was observed.

It was Alexander's opinion, based on witness statements, that something had been seen. He thought the object was a meteor of unusual brilliance and that it probably burned up completely. Had it not, he thought that it might have hit the ground to the southwest of Wichita Falls, near the Texas–New Mexico border.

> [Alexander] thought the object was a meteor of unusual brilliance and that it probably burned up completely.

Alexander thought the fine material, which in UFO circles would be known as Angel Hair, might have been spider web. Young spiders sometimes "ballooned" on strands of web, letting the wind disperse them. He thought there was no connection between the UFO sighting and the fall of material, and in this, he was probably correct. However, there is no analysis of the material in the government files.

This case would be of little interest if it wasn't for the reference to Project Moon Dust. According to other documentation, Moon Dust was classified, as was the name. To find it in a document that is unclassified is a violation of regulations. Of course, the Project Blue Book files, in 1960, were not open for public scrutiny and therefore the violation was of little importance.

The Official End of UFO Investigation

As has been noted, in December 1969 the Air Force announced the end of their UFO investigations. In January the following year, Project Blue Book was closed, and the requirement, by regulation, for the investigation of UFOs no longer applied. When Blue Book ended, Air Force Regulation 80-17 was rescinded. That was the end of official UFO Investigations.

Project Moon Dust

In the UFO community, it has been a matter of record for decades that Project Moon Dust began in November 1961. A document from the government files, with the subject of "AFCIN Intelligence Team Personnel," appeared to define what Moon Dust was intended to be and how it was to be implemented.

According to the opening statement, the objective was "To provide qualified personnel to AFCIN intelligence teams." After a paragraph that has been redacted, paragraph 2, subsection C, said, "In addition to their staff duty assignments, intelligence team personnel have peacetime duty functions in support of such Air Force Projects as Moon Dust, Blue Fly, and UFO, and other AFCIN directed quick reaction projects which require intelligence team operational capabilities (see Definitions)."

Paragraph 5 is labeled "Definitions." It lays out who will participate in these missions and the ties in the UFOs. It said:

e. Unidentified Flying Objects (UFO): Headquarters USAF has established a program for investigation of reliably reported unidentified flying objects within the United States. AFR [Air Force Regulation] 200-2 delineates 1127th collection responsibilities.

f. Blue Fly: Operation Blue Fly has been established to facilitate expeditious delivery to FTD of Moon Dust or other items of great technical intelligence interest. AFCIN SOP for Blue Fly operations, February 1960, provides for 1127th participation.

g. Moon Dust: As a specialized aspect of its over-all material exploitation program, Headquarters USAF has established Project Moon Dust to locate, recover and deliver descended foreign space vehicles. ICGL [inclosure] #4, 25 April 1961, delineates collection responsibilities.

There is additional information in the document about the Moon Dust teams, underscoring its role in the investigation of UFOs. Under "Discussion" it said:

a. Headquarters USAF (AFCIN) maintains intelligence teams as a function of AFCIN-1E (1127th USAF Field Activities Group). Personnel comprising such teams have normal AFCIN-1E staff duties, and their maintenance of qualification for intelligence team employment is in addition to their normal staff duties. For example, the Chief of

AFCIN-1E-OD, the Domestic Operations Section, additionally participates in approximately 18 hours of training per month for intelligence team employment. Such training includes physical training, classroom combat intelligence training, airborne operations, field problems, etc.

b. Intelligence teams are comprised of three men each, to include a linguist, a tech man, and an ops man. All are airborne qualified. Cross-training is provided each team member in the skills of the other team members to assure a team functional capability despite casualties which may be incurred in deployment.

c. Peacetime employment of AFCIN intelligence team capability is provided for in UFO investigation (AFR 200-2) and in support of Air Force Systems Command (AFSC) Foreign Technology Division (FTD) Projects Moon Dust and Blue Fly. These three [sic] peacetime projects all involve a potential for employment of qualified field intelligence personnel on a quick reaction basis to recover or perform field exploitation of unidentified flying objects, or known Soviet/Bloc aerospace vehicles, weapons systems, and/or residual components of such equipment. The intelligence team capability to gain rapid access, regardless of location, to recover or perform field exploitation, to communicate and provide intelligence reports is the only such collection capability available to AFCIN, and is vitally necessary in view of current intelligence gaps concerning Soviet/Bloc technological capabilities.

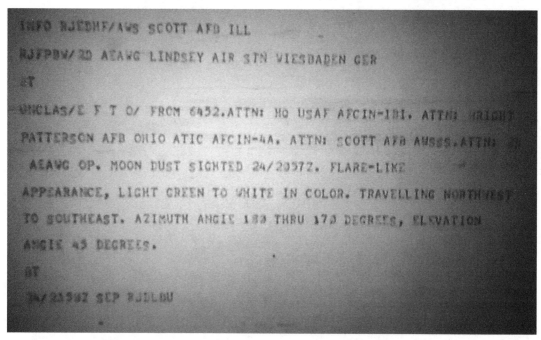

The Air Force memo that mentions Project Moon Dust.

This document, recovered through a FOIA request, shows that projects focused on the recovery of alien space craft did exist and that specific units had been created for this purpose. True, they had another mission, spelled out in the document as a wartime mission of capture and interrogation of enemy flight crews. At one point in the document, there is a discussion about the lack of Russian linguists available to the Air Force. Only five were available, and of those, only two were native speakers, meaning they had learned the language in Russia.

But the document seemed to be focused on UFOs, defining the missions and command and control structures for the deployment of these teams. While a wartime mission is discussed, it seems that it was the peacetime mission that was most important.

The document, however, has circulated inside the UFO community in two forms. One was marked as "Draft," but the other is not. Skeptics have suggested that UFO researchers "whited out" the draft and then circulated the document as if it was something that was implemented. Some researchers claimed that skeptics marked the document as a draft to reduce its impact when it was read by others.

The thinking is that this document marked the beginning of Project Moon Dust and Blue Fly but such is not the case. Documents in the Project Blue Book files mention Moon Dust. One of them, a letter from 1958, used Moon Dust in the subject line. Clearly this proves that the document from 1961 was not a suggestion for the creation of the teams, but a document created to define the various missions of those teams.

In fact, this can be taken a step further. On April 25, 1961, in a confidential document recovered from the government files and issued by the Department of the Air Force, there are instructions on "Intelligence Collection Guidance" in what is called "Letter No. 4." The subject, in an unclassified paragraph, is "MOON DUST Reporting."

This letter is clearly about "MOON DUST Alerts," and is "applicable worldwide for initiative reporting." The background is given as:

> Based on estimates of the time and place of foreign earth satellite vehicle (ESV) atmospheric re-entries, Headquarters USAF (AFCIN) initiates MOON DUST Alerts. They are issued as far in advance as practicable (normally 10 days) and automatically cancelled three (3) days after the re-entry prediction date stated in the alert message. It is necessary that the alerts be issued on a world-wide basis until such time as techniques are developed that will make possible the prediction of precise time and place of impact.

One section details the "instructions and guidance" and even provides some interesting information about what the reentries would look like. It said:

> The following guidance may assist in reporting observations of space vehicle re-entry. The re-entry of a space vehicle can be seen over great distances, and even the qualified observer cannot estimate from point of observation to the sighted object with any great degree of certainty. At these distances,

the re-entry would appear to resemble a meteor travelling in a near horizontal or descending path and, as the distance decreased, would appear as a brilliant object or cluster of objects visible during daylight conditions. In addition, an audible rumbling sound like thunder, arid [sic] possibly sharp explosion-like sounds might be correlated with the sighting.

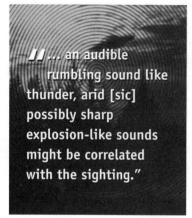

" *... an audible rumbling sound like thunder, arid [sic] possibly sharp explosion-like sounds might be correlated with the sighting."*

Under "Classification Aspects," the letter indicates the thinking that they anticipated recovering Soviet-made space vehicles and because of this, the overall project is classified as "Confidential." The reasoning seems to be that this was done because of "intelligence association with decay estimates." Sightings, however, would be unclassified.

Although it is clear from the letter that its intent was to create a policy for the retrieval of information about, and the recovery of, Soviet-manufactured space vehicles, Moon Dust covered other operations as well. As will be seen, some of the Moon Dust sightings were sent onto Project Blue Book, and later documents incorporated UFOs into the categories that required reporting.

Project Blue Book and Project Moon Dust

Project Blue Book files indicate that there was coordination between Blue Book and Moon Dust. Several cases reference Moon Dust even though they seem to have conventional explanations. According to the government files, there were several cases that were labeled as reported by Moon Dust in September 1960. The first of these came from Ramey Air Force Base, Puerto Rico, on September 15, 1960. The government files, which noted one of the addressees on the message as Moon Dust, said:

> Round object with a tail, size reports vary from the size of a pea to half dollar, color reports vary from bluish-white to dusky red. Tail aprox [sic] 3-5 times the size of the object. No sound. Object reported to have broken up into several fireballs. One report stated that object finally fell into ocean.

> It is possible that this object was a very slow meteor. However it is more probably a reentry of the 1960 Epsilon vehicle, parts of which reentered during Sep and Oct 1960. Epsilon had an inclination of 64 [degrees], therefore the heading would be about 26 degrees.

A series of sightings on September 21, 22, and 23, 1960, from Bermuda were listed as "ATIC possible Mon [sic] Dust." The witnesses are identified only as civilians. The government files said, "Reported sightings by local people of dull orange object on 21, 22, 23 Sep [sic] accompanied by weird [sic] whirring sound, in evening." The original message said that further investigation was being conducted but no follow-up information had been received. There was insufficient data for any sort of scientific analysis.

The first case about Moon Dust came from Ramey Air Force Base in Puerto Rico in 1960.

Another sighting took place on September 23, 1960, at Bitburg AB, Germany. The source of the sighting was listed as "Moon Dust." It said:

> Luminous streak, like shooting star, colors red and yellow. Object left a trail. Object appeared very suddenly and was red in color, gradually changing to bright yellow. Appeared much larger than meteor.... Path momentarily broken and when reappeared was red in color, no smoke but numerous sparks.

> Description conforms to satellite reentry. As to direction, color and breaking up. 1960 Lambda II (rocket body) reentered this date. Case evaluated as satellite reentry based upon general description, although duration of sighting was omitted.

This seems to be a reasonable explanation, especially since there was documentation to back up the solution. A few days later, on September 26, 1960, northeast of Bermuda, an object that was yellowish-green and described as a "falling star or object" was seen.

A teletype in the government files, received on September 26, 1960, said, "PD Moon Dust falling star or object sighted by GULL special at 0527Z 26 Sep." There was no explanation or definition of GULL. It might have been the name of the mission or the name of the witness. It was in sight for one second.

According to the government files, the source of the sighting was "military" and under "Type of Observation" someone had typed Moon Dust. The sighting wasn't important other than the reference to Moon Dust.

This Project Blue Book card mentions Moon Dust and the sighting in Wethersfield, England.

A Moon Dust case with little information came from Thule, Greenland. A teletype message said, "Bright comet like object presumably MOONDUST sighted at Thule AB Greenland … on 24 Sep 60. Estimated elevation less than ten degrees. Direction: Appeared from southeast and disappeared into the west…. Observed time 5 seconds." It was written off as a possible meteor.

Finally, in September, a sighting was made in Wethersfield, England. The project card in the government files listed the case as Moon Dust. The teletype message said, "Flare-like appearance, light green to white in color. Travelling northwest to southeast." It was noted that the "Information too limited for valid conclusion."

What this suggests is that Moon Dust was in operation prior to the document dated November 1961. Information was being shared with Project Blue Book, but that information was of cases that had little overall importance and certainly no national security impact. But it also suggests that the document, while it was just a draft, was created to more clearly define what Moon Dust was. It is no longer a question of whether the ideas in that document were implemented or not. It is a question about the reality of Moon Dust and its overall mission.

✳

The Beginning of Moon Dust

The question becomes: Exactly when did Moon Dust begin? Since the evidence proves that Moon Dust existed before the November 1961 Team Personnel instructions, and since there is documentation that pre-dates it, that is obviously not the beginning of Moon Dust.

According to some researchers, there is documentation that Moon Dust existed as early as January 1950. There is a September 8, 1950 letter issued by the Director of Air Force Intelligence called, "Reporting of Information on Unconventional Aircraft." It said, "The United States Air Force has a continuing requirement for the reporting and technical analysis of observations of unconventional aircraft which might indicate an advance in progress of a foreign power. An unconventional aircraft, within the meaning of this directive, is defined as any aircraft or airborne object which by performance, aerodynamic characteristics, or unusual features, does not conform to any presently known aircraft type."

While this does not specifically mention UFOs, it is virtually the same definition given to UFOs in other documents available from the government files. It is obviously a requirement to report UFO sightings, but it also suggests a cover story for them. They weren't spacecraft, they were unconventional aircraft.

This underscores the Air Force mission and can also be seen as support for Project Sign, which had begun in 1948. It does not give us a starting date for Moon Dust, only that the Air Force is still interested in UFOs.

Another starting date offered is that of January 3, 1953. This is the date that the 4602nd Air Intelligence Service Squadron was created. From the documentation available in the government files, the 4602nd was created in response to the need for trained intelligence personnel to conduct interrogations of downed enemy flight crews and the recovery of their wrecked aircraft. It was probably an outgrowth of the Korean War.

> *It is obviously a requirement to report UFO sightings, but it also suggests a cover story for them. They weren't spacecraft, they were unconventional aircraft.*

The wartime mission, at least in the documentation, suggests that the primary mission was wartime, but in peacetime, the assets could be used for UFO investigation as a method of training. Get the 4602nd personnel out in the field and have them attempt to get coherent information from those who thought they saw UFOs.

This suggests that there was an investigation underway and a team was created for quick reaction. But it is also entirely possible that the whole organization was set up in response to a need in Korea and in preparation for the coming of World War III. The belief was that long range bombers would be used to attack the United States by air. If that happened, there would be downed aircraft and crews, and personnel trained to handle these situations would be an asset. All of this was simply an attempt to create that pool of trained individuals to meet a perceived future need.

There is a document, available in the government files from Headquarters, U.S. Air Force Message #54322 and dated December 23, 1957, which discussed a new Project called Moon Dust. The mission was "to collect and analyze raw intelligence reports from the field on fallen space debris and objects of unknown origin."

This letter was dated about ninety days after the launch of Sputnik, which means that satellite reentries were now a real possibility. There would be returning space debris. Soviet satellite orbits might decay and the satellites could fall to the ground, providing an opportunity for recovery and analysis if there were teams already in place and were prepared for it.

The best evidence, currently available through the government files, is that Moon Dust began at the end of 1957. By 1960, Moon Dust information was being periodically fed into the Project Blue Book system.

More Moon Dust Activities

Documents from the government files located in the Department of State provide a number of Moon Dust related events. Although some of them cover the period of operation for Project Blue Book, these cases did not make it into those files. Some of them have obvious terrestrial explanations, but others remain mysterious. The list of sightings pulled from these government sources is:

January 22, 1965—Rajasthan, India

January 11, 1967—Agadir, Morocco: An object fell into the sea.

March 28, 1967—Kasba Tadia, Morocco: An 8.5 mm in diameter object landed on the roof of a house and then took off again.

August 17, 1967—Sudan: Cube shaped satellite weighing about three tons was found fifty miles from Kutum.

March 25, 1968—Katmandu, Nepal: Four objects were found.

August 7, 1970—Lai, Chad: Eighteen inch in diameter sphere weighing 20 to 25 pounds. It appeared to have been in two halves, welded together and resembled a pressurized fuel tank.

April 7, 1972—New Zealand: Space Defense Center reported that two objects had "deorbited" and fell to the ground.

October 20, 1973—New Zealand: A cylindrical object two feet long and seven inches in diameter was found.

May 6, 1978—Bermejo, Bolivia: An egg-shaped object made of metal and nearly five feet in diameter was found.

October 23, 1978—Ashburton, New Zealand: Two spheres were located.

It is clear from the descriptions of some of these recoveries that the objects were not extraterrestrial but debris that had fallen off aircraft or returning space objects manufactured on Earth. Even these reports are interesting because they demonstrate that the government, using various entities and agencies, had been working to recover the material for analysis for decades. Often the final reports and the existence of the material have been classified, released only under FOIA requirements.

One of those interesting cases, found in government files located in the Department of State and the Central Intelligence Agency, concerned an object that fell near Bermejo River in the Taija Province, Bolivia, on May 6, 1978. According to a document from the American Embassy in La Paz to the Department of State:

1. The Bolivian newspapers carried this morning an article concerning an unidentified object that apparently recently fell from the sky. The paper quotes a "Latin" correspondent's story from the Argentine city of Salta. The object was discovered near the Bolivian city of Bermejo and was described as egg-shaped, metal and about four meters in diameter.

2. The Bolivian Air Force plans to investigate to determine what the object might be and from where it came. I have expressed our interest and willingness to help. They will advise.

3. Request department check with appropriate agencies to see if they can shed some light on what this object might be. The general region has more than its share of reports of UFOs this past week. Requests a reply ASAP.

This suggests a real interest in UFO sightings. Something strange found in the jungle shouldn't have come to the attention of the ambassador, but it did, which implies that they may have been looking.

That the sighting was important becomes clearer when a CIA document, dated May 15, 1978, is examined. It said, in part:

This photo shows the Soviet satellite Sputnik opened up to show some of its interior. Sputnik was the first artificial satellite, ushering in not only the Space Age but also the possibility that some UFOs would be attributable to satellites reentering the atmosphere.

Many people in this part of the country [Bolivia] claim they saw an object which resembled a soccer ball falling behind the mountains on the Argentine–Bolivian border, causing an explosion that shook the earth. This took place on May 6. Around that time some people in San Luis and Mendoza provinces reported seeing a flying saucer squadron flying in formation. The news from Salta confirms that the artificial satellite fell on Taire Mountain in Bolivia, where it has already been located by authorities. The same sources said that the area where the artificial satellite fell has been declared an emergency zone by the Bolivian Government.

The next day, on May 16, 1978, the CIA added more information. The document, "Conflict on Details of Fallen Object," said:

" ... [T]he area where the artificial satellite fell has been declared an emergency zone by the Bolivian Government."

We have received another phone call from our audience requesting confirmation of reports that an unidentified object fell on Bolivian territory near the Argentine border. We can only say that the Argentine and Uruguayan radio stations are reporting on this even more frequently, saying that Bolivian authorities have urgently requested assistance from the U. S. National Aeronautics and Space Administration in order to determine the nature of that which crashed on a hill in Bolivian territory. Just a few minutes ago Radio El Espectador of Montevideo announced that there was uncertainty as to the truth of these reports. Argentine sources indicated that the border with Bolivia had been closed but that it might soon be reopened. They also reported that an unidentified object had fallen on Bolivian soil near the Argentine border and that local Bolivian authorities had requested aid from the U.S. National Aeronautics and Space Administration to investigate the case.

A La Paz newspaper said today that there is great interest in learning about the nature of the fallen object, adding that local authorities for security reasons had cordoned off 200 km around the spot where the object fell. The object is said to be a mechanical device with a diameter of about 4 meters which has already been brought to Tarija. There is interest in determining the accuracy of these reports which have spread quickly throughout the continent, particularly in Bolivia and its neighboring countries. Is it a satellite, a meteorite, or a false alarm?

On May 24, another message was sent from the embassy in La Paz. This one, from the Defense Attaché, was sent to several military agencies, including the Department of the Air Force, NORAD, and the Department of State. It said:

This office has tried to verify the stories put forth in the local press. The Chief of Staff of the Bolivian Air Force told DATT/AIRA [Defense Attaché/Air Attaché] this date that planes from the BAF have flown over the area where the object was supposed to have landed and in their search they drew a blank. Additionally, DATT/AIRA talked this date with the Commander of the Bolivian Army and informed DATT that the Army's search party directed to go into the area to find the object had found nothing. The Army has concluded that there may or not be an object, but to date nothing has been found.

Leonard Stringfield in his *The UFO Crash/Retrieval Syndrome, Status Report II: New Sources, New Data* published in January 1980, noted in Item B-8:

The case of the mysterious flying object crashing into the mountains bordering Argentina and Bolivia, May 8, 1978 [sic], is well known by researchers. Was it a meteorite, part of a satellite or spacecraft? Rumors say nothing was ever found after extensive search on the precipitous slopes by Bolivian and Argentine military teams and by NASA.

In June 1979, I [Stringfield] received a stack of clippings from Argentine newspapers with stories that claim otherwise. The sender, Nicholas M. Ojeda of Rosario, Argentina, stated in his letter, "... As you know, our country is one of the most visited areas in the world by OVNIs [UFOs] as we call them in Latin America. Last year, May 8, we had a very significant case in the Salta Province in the north of the country. A long object crashed into the mountains. Although some people thing it was a meteor or part of a satellite, this case is not closed yet. There is a report of a group of investigators who vanished mysteriously in the area. I really think something big happened in Salta. NASA investigated, but there was not news of it. I have to tell you that in La Paz, Bolivia, a huge USAF Hercules C-130 carried 'something' from the area where the UFO crashed. What was it?"

When this question and the news of the cargo plane being there was put to Bob Barry's former C.I.A. contact, he confirmed the flight and admitted, "I was aboard the plane." He offered no answer to, "what was aboard?"

Antonio Huneeus, a science journalist fluent in Spanish provided additional, clarifying information about the case. Given his contacts in South America, his accounts of what happened there might be considered the very best. Huneeus wrote, first in the winter 1994 issue of *UFO Universe* and later in a 2011 issue of *Open Minds*:

At 4:30 PM on May 6, 1978, a UFO—whether natural, man-made or unknown origin—crashed in South America on the hill at El Taire near the Bermejo River, which divides Bolivia's remote Tarija Department with the province of Salta in Argentina. The crash was first felt as a shattering explosion—a sonic boom that was heard within a range of 120 miles and which shattered windows of villages 30 miles from the target site....

It was reported that the explosion had shaken the village of Mecoya.... The sonic boom, on the other hand, was heard over a radius of 150 km inside Argentina.... Patrols of the 20th Detachment of the "Gendarmeria" (Border Police) of Oran were dispatched towards the rugged terrain around the river Bermejo, where it was believed the object had crashed. The town of Aguas Blanca in the Department of Santa Victoria in Salta rapidly brought a swarm of reporters following the patrols. An increasing number of eyewitness accounts followed the reporters.... It [the object] was sometimes described as a "fireball" the size of a soccer ball. For the most part, however, people described the UFO as an artificial-looking shiny space object.

Science journalist Antonio Huneeus covered the Bermejo, Bolivia, sighting of 1978, writing the best account of the incident that was published in *UFO Universe*.

There were a number of eyewitnesses interviewed by a variety of people, including the military representatives of Bolivia and Argentina, reporters from several countries, and eventually by American officers who might have been working at the request of NASA and who were certainly operating under the banner of Moon Dust.

The highest ranking military official on the scene was Corporal Natalio Farfan Ruiz, who told reporters, "I don't know what would have happened if the UFO had fallen on their houses. Can you imagine? ... It was around 4:30 when a cylinder shook the Earth.... I believed the end of the world was coming."

Huneeus reported that Velez Orozco, trained as an engineer, had seen the cylindrical object as well. He thought it was four meters [about fifteen feet] in diameter and had a conical shape in front.

As communications from the area continued, two Americas arrived for an inspection or investigation. Huneeus wrote:

> Clarin and other news media from the continent reported that two "NASA experts," Colonel Robert Simmons and Major John Heise, arrived in Tarija. Though the officers were allegedly "on vacation," their mission was actually to take the object, or parts of it, to a USAF Hercules C-130 cargo plane waiting at La Paz to carry pieces back to the United States.

> Naturally, the American Embassy in La Paz vehemently denied this story. Ernesto Uribe, chief of the Embassy's Information Service, was quoted in the press as saying that no satellite had been found....

> However, according to recently declassified documents [government files that were declassified in 1994], it appears that Simmons and Heise were from the Defense Attaché Office in La Paz, and that they did fly to Tarija with Bolivian Air Force officers as part of the "Moon Dust" project.

While there is good documentation in the government files that something was seen and reported, there is no documentation of an explanation. The newspaper articles, while certainly a form of documentation, are based on eyewitness reports without benefit of other evidence or real investigation. Stringfield's report was based on a source that was identified only as Bob Barry's CIA contact, which does not allow any additional verification and does nothing to validate the event.

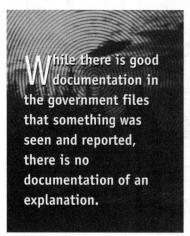

While there is good documentation in the government files that something was seen and reported, there is no documentation of an explanation.

There are some details that apparently weren't reported at the time. Huneeus wrote that a Bolivian UFO researcher, Jorge Arias Gonzalez, told the Argentinian UFO Congress in Santa Fe that government sources had told him that "a large dark object, 80 or 100 meters long," had been seen and that "two peasants and herds of sheep and goats were found dead by the Commission some 60 meters away from the crater...."

Huneeus interviewed Bob Pratt, an American UFO researcher who had traveled into the remote area and who interviewed many of the witnesses in the months that followed.

According to Huneeus, Pratt had trouble getting into the area at first. He eventually reached the site and told Huneeus:

> A lot of misinformation has been published about this incident. I am certain, however, that the area was not cordoned off by the military, that no object was recovered by NASA or anyone else, that no Hercules picked up anything and there was no news blackout … the "crash" area is in such rugged, remote territory that it would have been difficult for anyone to retrieve anything without the use of a large helicopter such as a CH-47, and had such an operation taken place, the people living in the area would have known about it. In the four weeks I spent in the area, including a total of seven days at the "crash" site itself, I never found anyone who had ever seen a helicopter or any stranger in the area, other than me and a few Argentine and Bolivian newsmen who tried to reach the crash site immediately after the incident occurred.

Pratt said, "I believe something crashed into the mountain and was buried under the landslide it created. But the six people I know who had personally inspected the site could find no debris of any kind. Whatever struck there is probably going to remain buried there."

More Moon Dust Missions

In July 1968, a document from the government files that was originally sent to the 1127th Air Activities Group at Ft. Belvoir and labeled as "Moon Dust (U)," which suggests that Moon Dust was the unclassified name, mentioned a recovery. Although heavily redacted, part one of the message said, "Ref a. Part Three, awaiting arrival of film, which FTD will process. Results of examination will determine whether dispatch of technical team would be necessary, and what you can tell … Defense Secretary as to identity of object. Agree film should remain unclassified. Will forward two copies all prints as you request."

There are notes at the bottom of the page that seems to expand on part of the message, though sections of it are redacted as well. It said:

> By ref a, [redacted] advised sequence [redacted] in obtaining MOON DUST specimens, advised film of nose cone photographed by DATT on 19 July being forwarded unprocessed to DIACO-2B [Defense Intelligence Agency Commanding Officer], and requested copies of prints of film for [redacted] as well as guidance as to what DATT can tell [redacted] as to identity of object photographed. By ref b. [redacted] requested permission to retransmit ref a. [redacted]. By ref c, FTD requested courier these items back to [redacted] and further requested [redacted] to attempt to obtain results of [redacted]. By ref e, [redacted] stresses need to protect our knowledge of [redacted] this matter, and state we cannot approach [redacted] on any of the objects which [redacted] had in their possession. MSG [message] above coordinated with DIACO-D in draft.

Most of the details in this case are hidden, but for this specific message that isn't the important part. It is the reference to the possibility of the dispatch of a technical team that is noteworthy, suggesting that these teams existed and that they were sent into various areas for analysis of the space debris.

On July 19, 1968, the embassy in Katmandu sent a message that dealt with Moon Dust. The message was in three parts and said:

Part I.

Full cooperation just affected [redacted] reveals history ... major actions regard objects as follows:

A. 23 Apr, RNA [Royal Nepalese Army] shows two objects to DATT.

B. 20 May, RNA gives photos of two objects to DATT.

C. 27 May, RNA shows three objects to [redacted]. Object not shown to DATT was oval shape, 10 X 15 inches and 2 inches thick (third object).

D. 29 May, RNA gives three objects to [redacted] and tells [redacted] that complete nose cone (fourth object) exists but cannot be seen.

E. 17 June, RNA tells DATT there is a complete nose cone but impossible to see.

F. 19 July, DATT invited to see fourth object. RNA CINC [Commander in Chief] asks [redacted] three objects back ASAP. Objects now expected back in Nepal OA [on or about] 28 July.

G. 22 July [redacted] still hasn't been able to see fourth object but receives small photo of same.

[Large section redacted on page two.]

B. Defense Secretary Chitta Bahadur K.C. asked DATT last night if origin of object had been determined and if we intended to send experts. Answer to both questions was that DATT did not yet know. Future access to fourth should be no problem but unknown as to first three.

Part II.

1. [Redacted] officer to POKHARA [city in Nepal] 15–25 June to investigate fall of objects. All four objects fell night 25–26 March at three locations E8358–N2816, E8402–N2819 from bearing of 020 RPT 020 degrees.

[Large section redacted]

1. In view of all the above, DATT now feels that technical team should not RPT not be sent unless visual examination of fourth object is felt essential.

2. If team is not RPT not sent, request guidance as to determination of objects is in order to close case.

3. Recommend prints requested by PARA 2, PART II, of REF MSG retain unclassified status. Film in registered pouch number 09 RPT 09.

Once again, there is mention of a technical team, again underscoring the fact that the structure of the Moon Dust teams and their deployment as discussed in the November 1961 document was being used. While the document in the hands of UFO researchers might well have been a draft, that doesn't mean that it was not implemented.

On July 30, 1968, in another Moon Dust message found in the government files, there was additional information. The message said, "No new developments here except [redacted] first secretary visited [redacted] on unsuccessful fishing expedition for info on space objects … DATT briefed ambassador yesterday on Moon Dust situation. Only point raised was desire that we give … positive info if at all possible due to: (Complete section has been redacted.)

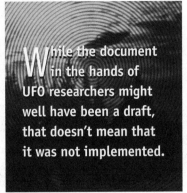

While the document in the hands of UFO researchers might well have been a draft, that doesn't mean that it was not implemented.

The Air Force Denies Moon Dust Existed

Clues about Moon Dust had been circulating for a long time. Although there were references to it in the Project Blue Book files, there were very few of them in the more than 12,000 cases released into the public domain. In June 1986, Barry Greenwood reported in *Just Cause* that they had learned more about Moon Dust. Greenwood wrote:

> In our last issue, we alluded to one of those many project code names which turn up from time to time in released government documents. Few of these are ever identified in more than brief detail. However, Project Moon Dust, as named in recently released DIA files is an exception. We have several documents which do seem to link UFOs with this colorfully named project. Our thanks to Robert Todd for providing us with the background information on his several-years-old research into Moon Dust.

Todd, a UFO researcher, filed hundreds of FOIA requests, and it was among those that the name Moon Dust first appeared. He filed additional FOIA requests with the Department of State, which resulted in a great deal of information being sent to him.

Cliff Stone, a retired Army Sergeant First Class, followed the same path, filing dozens of requests for additional information. Stone wrote that in December, 1989 he asked the Air Force for information on Project Moon Dust and Operation Blue Fly. In January, 1990 they responded that they had no information. Several months later, they sent another letter saying they had two documents that were responsive to Stone's request, but they were properly classified.

Stone, unhappy with the responses from the Air Force, eventually contacted U.S. Senator Jeff Bingaman, who in turn wrote to the Air Force. Their reply, from Lieutenant Colonel John E. Madison of the Congressional Inquiry Division, Office of Legislative Liaison, was, "There is no agency, nor has there ever been, at Fort Belvoir, Virginia, which would deal with UFOs or have any information

U.S. Senator Jeff Bingaman of New Mexico contacted the Air Force on Cliff Stone's behalf, but the military still denied that any agency handling UFOs at Fort Belvoir.

about the incident in Roswell. In addition, there is no Project Moon Dust or Operation Blue Fly. Those missions have never existed."

The government files, from Project Blue Book to the Department of State, prove that Madison's statement was in error. Documents labeled as Moon Dust have been found in various locations, all with the proper provenance. There is no doubt that Moon Dust existed and that it dealt with UFOs, at least in part.

Bingaman wrote back to the Air Force, this time including documents from the Department of State, proving that Moon Dust did exist. Colonel George M. Mattingley, Jr., wrote, "This is in reply to your inquiry on behalf of Mr. Clifford E. Stone on the accuracy of the information previously provided to your office. Upon further review of the case (which was aided by the several attachments to Mr. Stone's letter), we wish to amend our last statements contained in the previous response to your inquiry."

Clearly the Air Force had been caught in what, at best, would be called a mistake. Given the classification level of Moon Dust, and its appearance in so many places, including the files of Project Blue Book, and that it was an Air Force project, it is surprising that Lieutenant Colonel Madison couldn't find information on it.

Mattingley now wanted to provide as much information as possible and wrote:

> In 1953, during the Korean War, the Air Defense Command organized intelligence teams to deploy, recover, or exploit at the scene of downed enemy personnel, equipment, and aircraft. The unit with responsibility for maintaining these teams was located at Fort Belvoir, Virginia. As the occasion never arose to use these air defense teams, the mission was assigned to Headquarters, United States Air Force in 1957 and expanded to include the following peace-time functions: a) Unidentified Flying Objects (UFOs), to investigate reliably reported UFOs within the United States; b) Project MOON DUST, to recover objects and debris from space vehicles that survived re-entry from space to earth; c) Operation BLUE FLY, to expeditiously retrieve downed Soviet Bloc equipment.... These teams were eventually disbanded because of a lack of activity; Project MOON DUST teams and Operation BLUE FLY missions were similarly discontinued. The Air Force has no information that any UFOs were ever confirmed downed in the United States.

The documents found in the government files reveal that Moon Dust was discussed at high levels, and that teams were requested. The evidence shows that Moon Dust began no later than 1957, and some of the units that supported it were organized in the early 1950s. There is documented evidence proving the existence of Project Moon Dust and the fact that one of its components related to UFOs. There is also evidence that Colonel Mattingley's response to Senator Bingaman was also in error.

The End of Moon Dust

Mattingley wrote that Project Moon Dust ended because of a lack of activity. A search of various government files proved that Moon Dust teams were used, and while not all their missions were related to UFOs, they were a part of their mission. Teams were deployed and there were requests for teams to be deployed. There is no documentation currently available on the number of teams and how many times they might have been deployed.

There is other information available, however, showing that Project Moon Dust was not discontinued. Robert Todd, having learned that the code name had been changed, wrote to the Air Force. In a letter from the Air Force dated July 1, 1987, he learned that the "nickname Project Moon Dust no longer officially exists." According to Colonel Phillip E. Thompson, deputy assistant chief-of-staff, Intelligence, "It [Project Moon Dust] has been replaced by another name that is not releaseable [sic]. FTD's [Foreign Technology Division, headquartered at Wright-Patterson] duties are listed in a classified passage in a classified regulation that is being withheld because it is currently and properly classified."

> [T]he Air Force was caught telling a senator that Moon Dust had been terminated, but other documentation shows that Moon Dust was now operating under another name.

This is a trick that the Air Force had used in the past. They announced that there had been a final report for Project Sign, implying that the project had ended, but they simply changed the name to Grudge. Later they announced that Grudge had been terminated, but continued to investigate under the name Blue Book. Now the Air Force was caught telling a senator that Moon Dust had been terminated, but other documentation shows that Moon Dust was now operating under another name.

Moon Dust seems to outline standard operating procedure for the Air Force in the recovery of returning space debris and objects of unknown origin. Their attitude was to tell the public one thing and do something else—say the project had ended but continue to work under a different name.

It also demonstrates that an interest in UFOs has been in existence since the 1940s. It is an interest that continued long past the end of Project Blue Book in 1969, and it is clearly an interest that continues until today. While Moon Dust no longer exists by that name, it was likely replaced by another project name. Without the code name, there is no way to learn anything more about it. All that is known is that it exists and that it is classified.

The Washington UFO Sightings—2002 Version

Fifty-two years after UFOs were seen over Washington, D.C., and chased by Air Force jets, the same scenario was replayed, with fewer witnesses, fewer jets, and a dispute over what was seen on radar. There is some confusion about the reason for jets to have been scrambled and the government files seem to be somewhat inconsistent.

According to Joan Woodward, in an article published in the *International UFO Reporter* in the winter 2002–2003 issue and a similar article in the *MUFON UFO Journal* in October 2002, it was about 1:00 A.M. when fighters with the 113th Wing of the Air National Guard were scrambled at NORAD's request.

According to the government files, as reported by Woodward, "Two F-16 jets from Andrews Air Force base were scrambled at approximately 0100 hours 26 Jul 02 after radar detected an unknown aircraft. The unidentified aircraft's track subsequently faded from the radar. The F-16's investigated, found nothing out of the ordinary and returned to the base."

Gary Dillman, who was working as a security guard that night, heard what he described as "fighter jets being scrambled … they were coming from the general direction of Andrews AFB." He thought they were somewhere between 2,000 and 5,000 feet and there were three or four of them. They seemed to be circling, some in very tight turns, giving Dillman the impression that they were following something or searching for something.

Dillman said that he had seen the aircraft operating from Andrews AFB during the five years he had worked as a security guard. These jets were not following the procedures he had seen before and he didn't believe there was anything routine about those flights. He called a local radio station, WTOP, to let them know that the Air Force was up and looking for something.

It is important to note that this event took place less than a year after the terrorist attacks of 9/11, and any unidentified aircraft in the area would trigger a quick military response. Civilian flight operations into the area would have required a flight plan or operations away from the various restricted areas.

After Dillman called the radio station, and while standing outside of his truck to watch the jets, he saw an orange, hard-edged ball that was "coming on a downward slant toward the earth in the southwest."

Dillman said that a fighter, coming out of the clouds, banked toward it and the object then changed course in a smooth curve.

For a moment, Dillman thought that it was a meteor. Dillman said that a fighter, coming out of the clouds, banked toward it and the object then changed course in a smooth curve. They flew to the south and then were lost in the clouds. He said that he could hear the roar of the fighter's jet engines, but no sound coming from the light.

About ten minutes later, Dillman again called the radio station, telling them what he had seen. He could still see the flashing strobe lights on the fighters. When he finished the call, he again saw the orange object, in the southwest part of the sky. As it maneuvered in smooth, banking turns, Dillman saw the circular shape of the craft. The shape seemed to change into a slim oval, but that was probably a matter of perspective.

One of the fighters was following the object and although it was maneuvering, the gentle turns don't suggest that it was attempting to evade the jet. Both the object and the fighter disappeared into the clouds in the southeastern sky. Dillman thought the whole sequence had lasted ten to fifteen seconds. He could hear the sound of the jet's engines but there didn't seem to be any sound coming from the UFO.

At about the time that Dillman was calling WTOP the first time, Renny Rogers had just returned from work. He heard the fighters, which wasn't all that unusual for the area. This time, however, it seemed that it was more than the normal two fighters. They were low enough and loud enough to rattle the windows of his house. He went outside to see if he could find out what was happening. He saw nothing to the south, so he walked around the house to look toward the north. There, in the north-northwest sky, he saw a bright, pale blue light moving at a high rate of speed.

Rogers thought the object dropped rapidly to about 2,000 feet, climbed again, and continued on a straight line until Rogers lost sight of it behind some trees. He ran back to the south and saw the light moving toward the southwest. A fighter flew over his house, following the path of the light to the southwest. Although the fighter seemed to be chasing the light, the pilot was not using his afterburners; at least that was what Rogers thought. Rogers didn't think that the fighter had a chance of catching the light.

Rogers thought the chase took place about 6,000 feet overhead. There were scattered clouds at about 3,000 feet and both the light and the jet sometimes disappeared behind the clouds. Although Rogers never lost sight of the jet, the object (or light), which was smaller, was sometimes completely obscured. Rogers thought he saw the light for about five or six seconds but he saw the fighter for a longer period.

A neighbor, only identified as Mike, saw Rogers outside and called over to him. He saw Rogers coming toward him and then saw the pale blue light and the fighter that was chasing it. The light and jet flew over him and he thought that the UFO was slowing, allowing the fighter to get closer to it. He lost sight of the objects behind the trees and saw the fighter was still far behind the light.

Mike said the light was very bright, an ice-blue color, with a pulsating rhythm that brightened and dimmed. Like the others, Mike heard no sound from the light. The only noise was the roar of the jet engines.

Just before two that morning, the fighters returned to Andrews Air Force Base. They were no longer chasing anything and landed at the base. No other fighters took off.

Ten minutes later, about two that morning, Rogers called the radio station to tell them that he and his neighbor had seen fighters chasing a bright blue light. The station reported it was a large blue light, but Rogers said that he had not used that word in his description.

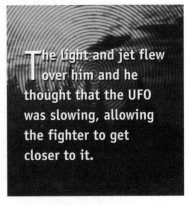

The light and jet flew over him and he thought that the UFO was slowing, allowing the fighter to get closer to it.

There were three witnesses on the ground. They did not describe the object in the same way, but they did describe the fighters attempting to intercept the UFO. The sightings lasted about an hour, with the object, or objects, in sight for only a fraction of that time. When the objects disappeared, the fighters returned to their base.

Radar, NORAD, and F-16s

One of the questions that was explored by the investigators, including Woodward and Kenny Young, was how the Air Force was alerted to the UFOs. According to them, the 113th Air National Guard, which is based at Andrews AFB, has the mission of maintaining the "alert fighters." That means they are one of the units that responds to NORAD's request for interception of unidentified targets. This, of course, identifies the unit that would have responded to the NORAD request for a scramble.

According to the story in the *International UFO Reporter* by Woodward, she interviewed "Maj. [Barry] Venable, NORAD ... [who] stated two F-16s were scrambled from Andrews about 1 am to investigate 'suspicious air activity over [Washington,] DC.' The pilots found nothing and returned to Andrews."

On July 26, both Fox News and CNN reported that two F-16s had been scrambled to investigate low-flying aircraft close to a restricted zone over Washington, D.C. Fox mentioned the "folks at NORAD saw something they couldn't identify ...," which would suggest some sort of monitoring, such as radar. CNN said that the aircraft appeared on radar in the restricted zone. A pair of jets had been scrambled.

Major Mike Snyder of NORAD said on July 27, 2002, that the radar track met the criteria of a "small private aircraft," and he said that it had never entered the restricted zone.

Given the timing of the events, that is, less than a year after 9/11, the reaction of NORAD is logical. Had the object, or objects, been a small private plane, they would have scrambled interceptors. Flight plans should have had to be filed for the private aircraft, and without those, and the close approach to, if not in, a restricted zone, the Air Force had to respond.

Woodward reported that Major Barry Venable said, "The facts: Two F-16 jets from Andrews Air Force Base were scrambled approximately 0100 hours 26 Jul 02 after radar detected an unknown aircraft. The unidentified aircraft's track subsequently faded from radar. The F-16s investigated found nothing out of the ordinary, and returned to base. For operational security reasons, NORAD will not discuss specific details...."

On July 27, the *Washington Post* published a report from Major Douglas Martin, also from NORAD, who said almost exactly what Venable had said earlier. Other newspapers also quoted Martin, which was the government line about the intercepts.

Woodward reported that she had spoken to Captain Smith at the 113th ANG and was told that the observations by the civilian witnesses were typical of

The headquarters for the North American Aerospace Command Center (NORAD) is located in Colorado Springs, Colorado. NORAD monitored two F-16s as they were scrambled to intercept a UFO near Washington, D.C., but the radar blip disappeared.

a training exercise. He apparently ignored questions about the low altitude and the use of afterburners. In other words, the government records, or the lack of them, do not support the various explanations for those late scrambles.

The government files, this time in the form of the tower logs at Reagan National tower, showed that they had been alerted to a scramble from Andrews and that the operators blocked the altitudes between 4,000 and 6,000 feet for the jets to use. In other words, Dillman's and Rogers' estimates of the altitudes for the jets were fairly accurate. In fact, the tower logs support the times for the aircraft take-offs and the other information given by the witnesses.

Woodward said that Robert Durant had filed a FOIA request on August 8, 2002, for the radar and voice recordings from Reagan National and Andrews for the early morning of July 26. He had done that because it was FAA policy to recycle all the tapes after two weeks, if there was nothing unusual on those tapes. Durant wanted to prevent the destruction of these tapes, but as late as February 2003, there had been no response.

Investigators at http://www.ufosnw.com performed their own investigation of the sightings and requested the same information as Durant. The four "principal investigators" are William "Bill" Puckett, Joe Ryan, Bradford Evans, and Tammy Calvano. About these sightings, in a story entitled, "FAA Denies Freedom of Information Request for Radar Data," and in a paragraph outlining "A Government Cover-up?" they wrote:

> Subsequent to hearing about this sighting which received exposure in the media (CNN and Fox News) I requested radar data from the primary FAA radar stations in the Washington, D.C., area. My intent was to compare the radar data with eyewitness reports and see if the radar data supported eyewitness testimony. My request was acknowledged, and I was told that the appropriate radar tapes would be set aside. (Normally the tapes are recycled every two weeks due to cost.) However, I did not receive any additional information from FAA for several weeks. Finally I called after about six weeks and was told that the person responsible to fulfill my request was on vacation and therefore the request wouldn't be processed until the employee's return. (This is against government regulations whereby agencies have to respond to FOIA requests in 20 days.) The next communication that I received was that the FOIA was transferred to another Region (from Washington D.C., to New York). The New York office told me that they couldn't respond to my request because the appropriate tapes had been recycled (the very problem that I was trying to avoid). Needless to say I was getting the "runaround". Under the guise of incompetence (with apologies galore) the FAA denied me the data. (I also found out from the FAA FOIA coordinator that several other requests for the same data were on her desk. I also learned through reading an article about the sightings that one researcher was also denied the data. This researcher was given the excuse that "a flood" destroyed the radar data.) Another interesting aspect to my request is that the FAA FOIA

coordinator kept referring to the July 26, 2002 aircraft scramble as "the incident." Does this suggest that she was given special instructions about to how handle requests for data regarding the July 26, sighting?

Chronology of a Cover-up:

- July 28, 2002—Submitted FOIA request to FAA, Washington for July 26 radar data.

- July 29, 2002—Called FAA in Washington, D.C., FAA acknowledged FOIA request.

- August 1, 2002—FAA acknowledged FOIA request via email.

- August 9, 2002—FOIA acknowledged via letter.

- September 17, 2002—Called and told FOIA coordinator on vacation until September 24.

- September 24, 2002—Called again. Was told FOIA "in processing."

- October 18, 2002—Received voice-mail saying that FOIA reassigned to Eastern Region (NY).

- October 21, 2002—Received letter with same message.

- October 23, 2002—Called New York and was told data not saved because tapes recycled.

- October 24, 2002—Called FAA manager of Evaluations & Investigations Branch and left voice-mail. (Call not returned.)

Concluding Remarks: First I wish to state that several FAA offices have been very helpful, responsive, and cooperative in providing radar data to support UFO investigations. This is the only office that has been uncooperative. Were they told to be uncooperative? Does the fact that NORAD now uses data from FAA primary radars result in the data being classified? Did NORAD instruct the FAA to not release any radar data? Perhaps these questions will never be answered. However, radar data combined with eye witness testimony on that given morning in Washington, D.C., could have revealed some very interesting results.

The FOIA requests, which would have accessed government files that should have been available, were denied. There is no reason for that denial, and Durant's request, filed within the fifteen day limit, should have ensured that the tapes were not destroyed. They should have been held until the FOIA request was resolved. At this late date, those tapes have yet to surface.

The Many Explanations Offered

As is the case in many UFO sightings, when governmental agencies are involved, they seem to follow the old adage that any explanation, no matter how many facts it ignores, is better than no explanation at all. Such is the case with these sightings.

As has been suggested in other UFO sightings around the United States, there were those who suspected that flares might have been the culprit. According to Kenny Young, "I had previously [been] informed that military jets will sometimes deploy flares for training purposes, and these flares are frequently mistaken for UFOs. It was my suspicion that flares might have been procedurally deployed by the returning pilots on July 26, causing the UFO sightings...."

Young reported that the emails sent to the public affairs officer went unanswered. He finally called the base and spoke to Captain Smith. The upshot was that the fighters carried flares, but there was no routine procedure for them to dump flares as they came in to land. Young reported that he tried to lead the discussion by giving Smith the opportunity to jump on the flare explanation to justify the sightings, According to Young, "... the DC ANG officials did not take the bait...."

A Black Hawk fires a flare in Afghanistan. Flares like this have also been blamed for causing people to report UFO sightings.

The government files available, that included the report of a radar track that looked like a small, private aircraft, suggest this is not a viable explanation. According to Woodward's analysis in the *International UFO Reporter*, the fighters scrambled had the capability to track the small aircraft in all weather and to separate it from the ground clutter. To land anywhere at night, the small aircraft would require a lighted strip. The only airstrip in the area searched by the fighters was small and privately owned and did not have lights. Further, given the altitudes used by the fighters and the UFOs, there should have been a flight plan, but none were found in the government files for the period in question.

The last possibility was a military training exercise, which often involves four fighters such as the witnesses reported. There would be no reason for the Air Guard to deny that training operations were in progress at the time of the UFO sightings if that would explain the sightings. But, according to the government records, there were no such exercises.

At this point, there are no explanations for the UFO sightings and the apparent attempted intercepts by fighters. That would suggest additional witnesses should be available. Among those would be the radar operators who initiated the interception. There should be the fighter pilots, who, according to the ground witnesses, were chasing the lights and objects. Woodward contacted the Charles County Sheriff's Office and the Maryland State Police but neither agency reported any telephone calls about the lights.

In the end, there are only three witnesses on the ground and an obvious response by the Air Guard. The sightings were not as robust as those reported in

1952, and had these not been reported fifty years later, they probably would have gone unnoticed.

Loring Air Force Base, 1975

On October 27, 1975, the security force including Sergeant Danny K. Lewis at Loring Air Force Base in Maine saw an object or craft penetrate the restricted area near the Weapons Storage Facility (WSA). It was flying low, at no more than 300 feet and it did approach the Weapons Storage Facility. It then flew off toward the north and was tracked by the base radar.

Lewis, as dictated by the Standard Operating Procedures, notified the 42nd Bomb Wing Command Post about what he had seen. Both Wing and Security personnel then converged on the WSA but they found no evidence of the intruder or anything that had been done to damage or to affect the weapons stored there.

Those in the Command Post called the tower to alert them. Sergeant Grover K. Eggleston was on duty. Alerted to the intruder, he began to watch it. The unknown was also indicated by radar and Eggleston noticed that it was circling about ten miles from the base. This lasted for about forty minutes when the object suddenly dropped from the screen, suggesting that it had slipped beneath radar coverage and that it might have landed. Radar contact was lost as the object, whatever it might have been, headed toward Grand Falls, New Brunswick, Canada.

In 1975 a UFO was spotted over Loring Air Force Base, where it got very close to the weapons storage facility.

The wing commander arrived within seven minutes and through the command post, requested fighter support from both the 21ˢᵗ NORAD Region and the 22ⁿᵈ. Both requests were denied. He had also alerted the Maine State Police, believing they might be able to identify the intruder, which he thought was a helicopter, based not on a description of the object but on its observed flight characteristics. It would hover for a while and then would drop suddenly.

As seen before, when the intrusions were reported at Malmstrom in 1967, the intrusion was reported to the National Military Command Center in Washington, D.C., the Air Force Chief of Staff, Strategic Air Command headquarters in Omaha, Nebraska, and the USAF Forward Operations Division at Fort Ritchie in Maryland. This intrusion was a matter of national security. It is difficult to believe that fighter support had been denied when requested by the base commander.

> "The object was solid and we could not hear any noise coming from it."

The next night, October 28, 1975, Sergeant Clifton W. Blakeslee and Staff Sergeant William J. Long, assigned to the 42ⁿᵈ Security Police Squadron, were on duty in the munitions storage area. With them was Lewis, who had seen the UFO the night before. At about 7:45 P.M. they all saw the lights of an aircraft approaching the base from the north, this time at about 3,000 feet. At one point the craft was about 150 feet from the end of the runway at only 150 feet altitude. They lost sight of it about forty-five minutes later.

Sergeant Steven Eichner and Sergeant R. Jones, who were crewmen on a B-52, were working out of what is known as a launch truck. Jones spotted a red and orange object over the flight line. It looked like a stretched out football. As Eichner and Jones watched, along with the rest of the crew, the object's lights went out and they lost sight of it.

And then it reappeared over the north end of the runway. Now it was moving in a jerky motion, and finally stopped and hovered. Eichner and his crew jumped into a truck and headed toward the object. They turned onto the road that lead to the Weapons Storage Facility and spotted the UFO hovering about five feet in the air and only about 300 feet from them. It glowed with a reddish-orange color, was about 40 or 50 feet long and made no noise.

According to Lawrence Fawcett and Barry Greenwood in *The UFO Cover-Up*, Eichner said:

> The object looked like all the colors were blending together, as if you were looking at a desert scene. You see waves of hear rising off the desert floor. This is what I saw. There were these waves in front of the object and all the colors blending together. The object was solid and we could not hear any noise coming from it.

They saw nothing on the object that would suggest windows or hatches. About that time, according to Eichner, the base came alive, with warning sirens going off and security police vehicles heading into the area. Eichner thought that it was time to get out. The security police did not try to stop them and they drove back to their original location. From there they watched as the security police searched for the UFO, but it had apparently turned off its lights and was not seen again that night.

Again, the proper messages were sent to the various command authorities and the wing commander, Colonel Richard E. Chapman, requested the support from a National Guard helicopter crew that was training on the base at the time. He wanted to be ready to chase the intruder if it returned the next night.

Since the helicopter, and the crew, belonged to the National Guard, permission to use them had to go up the chain of command, to a point where the request could be handed to the National Guard and then passed to the appropriate approval authority. This was done, with the caveat that the helicopter would not cross an international boundary, Loring being close to the Canadian border, and that it would only carry military personnel. The FBI, the FAA, and agents of the Border Patrol were all considered military for the purpose of this mission.

The pilots, from the 112th Army National Guard Medical Company (Air Ambulance), were assigned the task of flying the helicopter. They were told they could make one telephone call to their wives and then have to drop out of communications. Fawcett interviewed Chief Warrant Officer Bernard Poulin, who said:

> Upon our arrival at Loring AFB, we were briefed by the Wing Commander, Colonel Richard Chapman. We were informed that all the sightings of the craft or whatever ... had been late at night or early morning. We launched the next morning.... The Air Police had a radio in the back of the helicopter and when the reports of the intruder started to come in, they would direct me to the location in which the object was seen. The reason the Maine State Police and the Canadian Police were aboard was that there had been a lot of drug operations going on in the area, and the powers to be thought that this was what was occurring ... but this never panned out....
>
> Well, we were launched on the first search mission after the ground personnel started to see or hear the, quote ... "UFO" go by. So, we would launch, and I believe that we were in the air for around 40 minutes looking for this thing, with the idea that if it was a rotary-type craft we were searching for. We were vectored in by ground personnel to different spots on the base where the ground personnel were seeing or hearing it. All this time we were being tracked by base radar [traffic control radar which is designed to pick up arcraft], and the radar was not painting the object that was being reported. Ground personnel would call and say the object is at this location, but radar would not pick it up.... [W]e hunted around, and we didn't see anything. Again they would call and say they could hear it at a location, and we would go there, but could not see it. We would then shut down and wait for the next call. And that went on for a couple of nights. This, again, was early evening or early morning. I can recall on the second night of the mission radar picked up a return, but it turned out to be a KC-135 tanker....

Poulin said that they were to sweep the area with their searchlight, but that he never saw anything. He knew that they were flying near some highly sensitive areas and that it was of great concern to the base command. Poulin remembered that Chapman told him: "We've got to keep the lid on the fact that someone has been able to penetrate in and around the bomb dump, and we don't know what's going on. We've got to find out what is going on and prevent it from happing again."

All this time we were being tracked by base radar and the radar was not painting the object that was being reported."

According to the government files, a message went out to the SAC bases mostly along the northern tier [Barksdale AFB is in Louisiana] of states, including Pease AFB in New Hampshire, Plattsburg AFB in New York, Wurtsmith AFB in Michigan, Kinchloe AFB in Michigan, Sawyer AFB in Michigan, Grand Forks AFB in North Dakota, Minot AFB in North Dakota, Malmstrom AFB in Montana, Fairchild AFB in Washington, and Barksdale AFB in Louisiana. The message concerned "Defense Against Helicopter Assault," and said:

> The past two evenings at one of our northern tier bases, an unidentified helicopter has been observed hovering over and in the near vicinity of the weapons storage area. Attempts to identify this aircraft have so far met with negative results. In the interest of nuclear weapons security, the action addresses will assume Security Option 3 during the hours of darkness until further notice. Actions also should be taken to re-establish liaison with local law enforcement agencies that could assist your base in the event of similar incident. Bases should thoroughly review and insure all personnel are familiar with actions to take in association with the helicopter denial portion of your 207-xx plan.

The Skeptics "Find a Solution"

The U.S. Air Force was locked onto the idea that the object was a helicopter. UFO debunker Philip Klass investigated the sightings and told reporter John Day of the *Bangor Daily News*, that "he investigated the 1975 Loring incident. Among other things, he was given access to base Telex communications during the four or five nights when the mysterious object repeatedly hovered over Loring's nuclear storage facility. According to Klass, the cable traffic shows that Loring officers had strong evidence that the mysterious object cited by Eichner was a helicopter. Their concern was not that the SAC base was being penetrated by spacemen, but that a radical anti-Vietnam group had rented a helicopter and was trying to steal a nuclear warhead."

Day wrote, "According to Klass, the cable traffic he obtained pertaining to the Loring UFO incident indicated that authorities established that a well-financed crew operating out of a motel near Moosehead Lake, was flying on the nights the mysterious object was observed hovering over Loring's nuclear stockpile.

"Klass has no proof that the Moosehead Lake helicopter was the object which buzzed Loring. He says it is unfortunate that the Air Force never followed up on their suspicions, or made public the results of their investigations."

Although Klass, in his book *UFOs: The Public Deceived*, isn't quite as direct, he is still of the opinion that a helicopter was responsible for the intrusion at Loring. For proof, he cites, as have those on the other side of the controversy, the government documents that have been released through FOIA.

According to the government files that Klass reviewed, the assumption made by the author of the report, Colonel William D. Myers, chief of security policy for SAC, was that the intruder was a helicopter. He labeled his report, "SUBJECT: Unidentified Helicopter Sightings, Loring AFB." It said:

27 Oct.'75   Helicopter sighted flying over weapons storage area. Attempts to contact, negative results. 42BMW [42 Bombardment Wing] Commander requested fighter coverage—request denied.

28 Oct.'75   42BMW Commander requested and received helicopter support from Maine Army National Guard. Helicopter again sighted, Maine National Guard Helicopter launched, but unidentified helicopter disappeared before acquisition. One and one-half hours later unidentified helicopter sighted again. Standby helicopter again launched, no contact made. Fighter launch again requested and denied. Local flight service inquired for possible identification, negative results. Radar contact on unidentified helicopter lost in vicinity of Grand Falls, N.B., Canada.

29 Oct.'75   Meeting with State Police, U.S. Border Patrol, Canadian authorities, OSI and National Guard—Plan and coordinate future actions. SAC/SP message to all SAC northern bases advising of possible threat—advised to increase security during hours of darkness and review helicopter denial plans.

30 Oct.'75   Maine Army National Guard helicopter replaced with Air Force helicopter from Plattsburgh. Placed on alert during hours of darkness.

31 Oct.'75   Several suspected sightings made—some visual sightings appeared to be substantiated by RAPCON radar. Alert helicopter launched—unsuccessful intercepts.

1–8 Nov 75   Alert helicopter and searchlight alert maintained during hours of darkness. No further activity reported or expected. All attempts to identify helicopter(s) throughout this period were negative. Although local USAF or Canadian authorities were unable to provide positive identification of helicopters the possibility exists that some type of game poaching or illegal smuggling across the borders could have been involved. At no time was the helicopter used in any manner which could have been interpreted as a hostile act against USAF resources.

The government files, then, show that there was an intrusion at Loring, and in at least one case, seemed to penetrate the weapons source area. Although they mention that it was a helicopter, they were unable to identify it, catch it, or apparently stop it. Violating the restricted area and flying over the weapons storage area would be a matter of national security and should have caused a more robust Air Force response. The government files suggest that they couldn't identify the helicopter, but they didn't work very hard to find out who had committed the crime.

Klass, in his commentary, pointed this out. He wrote, "If *Parade,* the *Washington Post,* or the *National Enquirer* [all of which carried stories about the sightings at Loring AFB] really believed what their stories implied, the USAF not only was derelict in its duties to defend the nation's airspace, but here was a coverup that dwarfed the Watergate scandal. It would have been an investigative reporter's dream."

And Klass would be correct, but what he does not say is that as a matter of national security, the investigation would have been highly classified. Such a matter would be beyond FOIA and any documents associated with the case could be legally withheld.

Could the UFO spotted over Moosehead Lake have been just a helicopter?

The Air Force, with all the state and federal resources available, still failed to identify the helicopter but Klass was able to learn about it. He mentioned that Somerset County Sheriff Francis B. Henderson had discovered that a helicopter with photo equipment on board had landed in Rockwood, about 120 miles from Loring. No evidence was offered that the helicopter operating in the Moosehead Lake or at the Moosehead Motel had anything to do with the object reported over Loring.

Klass reported that a former deputy named Ivon Turmell told him that a red and white Hughes helicopter had landed outside the Moosehead Motel. According to Klass, Turmell said that when he, Turmell, called the motel owner, he was told the whole thing was "very hush-hush."

Klass then asked, "Could Rockwood's 'mysterious helicopter' have been the same craft that reportedly penetrated Loring's airspace on the night of October 27?"

This is little more than a red herring. Klass, in his analysis, is off on several tangents, most of which are irrelevant to the Loring case. The Moosehead Lake helicopter is just one of those tangents. Although he mentions that the Air Force was never able to identify the helicopter, he makes much of their repeated claim that the Air Force used that term in many of the official government files.

A Final Analysis

After all the investigation by the military, UFO investigators, including those who consider themselves skeptics, there was no solution for the case. The

Air Force called it an unidentified helicopter, but given the area of the sightings, that is wholly unsatisfactory. This was a matter of national security, and while Colonel William D. Myers repeatedly called it an unidentified helicopter in his report, the Air Force never found it.

Klass claimed that he had found it, but the helicopter was based more than 120 miles away and didn't appear on the scene at Moosehead Lake until weeks after the Loring penetration. There is no reason to assume that the private helicopter had anything to do with the UFO sightings at Loring.

As mentioned, with the UFO hovering over the Weapons Storage Facility, this became a matter of national security. To the Air Force, the UFO sighting was secondary. What concerned them was that the facility had been penetrated by someone or something that was unauthorized. Their response to that should have been extreme because they would want to know who was flying over those restricted areas. They would have played the string all the way out and wouldn't have stopped until they learned the truth or they had nowhere else to look.

When Klass investigated, he suggested, based on the documentation he saw, that the Air Force didn't do much with the information. They were half-hearted in their investigation. The truth is the Air Force wouldn't be sharing these highly classified documents with Klass. Since this was a matter of national security, the investigative documentation would not be available to Klass.

Loring represents just one more example of UFOs affecting equipment that should have been outside their influence or being seen over areas where they shouldn't have been. In other words, they were in violation of the law and they were challenging national security. The Air Force would have taken that seriously, no matter what they said about the case in public.

In the end, there is no satisfactory explanation for what was seen over Loring. Likewise, there is no satisfactory explanation for the objects seen in restricted areas near Washington, D.C. The best that can be said is that the objects or lights are unidentified. Their performance suggests something that was alien, but that doesn't prove it was alien. All that can be said is that something was flying around where it shouldn't have been.

The SETI Protocols

It would seem that an organization that calls itself the Search for Extraterrestrial Intelligence (SETI) would be interested in the possibility that some UFO reports are related to alien visitation. It would seem that those at SETI, who often proclaim that there are other civilizations out there, that the galaxy might be teeming with life, would want to explore the idea that some of those civilizations have developed interstellar travel capabilities. It would seem logical, but it would be incorrect.

Those at SETI have suggested that "In addition to the unlikelihood that we have been visited by extraterrestrials, there is no scientific evidence to prove it. Personal accounts are not physical or verifiable evidence. These reasons are sufficient to exclude UFO's from the research objectives of the SETI Institute."

And if that statement is true, then there would be sufficient reason, but for an organization that predicates its existence on the idea that alien civilizations exist, it seems to be a very narrow view. There are many good cases that go beyond just personal accounts, but for some reason those cases are always overlooked in the rush to dismiss UFOs.

Minot Air Force Base, North Dakota

While a single witness, personal account might not be much good as evidence, it would seem that a multiple witness case in which the witnesses were separated by distance, along with observations using instruments might be considered evidence. On October 24, 1968, there was a series of sightings that fit into this category. There were witnesses on the ground, in the air, and observations made by those using radar. The Blue Book project card identified the sightings as: "Ground-visual: 1. Probable (Aircraft) (B-52). 2. Probable Astro (Sirius). Radar: Possible (Plasma). Air-Visual: Possible (Plasma)."

The government files revealed, "The ground visual sightings appear to be of the star Sirius and the B-52 which was flying in the area. The B-52 radar contact and temporary loss of UHF transmission could be attributed to plasma, similar to ball lightning. The air-visual from the B-52 could be the star Vega which was on the horizon at the time, or it could be a light on the ground, or possibly a plasma."

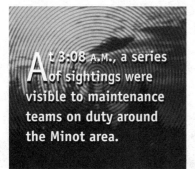

At 3:08 A.M., a series of sightings were visible to maintenance teams on duty around the Minot area.

Or, in other words, the investigators threw everything at the wall to see what would stick. It would seem that no one revisited this case to see if a plausible solution could be found, especially in a climate in which any solution was better than no solution.

According to the government file, the first sighting was made for about thirty minutes on October 24 by an airman named Isley (only the last names are available in the Project Blue Book files). He said he saw only a bright light in the east.

Two hours later, Airman First Class (A/1C) O'Connor saw a bright light. At about the same time, about 2:30 A.M., Staff Sergeant Smith said that he had seen a bright star. Both Isley and Smith thought the lights looked unusual and were unable to easily identify them.

At 3:08 A.M., a series of sightings were visible to maintenance teams on duty around the Minot area. O'Connor, the maintenance team chief, said that all members of his team saw a lighted object that was a reddish-orange in color. They thought it was a large object with flashing green and white lights on it. According to the government files:

> After they [O'Connor and his maintenance team members] entered N-7 LF [a field site at Minot] the object came directly overhead with the sound of jet engines ... SSGT Bond, the FSC at Nov Flt [November Flight, a unit designation] stated that the object which looked to him as the sun, came near the handred antenna at Nov—1 [missile silo]. It then moved to the right and he sent the SAT out to check and see what it was. The object then moved about one mile away with the Nov SAT following. They came within a ½ mile from where it appeared to be landing. When it reached the surface the lights became dimmer and finally went out. After this they could see nothing. SSGT Smith at Oscar—1 [missile silo belonging to Oscar Flight] saw the object separate into two parts and go in opposite [sic] directions and return and pass under each other. At this time Juliet Flight and Mike Flight Team observed the same things and described it the same way. The approximate grid coordinates of the apparent landing was AA-43. The entire observation period as near as can be determined was about 45 minutes.

Sixteen minutes later, at 3:24 A.M., SSGT Wagla, A/1C Allis, and A/1C Deer said they saw a UFO. A minute later, SSGT Halko, A/1C Halko, A/1C Jenkins, and A/1C Richardson saw the UFO. Ten minutes later the crew of a B-52, entered the case.

The transcript of the conversations between the tower and the aircraft are available in the government files. The times in the transcript are all originally given as Greenwich Mean Time (Zulu), but have been corrected to local time in North Dakota for continuity.

At 3:30 A.M., the controllers received information that there was a UFO 24 miles to the northwest. Four minutes later, JAG-31 [JAG Thirty-one, call sign of a B-52] made a request and said that they were at "Flight Level 200. The transcript said:

MIB [Minot] approach control does JAG 31 have clearance to WT fix at Flight Level 2000?

JAG 31, roger, climb out on a heading of 290 climb and maintain 5000. Stand by for higher altitude. We're trying to get it from center now.

[At 0335], And JAG 31 on your way out to the WT fix request you look out toward your one o'clock position for the next fifteen or sixteen miles and see if you see any orange glows out there.

Roger, roger … glows. 31 [Which meant the pilot understood that he was to look for an orange glow, and ended the transmission with the aircraft number].

Someone is seeing flying saucers again.

Roger, I see a … [rest of the transmission is garbled].

[0352] Three one, the UFO is being picked up by weather radar also. Should be at our one o'clock position three miles now.

[Pilot] We have nothing on our airborne radar and I'm in some pretty thick haze right now and unable to see out that way.…

[0400] JAG Three one, if you hear me squawk ident [meaning that the pilot was being requested to send a transponder signal that would display the aircraft on the radar screen in a bold double green line … this was being done because the controller had lost radio contact with the aircraft. This was a way of determining that the pilot could hear the instructions being given.] … JAG Three one ident observed. Cleared for approach attempt.

[0402 Pilot] Our UFO was off to our left there when we started penetration.

We had a radar return at about a mile and a quarter, nine o'clock position for about the time we left [flight level] 200 to about 14.…

[0403 Controller] Affirmative. I was wondering how far out did you see that UFO?

He was about one and a half miles off our left wing at 35 miles when we started in and he stayed with us 'til about 10.

I wonder if that could have been your radio troubles.

I don't know … but that's exactly when they started.

[0413] JAG Three one, are you observing any more UFOs?

Negative on radar. We can't see anything visually.

JAG Three one, roger. The personnel on from the missile site advise they don't see anything anymore either.

[0421] JAG Three one … [garbled] requests that somebody from your aircraft stop in at base ops after you land.…

All this demonstrates that a series of sightings were made by men on the ground, at the various missile sites scattered around the Minot Air Force Base

> These were a series of sightings, made by a number of men, in widely scattered locations, and they were apparently not in communications with one another.

that seem to be predictive of those to come in the 1970s, and that were corroborated by radar on the ground and in the aircraft. That ground-based radar is never fully identified in the government files. The sightings were continuous; they covered a period from just after midnight until about four in the morning and included the flight crew of an airborne B-52. These were a series of sightings, made by a number of men, in widely scattered locations, and they were apparently not in communications with one another.

Project Blue Book at Wright-Patterson AFB was alerted about the sightings that same day. In a memo for the record, found in the government files and dated October 24, an officer identified only as Lieutenant Marano began to receive telephone calls. He learned that the base commander at Minot and Major General Nichols at 15th Air Force Headquarters were interested in the sightings. An officer identified only as Lieutenant Colonel Werlich had been appointed as the Minot UFO officer. He would conduct an investigation into the sightings.

According to the memo for the record, as found in the government files, the situation was described as:

At about 0300 hours local, a B-52 that was about 39 miles northwest of Minot AFB and was making practice penetrations sighted an unidentified blip on their radar. Initially the target traveled approximately 2½ miles in 3 sec or about 3000 mi/hr. After passing from right to the left of the plane, it assumed a position off the left wing for the [B] 52. The blip stayed on the left wing for approximately 20 miles at which point it broke off. Scope photographs were taken. When the target was close to the B-52 neither of the two transmitters in the B-52 would operate properly but when it broke off both returned to normal function.

About this time a missile maintenance man called in and reported sighting a bright orangish-red object. The object was hovering about 1000 ft or so, and had a sound similar to a jet engine. The observer stopped his car, but he then started it up again. As he started to move, the object followed him then accelerated and appeared to stop at about 6–8 miles away. The observer shortly afterward lost sight of it.

In response to the maintenance man's call the B-52, which had continued its penetration run, was vectored toward the visual which was about 10 miles northwest of the base. The B-52 confirmed having sighted a bright light of some type that appeared to be hovering over or on the ground.

The government file then reveals, "Fourteen other people in separate locations also reported sighting a similar object. Also, at this approximate time, the security alarm for one of the sites was activated. This was an alarm for both the outer and inner ring. When guards arrived at the scene they found that the outer door was open and the combination lock on the inner door had been moved."

The government files reveal that on October 30, 1968, Lieutenant Colonel Hector Quintanilla, who was the chief of Project Blue Book at the time, had a telephone conversation with Colonel Pullen at SAC Headquarters in Omaha. When Quintanilla was asked if he had sent anyone up to Minot to investigate the sighting, Quintanilla said, "We did not send anybody up because I only have four people on my staff, myself, an assistant, a secretary, and an admin sergeant. I talked to Col Werlich for over thirty minutes and since this didn't appear unusual I didn't send anyone up."

This statement is quite revealing given the number of witnesses, the locations of those witnesses, and the radar confirmation of the object. The sighting is anything but usual. It demanded a response if only because of the penetration of restricted areas, including one of the missile sites. This should have been considered a matter of national security, just as the sightings at Malmstrom and Loring would be in the future.

The Air Force investigation seems to have been rather cavalier. Colonel Werlich, the officer on the ground at Minot conducting the investigation, reported that he had the witnesses fill out the Air Force Form 117, which was a several page-long form used to gather data about UFO sightings.

Werlich, according to the government files, told Marano at Wright-Patterson, "I monitored them while they filled them out [AF Form 117], but I can't see where the navigator can help...."

Marano noted, "The one we are mainly interested in is the one that cannot be identified. The one of radar and the aircraft correlated pretty well."

Studying the area and using the best maps they had, they attempted to identify the low-flying light. According to the report, "There is nothing there that would produce this type of light. The same for O'Conner and Nicely from November 7 [that is, two of the maintenance men from the silo that had been designated at November 7] which is near Greno."

Then, in an account in the government files which seems to capture the schizophrenic nature of the Air Force investigation in 1968, the memo for the record shows, "Almost 80 percent were looking at the B-52. If you would look at an aircraft at 20,000 ft, then you wouldn't see much but I'm an [sic] to place logic in that it was there and what they saw was there. There is enough there that it is worth looking at. Nobody can definitely say that these people definitely saw the aircraft, but within reason they probably saw it."

It seems that the investigators are suggesting that the officers at Minot think the ground sightings might be of the B-52, but they're not sure. They seem to realize that they are saying that the men stationed at Minot are incapable of identifying a large bomber that is assigned to SAC. How could these men,

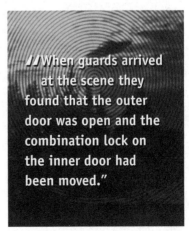

// When guards arrived at the scene they found that the outer door was open and the combination lock on the inner door had been moved."

some of whom had been around SAC and B-52s for years, suddenly not be able to recognize a B-52, even if it was night and the bomber was flying at 20,000 feet?

Having disposed of some of the ground sightings, sort of, the investigators attacked the radar part of the case. Werlich, in a telephone conversation with those at Blue Book, said:

> I only stated one radar in the message because there was only one radar set. The ECM [electronic counter messages] equipment hadn't been used. RAPCOM [radar facility] was painting [operating]. IFF [identification friend or foe] was operating in the airplane. It's a fairly good sized blip. There is a Sage site [another radar facility] to the south. They do not remember any unidentified paints [blips]. The only one that I have is the one on the plane. The unusual part is the B-52 was in the middle of a sentence and the voice just quit transmitting right in the middle of a word....

Colonel Werlich seems to suggest that there was only a single radar corroboration for the sighting, but he also suggests that if the UFO was close to the B-52, then the transponder equipment emits a signal so strong that an object close to the aircraft would be obscured by that signal. He then said that other radar controllers don't remember any unidentified blips, which does not mean that there were no blips.

Going through the government files on this case, there is a mention of weather radar, but there is no identification of this facility. Someone reading the file added a penciled question mark above the notation for the weather radar. If the weather radar picked up the blip, as suggested by the file, and the B-52's radar also detected it, then, at the very least, two separate radars "painted" the UFO.

A second important point made during that telephone conversation was that the communications between the aircraft and the ground had shut down. Electromagnetic effects are a well-known consequence of close encounters with UFOs. This suggests that the UFO, whatever it might have been, was interacting with the environment.

Werlich underscored this, after a fashion, when he said, "My personal opinion is that it couldn't be a malfunction because they transmitted before and afterwards. The aircraft was not checked out afterward because the transmission [sic] was working."

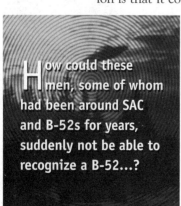

How could these men, some of whom had been around SAC and B-52s for years, suddenly not be able to recognize a B-52...?

In any proper investigation, the aircraft and its electrical equipment would have been checked out. The close approach of the UFO and the shutting down of the communications equipment might have been a coincidence, but no one bothered to see if there was some sort of transient event that would explain the malfunction.

During the telephone discussion, someone mentioned the possibility of a temperature inversion. They eventually forgot about that, but Lieutenant Marano then said that "the many astronomical bodies that were over the area at the time and when there is quite an inversion they are magnified even greater."

On November 1, 1968, in a memo for the record, it was noted, "Talked to Mr. Goff … who is quite familiar with airborne radars. Mr. Goff said that from the evidence at this time it would appear to him that the sightings may have been precipitated by some type of ionized air plasma similar to ball lightning. He felt that a plasma could account for the radar blip, loss of transmission and some of the visual sightings.…"

This theory, that plasmas were responsible for many of the UFO sightings, had been advanced in a 1968 book by Philip Klass, an aviation writer with *Aviation Week* and *Space Technology*. These plasmas, usually generated

A B-52's radar detected the UFO, as did a weather radar.

near electrical lines, could also be generated by other factors and were a natural phenomenon that could explain many UFO cases had been listed as unidentified in the past. In October, 1968, this theory was in vogue and used frequently to dispose of otherwise mysterious UFO sightings.

But that suggestion wasn't universally accepted. A physics professor at the University of Nebraska asked why, if this is the explanation in Minot, it wasn't reported more frequently. In other words, if plasmas were a good explanation, then similar things should be seen around airports and airfields all over the world. There should be reports of failures of transmitters, airborne radars filled with false images, and reports of lights all around them. Of course that's not the situation.

The final nail in the plasma coffin, according to the physicist, was that if there wasn't some additional mechanism, they would not glow. The air could be filled with plasmas, but no one would see them because they don't routinely glow. There would be nothing for anyone to see.

But the science of plasmas didn't concern the Air Force. In a teletype message from Quintanilla to Colonel Pullen at SAC and available in the government files, he wrote:

> It is my feelings, after reviewing preliminary information submitted by Monot [Minot], that the UFO painted by B-52 on radar and also observed visually by IP [instructor pilot] and personnel on the ground is probably a plasma of the ball-lightning class. Plasmas of this type will paint on radar and also affect some electronic equipment at certain frequencies.…

> Plasmas are not uncommon, however, they are unique and extremely difficult to duplicate in the laboratory.… Also, because of duration, feel strongly that some security guards and maintenance crew were observing some first magnitude celestial bodies which were greatly magnified by the inversion layer and haze which was present at Minot during the time of

An E-2C Hawkeye carrying radar equipment takes off from the USS *Kitty Hawk*. Airborne radars like this would receive false signals if the theory about plasma were correct, but that has not been the case.

the UFO observations.... I consider the UFO reports as fairly routine, except of the plasma observation which is interesting from a scientific point of view. We will study this report in more detail when we receive the raw data from Minot.

On November 13, 1968, Quintanilla provided the final solutions, at least as seen in the government files. He wrote, "The following conclusions have been reached after a thorough study of the data submitted to the Foreign Technology Division. The ground visual sightings appear to be of the star Sirius and the B-52 which was flying the area. The B-52 radar contact and the temporary loss of the UHF transmission could be attributed to a plasma similar to ball lightning. The air visual from the B-52 could be the star Vega which was on the horizon at the time or it could be a light on the ground, or possibly a plasma ... No further investigation by the Foreign Technology Division is contemplated."

In the world today it is clear that the explanations offered for this case do not fit the facts. It is clear that in 1968, the rage in the UFO world was the idea that glowing plasmas could explain many UFO sightings, but in the world today, it is clear that such an explanation fails.

This is a case that deserved better investigation in 1968, but at that point it was clear the Air Force mission was to explain UFOs. If an explanation sounded scientific and if the general population were unaware of the facts that contradicted the explanation, no one cared. Explain the sighting and move on was the attitude.

SETI rejects the idea of alien visitation because "there is no scientific evidence to prove it. Personal accounts are not physical or verifiable evidence." But this case would have provided some of that evidence if the investigation had been conducted in an unbiased manner. The evidence would not be sufficient to prove alien visitation, but it would prove that something was happening. The case should be investigated with an open mind rather than a statement about the lack of scientific evidence. What this proves is that an unbiased investigation might change some attitudes.

The History of SETI

Although it can be said that the idea of SETI began at the turn of the twentieth century, when Nikolai Tesla suggested that radio might be a way to communicate with alien intelligence, the real history can be traced to Frank Drake and the Order of the Dolphin. At a conference in 1961, in which the idea of the search for extraterrestrial intelligence (SETI) became a legitimate scientific pursuit, the attendees dubbed themselves the Order of the Dolphin.

In fact, Drake had made a limited search for alien radio signals in 1960, targeting the nearby stars Tau Ceti and Epsilon Eridani using the radio telescope at Green Bank, West Virginia. He scanned the radio band known as the water hole because of its proximity to the hydrogen and hydroxyl radical spectral lines, believing that an alien race intent on interstellar communication would broadcast in that region of the spectrum. He found nothing of great interest.

In November 1961, the first SETI conference took place. It was here that the idea of attempting to contact alien races was brought into prominence. Drake presented his equation, which was a way of determining how many civilizations might exist in the galaxy. It was filled with variables that, when the equation was created, couldn't be answered. For example, he plugged in the number of inhabitable planets in the galaxy. At the time, there was no scientific evidence that there were planets around other stars. The Solar System might be a rarity if not unique.

To understand Drake's equation and its impact, it needs to be examined. Written out, it looks like this:

SETI dishes like this one have been built for the sole purpose of detecting signals from outer space that may have been generated by alien civilizations.

$$N = R^* \, fp \, ne \, fl \, fi \, fc \, L$$

The values for each are:

N = The number of communicative civilizations.

R^* = The rate of formation of suitable stars (such as our Sun)

fp = The fraction of those stars with planets. (Current evidence indicates that planetary systems may be common for stars like the Sun. In fact, planetary systems have been found where astronomers had once believed that they couldn't exist.)

ne = The number of Earth-like worlds per planetary system

fl = The fraction of those Earth-like planets where life actually develops

fi = The fraction of those planets on which life develops where intelligence develops

fc = The fraction of communicative planets (those on which communications technology develops that might be something like radio, or something that involves light)

L = The "lifetime" of communicating civilizations

Drake himself seemed to think that there were about ten thousand worlds in our galaxy that were, what he called, communicative civilizations. Which means that 10,000 worlds have an industrial civilization sufficiently advanced that it could, theoretically, communicate with its neighbors. Earth would be an example of this type of world.

This became an accepted part of the SETI environment, with various individuals changing the figures. For some, it suggested a relatively low number of other civilizations, while others found figures in the tens of thousands. The size of the galaxy suggested to many that even if there were tens of thousands of civilizations out there, their radio signals might be so faint as to be undetectable by radio astronomers, that a civilization that was sufficiently advanced might communicate with other methods, or that the aliens might never have invented radio using some other method of communication.

As technology advanced, SETI evolved, applying other methods for the search, and able to scan much larger areas in a fraction of the time taken by the original searches. There were a number of cases in which a signal, thought to be from an alien radio source, led to the discovery of an astronomical object.

The first pulsar was discovered on November 28, 1967, by Jocelyn Bell Burnell and Antony Hewish. They could find no corresponding objects in space and the pulses came too fast for a spinning object, so it seemed. Burnell said that she and Hewish "did not really believe that we had picked up signals from another civilization, but obviously the idea had crossed our minds and we had no proof that it was an entirely natural radio emission." Even so, they called the first discovery "LGM-1" meaning, "Little Green Man," a term that referenced an alien source.

The discovery of a second pulsar in another part of the sky eliminated the idea that these were signals from aliens.

There have been other false positives, some of which lead to other natural phenomena. And, SETI has also suggested lasers might be a better way of searching extraterrestrial civilizations, though the sky is still scanned for radio waves. In all the time since the middle of the last century, and with all the work that has been done, there have been few signals detected that would suggest the presence of aliens.

The WOW Signal

On August 15, 1977, a signal that is still thought to be of extraterrestrial origin was detected at The Big Ear radio telescope at Ohio State University by Dr. Jerry Ehman, working in conjunction with SETI. He was so excited by the signal that on a computer printout of the data, he circled the short segment and wrote, "Wow!" next to it.

Although the configuration of the equipment and a delay between the reception of the signal and the discovery on the computer printout made finding the precise location difficult, it was determined that the source was in Sagittarius or more precisely, about 2.5 degrees south

There are 300 billion stars in our galaxy, which means that even if only a tiny fraction harbor intelligent life, there could be tens of thousands of extraterrestrial civilizations.

of the fifth-magnitude star, Chi Sagittarii, in the constellation of Sagittarius. The signal lasted for seventy-two seconds, and was not repeated.

Naturally, as equipment and capabilities improved, they searched for the signal again. In 1987 and in 1989, Robert Gray searched, but didn't find anything. Gray, using the Very Large Array tried again in 1995 and 1996, with no results. And in 1999, Gray, with Dr. Simon Ellingsen, used the University of Tasmania's Hobart 26m radio telescope in six fourteen-hour observations and detected nothing.

On the thirtieth anniversary of finding the signal, Ehman updated the findings and his opinions on the Wow! signal. He wrote:

> Thus, since all of the possibilities of a terrestrial origin have been either ruled out or seem improbable, and since the possibility of an extraterrestrial origin has not been able to be ruled out, I must conclude that an ETI (ExtraTerrestrial Intelligence) *might* have sent the signal that we received as the Wow! source. The fact that we saw the signal in only one beam could be due to an ETI sending a beacon signal in our direction and then send-

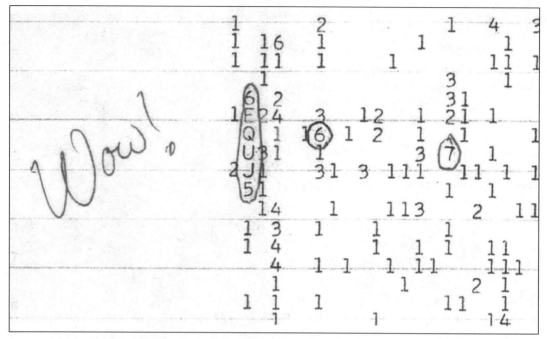

This is the printout showing the signal received by the Big Ear radio telescope that Dr. Jerry Ehman of Ohio State University interpreted to be of alien origin.

ing it in another direction that we couldn't detect. Of course, being a scientist, I await the reception of additional signals like the Wow! source that are able to be received and analyzed by many observatories. Thus, I must state that the origin of the Wow! signal is still an open question for me. There is simply too little data to draw many conclusions. In other words, as I stated above, I choose not to "draw vast conclusions from 'half-vast' data."

But even if the source was an extraterrestrial intelligence, which by itself would be an astounding discovery, it does not translate into the capability to travel interstellar distances. We have been radiating radio signals for more than a hundred years, which means, of course, that none of our signals could have reached any of the stars in the small cluster *Chi Sagittarii*. That means they wouldn't be looking for us and wouldn't know about us. And even if they had discovered our radio signals, we cannot reach them and that might mean they can't reach us.... Yet.

The Brookings Institution Study

With the theory that there should be signals of some sort from alien intelligences comes the question of what do to if a signal is detected? How will the scientific community respond? But more important is how will the rest of the world respond?

In 1960, NASA commissioned the Brookings Institution to study the effects of space exploration. That study, entitled *Proposed Studies on the Implications of Peaceful Space Activities for Humans*, discussed the need for research on a variety of issues related to space exploration. In a very short section, the study touched on the possibility of the discovery of extraterrestrial life, suggesting that the best course of action might be to hide that discovery, though it doesn't say that in so many words.

In the report it said: "While face-to-face meetings with it [alien life forms] will not occur within the next twenty years (unless its technology is more advanced than ours, qualifying it to visit earth), artifacts left at some point in time by these life forms might possibly be discovered through our space activities on the Moon, Mars or Venus."

It is interesting that in this government file the authors suggest visitation by extraterrestrial life but do not seem to include the possibility that alien life already has visited Earth. Carl Sagan had suggested that we could expect one visitation every ten thousand years, but when it comes to the world of the UFO, no one at this level considers that possibility.

The danger in alien visitation, or even mere detection, is outlined in the file. They wrote:

> Anthropological files contain many examples of societies, sure of their place in the universe, which have disintegrated when they have had to associate with previously unfamiliar societies espousing different ideas and different life ways; others that survived such an experience usually did so by paying the price of changes in values and attitudes and behavior.

> Since intelligent life might be discovered at any time via the radio telescope research presently underway, and since the consequences of such a discovery are presently unpredictable because of our limited knowledge of behavior under even an approximation of such dramatic circumstances, two research areas can be recommended:

>   1. Continuing studies to determine emotional and intellectual understanding, and attitudes—and successive alterations of them if any—regarding the possibility and consequences of discovering intelligent extraterrestrial life.

>   2. Historical and empirical studies of the behavior of peoples and their leaders when confronted with dramatic and unfamiliar events or social pressures. Such studies might help provide programs for meeting and adjusting to the implications of such a discovery. Questions one might wish to answer by such studies would include: How might such information, under what circumstances, be presented to or withheld from the public to what ends? What might be the role of the discovering scientists and other decision makers regarding release of the fact of discovery?

> An individual's reactions to such a radio contact would in part depend on his cultural, religious, and social background, as well as on the actions

of those he considered authorities and leaders, and their behavior, in turn would in part depend on their cultural, social and religious environment. The discovery would certainly be front-page news everywhere; the degree of political or social repercussion would probably depend on leadership's interpretation of (1) its own role, (2) threats to that role, and (3) national and personal opportunities to take advantage of the disruption or reinforcement of the attitudes and values of others. Since leadership itself might have great need to gauge the direction and intensity of public attitudes, to strengthen its own morale and for decision making purposes, it would be most advantageous to have more to go on than personal opinions about the opinions of the public and other leadership groups.

The knowledge that life existed in other parts of the universe might lead to a greater unity of men on earth, based on the "oneness" of man or on the age-old assumption that any stranger is threatening. Much would depend on what, if anything, was communicated between man and the other beings....

The positions of the major American religious denominations, the Christian sects, and the Eastern religions on the matter of extraterrestrial life need elucidation. Consider the following: "The Fundamentalist (and anti-science) sects are growing apace around the world.... For them, the discovery of other life—rather than any other space product—would be electrifying ... some scattered studies need to be made both in their home centers and churches and their missions, in relation to attitudes about space activities and extraterrestrial life."

If plant life or some subhuman intelligence were found on Mars or Venus, for example, there is on the face of it no good reason to suppose these discoveries, after the original novelty had been exploited to the fullest and worn off, would result in substantial changes in perspectives or philosophy in large parts of the American public, at least any more than, let us say, did the discovery of the coelacanth or the panda.

If super intelligence is discovered, the results become quite unpredictable. It is possible that if the intelligence of these creatures were sufficiently superior to ours, they would choose to have little if any contact with us. On the face of it, there is no reason to believe that we might learn a great deal from them, especially if their physiology and psychology were substantially different from ours.

It has been speculated that, of all groups, scientists and engineers might be the most devastated by the discovery of relatively superior creatures, since these professions are most clearly associated with the mastery of nature, rather than with the understanding and expression of man. Advanced understanding of nature might vitiate all our theories at the very least, if not also require a culture and perhaps a brain inaccessible to earth scientists.

It is perhaps interesting to note that when asked what the consequences of the discovery of superior life would be, an audience of *Saturday Review* readership chose, for the most part, not to answer the question at all, in spite of their detailed answers to many other speculative questions.

Undoubtedly, any civilization capable of interstellar travel would be far in advace of our own. Encountering other beings with superior intelligence could cause serious social up-heavals here on Earth.

A possible but not completely satisfactory means for making the possibility "real" for many people would be to confront them with present speculations about the I.Q. of the porpoise and to encourage them to expand on the implications of this situation.

Such studies would include historical reactions to hoaxes, psychic manifestations, unidentified flying objects, etc. Hadley Cantril's study, *Invasion from Mars* (Princeton University Press, 1940), would provide a useful if limited guide in this area. Fruitful understanding might be gained from a comparative study of factors affecting the responses of primitive societies to exposure to technologically advanced societies. Some thrived, some endured, and some died.

While they seem to rule out the idea of alien visitation they seem amenable to the idea of alien communication via radio. They are suggesting that in the communications between a technologically superior civilization with a technologically inferior civilization, the technologically inferior civilization ceases to exist. They are suggesting that the destruction of those civilizations isn't necessarily through conquest, but is likely due to the introduction of that superior technology.

A society that has no firearms, for example, would change with the introduction of firearms. It would soon become obvious that firearms are superior than bows and arrows, but more importantly, the firearms require a manufacturing base. They need powder in order to work, and the bow and arrow technology simply would be overwhelmed. They would depend on the manufacturers to reproduce the firearms, to repair them and supply the powder to make them operate.

There is also the story of the anthropologist who began to live with a primitive tribe for his research. The tribe used stone axes, but the anthropologist had brought a supply of steel axes with him. To induce the population to speak with him and share the secrets of their society, he would give individuals a steel ax after the interview. What he didn't know was that only the leaders of that society were allowed to possess and use an ax, while the rest of the people had to ask permission of the leaders to borrow an ax. With the anthropologist handing out steel axes, that social underpinning was destroyed. An alteration of the societal structure ended up destroying that structure.

History suggests that face-to-face contact with aliens would be disastrous because, by definition, the aliens would be from a technologically superior civilization. They would have the ability to cross interstellar space. The introduction of that technology to society on Earth would alter our society.

> History suggests that face-to-face contact with aliens would be disastrous because, by definition, the aliens would be from a technologically superior civilization.

But those who wrote this section of the report didn't believe that the confrontation would be face-to-face and chose to ignore the material about unidentified flying objects. Instead they were concerned with the detection of a radio signal from another solar system. They weren't sure what the reaction would be, but thought it might be wise to keep word of the discovery hidden from the general population. They asked, "How might such information, under what circumstances, be presented to or withheld from the public to what ends?"

Early on, then, there was discussion, according to the government files, about the implications of alien communications and a suggestion that it would be best to withhold information of alien contact. Even with the aliens light years from Earth and of no immediate threat, they were concerned with the effect on modern society. Maybe it would be best for those in charge to keep the information as classified and hidden. If nothing else, it would give them an advantage over the rest of the human race.

The SETI Protocols

Over the next few decades, as interest in SETI expanded, the organization also expanded information about SETI. They produced what they called the *Declaration of Principles Concerning the Conduct of the Search for Extraterrestrial Intelligence*. This said:

> The parties to this declaration are individuals and institutions participating in the scientific Search for Extraterrestrial Intelligence (SETI).

> The purpose of this document is to declare our commitment to conduct this search in a scientifically valid and transparent manner and to establish uniform procedures for the announcement of a confirmed SETI detection.

This commitment is made in recognition of the profound scientific, social, ethical, legal, philosophical and other implications of a SETI detection. As this enterprise enjoys wide public interest, but engenders uncertainty about how information collected during the search will be handled, the signatories have voluntarily constructed this declaration. It, together with a current list of signatory parties, will be placed on file with the International Academy of Astronautics (IAA).

Principles

1. *Searching*: SETI experiments will be conducted transparently, and its practitioners will be free to present reports on activities and results in public and professional fora. They will also be responsive to news organizations and other public communications media about their work.

2. *Handling candidate evidence*: In the event of a suspected detection of extraterrestrial intelligence, the discoverer will make all efforts to verify the detection, using the resources available to the discoverer and with the collaboration of other investigators, whether or not signatories to this Declaration. Such efforts will include, but not be limited to, observations at more than one facility and/or by more

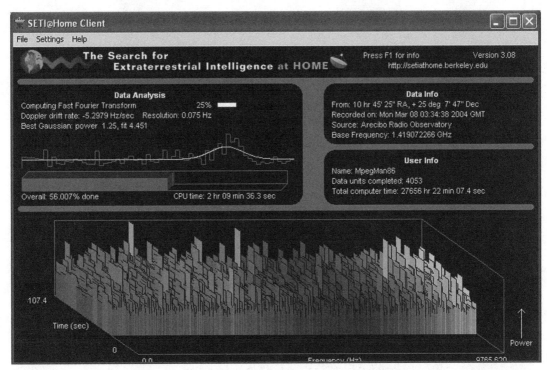

The screen display for the SETI home version. Anyone with a computer at home and sufficient hard drive memory can download this program, which analyzes data gathered by SETI dishes.

than one organization. There is no obligation to disclose verification efforts while they are underway, and there should be no premature disclosures pending verification. Inquiries from the media and news organizations should be responded to promptly and honestly.

Information about candidate signals or other detections should be treated in the same way that any scientist would treat provisional laboratory results. The Rio Scale, or its equivalent, should be used as a guide to the import and significance of candidate discoveries for the benefit of non-specialist audiences.

3. *Confirmed detections:* If the verification process confirms—by the consensus of the other investigators involved and to a degree of certainty judged by the discoverers to be credible—that a signal or other evidence is due to extraterrestrial intelligence, the discoverer shall report this conclusion in a full and complete open manner to the public, the scientific community, and the Secretary General of the United Nations. The confirmation report will include the basic data, the process and results of the verification efforts, any conclusions and interpretations, and any detected information content of the signal itself. A formal report will also be made to the International Astronomical Union (IAU).

4. All data necessary for the confirmation of the detection should be made available to the international scientific community through publications, meetings, conferences, and other appropriate means.

5. The discovery should be monitored. Any data bearing on the evidence of extraterrestrial intelligence should be recorded and stored permanently to the greatest extent feasible and practicable, in a form that will make it available to observers and to the scientific community for further analysis and interpretation.

6. If the evidence of detection is in the form of electromagnetic signals, observers should seek international agreement to protect the appropriate frequencies by exercising the extraordinary procedures established within the World Administrative Radio Council of the International Telecommunication Union.

7. *Post Detection:* A Post-Detection Task Group under the auspices of the IAA SETI Permanent Study Group has been established to assist in matters that may arise in the event of a confirmed signal, and to support the scientific and public analysis by offering guidance, interpretation, and discussion of the wider implications of the detection.

8. *Response to signals:* In the case of the confirmed detection of a signal, signatories to this declaration will not respond without first seeking guidance and consent of a broadly representative international body, such as the United Nations.

This document was unanimously adopted by the SETI Permanent Study Group of the International Academy of Astronautics at its annual meeting in

Prague, Czech Republic, on September 30, 2010. They were intended to replace the protocols that had been adopted in 1989.

These protocols were established by the scientific community to ensure that everyone had access to the information, whether it was merely the knowledge that an alien race existed, or to the actual content of the message. It is an ideal situation but one that could easily run afoul of various government agencies and entities.

There is that note in the government files, from the Brookings Institution report, that suggested it might be in the best interest of the world to keep the discovery of an alien signal secret, and while it can be argued that a signal from space could be detected by scientists in any country who had the capability of searching, the sad fact is that many of those scientists are not looking for alien signals. It might be that a single country could control the information, at least for a period of time.

A report from the Brookings Institution in Washington, D.C., suggested that it might be best to keep secret any proof that aliens exist.

The announcement of detection is directly related to who detects it and who they happen to work for. A government-sponsored agency could have a specific protocol in place to restrict the announcement until certain circumstances are met, taking the decision to announce out of the hands of those who make the discovery.

On the other hand, if the discovery is made by a private concern, such as a university, then the protocols adopted by SETI would come into play. By the time a government was involved, it might simply be too late.

O'Hare and Stephenville Sightings

Few UFO sightings in the modern world receive any sort of national and international coverage, but there are some exceptions. The reason for the lack of coverage is often unclear, but in some cases it is related to the number of witnesses and their location. On November 7, 2006, employees of United Airlines at Chicago's O'Hare International Airport saw something that did receive international attention. That attention came several weeks late, often couched in obscure language, with witness names left out, but the information did travel around the world.

According to a massive report prepared by Dr. Richard F. Haines, along with K. Efishoff, D. Ledger, L. Lemke, S. Maranto, W. Puckett, T. Roe, M. Shough, and R. Uriarte titled *Report on an Unidentified Aerial Phenomenon and its Safety Implications at O'Hare International Airport on November 7, 2006*, a series of sightings began about four in the afternoon. The government files from the FAA reveal an FAA inbound ground controller mentioned a UFO at 3:58 P.M., about seventeen minutes before the majority of the sightings began. This was the only mention of a UFO by an inbound or an outbound flight on November 7.

According to Haines' report, "The earliest known witness was Mr. X.X. [Haines, and other who have reported on this incident have removed the names of the witnesses at their request ... all feared for their jobs if they were publically identified in the press accounts] who was assisting the push-back of a B-737-500 from gate C17 [on the "C" concourse at O'Hare]. He was standing on the tarmac beside the nose of the jet with his communication headset cable plugged into a connection port in the nose of the airplane.... At about 4:30 pm [sic] [he] said that '... he was compelled to look straight up for some reason and was startled to see the craft hovering silently.'"

He said that he thought the object was between 500 and 1,000 feet in the air and that it was directly above his gate. He thought that it was spinning and after two minutes, it shot straight upward, through the clouds, leaving a hole behind it.

He told the flight crew what he was seeing and, according to the witness, either one or both of the flight crew saw the object. Haines reported that this couldn't be confirmed.

The witness also made a call to the airline's operations center, where Sylvia, in United Airlines Zone 5, who was responsible for ten gates.

The next witnesses, according to Haines, were two United aviation mechanics who were cleared to taxi aircraft from the gates to the maintenance facilities and back again. Although not rated flight crew, the mechanics have a responsible job when taxiing aircraft. While their versions of the events vary slightly, there are no significant discrepancies in what they told those who interviewed them later. According to Haines' report:

> In the first version, the details provided to NARCAP [National Aviation Reporting Center on Anomalous Phenomena] by witness B [the mechanic in the left (command) seat] are given. He said that while they were parked they both overheard a radio message from the flight crew of the B-737-500 at gate C17 talking on their company frequency about, "... a circle or disc shaped [sic] object hovering over [the] gate. This fact tends to confirm that at least one of the two cockpit crewmen in the B-737-500 looked up at the object...."

> Witness B continued, "At frist [sic] we laughed [sic] to each other and then the same pilot said again on the radio that it was about 700 feet agl [sic] (above ground level) ... the radio irrupted [sic] with chatter about the object and the ATC controller that was handling ground traffic made a few smart comments about the alleged UFO siting [sic] about the C terminal."

> According to witness B then they began to taxi the airplane to the west around taxiway Alpha ... Radio communications with the inbound ground controller showed that they began to taxi at 3:57:30 pm [sic].... During their taxiing witness C [in the right seat] was in radio contact with inbound ground control for directions to their destination, he would have used the call sign "United maintenance-44.

Dr. Richard J. Haines was coauthor of the extensive report about the O'Hare Airport UFO sighting in 2006.

The interview boils down to the witnesses, two members of the United maintenance team known as aviation mechanics, who believe they saw a disc-shaped object hovering below the cloud deck. They heard some talk about it over the ground control frequencies. More important was the allegation that the controller was making "smart comments" about the sighting. This underscores the attitudes of those working around airports, if that allegation could be proven.

The government files, recovered by Haines using FOIA after two attempts, showed that one of the controllers did make a "smart remark." It was a single instance, but the tape revealed that the first sighting happened just before four in the afternoon.

The attitude of the United management regarding the sighting was also revealed during the investigation. Haines noted that witness C refused to cooperate with the investigation because of management and his co-workers. He wouldn't even fill out a questionnaire about the case.

The two aviation maintenance men were taxiing for about twenty minutes. They could see the object hovering about 100 to 200 feet below the clouds. Witness B, according to Haines, said that the object didn't appear to be rotating. He thought it was hazy on the bottom and at both ends. It didn't change color or brightness while he watched it. He said it wasn't a blimp and it was not any type of airplane.

After they parked the airplane at about 4:22 P.M. both men looked back to where the UFO had been. They could see a "smooth round hole" in the clouds but there was no UFO.

At about 4:30, according to information uncovered by Peter Davenport at the National UFO Reporting Center, another witness who wishes to remain anonymous, was working in his office when he heard the announcement about the UFO over the company's radio frequency. He said that he walked outside and saw the object. He wasn't sure what to think, trying to figure out what it was. He said, "I knew no one would make a false call like that ... if someone was bouncing a weather balloon or something ... we had to stop it because it was in very close proximity to our flight operations."

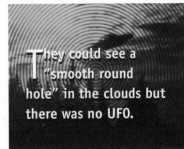

They could see a "smooth round hole" in the clouds but there was no UFO.

He thought the UFO was small, not much larger than six to ten feet in diameter. Importantly, he said that it had taken him a few seconds to spot it and he saw it only because he knew where to look, which might explain why there were not many other witnesses. He said it was an elliptically shaped sphere and seemed to be made of dark metal. He saw the object rise upwards and disappear almost instantaneously.

This man wasn't alone. He said that another United employee watched the UFO for about thirty seconds. This second man thought the UFO was nothing more than a bird so he walked away.

A few minutes later, there were additional sightings, according to what Haines learned through a FOIA of the government files. He was provided with a copy of a tape of a conversation among three groups at O'Hare. These were two aircraft and the inbound ground controller. It said:

IGC (inbound ground controller): Gateway 5668

5668 (Gateway flight 5668): Gateway 5668

IGC: Yeh ... look out your window. Do you see anything about United concourse? They actually, believe it or not, they called us and said somebody observed a flying disc about a thousand feet above the, ah ... gate Charley 17. Do you see anything over there?

5668: (After a five second delay) Not that I can tell. I thought my job was stressful.

44 (the United aircraft carrying witnesses B and C): Oh, we saw it a half hour ago.

IGC: Who saw it?

44: A whole bunch of us over at the Charley concourse.

IGC: Really? You guys did? Who is this?

44: United taxi mechanics ... We thought it was a balloon but we're not sure.

While all this was going on, the zone controller at United asked if the object was still present. She called the control tower to learn more about it. Leslie Kean, in her book, *UFOs: Generals, Pilots and Government Officials Go On the Record*, wrote that at first both the FAA and United denied the incident had taken place, but later said that tapes did exist. She had listened to the tapes and reported:

"Hey, did you see a flying disc out by C17?" asked the supervisor, giving her name as Sue. Laughter is audible from tower operator Dave and a second person nearby. "That what a pilot in the ramp area at C17 told us," she continues. "They saw some flying disc above them. But we can't see about us." The laughter continues nervously, and Dave replies, "Hey, you guys been celebrating the holidays or anything, or what? You're celebrating Christmas today? I haven't seen anything, Sue, and if I did, I wouldn't admit to it. No, I have not seen any flying disc at gate C17."

About fifteen minutes later, Sue calls back again, this time reaching operator Dwight. The conversation is as follows:

Sue: This is Sue from United. (Laughter)

Tower: Yes (serious tone)

(12 second pause)

S: There was a disc out there flying around.

T: There was a what?

S: A disc.

T: A disc?

S: Yeah.

T: Can you hang on one second?

S: Sure.

(pause, 33 seconds)

T: Okay. I'm sorry, what can I do for you?

S: I'm sorry, there was, I told Dave, there was a disc flying outside above Charley 17 and he thought I was pretty high. But, um, I'm not high and I'm not drinking.

T: Yeah

S: So, someone got a picture of it. So, if you guys see it out there—

T: A disc, like a Frisbee?

S: Like a UFO type thing.

T: Yeah, okay.

S: He got a picture of it. (laughs)

T: How, how, how high above Charley 17?

S: So, if you happen to see anything … (she continues to laugh)

T: You know, I'll keep a peeled eye for that.

S: Okay.

There are three important points that come out of this. First is the derision with which the report was met by those in the tower. Even though the description was of a disc, it was an intrusion into restricted airspace and could have been a hazard to aerial navigation. Those in the control tower are there to ensure that traffic flow is safe, yet when an intruder was reported, they thought nothing of it based solely on the description. According to Kean, the construction of the control tower was such that they couldn't see an object in the position reported.

Second, there is Sue's mention of a photograph. Since that time, several have surfaced, but all of those seem to be faked. No one has found the photo to which she referred. Given the nature of the reporting on this event, whoever has the photograph must be worrying about either holding onto his or her job, or the accompanying ridicule that will follow the revelation. No photograph that was taken at the time in Chicago has surfaced.

> [I]t seems that neither the FAA nor United were overly concerned with the intrusion of their airspace.

Finally, it seems that neither the FAA nor United were overly concerned with the intrusion of their airspace. Such a safety violation should have required immediate action and a follow-up investigation. There is no evidence that such was done until the media became involved in the sighting, several weeks after the event.

The Media Learns of the UFO

This incident would have slid into obscurity had it not been for Peter Davenport. His National UFO Reporting Center heard about the sighting. Davenport convinced one of the witnesses to appear on a radio show hosted by Jeff Rense, and that is detailed at rense.com. According to Rense, on December 12, just over a month after the sightings, the eyewitness described a perfect disc that he and a co-worker watched for several minutes as it hovered just under the cloud deck at 1,900 feet. This witness was described as one of the two ferrying a large jet to the maintenance or hangar area.

Davenport was also responsible for the story that appeared in the *Chicago Tribune* on January 1, 2007. He contacted Jon Hilkevitch, who wrote the story, published under the headline, "In the sky! A bird? A plane? A … UFO?"

The lead of the story was important. Hilkevitch wrote, "It sounds like a tired joke—but a group of airline employees insist they are in earnest, and they are upset that neither their bosses nor the government will take them seriously."

Hilkevitch reported that officials at United said they didn't know a thing about the sighting. He did note that when they, meaning the *Tribune* reporters, or in reality Hilkevitch, began to ask questions, those in the control tower said they did receive a call from a United supervisor who was asking questions about a "mysterious elliptical-shaped craft." The controllers said that a preliminary check with the radar showed nothing, according to FAA spokeswoman Elizabeth Isham Cory. She added that there were no plans for a follow up investigation and that the theory was that the sighting was caused by a "weather phenomenon."

Craig Burzych, a controller and union official was quoted as saying, "To fly 7 million light years to O'Hare and then have to turn around and go home because your gate was occupied is simply unacceptable."

Hilkevitch described the sightings, reporting that some said it looked like a rotating Frisbee while others said it did not rotate. It made no noise and remained where it was, just under the bottom of the clouds before shooting upwards and disappearing. "It was like somebody punched a hole in the sky," a witness said. Hilkevitch interviewed the two mechanics who had been taxiing the jet, the manager who had run outside to look for himself, and information from several pilots who said that they were sure it was not anything found on Earth.

> *"To fly 7 million light years to O'Hare and then have to turn around and go home because your gate was occupied is simply unacceptable."*

United said there was no UFO report. A spokeswoman, Megan McCarthy, said that there was nothing in the manager's log, there was no record of a UFO report and officials did not remember discussing the event. But, according to Hilkevitch, "Some [United employees] said they were interviewed by United officials and instructed to write reports and draw pictures of what they observed, and that they were advised by United officials to refrain from speaking about what they saw."

Hilkevitch wrote, "Like United, the FAA originally told the Tribune that it had no information on the alleged UFO sighting."

If nothing else, these denials should have revealed the way some organizations and parts of the government regarded UFO sightings. Rather than providing information about the source of the sightings, rather than offering a good explanation for them, they denied that the sightings took place. But a FOIA request forced the FAA to change its original statement.

The government files, in this case, the FAA tapes, revealed the call by the United supervisor to the tower, which proved that both organizations had been less than honest. Clearly, a United official knew about the sightings, and clearly, they had been reported to the FAA.

Cory told Hilkevitch, "Our theory on that was it was a weather phenomenon. That night was a perfect atmospheric condition in terms of low [cloud] ceiling and a lot of airport lights. When the lights shine up into the clouds, sometimes you can see funny things. That's our take on it."

And while all that might be true, the events began in daylight, though overcast. There wouldn't have been airport lights shining up into the clouds, not to mention that airport employees, especially those who had worked at O'Hare for many years, would have been familiar with the look of lights on the clouds.

Also in January, 2007, according to Leslie Kean, FAA spokesman Tony Molinaro, said that the absence of any kind of factual evidence, including the fact that no FAA controller saw anything and there was nothing detected by radar precluded any sort of investigation. He did say that the witnesses could have seen a "hole-punch cloud … with vapor going up into it."

Kean said that these are natural clouds that have ice crystals falling through them, and they can only form at below-freezing temperatures. It was forty-eight degrees at O'Hare at the time of the sightings.

John Callahan, who was a division chief of accidents and investigations and who was involved in the investigation of the JAL 1628 in the 1980s, said that it

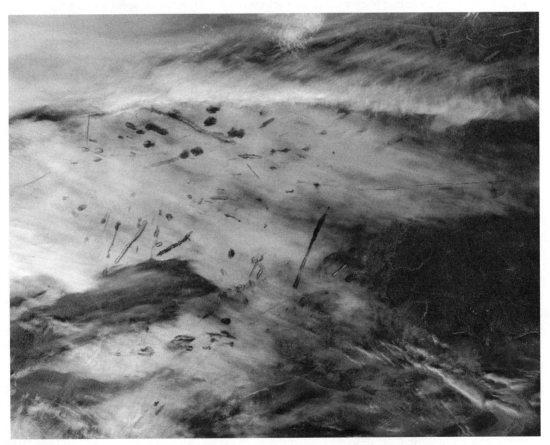

Hole-punch clouds, like these spotted in 2007 over Louisiana, are rare phenomena that may be caused by a combination of air traffic, cold temperatures, and atypical atmospheric stability.

wasn't surprising that the FAA radar did not detect anything at O'Hare but that it didn't mean anything. Some experts said that the radars do not pick up strange objects with bizarre flight capabilities, not to mention one that was directly over the facility.

According to Kean, Callahan said that the official response was predictable. He said, "The FAA will offer a host of other explanations, as if wearing a blindfold. It's always something else so it can't be what it is."

Government files, in this case the *FAA Aeronautical Information Manual*, tell its employees what to do if they are "wanting to report UFO/Unexplained Phenomena activity." They should contact an organization such as NUFORC, which is a civilian agency with no governmental support.

The advice continues. If "concern is expressed that life or property might be endangered, report the activity to the local law-enforcement department."

It is interesting that, like the Air Force, the FAA is abrogating part of its responsibility to civilian organizations or law enforcement agencies that have nothing to do with aviation. The FAA, which will investigate trivial incidents on aircraft that might affect aviation safety, will ignore the intrusion of an object over a major airport. Instead of investigating, they will deny the event took place and then when their own files, released under Freedom of Information Act requests, prove they have lied about an event, they will invent an excuse, such as weather phenomenon. They simply won't investigate, at least in a public arena.

The FAA and the CIA: This Never Happened

In 2011, the FAA issued new instructions for the reporting of UFOs. On page 401 of their manual, they wrote, "Persons wanting to report UFO/unexplained phenomena activity should contact a UFO/unexplained phenomena reporting data collection center, such as Bigelow Aerospace Advanced Space Studies ... the National UFO Reporting Center...."

Basically, the FAA is asking their employees to report UFO sightings to civilian and local law-enforcement agencies. They do not have a system for reporting UFOs that endanger aerial navigation. Based on discussions with some people who worked with the FAA, the agency's internal attitude is that there is nothing extraterrestrial about UFOs and those who think there is suffering from some kind of problem. When Sue called the control tower at O'Hare, her observation was met with derision. Who would call in a UFO report to his or her superiors, knowing that the corporate attitude was so negative towards such reports?

In the 2011 statement, the FAA addressed John Callahan's statements that he had been told by members of the CIA at a meeting held at the White House that the JAL 1928 event never happened. They noted that, "At this point, Callahan's credentials and story has never been independently confirmed." The flip side is that his credentials and story have also never been successfully challenged.

As well, Callahan had copies of the radar data, flight logs, and witness testimony about the UFO sighting.

CIA Science Analyst Ron Pandolfi said that both he and UFO researcher and retired Navy physicist Bruce Maccabee had attended similar meetings. Pandolfi didn't remember anyone making statements refuting that the events ever took place. Of course, he was not present at the meeting in which this specific UFO case was discussed.

Callahan's case was a single incident and it is possible that mistakes were made or statements misunderstood in his particular instance. The question becomes, are there other incidents that might shed some light on this? That is, apart from the report from the FAA denying that something was reported to their tower crew at O'Hare in 2006.

> When Sue called the control tower at O'Hare, her observation was met with derision.

On January 8, 2013, people in Amherst and Pelham, Massachusetts, reported a low-flying pyramid-shaped object, moving slowly and silently sometime between 5:45 P.M. and 6:30 P.M. The *Hampshire Gazette* reported that an FAA spokesman said, "The only aircraft that was operating in the area was a military aircraft doing practice approaches to Westover...."

The Air Force said, at first, they had nothing operating in the area at the time of the sighting, but Lieutenant Colonel James Bishop said that an Air Force C-5 did depart from Westover Air Reserve Base about 5:30 P.M.. It left the local area and didn't return until 9:30 P.M. that night.

Bishop said that he didn't think the C-5 explanation was viable. The witnesses had reported something that was low, remained in the area, was pyramid shaped and silent. The C-5 did not remain in the area and was anything but silent. Had it been flying low, as the witnesses suggested, they would have heard noise from it. No one seemed to be satisfied with the explanation except the FAA.

According to a story written by Rebecca Everett of the *Daily Hampshire Gazette*, "The Federal Aviation Administration says a military aircraft was flying over Amherst Jan 8 when residents reported seeing a mysterious object flying silently overhead."

There is nothing to link the Air Force cargo jet to the reported sighting of the UFO, except that a jet took off from Westover at 5:30 P.M., some fifteen minutes before the UFO sightings began.

Stephenville, Texas, January 8, 2008

Some five years earlier, and almost to the exact time of day, about 6:10 P.M., a truck driver named Harlan Cowan was heading east toward Stephenville when he said he saw two stationary lights directly ahead of him. They were as bright as welding arcs.

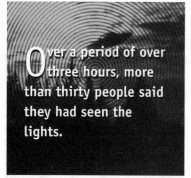

Over a period of over three hours, more than thirty people said they had seen the lights.

At about 6:15 P.M., a private pilot, Steve Allen, who was five miles southeast of Stephenville, saw something similar. He said that four bright lights came out of the northeast at a speed much faster than a military jet. They slowed suddenly, hovered, and then four lights visible in a horizontal position changed into seven lights in a vertical position. Then, still hovering, they flashed bright white and disappeared.

Over a period of over three hours, more than thirty people said they had seen the lights. The witnesses included Stephenville police officers, a former air traffic controller, and the chief of police in another county. Given the timing of the sightings, over such a long period, and by some who were quite familiar with aircraft, there was no good explanation offered.

Reporter Angelia Joiner called the Naval Air Station Joint Reserve Base, previously known as Carswell Air Force Base. Major Karl Lewis told Joiner that he might be able to solve the mystery. Then, on January 11, 2008, Lewis said, "I think it was a consortium of lights. It sounds like the sun reflection off of an aircraft traveling at high altitude."

Which might have been a possibility, except that the sightings were reported over a period of three hours and the sun had set at least an hour before the first sighting was reported.

Lewis also said that there were no F-16s from the 301st Fighter Wing flying at the time and that no other fighter pilots had reported a UFO.

Two weeks after the sightings, on January 23, 2008, the Air Force released an official statement:

In the interest of public awareness, Air Force Reserve Command Public Affairs realized an error was made regarding the reported training activity of military aircraft. Ten F-16s from the 457th Fighter Squadron were performing training operations from 6 to 8 P.M., Tuesday, January 8, 2008, in the Brownwood Military Operating Area (MOA), which includes the airspace about Erath County.

At that point, Air Force cooperation ended, and Major Karl Lewis refused to answer additional questions. When Joiner asked him about what had happened, Lewis would read the press release. He would not say anything more. It is clear that someone higher up the chain of command had spoken to him and he wasn't going to say anything that might get him into some kind of trouble.

Glen Schulze, an electrical engineer and radar expert, filed a FOIA request with the FAA for the raw radar data from the Stephenville area for January 8. He believed, along with Robert Powell, that the data would allow them to accurately plot where everything was that night. They would be able to identify the jets, commercial airliners, or anything else in the sky.

According to the report on these analyses included in Swords' *UFO and Government*:

The radar results were detailed and striking in regards to the Air Force activity in the area of interest. Radar had recorded the location and time transit of every F-16 within 100 miles of Stephenville. It was clear that the unknown lights seen by the witnesses were not related to the F-16s. The amount of Air Force activity was unusual. Ten F-16s and an apparent AWACS jet showed up on FAA radar and made figure 8s over the area of interest from 4 P.M. to 8 P.M. At 7:30 P.M. two F-16s that were in Military Operating Area (MOA) 200 miles to the north of Stephenville in Oklahoma left their MOA. They did not proceed directly back to their point of origin at NASJRB [the former Carswell AFB] in Fort Worth, which was 150 miles southeast of their location. Instead they proceeded 200 miles to the south and directly towards the area where the unknown lights were seen. They did not travel into the MOA, which was only a few miles farther to the south. Instead, their route took them directly over Stephenville on their out-of-the-way journey back to Ft. Worth....

But the radar results showed more than just the Air Force activity that day. At 6:15 P.M., the approximate time that Steve Allen had reported the extremely fast moving object moving from northeast of his position to the northwest, radar made contact with an object four miles south of Allen and then twenty seconds later it was twelve miles northwest of his position. The calculated speed from radar was 2100 mph. And there were more radar confirmations of witness testimony.

Radar at two separate sites picked up another unknown, this one matching the time and location provided by law enforcement officer Lee Roy Gaitan. He described a silent, reddish-orange light that hovered above a tree line to the south of his home. He went inside to tell his wife, but when he came back out, the single light was gone, replaced by white balls that were higher in the sky.

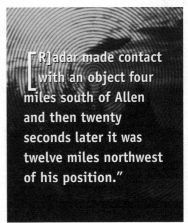

[R]adar made contact with an object four miles south of Allen and then twenty seconds later it was twelve miles northwest of his position."

Gaitan said that as he watched them through binoculars, the balls were moving at random. They covered much of the sky. The lights suddenly moved in tandem and disappeared to the northeast at an "extremely high rate of speed." Radar tracks received from the FAA confirmed the sighting.

There was additional confirmation of other sightings by the FAA radar tracks. According to Swords in *UFOs and Government*:

A most interesting radar track began at 6:51 P.M. What makes it interesting is the Air Force's "response" and "lack of response." An unknown object, *without a transponder signal* [emphasis in original], was tracked with FAA radar for over an hour. It was a real object as two different radar systems (one near Ft. Worth and one near Temple) made contact with the object 187 times as the object covered a distance of about fifty miles on a constant trajectory to the southeast. Its speed varied from stationary, to accelerating to 532 mph in thirty seconds, to de-accelerating [sic] from

532 mph to 49 mph in ten seconds. The unknown bogey without a transponder was traveling on a direct course to President George W. Bush's Western White House in Crawford, Texas. At 8 P.M. it was ten miles from Crawford Ranch and would be directly over the ranch in a few more minutes. Two witnesses riding bikes about two miles from Crawford Ranch reported a bright object in the direction of the president's ranch that slowly descended and then suddenly made a ninety degree angle turn and accelerated out of sight within one to two seconds. This was restricted and sensitive air space. The no-fly zone was restricted to a twenty mile radius when the president was present and a six mile radius when he was not present. Once an aircraft violates that controlled air space, a response from military aircraft will occur. Previous intrusions by aircraft into the same no-fly zone resulted in pursuit by F16 [sic] jets and handcuffing of the trespassing pilot after landing [reference to the *Wall Street Journal*, "Don't Go There: The President Takes a No-Fly Zone Wherever He Goes," August 22, 2002]. What was the military's response in this incident? (The object was observable on FAA radar located 70 miles away, so it must have shown up on the F16's radar that came within two miles of the object at one point in time, the AWACS radar, and radar at Ft. Hood only thirty miles distant.) But the response from the Air Force was zero. Analysis of the FAA radar data showed no attempt by any of the F16s in the area to divert and investigate an unknown aircraft, without any transponder, closing in on the president's ranch.

Due to the lack of response from the Air Force, a letter was sent in November of 2008 by Robert Powell to General Renuart, the Commander of NORAD, and Michael Chertoff, the Secretary of Homeland Security, with copies to the FAA and the ranking chairmen of the Senate and House Committees on Homeland Security. The letter asked for an investigation into the violation of restricted air space by an "unknown aircraft" in light of the tragic events of September 11, 2001. A response was received and it came from Major General John Bordelon, the Chief of Staff of NORAD. As might be expected, the Air Force claimed no knowledge of an unknown aircraft in the area on that date even though they had access to the same FAA radar data through the Joint Surveillance System. Surprisingly, General Bordelon called the "unidentified aircraft" a UFO. He even referred the author to the FAA guidelines for UFO reports as well as Peter Davenport's National UFO Hotline. Powell [co-author of *UFOs and Government with Swords*, and writer of the original letter] called the object on radar an *unknown aircraft* [emphasis in original] yet the General chose to refer to it as a *UFO* [emphasis in the original] … One wonders if this was a slip of the tongue that perhaps epitomizes the Air Force approach to the investigation of this phenomenon.

The importance of these sightings isn't the nature of the object or the lights seen, but the response to them. While witnesses on the ground might have called the local law enforcement to report the sightings, the radar tracks, which confirmed that something was in the air, demanded a response from the Air Force, one that didn't happen.

Breakdown of Armed Response

Over the last several decades, there have been UFO sightings that should have elicited some sort of response by the military or the various government agencies charged with aviation safety. Rules, regulations, and laws dictate some of those responses. Sometimes the situation requires a response, but has been ignored. Why?

At Loring Air Force Base, an unidentified intruder flew over their weapons storage facility and the best explanation the Air Force could offer was a policy about helicopters. Any intrusion over that area would have called for the Air Force to respond with armed security police and an investigation into who was flying the alleged helicopter and for what purpose. Instead, requests for aviation support were met with a less than adequate response, and the local commander had to coordinate with the Army National Guard for the use of a medical helicopter. There was no follow up, at least available in the government files released into the public arena, and no one was arrested or charged with a violation of that airspace.

> The attitude seems to be that if we don't acknowledge it, then it never happened....

Later ICBMs at Malmstrom Air Force Base go off-line, meaning they were no longer available for a retaliatory response after a strange object is reported in the area. The investigation suggested some sort of a transitory electrical failure at the Launch Control Facility, but that failure has never been satisfactorily explained. Government documents suggest the investigation was suspended before an answer was found.

Air space near the Western White House was violated, there was radar confirmation on two separate radars of the intruder, there were Air Force jets in the air, but nothing was done. In other such incidents, pilots who violated that air space were arrested upon landing. In this case, the Air Force didn't know the violation happened, or that is what they suggest publicly.

There was also the object seen by several witnesses over O'Hare International Airport in Chicago. Again, the FAA denied that anything had been reported to them.

The government files reveal that these various events occurred, but the agencies with responsibility to investigate them failed to do so. There has been no satisfactory resolution for any of these and hundreds of other, similar events. The attitude seems to be that if we don't acknowledge it, then it never happened, and if it never happened, there was nothing for us to do. The agencies are then off the hook, but the situation hasn't changed. All we know is that they are not doing the jobs they were paid to do ... but who cares? These things do not exist.

Conclusions

In the examination of government files relating to all aspects of UFO phenomena, one thing has become clear. People running the investigations and those controlling the flow of information are either hiding something or they are completely incompetent. It is clear that there is something going on. It is possible that those in the know about UFOs have been busy trying to keep everyone else from finding out much of anything. They are happy with the status quo and are working to keep things unchanged. They do not want disclosure.

As we have seen, the beginning of the modern era of UFO sightings didn't begin in June, 1947, with the Kenneth Arnold sighting and the government investigation of these things wasn't sparked by that sighting. The evidence we have seen, much of it from the government files, shows that interest in these unidentified aerial phenomena goes back to the very beginning of World War II. At that time, no one was thinking in terms of objects that did not originate on Earth—everyone was focused on enemy research and development.

In 1944, when the Foo Fighters caused great concern, the Allies formed a group to resolve the issue. Colonel Howard McCoy was a member of that group. When the war ended, and the pressure was off, that investigation stagnated and then simply ended because there was no longer an imperative to find an answer.

When the Ghost Rocket sightings began in 1946, there was concern that they were connected to some sort of Soviet technology under development, and the U.S. government became concerned once again. One of the men who was involved in that investigation was Howard McCoy.

In December, 1946, McCoy, with Albert Deyarmond, set up an investigation at Wright Field. This was an unofficial investigation, conducted in secret, with extremely limited access to the information collected. This investigation preceded Arnold's by over six months, so when the Arnold sighting hit the newspapers, the investigative tools needed to explore the sighting were already in place. All McCoy and Deyarmond had to do was sanitize their files and open their doors.

The government files prove that some sort of sanitation took place. Most of the Ghost Rocket reports disappeared, although there was good evidence that the information had been collected and had been available at one time. Early sightings, especially those of disk-shaped craft, disappeared from the files, but the sanitation wasn't totally effective. In the Project Grudge Final Report, there is a reference to Case No. 79. These are the sightings made by Walter Minczewski at the Richmond, Virginia, weather bureau. Clearly they had been in the official files at some point, but by the time these files were released into the public arena, that information was gone.

An examination of the records shows the same pattern over the years about other UFO cases, too. The Green Fireballs seemed to be inexplicable. The leading authority on meteors, Dr. Lincoln La Paz, said that the Fireballs were not meteors, and he had seen one himself. In the end, the study concluded that the sightings were of meteors.

Ed Ruppelt had written that no photographs had ever been taken of any of the Fireballs, but the government files show that to be untrue. This doesn't mean that Ruppelt was lying; only that he was unaware a Fireball had been photographed. That photograph or photographs have not surfaced in the public record, meaning that although there are references to it in the documentation available, the photograph itself is not.

This sort of duplicity, whether intentional or not, has dominated the UFO research from the beginning. In July 1947, George Garrett produced a "mini" Estimate of the Situation and asked for the assistance from the Air Materiel Command in reviewing it. Lieutenant Nathan F. Twining, as the commanding officer, signed the letter that was written by one of his staff officers. That letter has been quoted by everyone on every side of the UFO controversy. But no one has ever taken the time to understand what the letter really meant.

Twining's response was that the "phenomena" was real, but the letter also mentioned "a lack of crash recovered debris." Skeptics use this statement as proof that nothing alien fell at Roswell in July, 1947, but what they fail to realize is that Twining's analysis was based on material provided to the AMC. They were asked to review the cases in the document forwarded to them, and that is exactly what they did. Since the document reviewed by the AMC did not discuss the case in question, their analysis did not address it, either. That is not proof that nothing alien fell in Roswell.

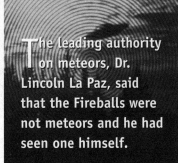

The leading authority on meteors, Dr. Lincoln La Paz, said that the Fireballs were not meteors and he had seen one himself.

The same problem exists in the discussion of the intrusions over military installations. Missileers, the men in the capsules with their fingers literally on the button, have reported that their missiles were affected by something on the outside. These intrusions, accompanied by UFO sightings, are a matter of national security. The missiles were clearly knocked offline by the UFOs and in some cases, it took hours to bring them back online. The Air Force denied most of this, except one instance, where they admitted the missiles were offline but insisted that there were no UFO sightings reported in the area at the time. What a strange comment to make.

In Belt, Montana, there were several UFO sightings as the missiles in one flight failed. Because there were so many sightings and so many civilians involved, the Air Force had no choice but to investigate. They did their best to limit what was known, but their own files contradict what they publicly said about the sightings. With access to the government files, we saw the duplicity.

It was the same case with Project Moon Dust, the documentation for which clearly proves that a component of the project dealt with UFOs. But when a U.S. senator asked about Moon Dust, he was told that no such project existed, and when documentation about Moon Dust was provided, the Air Force said the proj-

The tens of thousands of pages in the government files strongly suggest that there *is* something to what witnesses are saying about UFOs, but that the government has chosen to sweep it away from the public eye.

ect was never deployed. Of course, other documents show that Moon Dust was definitely deployed. True, many of the items recovered by Moon Dust were of terrestrial manufacture, but there are hints that other things were found. There are hints of alien creatures being involved.

This examination of the government files found the paperwork trail. Officers involved from the very beginning, in the early 1940s, and evidence of a compartmentalized investigation prevented any one individual from putting everything together and understanding the whole history of the UFO investigations. Documents that were created with little expectation that they would be seen by anyone outside a select and very small circle of influential people are now part of the public arena to be examined by everyone.

There are tens of thousands of pages that still need to be reviewed and that takes time and patience. I discovered the connection between Project Blue Book and Project Moon Dust by accident. While searching for a specific UFO sighting in the Blue Book files, I scanned past another sighting and the words, "Moon Dust" caught my attention. I stopped to take a look and was able to find several other cases that had been labeled as Moon Dust.

By searching the files carefully, and using documents from a variety of sources, including unit histories, I discovered that Moon Dust began just after the launch of Sputnik. Others, such as Robert Todd and Cliff Stone, added much to that aspect of the investigation. It proves, again, that these investigations were shrouded in secrecy and were hidden from the public through lies and deception.

The evidence was overwhelming. John Callahan, a high-ranking member of the FAA, provided documentation about a UFO sighting by a Japanese airline crew over Alaska, but was told the event never happened and that the CIA was never at the briefing.

The Condon Committee, launched in 1967 at the University of Colorado, was not a scientific investigation of UFOs, but an Air Force propaganda operation designed to end the public Air Force investigation and to convince the public that UFOs didn't exist outside the minds of the deluded, fans of science fiction, or the poorly educated. The government files prove that the conclusions of the

Condon Committee were untrue, that UFOs did impact national security, there were secret studies and secret investigations, and there was very good evidence that something happened.

In fact, found in the government files is a letter from an Air Force officer telling the members of the Condon Committee what they are supposed to report, and a confirmation by Robert Low that the committee understood what they were being asked to say. Their report was not intended to be a scientific study, but it was to be a way of ending the UFO investigations, at least publicly, making it look as if the Air Force had been doing a good job.

Condon, of course, said that there was no evidence that anything was going on, and that it was a waste of time, money, and effort to continue to record UFO sightings. The activity should be discouraged because it created a distrust of science, and as notorious debunker Phil Klass said, it suggested that the government couldn't be trusted.

The government files are filled with cases that demanded better investigation at the time of the events. The files are filled with physical evidence cases, photographic cases, and radar cases. There are reports from pilots, scientists, soldiers, sailors, from police officers, doctors, lawyers, and people who didn't finish high school. Added together, this results in a solid body of evidence that leads to a very realistic conclusion. There is something going on, and we have not been told what that is.

For some reason, the government, our leaders, and those in power, have decided that we are not to be told the truth. They have stuck with a policy of conceal and deceive but the evidence is out there in the government files. The conclusion is obvious and the government files prove it.

We have been visited.

BIBLIOGRAPHY

Air Defense Command Briefing, January 1953, Project Blue Book Files.

Air Intelligence Report No. 100-201-79, "Analysis of Flying Object Incidents in the U.S.," 10 December 1948.

Aldrich, Jan. "Investigating the Ghost Rockets." *International UFO Reporter* 23, 4 (winter 1998): 9–14.

———. "Project 1947: An Inquiry into the Beginning of the UFO Era," *International UFO Reporter* 21, 2 (summer 1996): 18–20.

Alexander, John B. *UFOs: Myths, Conspiracies, and Realities.* New York: St. Martin's Press, 2011.

Allan, Christopher D. "Dubious Truth about the Roswell Crash," *International UFO Reporter* 19, 3 (May/June 1994): 12–14.

Anderson, Michele. "BIOSPEX: Biological Space Experiments," *NASA Technical Memorandum 5821* 7, NASA, Washington, D.C., 1979.

Andrus, Walt. "Air Intelligence Report No. 100-203-79," *MUFON UFO Journal* 207 (July 1985): 3–19.

Asimov, Isaac. *Is Anyone There?* New York: Ace Books, 1967

ATIC UFO Briefing, April 1952, Project Blue Book Files.

"The Aurora, Texas Case," *The APRO Bulletin* (May/June 1973): 1, 3–4.

Barker, Gray. "America's Captured Flying Saucers—The Cover-up of the Century," *UFO Report* 4, 1 (May 1977): 32–35, 64, 66–73.

———. "Archives Reveal More Crashed Saucers," *Gray Barker's Newsletter* (14 March 1982): 5–6.

———. "Chasing Flying Saucers," *Gray Barker's Newsletter* 17 (December 1960): 22–28.

———. "Von Poppen Update," *Gray Barker's Newsletter* (December 1982): 8.

Basterfield, Keith. "Angel Hair: An Australian Perspective," *International UFO Reporter* 27, 1 (spring 2002): 6–9, 32.

Baxter, John, and Atkins Thomas. *The Fire Came By.* Garden City, NY: Doubleday, 1976.

Berliner, Don. "The Ghost Rockets of Sweden," *Official UFO* 1, 11 (October 1976): 30–31, 60–64.

Berliner, Don, with Marie Galbraith and Antonio Huneeus. *Unidentified Flying Objects Briefing Document: The Best Evidence Available.* Washington, D.C., 1995. 33–35.

Berlitz, Charles, and William L. Moore. *The Roswell Incident.* New York: Berkley, 1988.

"Big Fire in the Sky: A Burning Meteor," *New York Herald Tribune* (10 December 1965).

Binder, Otto. *What We Really Know about Flying Saucers.* Greenwich, CT: Fawcett Gold Medal, 1967.

———. *Flying Saucers Are Watching Us.* New York: Tower, 1968.

———. "The Secret Warehouse of UFO Proof," *UFO Report* 2, 2 (winter 1974): 16–19, 50, 52.

Bloecher, Ted. *Report on the UFO Wave of 1947*. Washington, DC: privately printed, 1967.

Bloecher, Ted, and Paul Cerny. "The Cisco Grove Bow and Arrow Case of 1964," *International UFO Reporter* 20, 5 (winter 1995): 16–22, 32.

Blum, Howard. *Out There: The Government's Secret Quest for Extraterrestrials*. New York: Simon & Schuster, 1991.

Blum, Ralph, with Judy Blum. *Beyond Earth: Man's Contact with UFOs*. New York: Bantam Books, 1974.

Bontempto, Pat. "Incident at Heligoland," *UFO Universe* 5 (spring 1989): 18–22.

———. "The Helgoland Crash: A Dissection of a Hoax." privately printed, 1994.

Bourdais, Gildas. *Roswell*. Agnieres, France: JMG Editions, 2004.

Bowen, Charles, editor. *The Humanoids*. Chicago: Henry Regency, 1969.

Braenne, Ole Jonny. "Legend of the Spitzbergen Saucer," *International UFO Reporter* 17, 6 (November/December 1992), 14–20.

Brew, John Otis, and Edward B. Danson. "The 1947 Reconnaissance and the Proposed Upper Gila Expedition of the Peabody Museum of Harvard University," *El Palacio* (July 1948): 211–222.

Briefing Document: Operation Majestic 12, November 18, 1952.

"Brilliant Red Explosion Flares in Las Vegas Sky," *Las Vegas Sun* (April 19, 1962): 1.

Britton, Jack, and George Washington, Jr. *Military Shoulder Patches of the United States Armed Forces*. Tulsa, OK: MCN Press, 1985.

Brown, Eunice H. *White Sands History*. White Sands, NM: Public Affairs Office, 1959.

Bullard, Thomas E. *The Myth and Mystery of UFOs*. Lawrence, KS: University of Kansas Press, 2010.

Burleson, Donald R. "Levelland, Texas, 1957: Case Reopened," *International UFO Reporter* 28, 1 (spring 2003): 3–6, 25.

———. "Deciphering the Ramey Memo," *International UFO Reporter* 25, 2 (summer 2000): 3–6, 32.

Cahn, J. P. "The Flying Saucers and the Mysterious Little Men," *True* (September 1952): 17–19, 102–112.

———. "Flying Saucer Swindlers," *True* (August 1956): 36–37, 69–72.

"California Man Besieged [sic] by 'Occupants,'" *The A.P.R.O. Bulletin* (July/August 1966): 5.

Candeo, Anne. *UFO's The Fact or Fiction Files*. New York: Walker 1990.

Cannon, Martin. "The Amazing Story of John Lear," *UFO Universe* (March 1990): 8.

Carey, Thomas J., and Donald R. Schmitt. *Witness to Roswell Revised and Expanded*. Pompton Plains, NJ: New Page Books, 2009.

Carpenter, Joel. "The Senator, The Saucer, and Special Report 14," *International UFO Reporter* 25,1 (spring 2000): 3–11, 30.

———. "The Ghost Rockets." Project 1947. http://www.project1947.com/gr/grchron1.htm. (Accessed January 20, 2014).

Catoe, Lynn E. *UFOs and Related Subjects: An Annotated Bibliography*. Washington, DC: Government Printing Office, 1969.

Cerny, Paul, and Robert Neville. "U.S. Navy 1942 Sighting," *MUFON UFO Journal* 185 (July 1983): 14–15.

Chaikin, Andrew. "Target: Tunguska," *Sky & Telescope* (January 1984): 18–21.

Chamberlain, Von Del, and David J. Krause. "The Fireball of December 9 1965—Part I," *Royal Astronomical Society of Canada Journal* 61 no. 4.

Chariton, Wallace O. *The Great Texas Airship Mystery*. Plano, TX: Wordware, 1991.

Chavarria, Hector. "El Caso Puebla," *OVNI*: 10–14.

Chester, Keith. *Strange Company: Military Encounters with UFOs in WW II*. San Antonio, TX: Anomalist Books, 2007.

Clark, Jerome. "The Great Unidentified Airship Scare," *Official UFO* (November, 1976).

———. "The Great Crashed Saucer Debate," *UFO Report* (October 1980): 16–19, 74, 76.

———. "Crashed Saucers—Another View," *Saga's UFO Annual 1981* (1981): 44–47, 66.

———. *UFO's in the 1980s*. Detroit: Apogee, 1990.

———. "The Great Crashed Saucer Debate," *UFO Report* 8, 5 (February 1980): 16–19, 74, 76.

———. "Crash Landings," *Omni* (December 1990): 92.

———. "UFO Reporters. (MJ-12)," *Fate* (December 1990).

———. "Airships: Part I," *International UFO Reporter* (January/February 1991): 4–23.

———. "Airships: Part II," *International UFO Reporter* (March/April 1991): 20–23.

———. "A Catalog of Early Crash Claims," *International UFO Reporter* (July/August 1993): 7–14 .

———. *The UFO Encyclopedia.* Detroit: Omnigraphics, 1998.

———. *Hidden Realms, Lost Civilizations, and Beings from Other Worlds,* Detroit: Visible Ink Press 2010.

Cohen, Daniel. *Encyclopedia of the Strange.* New York: Avon, 1987.

———. *The Great Airship Mystery: A UFO of the 1890s.* New York: Dodd, Mead, 1981.

———. *UFOs—The Third Wave.* New York: Evans, 1988.

Committee on Science and Astronautics, report, 1961.

Cooper, Milton William. *Behold a Pale Horse.* Sedona, AZ: Light Technology, 1991.

"Could the Scully Story Be True?," *The Saucerian Bulletin* 1, 2 (May 1956): 1.

Creighton, Gordon. "Close Encounters of an Unthinkable and Inadmissible Kind," *Flying Saucer Review* (July/August 1979).

———. "Further Evidence of 'Retrievals,'" *Flying Saucer Review* (January 1980).

———. "Continuing Evidence of Retrievals of the Third Kind." *Flying Saucer Review* (January/February 1982).

———. "Top U.S. Scientist Admits Crashed UFOs," *Flying Saucer Review* (October 1985).

Davies, John K. *Cosmic Impact.* New York: St. Martin's, 1986.

Davis, Richard. "Results of a Search for Records Concerning the 1947 Crash Near Roswell, New Mexico." Washington, DC: GAO, 1995.

Davison, Leon, editor. *Flying Saucers: An Analysis of Air Force Project Blue Book Special Report No. 14.* Clarksburg, VA: Saucerian Press, 1971.

DeGraw, Ralph C. "Did Two Iowans Witness the Famous Socorro Landing?," *The UFO Examiner* 3, 6 (1982): 18–20.

Dennett, Preston. "Project Redlight: Are We Flying The Saucers Too?," *UFO Universe* (May 1990): 39.

"Did A UFO Blast a Hole in Russia?," *The New UFO Magazine* 13, 4 (November/December 1994): 8–9, 46–49.

Dobbs, D. L. "Crashed Saucers—The Mystery Continues," *UFO Report* (September 1979): 28–31, 60–61.

"DoD News Releases and Fact Sheets." Washington, DC: U.S. Department of Defense, 1952–1968.

Dolan, Richard M. *UFOs and the National Security State.* Charlottesville, VA: Hampton Roads Publishing Company, 2000.

———. *UFOs and the National Security State: The Cover-Up Exposed, 1973–1991.* Rochester, NY: Keyhole Publishing, 2009.

Douglas, J. V., and Henry Lee. "The Fireball of December 9, 1965—Part II,"*Royal Astronomical Society of Canada Journal* 62, 41.

Earley, George W. "Crashed Saucers and Pickled Aliens, Part I," *Fate* 34, 3 (March 1981): 42–48.

———. "Crashed Saucers and Pickled Aliens, Part II," *Fate* 34, 4 (April 1981): 84–89.

———. "The Scam That Failed: Fred Crisman and the Maury Island Incident," *UFO* 24, 1 (October 1, 2010): 12–13, 65.

———. "The Scam that Failed: Fred Crisman and the Maury Island Incident, Part Two," *UFO* 24, 2 (January 2011): 12–13.

———. "The Maury Island Hoax, Part Four and Conclusion," *UFO* 24, 4 (October 2011): 38–52.

———. "The Scam That Failed: Fred Crisman and the Maury Island Incident, Part I," *UFO* 24, 1 (October 1, 2010): 12–13, 65.

Eberhart, George, *The Roswell Report: A Historical Perspective.* Chicago: CUFOS, 1991.

Edwards, Frank. *Flying Saucers—Here and Now!* New York: Bantam, 1968.

———. *Flying Saucers—Serious Business.* New York: Bantam, 1966.

———. *Strange World.* New York: Bantam, 1964.

"Effect of the Tunguska Meteorite Explosion on the Geomagnetic Field," Office of Technical Services U.S. Department of Commerce, 21 December 1961.

Eighth Air Force Staff Directory. Texas: June 1947.

"Evidence of UFO Landing Here Observed," *El Defensor Chieftain* [Socorro, New Mexico] (April 28, 1964).

"Experts Say a Meteor Caused Flash of Fire," *Deseret News* (April 19, 1962): 1.

Fact Sheet, "Office of Naval Research 1952 Greenland Cosmic Ray Scientific Expedition" (October 16, 1952).

Farish, Lucius, and Jerome Clark. "The Mysterious 'Foo Fighters' of World War II," *Saga's UFO Report* 2, 3 (spring 1974): 44–47, 64–66.

———. "The 'Ghost Rockets' of 1946," *Saga's UFO Report* 2, 1 (fall 1974): 24–27, 62–64.

Fawcett, Lawrence, and Barry J. Greenwood. *Clear Intent: The Government Cover-up of the UFO Experience.* Englewood Cliffs, NJ: Prentice-Hall, 1984.

Final Report, "Project Twinkle," Project Blue Book Files, November 1951.

Finney, Ben R., and Eric M. Jones. *Interstellar Migration and the Human Experience.* Berkeley, CA: University of California Press, 1985.

"Fireball Explodes in Utah," *Nevada State Journal* (April 19, 1962): 1.

First Status Report, Project STORK (Preliminary to Special Report No. 14), April 1952.

Foster, Tad. Unpublished articles for Condon Committee Casebook. 1969

"Flying Saucers Are Real," *Flying Saucer Review* (January/February 1956): 2–5.

Fowler, Raymond E. *Casebook of a UFO Investigator.* Englewood Cliffs, NJ: Prentice-Hall, 1981

Gevaerd, A. J. "Flying Saucer or Distillation Machine?," *Brazilian UFO Magazine* (November 2006).

Gillmor, Daniel S., editor. *Scientific Study of Unidentified Flying Objects.* New York: Bantam Books, 1969.

Good, Timothy. *Above Top Secret.* New York: Morrow, 1988.

———. *The UFO Report.* New York: Avon Books, 1989.

———. *Alien Contact.* New York: Morrow, 1993.

Gordon, Stan. "After 25 Years, New Facts on the Kecksburg, Pa., UFO Retrieval are Revealed." *PASU Data Exchange #15* (December 1990): 1.

———. "Kecksburg Crash Update," *MUFON UFO Journal* (September 1989).

———. "Kecksburg Crash Update," *MUFON UFO Journal* (October 1989): 3–5,9.

———. "The Military UFO Retrieval at Kecksburg, Pennsylvania," *Pursuit* 20, 4 (1987): 174–179.

Gordon, Stan, and Vicki Cooper. "The Kecksburg Incident," *UFO* 6, 1 (1991): 16–19.

Graeber, Matt. "The Reality, the Hoaxes and the Legend." Privately printed, 2009.

Greenwell, J. Richard. "UFO Crash/Retrievals: A Critique," *MUFON UFO Journal* 153 (November 1980): 16–19.

Gribben, John. "Cosmic Disaster Shock," *New Scientist* (March 6, 1980): 750–752.

"Guidance for Dealing with Space Objects Which Have Returned to Earth," Department of State Airgram, July 26, 1973.

Hall, Michael. "Was There a Second Estimate of the Situation?," *International UFO Reporter* 27, 1 (spring 2002): 10–14, 32.

Hall, Michael, and Wendy Connors. "Alfred Loedding: New Insight on the Man behind Project Sign," *International UFO Reporter* 23, 4 (winter 1999): 3–8, 24–28.

Hall, Richard. "Crashed Discs—Maybe," *International UFO Reporter* 10, 4 (July/August 1985).

———. *Uninvited Guests.* Santa Fe, NM: Aurora Press, 1988.

———, editor. *The UFO Evidence.* Washington, DC: NICAP, 1964.

————. "Pentagon Pantry: Is the Cupboard Bare?," *MUFON UFO Journal* 108 (November 1976): 15–18.

————. *Contributions of Balloon Operations to Research and Development at the Air Force Missile Development Center 1947–1958*. Alamogordo, NM: Office of Information Services, 1959.

Hastings, Robert. *UFOs and Nukes*. Bloomington, IN: Author House, 2008.

Haugland, Vern. "AF Denies Recovering Portions of 'Saucers,'" *Albuquerque New Mexican* (March 23, 1954).

Hazard, Catherine. "Did the Air Force Hush Up a Flying Saucer Crash?," *Woman's World* (February 27, 1990): 10.

Hegt, William H. Noordhoek. "News of Spitzbergen UFO Revealed," *APRG Reporter* (February 1957): 6.

Henry, James P., and John D. Mosely. "Results of the Project Mercury Ballistic and Orbital Chimpanzee Flights," *NASA SP-39*, NASA, 1963.

Hessmann, Michael, and Philip Mantle. *Beyond Roswell: The Alien Autopsy Film, Area 51 and the U.S. Government Cover-up of UFOs*. New York: Marlowe & Company, 1991.

Hippler, Robert H. "Letter to Edward U. Condon," January 16, 1967.

"History of the Eighth Air Force, Fort Worth, Texas" (microfilm), Air Force Archives, Maxwell Air Force Base, AL.

"History of the 509th Bomb Group, Roswell, New Mexico" (microfilm), Air Force Archives, Maxwell Air Force Base, AL.

Hogg, Ivan U., and J. B. King. *German and Allied Secret Weapons of World War II*. London: Chartwell, 1974.

Houran, James, and Kevin Randle. "Interpreting the Ramey Memo," *International UFO Reporter* 27, 2 (summer 2002): 10–14, 26–27.

Hughes, Jim. "Light, Boom a Mystery," *Denver Post*. (January 12, 1998).

Humble, Ronald D. "The German Secret Weapon/UFO Connection," *UFO* 10, 4 (July/August 1995): 21–25.

Huneeus, J. Antonio. "Soviet Scientist Bares Evidence of 2 Objects at Tunguska Blast," *New York City Tribune* (November 30, 1989): 11.

————. "Great Soviet UFO Flap of 1989 Centers on Dalnegorsk Crash," *New York City Tribune* (June 14, 1990).

————. "Spacecraft Shot Out of South African Sky—Alien Survives," *UFO Universe* (July 1990) 38–45, 64–66.

————. "Roswell UFO Crash Update," *UFO Universe* (winter 1991): 8–13, 52, 57.

————. "A Full Report on the 1978 UFO Crash in Bolivia," *UFO Universe* (winter 1993).

"Hunting Old and New UFOs in New Mexico," *International UFO Reporter* 7, 2 (March 1982): 12–14.

Hurt, Wesley R., and Daniel McKnight. "Archaeology of the San Augustine Plains: A Preliminary Report," *American Antiquity* (January 1949): 172–194.

Hynek, J. Allen. *The UFO Experience: A Scientific Inquiry*. Chicago: Henry Regency, 1975.

————. *The Hynek UFO Report*. New York: Dell 1977.

Hynek, J. Allen, and Jacques Vallee. *The Edge of Reality*. Chicago: Henry Regency, 1972.

"Ike and Aliens? A Few Facts about a Persistent Rumor," *Focus* 1, 2 (April 30, 1985): 1, 3–4.

"International Reports: Tale of Captured UFO," *UFO* 8, 3 (1993): 10–11.

"It Whizzed Through the Air; Livonia Boys Find Fireball Clues," *Livonian Observer & City Post* (December 16, 1965).

Jacobs, David M. *The UFO Controversy in America*. New York: Signet, 1975.

Johnson, J. Bond. "'Disk-overy' Near Roswell Identified as Weather Balloon by FWAAF Officer," *Fort Worth Star-Telegram* (July 9, 1947).

Jones, William E., and Rebecca D. Minshall. "Aztec, New Mexico—A Crash Story Reexamined," *International UFO Reporter* 16, 5 (September/October 1991): 11.

Jung, Carl G. *Flying Saucers: A Modern Myth of Things Seen in the Sky*. New York: Harcourt, Brace, 1959.

Kean, Leslie. "Forty Years of Secrecy: NASA, the Military, and the 1965 Kecksburg Crash," *International UFO Reporter* 30, 1 (October 2005): 3–9, 28–31.

Keel, John. "Now It's No Secret: The Japanese 'Fugo Balloon,'" *UFO* (January/February 1991): 33–35.

———. *UFOs: Operation Trojan Horse*. New York: G. P. Putnam's Sons, 1970.

———. *Strange Creatures from Space and Time*. New York: Fawcett, 1970.

Kennedy, George P. "Mercury Primates," *American Institute of Aeronautics and Astronautics* (1989).

Keyhoe, Donald E. *Flying Saucers from Outer Space*. New York: Henry Holt, 1953.

———. *Aliens from Space*. New York: Signet, 1974.

Klass, Philip J. *UFOs Explained*. New York: Random House, 1974.

———. "Crash of the Crashed Saucer Claim," *Skeptical Inquirer* 10, 3 (1986).

———. *The Public Deceived*. Buffalo, NY: Prometheus Books, 1983.

Knaack, Marcelle. *Encyclopedia of U.S. Air Force Aircraft and Missile Systems*. Washington, DC: Office of Air Force History, 1988.

LaPaz, Lincoln, and Albert Rosenfeld. "Japan's Balloon Invasion of America," *Collier's* (January 17, 1953): 9.

Lasco, Jack. "Has the US Air Force Captured a Flying Saucer?," *Saga* (April 1967): 18–19, 67–68, 70–74.

Lester, Dave. "Kecksburg's UFO Mystery Unsolved," *Greenburg Tribune-Review* (December 8, 1985): A10.

Library of Congress Legislative Reference Service, "Facts about UFOs," May 1966.

"Little Frozen Aliens," *The APRO Bulletin* (January/February 1975): 5–6.

Lore, Gordon, and Harold H. Deneault. *Mysteries of the Skies: UFOs in Perspective*. Englewood Cliff, NJ: Prentice-Hall, 1968.

Lorenzen, Coral, and Jim Lorenzen. *Flying Saucers: The Startling Evidence of the Invasion from Outer Space*. New York: Signet, 1966.

———. *Flying Saucer Occupants*. New York: Signet, 1967

———. *Encounters with UFO Occupants*. New York: Berkley Medallion Books, 1976

Low, Robert J. "Letter to Lt. Col. Robert Hippler," January 27, 1967.

Maccabee, Bruce. "Hiding the Hardware," *International UFO Reporter* (September/October 1991): 4.

———. "What the Admiral Knew," *International UFO Reporter*. (November/December 1986).

"The Magical Meteor," *Nebraska State Journal* (June 10, 1884).

Mantle, Phillip. *Roswell Alien Autopsy*. Edinburg, TX: RoswellBooks, 2012.

———. "Alien Autopsy Film, R.I.P.," *International UFO Reporter* 32, 1 (August 2008): 15–19.

Marcel, Jesse, and Linda Marcel. *The Roswell Legacy*. Franklin Lakes, NJ: New Page Books, 2009.

Matthews, Mark. "Armageddon at Tunguska!," *Official UFO* (May 1979): 28–30, 58, 60.

McAndrews, James. *The Roswell Report: Case Closed*. Washington, DC: Government Printing Office, 1997.

McCall, G. J. H. *Meteorites and Their Origins*. New York: Wiley & Sons, 1973.

McClellan, Mike. "The Flying Saucer Crash of 1948 Is a Hoax," *Official UFO* 1, 3 (October 1975): 36–37, 60, 62–64.

"McClellan Sub-Committee Hearings," March 1958.

"McCormack Sub-Committee Briefing," August 1958.

McDonald, Bill. "Comparing Descriptions, An Illustrated Roswell," *UFO* 8, 3 (1993): 31–36.

McDonough, Thomas R. *The Search for Extraterrestrial Intelligence*. New York: Wiley & Sons, 1987.

Menzel, Donald H., and Ernest Taves. *The UFO Enigma*. Garden City, New York: Doubleday, 1977.

Menzel, Donald H., and Lyle G. Boyd. *The World of Flying Saucers*. Garden City, NY: Doubleday, 1963.

THE GOVERNMENT UFO FILES: THE CONSPIRACY OF COVER-UP

Michael, Donald N., et. al. "Proposed Studies on the Implications of Peaceful Space Activities for Human Affairs." The Brookings Institution (December 1960): 182–184.

Michel, Aime. *The Truth about Flying Saucers*. New York: Pyramid, 1967.

Moore, Charles B. *The New York University Balloon Flights during Early June, 1947*. privately printed, 1995.

Moore, Charles B., Benson Saler, and Charles A. Ziegler. *UFO Crash at Roswell: Genesis of a Modern Myth*. Washington, DC: Smithsonian Institute Press, 1997.

Moseley, James W., and Karl T. Pflock. *Shockingly Close to the Truth*. Amherst, NY: Prometheus Books, 2002.

Mueller, Robert. *Air Force Bases: Volume 1, Active Air Force Bases within the United States of American on 17 September 1982*. Washington, DC: Office of Air Force History, 1989.

Murphy, John, "Object in the Woods," WHJB Radio, broadcast December 1965.

National Security Agency. Presidential Documents. Washington, DC: Executive Order 12356, 1982.

Neilson, James. "Secret U.S./UFO Structure," *UFO* 4, 1 (1989): 4–6.

"New Explanation for 1908 Siberian Blast," *Cedar Rapids Gazette*. (January 25, 1993).

NICAP. *The UFO Evidence*. Washington, DC: NICAP, 1964.

Nickell, Joe. "The Hangar 18 Tales,"*Common Ground* (June 1984).

"No Reputable Dope On Disks," *Midland [Texas] Reporter Telegram* (July 1, 1947).

Northrup, Stuart A. *Minerals of New Mexico*. Albuquerque: University of New Mexico, 1959.

"No Sign of 'UFO,'" *NSRI News* 24, 5 (May 2006).

Oberg, James. "UFO Update: UFO Buffs May Be Unwitting Pawns in an Elaborate Government Charade," *Omni* 15, 11 (September 1993): 75.

Oldham, Chuck, and Vicky Oldham. *The Report on the Crash at Farmington*. Lansdowne, PA: privately printed, 1991.

Olive, Dick. "Most UFO's Explainable, Says Scientist," *Elmira [NY] Star-Gazette* (January 26, 1967): 19.

Packard, Pat, and Terry Endres. "Riding the Roswell-Go-Round," *A.S.K. UFO Report* 2 (1992): 1, 1–8.

Papagiannis, Michael D., editor. *The Search for Extraterrestrial Life: Recent Developments*. Boston: 1985.

Peebles, Curtis. *The Moby Dick Project*. Washington, DC: Smithsonian Institution Press, 1991.

———. *Watch the Skies!* New York, NY: Berkley Books, 1995.

Pflock, Karl. *Roswell in Perspective*. Mt. Rainier, MD: FUFOR, 1994.

———. "In Defense of Roswell Reality." *HUFON Report* (February 1995): 5–7.

———. "Roswell, a Cautionary Tale: Facts and Fantasies, Lessons and Legacies." In Walter H. Andrus, Jr., ed. *MUFON 1995 International UFO Symposium Proceedings*. Seguin, TX: MUFON, 1990: 154–168.

———. "Roswell, The Air Force, and Us," *International UFO Reporter* (November/December 1994): 3–5, 24.

———. *Roswell: Inconvenient Facts and the Will to Believe*. Amherst, NY: Prometheus Books, 2001.

"Physical Evidence: Landing Reports," *The U.F.O. Investigator* 2, 11 (July/August 1964): 4–6.

Press Conference—General Samford, Project Blue Book Files, 1952.

"Press Release—Monkeynaut Baker Is Memorialized," Space and Rocket Center, Huntsville, AL (December 4, 1984).

"Project Blue Book" (microfilm). RG [Record Group] 341, T-1206 National Archives, Washington, DC.

Prytz, John M. "UFO Crashes," *Flying Saucers* (October 1969): 24–25.

Randle, Kevin D. "Mysterious Clues Left Behind by UFOs," *Saga's UFO Annual* (summer 1972).

———. "The Pentagon's Secret Air War Against UFOs," *Saga* (March 1976).

———. "The Flight of the Great Airship," *True's Flying Saucers and UFOs Quarterly* (spring 1977).

———. *The October Scenario*. Iowa City, IA: Middle Coast Publishing, 1988.

————. *The UFO Casebook*. New York: Warner, 1989.

————. *A History of UFO Crashes*. New York: Avon, 1995

————. *Conspiracy of Silence*. New York: Avon, 1997.

————. *Project Moon Dust*. New York: Avon, 1998.

————. *Scientific Ufology*. New York: Avon, 1999.

————. *Roswell Encyclopedia*. New York: Avon, 2000.

————. *Roswell Revisited*, Lakeville, MN: Galde Press, 2007.

————. *Crash: When UFOs Fall from the Sky*, Franklin Lakes, NJ: 2010.

————. "MJ-12's Fatal Flaw and Robert Willingham," *International UFO Reporter* 33, 4 (May 2011): 3–7.

————. *Reflections of a UFO Investigator*, San Antonio, TX: Anomalist Books, 2012.

————. *Roswell, UFOs and the Unusual*. Kindle eBooks, 2012.

Randle, Kevin D., and Donald R. Schmitt. *UFO Crash at Roswell*. New York, NY: Avon, 1991.

————. *The Truth about the UFO Crash at Roswell*. New York, NY: M. Evans, 1994.

Randle, Kevin D., and Robert Charles Cornett. "Project Blue Book Cover-up: Pentagon Suppressed UFO Data," *UFO Report* 2, 5 (fall 1975).

————. "Siberian Explosion, Comet or Spacecraft?," *Quest UFO* 1, 1 (1977): 10–15.

Randle, Kevin D., and Russ Estes. *Spaceships of the Visitors*. New York: Fireside Books, 2000.

Randles, Jenny. *The UFO Conspiracy*. New York: Javelin, 1987.

Ramsey, Scott, and Suzanne Ramsey. *The Aztec Incident: Recovery at Hart Canyon*. Mooresville, NC: Aztec 48 Productions, 2012.

Redfern, Nick. "Tunguska: 100 Years Latter [sic]." In *6th Annual UFO Crash Retrieval Conference*. Broomfield, CO: Wood and Wood Enterprises, 2008.

————. *On the Trial of the Saucer Spies*. San Antonio, TX: Anomalist Books, 2006.

————. *The Real Men in Black*. Pompton Plains, NJ: New Page Books, 2011.

Reichmuth, Richard. "The Cisco Grove Bow and Arrow Alien Encounter." *MUFON UFO Journal* 468 (April 2007): 3–6.

"Report of Air Force Research Regarding the 'Roswell Incident,'" July 1994.

"Rocket and Missile Firings," White Sands Proving Grounds, Jan–Jul 1947.

"Rocket Craft Encounter Revealed by World War 2 Pilot," *The UFO Investigator* 1, 2 (August/September 1957): 15.

Rodeghier, Mark. "Roswell, 1989," *International UFO Reporter*. (September/October 1989): 4.

Rodeghier, Mark, and Mark Chesney. "The Air Force Report on Roswell: An Absence of Evidence," *International UFO Reporter* (September/October 1994).

Rosignoli, Guido. *The Illustrated Encyclopedia of Military Insignia of the 20th Century*. Secaucus, NJ: Chartwell, 1986.

Ruppelt, Edward J. *The Report on Unidentified Flying Objects*. New York: Ace, 1956.

Russell, Eric. "Phantom Balloons Over North America," *Modern Aviation* (February 1953).

Rux, Bruce. *Hollywood vs. the Aliens*. Berkeley, CA: Frog, Ltd., 1997.

Sagan, Carl, and Thornton Page, eds. *UFO's: Scientific Debate*. New York: Norton, 1974.

Sanderson, Ivan T. "Meteorite-like Object Made a Turn in Cleveland, O. Area," *Omaha World-Herald* (December 15, 1965).

————. *Uninvited Visitors*. New York: Cowles, 1967.

————. *Invisible Residents*. New York: World Publishing, 1970.

Saunders, David, and R. Roger Harkins. *UFOs? Yes!* New York: New American Library, 1968

Schmitt, Donald R. "New Revelations from Roswell." In Walter H. Andrus, Jr., ed. *MUFON 1990 International UFO Symposium Proceedings* Seguin, TX: MUFON, 1990: 154–168.

Schmitt, Donald R., and Kevin D. Randle. "Second Thoughts on the Barney Barnett Story." *International UFO Reporter* (May/June 1992): 4–5, 22.

Scully, Frank. "Scully's Scrapbook," *Variety* (October 12, 1949): 61.

———. *Behind the Flying Saucers*. New York: Henry Holt, 1950.

"The Search for Hidden Reports," *The U.F.O. Investigator* 4, 5 (March 1968): 7–8.

Sheaffer, Robert. *The UFO Verdict*. Buffalo, NY: Prometheus, 1981.

Simmons, H. M. "Once Upon a Time in the West," *Magonia* (August 1985).

Skow, Brian, and Terry Endres. "The 4602d Air Intelligence Service Squadron." *International UFO Reporter* 20, 5 (winter 1995): 9–10.

Slate, B. Ann. "The Case of the Crippled Flying Saucer," *Saga* (April 1972): 22–25, 64, 66–68, 71, 72.

Smith, Scott. "Q & A: Len Stringfield," *UFO* 6,1, (1991): 20–24.

Smith, Willy. "The Curious Case of the Argentine Crashed Saucer," *International UFO Reporter* 11, 1 (January/February 1986): 18–19.

"The Space Men at Wright-Patterson." UFO Update. Special Report No. 14 (Project Blue Book), 1955.

Spencer, John. *The UFO Encyclopedia*. New York: Avon, 1993.

Spencer, John, and Hilary Evans. *Phenomenon*. New York: Avon, 1988.

Stanyukovich, K. P., and V. A. Bronshten. "Velocity and Energy of the Tunguska Meteorite," *National Aeronautics and Space Administration* (December 1962).

Status Reports, "Grudge—Blue Book," Nos. 1–12.

Steiger, Brad. *Strangers from the Skies*. New York: Award, 1966.

———. *Project Blue Book*. New York: Ballantine, 1976.

———. *UFO Missionaries Extraordinary*. New York: Pocket Books, 1976.

———. *The Fellowship*. New York: Dolphin Books, 1988.

Steiger, Brad, and Sherry Hanson Steiger. *The Rainbow Conspiracy*. New York: Pinnacle, 1994.

———. *Conspiracies and Secret Societies*. Detroit: Visible Ink Press, 2006.

———. *Real Aliens, Space Beings, and Creatures from Other Worlds*. Detroit: Visible Ink Press, 2011.

Stone, Clifford E. *UFO's: Let the Evidence Speak for Itself*. CA: privately printed, 1991.

———. "The U.S. Air Force's Real, Official Investigation of UFO's." Privately printed, 1993.

Stonehill, Paul. "Former Pilot Tells of Captured UFO," *UFO* 8, 2 (March/April 1993): 10–11.

Story, Ronald D. *The Encyclopedia of UFOs*. Garden City, NY: Doubleday, 1980.

———. *The Encyclopedia of Extraterrestrial Encounters*. New York: New American Library, 2001.

Stringfield, Leonard H. *Situation Red: The UFO Siege!* Garden City, NY: Doubleday, 1977.

———. *Inside Saucer Post… 3-0 Blue*. Cincinnati, OH: Civilian Research, Interplanetary Flying Objects, 1975.

———. *UFO Crash/Retrieval Syndrome: Status Report II*. Seguin, TX: MUFON, 1980.

———. *UFO Crash/Retrieval: Amassing the Evidence: Status Report III* Cincinnati, OH: privately printed, 1982.

———. *UFO Crash/Retrievals: The Inner Sanctum Status Report VI*, Cincinnati, OH: privately printed, 1991.

———. "Retrievals of the Third Kind." In *MUFON Symposium Proceedings* (1978): 77–105.

———. "Roswell & the X-15: UFO Basics," *MUFON UFO Journal* 259 (November 1989): 3–7.

Sturrock, P. A. "UFOs—A Scientific Debate," *Science* 180 (1973): 593.

Sullivan, Walter. *We Are Not Alone*. New York: Signet, 1966.

Summer, Donald A. "Skyhook Churchill 1966," *Naval Reserve Reviews* (January 1967): 29.

Svahn, Clas. "The 1946 Ghost Rocket Photo," *International UFO Investigator* 27, 3 (fall 2002): 12–14, 23.

Svahn, Clas, and Anders Liljegren. "Close Encounters with Unknown Missiles," *International UFO Reporter* 19, 4 (July/August 1994): 11–15.

Swords, Michael, et.al. *UFOS and the Government: A Historical Inquiry*. San Antonio, TX: Anomalist Books, 2012.

———. "Too Close for Condon: Close Encounters of the 4th Kind," *International UFO Reporter*, 28, 3 (fall 2003): 3–6.

Tafur, Max. "UFO Crashes in Argentina," *INFO Journal* 75 (summer 1996): 35–36.

Tech Bulletin, "Army Ordnance Department Guided Missile Program," January 1948.

Technical Report, "Unidentified Aerial Objects, Project SIGN," February 1949.

Technical Report, "Unidentified Flying Objects, Project GRUDGE," August 1949.

Templeton, David. "The Uninvited," *Pittsburgh Press* (May 19, 1991): 10–15.

Thomas, Dick. "'Flying Saucers' in New Mexico," *Denver Post* (May 3, 1964).

Thompson, Tina D., editor. *TRW Space Log*. Redondo Beach, CA: TRW 1991.

Torres, Noe, and Ruben Uriarte. *The Other Roswell*. Edinburg, TX: Roswell Books, 2008.

———. *Aliens in the Forest*. Edinburg, TX: RoswellBooks.com, 2011.

"Tunguska and the Making of Pseudo-scientific Myths," *New Scientist* (March 6, 1980): 750–751.

"Two Dubuquers Spot Flying Saucer," *Dubuque* [Iowa] *Telegraph Herald*. (April 29, 1964): 1.

"UAO Landing in New Mexico," *The A.P.R.O. Bulletin* (May 1964): 1, 3–10.

"UFOs and Lights: 12 Aliens on Ice in Ohio?," *The News* 10 (June 1975): 14–15.

U.S. Congress, House Committee on Armed Forces. Unidentified Flying Objects. Hearings, 89th Congress, 2nd Session, April 5, 1966. Washington DC: U.S. Government Printing Office, 1968.

Vallee, Jacques. *Anatomy of a Phenomenon*. New York: Ace, 1966.

———. *Challenge to Science*. New York: Ace, 1966.

———. *Dimensions*. New York: Ballantine, 1989.

———. *Revelations*. New York: Ballantine, 1991.

War Department. Meteorological Balloons (Army Technical Manual) Washington, DC: Government Printing Office, 1944.

Weaver, Richard L., and James McAndrew. *The Roswell Report: Fact vs Fiction in the New Mexico Desert*. Washington, DC: Government Printing Office, 1995.

Webber, Bert. *Retaliation. Japanese Attacks and Allied Countermeasures on the Pacific Coast in World War II*. Corvallis, OR: Oregon State University Press, 1975.

Wilkins, Harold T. *Flying Saucers on the Attack*. New York: Citadel, 1954.

———. *Flying Saucers Uncensored*. New York: Pyramid, 1967.

———. "The Strange Mystery of the Foo Fighters," *Fate* 4, 6 (August/September 1951): 98–106.

Wise, David, and Thomas B. Ross. *The Invisible Government*. New York: 1964.

Wood, Robert M. "Forensic Linguistics and the Majestic Documents." In *6th Annual UFO Crash Retrieval Conference*. Broomfield, CO: Wood and Wood Enterprises, 2008, pp. 98–116.

———. "Validating the New Majestic Documents." In *MUFON Symposium Proceedings* (2000): 163–192.

Wood, Ryan. *Majic Eyes Only*. Broomfield, CO: Wood Enterprises, 2005

"World Round-up: South Africa: Search for Crashed UFO," *Flying Saucer Review* 8, 2 (March/April 1962): 24.

Zabawski, Walter. "UFO: The Tunguska Riddle." *Official UFO* (May 1977): 31–33, 59–62.

Zeidman, Jennie. "I Remember Blue Book." *International UFO Reporter* (March/ April l 1991): 7.

THE GOVERNMENT UFO FILES: THE CONSPIRACY OF COVER-UP

INDEX

Note: (ill.) indicates photos and illustrations.

Palmer, Ray, 56 (ill.), 56–59, 58 (ill.), 258
Pandolfi, Ron, 329
Patrick, Don, 168
Patterson, William, 139, 141
Pearson, Drew, 162, 162 (ill.)
Pelham, Massachusetts, 329
Petersen, James C., 113
Peterson, Don, 212
Peterson, Ellen, 105
Phillips, C. L., 109
Phoenix, Arizona, 105, 159
Pickering, Jack, 254
Pierman, Casey, 136–37, 141
pirate bodies, 13
Pittsburg, Kansas, 197–200, 199 (ill.)
Platt, Raymond P., 110, 112, 114
Port Hope, Ontario, 252
Portugal, Ghost Rocket sightings in, 37
Poulin, Bernard, 296–97
Pounders, Robert, 211
Powell, Jody, 174, 174 (ill.)
Powell, Robert, 83, 91, 330, 332
Powers, Dick, 233
Pratt, Bob, 280–81
Preucil, Charles, 53
Project Blue Book
    end of, 267
    first American UFO investigation, 39–42,
        40 (ill.)
    Oak Ridge laboratories, 170–72
    Project Moon Dust, 272–74
Project Blue Fly, 269, 270, 271
Project Grudge, 41–42, 50, 78, 127–28
Project Moon Dust
    Angel Hair, 266
    background, 269–72, 270 (ill.)
    end of, 285
    government's denial of existence of, 283–
        85, 335–36
    missions, 281–83
    origins of, 274–76
    Project Blue Book, 272–74
    sightings, 276–81
Project Saucer, 92–94
Project Sign, 39, 47, 71–72, 73, 81, 95–103
Project Stork, 150–53
Project Twinkle, 119–24
Pruett, J. Hugh, 105
Puckett, Jack, 48–49
Puckett, William "Bill," 291, 321
Puerto Rico, UFO sightings in, 272
Pullen, Colonel, 305, 307–8
Putt, Donald, 77, 101

Q–R

Quintanilla, Hector, 40, 40 (ill.), 188–94, 196,
    220, 305, 307–8
Raftery, Bernard G., 118
Ramey, Roger, 88 (ill.)
    flying saucer statement, 84
    Roswell crash, 86, 87, 88–89, 90, 159
    Washington National Airport UFO sight-
        ings, 144
Randle, Kevin, 132–33, 138, 143, 237
Ravndal, Christian M., 27
Reagan, Ronald, 242
Rees, Doyle, 107, 108, 115–16, 118, 119

Rehoboth Beach, Delaware, 96–97
Reichmuth, Steven, 179, 180
Rense, Jeff, 325
Renualdi, Dan, 211
Renuart, General, 332
Reuterswärd, Åsa, 23
Reuterswärd, Erik, 23–24, 36 (ill.), 46
Reynolds, S. W., 63, 65, 91, 155–56, 158
Rhodes, William, 58, 59–60
Rhodes photographs, 59–60, 159, 162
Rice, Ron, 204, 205
Richardson, Airman, 302
Richardson, James, 247
Rickard, D. M., 117
Rickett, Lewis "Bill," 110, 113, 114
Riley, Albert, 74
Ringwald, F., 10
Riordan, Larry, 168, 169
Robertson, Howard, 12, 13
Robertson Panel, 13
Robinson, W. I., 128
Roe, T., 321
Rogers, Mrs. F. A., 129
Rogers, Mrs. R. A., 129
Rogers, Renny, 288–89
Roseville, California, 252–53
Roswell, New Mexico, crashes, 84–90, 85 (ill.),
    87 (ill.), 88 (ill.), 89 (ill.), 93 (ill.), 110,
    111–17, 335
Royal Air Force, 3
Ruiz, Natalio Farfan, 280
Ruppelt, Edward, 50 (ill.)
    Air Intelligence Service Squadron
        (AISS), 4602nd, 246, 248–49
    Alabama UFO sighting, 65
    Arnold sighting, 57, 58
    Blue Book Special Reports, 127–28
    Estimate of the Situation, 63, 64 (ill.), 75,
        77–78
    green fireballs, 105–6, 335
    Lubbock Lights, 130, 132–33
    private papers, 50
    Project Sign, 71, 78, 79
    Project Twinkle, 119–20, 121
    Real Special Report No. 13, 150
    Washington National Airport sightings,
        134, 135, 137, 139, 140, 141, 142
Ryan, Joe, 291
Ryan, Paul L., 111
Rymer, Edward D., 168, 170, 171, 172

S

Sadowski, Vernon L., 246
Safeer, Harvey, 241
Sagan, Carl, 313
Sagittarius (constellation), 311
Salas, Robert, 208, 209 (ill.), 217, 218, 219,
    225, 227
Samford, John A., 140, 140 (ill.), 144
Sandia Peak, 106, 107 (ill.), 108–11
Saucerian Bulletin, 95 (ill.)
Schindele, David D., 223–25
Schluter, Edward, 10–11
Schmidt, Lieutenant, 10
Schmitt, Don, 148
Schraff, Major, 210
Schulgen, George F.

Estimate of the Situation, 61, 63–64, 65,
    69, 91–92
FBI, 155–56, 158, 159
Schulze, Glen, 330
Schweizer, John W., 118
Scully, Frank, 160
Search for Extraterrestrial Intelligence (SETI),
    301
    history of, 309 (ill.), 309–11, 311 (ill.)
    protocols, 316–19, 317 (ill.)
    WOW signal, 311–12, 312 (ill.)
Seely, Ben, 118
Semitjov, Eugen, 43
Sessions, William S., 175
73rd Bombardment Wing, 9
Sewell, Louis, 16
Shavery Mystery, 56, 57 (ill.)
Shaw, Chester A., 220
Shoop, Richard R., 76
Shough, M., 321
Shreveport, Louisiana, 94
Shrum, Donald, 177–82
Shrum, Judy, 180
Simmons, Robert, 280
Simpson, Captain, 21
61 Squadron, 4
skyhook balloons, 95
Smith, Captain, 290–91, 293
Smith, E. J., 48, 57, 65, 67
Smith, Howard, 116
Smith, R. H., 163
Smith, Staff Sergeant, 302
Smith, T. J., 82
Smith, Val, 219, 220, 225
Sneider, Robert, 74, 93, 94
Snyder, Mike, 289
Socorro, New Mexico, 188–96, 201
Sorensen, Hans, 43
South Carolina, UFO sightings in, 246–48
South Dakota, UFO sightings in, 301–9, 307
    (ill.), 308 (ill.)
Soviet Union
    flying discs, 155, 156
    Ghost Rocket speculation, 22–23, 27, 28–
        29, 32–33, 36–37
Spaatz, Carl, 13, 29, 29 (ill.)
Sparks, Brad, 150
Springer, Lieutenant Colonel, 165
Sputnik, 277
Squyers, William, 198
St. Elmo's fire, 4, 4 (ill.), 15
Stahl, John, 107–8
Stancombe, Marilyn, 40 (ill.), 192
Stefanopoulos, Stefanos, 37
Stephenville, Texas, 329–33
Steucke, Paul, 235–36, 237, 238
Stevens, Captain, 237
Stevens, Ralph, 48, 65, 67
Stone, Cliff, 283, 284, 336
Strasbourg, France, 10–11
Stratmeyer, Lieutenant General, 163
Strentz, Herbert, 40
Strepp, John Paul, 76
Stringfield, Leonard, 5–6, 15, 278, 280
Sudan, UFO sightings in, 276
Sutton, Aline, 188
Sutton, Elmer, 187, 188

THE GOVERNMENT UFO FILES: THE CONSPIRACY OF COVER-UP